THE FUTURE OF CORRECTIONAL REHABILITATION

Since the founding of the penitentiary nearly two centuries ago, modern correctional systems have been marked by the belief that offenders should not only be punished but also rehabilitated. This uplifting goal, however, involves a very practical challenge: knowing how to save offenders from a life in crime.

In the aftermath of Martinson's 1974 "nothing works" doctrine, scholars have made a concerted effort to develop an evidence-based corrections theory and practice to show "what works" to change offenders. Perhaps the most important contribution to this effort was made by a group of Canadian psychologists, most notably Donald Andrews, James Bonta, and Paul Gendreau, who developed a treatment paradigm called the Risk–Need–Responsivity (RNR) model, which became the dominant theory of correctional treatment. This approach was more recently challenged by a perspective developed by Tony Ward, Shadd Maruna, and others, called the Good Lives Model (GLM). Based in part on desistance research and positive psychology, this model proposes to rehabilitate offenders by building on the strengths offenders possess. GLM proponents see the RNR model as a deficit model that fixes dynamic risk factors rather than identifying what offenders value most, and using these positive factors to pull them out of crime.

Through a detailed examination of both models' theoretical and correctional frameworks, *The Future of Correctional Rehabilitation: Moving Beyond the RNR Model and Good Lives Model Debate* probes the extent to which the models offer incompatible or compatible approaches to offender treatment, and suggests how to integrate the RNR and GLM approaches to build a new and hopefully more effective vision for offender treatment. A foreword by renowned criminologist Francis T. Cullen helps put the material into context. This book will be of much interest to scholars and students interested in correctional rehabilitation as well as practitioners working with offenders.

Ronen Ziv, PhD, is a research fellow of the University of Cincinnati Corrections Institute and a teaching fellow in the Department of Social Sciences, School of Criminology, at the University of Haifa, Israel. He received his MS (2012) and PhD (2016) in criminal justice from the University of Cincinnati. Previously, he received his LLB (2005) and LLM (2006) in Law from Tel-Aviv University and worked as a criminal defense lawyer. His current research interests are in developing and testing the evidence-based approach to correctional rehabilitation, the integration of motivational theories in correctional intervention, and the capacity of correctional agencies to implement a promising correctional framework that aims to rehabilitate offenders.

THE FUTURE OF CORRECTIONAL REHABILITATION

Moving Beyond the RNR Model and Good Lives Model Debate

Ronen Ziv

Routledge
Taylor & Francis Group

NEW YORK AND LONDON

First published 2018
by Routledge
711 Third Avenue, New York, NY 10017

and by Routledge
2 Park Square, Milton Park, Abingdon, Oxon, OX14 4RN

Routledge is an imprint of the Taylor & Francis Group, an informa business

Library of Congress Cataloging-in-Publication Data
Names: Ziv, Ronen, author.
Title: The future of correctional rehabilitation : moving beyond the RNR model and good lives model debate / Ronen Ziv.
Description: New York, NY : Routledge, 2018.
Identifiers: LCCN 2017019045 | ISBN 9781138095960 (hardback) | ISBN 9781138095984 (pbk.)
Subjects: LCSH: Criminals—Rehabilitation—United States. | Corrections—United States.
Classification: LCC HV9304 .Z58 2018 | DDC 365/.6610973—dc23
LC record available at https://lccn.loc.gov/2017019045

ISBN: 978-1-138-09596-0 (hbk)
ISBN: 978-1-138-09598-4 (pbk)
ISBN: 978-1-315-10550-5 (ebk)

Typeset in Bembo
by Apex CoVantage, LLC

To my family and the people in the field of correctional rehabilitation.

CONTENTS

TABLES

FOREWORD

I entered the field of criminology in the mid-1970s and eventually was moved, with Karen Gilbert in 1982, to write *Reaffirming Rehabilitation*. At this time, I was in a distinct minority in arguing that the rehabilitative ideal should remain the guiding correctional paradigm. Virtually every scholar I encountered, including most of my criminological friends, believed that offender treatment was an intractably flawed and failed enterprise. The dismal state of the nation's "correctional" institutions, marked most notably by the lethal suppression of the Attica inmate uprising, made it difficult to imagine that these could ever be therapeutic communities. Most troubling, Robert Martinson's summary of 231 evaluations in *The Public Interest* reported that no reliably effective intervention reduced recidivism. With his study, evidence-based corrections had arrived and delivered a stunning message: "nothing works" in offender treatment.

While a graduate student at Columbia University, I interviewed with Martinson for a researcher position on a follow-up study to his nothing works project. My lack of computer skills undermined my employability, but it was still a thrill to meet him. At that time, I was writing a lot on labeling theory, a perspective that reminded us that state intervention not only did not work but also made offenders worse off. I was a committed member of the nothing works gang.

But I would change my mind a few years later. In the summer of 1979, I was attending a seminar at the University of Virginia funded by the National Endowment for the Humanities and run by Gresham Sykes. I decided to write a seminar paper critical of correctional rehabilitation. For some reason that still escapes me, a disquieting thought popped into my mind: Why would we expect a system that explicitly tried to punish offenders to be more just and effective than a system that at least aspired to rehabilitate them? My sense was that critics of treatment did not consider the unanticipated consequences of their policy alternatives, especially the embrace of determinate sentencing and the abolition of parole release. In *Reaffirming Rehabilitation*, Karen and I predicted that greater punitiveness could result. Unfortunately, we proved prescient.

Still, the Martinson study remained. Even if my dire warnings had merit, how could I support something that did not work? Practicing a lot of confirmation bias, I soon took solace in reading rebuttals to the nothing works doctrine that listed tens of effective programs—especially those written by Ted Palmer and by Paul Gendreau and Robert Ross. I chose to believe that the glass was half full and not half empty. Paul, in particular, became a close friend—his letter to me following the publication of *Reaffirming Rehabilitation* leading to more exchanges and then to collaborations. Eventually, a series of meta-analyses appeared, most notably by Mark Lipsey and colleagues, which showed more definitively that rehabilitation programs were effective. They also revealed that punishment-oriented programs—those that sought to change offenders through scare tactics, discipline, threats, intensive supervision—were dismal failures. Alas, in the end, we learned that rehabilitation works and punishment does not.

Thus, a good part of my career was spent trying to move rehabilitation beyond the nothing works doctrine. In the beginning chapters, Ronen Ziv does an excellent job telling the story of how the emerging data eventually led to the rejection of the idea that offenders could not be cured by correctional interventions. But he also realizes that the future of rehabilitation must move beyond the increasingly sterile question of, "Does rehabilitation work?" to the more pressing question of, "What works to rehabilitate offenders?"

His remarkable book addresses this query. We reside in a field that cherishes the study of criminological theory—a good thing since I publish books in this area! But the cost of this focus is that less interest has been devoted to designing treatment theories that can lead to the effective reform of the wayward. Put another way, we spend more time testing how well control theory versus social learning theory explains delinquency among school kids, but much less time studying how to save a high-risk offender from a life in crime. It is important that this latter task be taken more seriously.

Professor Ziv does us all a service in exploring the two major theoretical developments in correctional rehabilitation: the Risk-Need-Responsivity (RNR) model and the Good Lives Model (GLM). In the tradition of Ruth Kornhauser's poignant analysis of criminological theories in *Social Sources of Delinquency*, he takes us on a guided tour through the theory and practice of these competing correctional paradigms. Many readers might be familiar with the three core principles of the RNR model, but there is much more to learn to achieve a comprehensive understanding of this perspective. Similarly, although newer and perhaps less prominent, the GLM offers a powerful thesis on how best to rehabilitate offenders: focus less on their fixing their deficits (or risk factors) and more on building upon their positive strengths, with the goal of helping offenders to live a "good life."

Readers of this volume thus will acquire an in-depth knowledge of the treatment enterprise that is available in few other places. More than this, Professor Ziv not only alerts us to the nature of the debate between the RNR model and the GLM but also shares his thoughts on the current status of this paradigmatic contest. His ultimate goal, however, is to articulate a vision for the future of rehabilitation. For all those who wish to know what next steps should be taken in offender treatment, this is a work that rises to the level of essential reading.

Francis T. Cullen
University of Cincinnati

ACKNOWLEGMENTS

Many scholars assisted me with this book. I especially want to thank my mentor, Frank Cullen, who helped me to explore the boundaries of rehabilitation with a unique combination of interest and joy. Pat Van Voorhis, Paula Smith, and Cheryl Jonson provided thoughtful advice that enriched the preparation of this manuscript. Essential contributions were also provided by Ed Latessa and others from the School of Criminal Justice at the University of Cincinnati. Finally, I will always cherish the support and inspiration that the University of Cincinnati Corrections Institute (UCCI) gave to this book.

PART I

Beyond Nothing Works

1

THE RISE AND FALL OF THE
REHABILITATIVE IDEAL

Since the founding of the penitentiary nearly two centuries ago, American corrections has been marked by the belief that offenders should not only be punished but also rehabilitated. This uplifting belief reflected Americans' wide agreement that rehabilitation should benefit both the public and the individual offenders, and bolstered by their confidence in the state's capacity to attain this goal. Starting in the late 1960s, however, ongoing social unrest in American social and political institutions triggered a deep challenge to the ideological hegemony of rehabilitation. At that time, both conservative and liberal scholars asserted that correctional rehabilitation had reached a dead end—that it did not work—and they joined forces to eliminate offender treatment as a guiding principle of the correctional system.

This concerted attack involved tempting reasons against the theoretical assumptions of rehabilitation and its manifestation in the correctional system. Scholars argued, for example, that rehabilitation is a futile theory because it is based on the assumption that the roots of crime lay in individual defects rather than in the defects of an inequitable social structure. In addition, scholars looked inside the correctional system and concluded that state officials were no longer committed to the rehabilitative ideal. Thus, by the mid-1970s, American scholars had closed ranks to attack corrections as a system that was both ineffective and unjust.

In a classic 1974 essay, Robert Martinson summarized the results of a comprehensive review of 231 studies evaluating rehabilitation programs. The dismal findings led him to question whether "nothing works" in corrections to reform offenders. This widely read and cited work provided critics with scientific confirmation that their loss of faith in rehabilitation was justified. His research project equipped policy makers and criminologists with a very rational reason to reject rehabilitation—correctional interventions cannot demonstrate success in changing offenders' behavior. Despite the dark future that Martinson's article cast on the field of correctional rehabilitation, his "nothing works doctrine" came with a silver lining. The status of offender treatment was now a matter of evidence. For rehabilitation to regain its legitimacy, advocates would have to produce scientific data showing that programs could reduce recidivism.

In the aftermath of the Martinson article, few scholars in the United States were inclined to embark on this task (see Cullen, 2005). However, a critical challenge to the "nothing works doctrine" would come from north of the border. Since the 1970s, a group of Canadian psychologists—most notably the late Donald Andrews, James Bonta, and Paul Gendreau—had worked across both university and correctional settings to design effective programming. Viewing themselves "scientist practitioners" (p. 15), they collaborated in the development of a theoretical framework that aimed to explain, predict, and influence criminal behavior. During the 1980s, they continued their scientific journey to demarcate the theoretical, empirical, and practical bases for intervening effectively with offenders. In the early 1990s, these Canadian scholars had accumulated sufficient research to propose a general correctional framework—a set of testable principles for correctional interventions designed to reduce reoffending (see Andrews & Bonta, 1994). Since then, their theoretical approach and recommended correctional practices have developed into a powerful treatment paradigm—the *Risk-Need-Responsivity* model. It is most often referred to by its acronym, the "RNR" model.

By the early 2000s, consensus grew that the RNR model had advanced the status of correctional rehabilitation and became the dominant theory of offender treatment (Ogloff & Davis, 2004). Nonetheless, a group of mostly non-American scholars questioned the RNR model's underlying theoretical premises. Based in part on desistance research and positive psychology, Tony Ward, Shadd Maruna, and others criticized the RNR model for using recidivism as its major measure of success while neglecting offenders' general well-being. They contended that any treatment model must include this essential psychological outcome. These scholars also criticized the RNR model for focusing on what was wrong with offenders—deficits or "criminogenic needs" that should be fixed—rather than on what was right with offenders—their strengths—and how these positive characteristics could be used to achieve reform (see Ward & Maruna, 2007). They also argued that beyond assessing the risks individuals posed, therapists should give priority to identifying what offenders want from their rehabilitative process and how to help them attain their "good life." These ideas coalesced into form an increasingly popular alternative framework for correctional rehabilitation, which Ward and colleagues called the *Good Lives Model*. It is now known by its acronym, the "GLM."

Taking together, advocates of the RNR model and GLM provide a broad outlook on the boundaries of offender treatment and enrich the field of correctional rehabilitation with two legitimate approaches to conducting interventions. The chapters that follow, describe the development and content of each of these treatment paradigms, and then detail the nature of the debate between the RNR and GLM approaches. This debate has raised important questions about the purpose of changing convicted offenders' behavior offenders through planned interventions and how to achieve this outcomes. Although often portrayed as rival and incompatible perspectives, the argument is made that they can also be considered as models that should be integrated. This book sets forth a conceptual integration of these models and ends with thoughts on the future of correctional rehabilitation.

As a prelude to this analysis, Part I provides an overview of the emergence and impact of the rehabilitative ideal. Within this overview, four historical periods are identified—the rehabilitative ideal's discovery, dominance, decline, and reaffirmation. Chapter 1 presents the first three historical periods. First, this discussion highlights how, during the 1800s, the rehabilitative ideal was discovered and developed. Thoughts of how best to reform offenders changed from a belief in the curative powers of the internal regimen of the prison to the view that the unique criminogenic circumstances of each offender must be treated individually. Second, the rehabilitative ideal then became the dominant correctional ideology, shaping the development of the criminal justice and juvenile justice systems and being consolidated with the rise of modern "corrections." Third, in a sudden reversal, the rehabilitative ideal came under withering attack during the late 1970s—notably not only from conservatives but also from liberals. In 1974, Robert Martinson published a classic essay in which he challenged the effectiveness of correctional treatment. This essay solidified the idea that "nothing works" to change offenders. At this point, the rehabilitative ideal was in steep decline (Allen, 1981; Cullen & Gilbert, 1982).

The Discovery of the Rehabilitative Ideal

As Rothman (1971) has documented, the origins of the rehabilitative ideal in the United States extend to the 1820s. Reformers in New York and Pennsylvania developed prisons—which they called penitentiaries—intended not to punish offenders but to rehabilitate them. According to Rothman, these institutions were created in response to a changing social context that resulted in new ideas about the causes of criminal conduct.

By the 1820s, the United States experienced unprecedented urban and economic growth, followed by social and geographical mobility. Americans viewed these social changes as a process that imposed a real threat to the order and cohesiveness of the nation. They claimed that social institutions (e.g., family, church, and school) were losing the capacity to stabilize the social order (Morris & Rothman, 1995). Americans of that era perceived the weakening of discipline and obedience in these institutions as an expression of social disorder. They argued that there was a link between the breakdown of traditional principles and criminal behavior. Although the actual crime rate "probably did not increase over these years," there was a broad consensus that the origins of crime locate in the society disorder (Rothman, 1971, p. 69).

Reformers created the prison as a way of addressing the problem of disorder causing crime. The prison was designed to be a model institution in which an orderly society might be recreated. Reformers believed that prison's walls would isolate offenders from the corruptive, disorderly environment that prevailed in the outer community. In addition, they argued, the prison's internal routine would regenerate the order and discipline offenders would need to be transformed into law-abiding citizens (Cullen & Gilbert, 1982). Overall, reformers agreed upon the rehabilitative goal of prison and on the theoretical outline to achieve this goal—isolation, discipline, obedience, and a steady routine of labor. However, reformers in New York and Pennsylvania implemented two rival approaches for achieving the goal of rehabilitation.

In Pennsylvania, the reformative discipline in prison was maintained through the solitary confinement of inmates, called the "separate" system. During their entire period behind walls, inmates "remained in solitary cells for eating, sleeping, and working, and entered private yards for exercise" (Rothman, 1971, p. 85). Under this regimen, the rehabilitation process had three phases. At the initial stage, offenders who entered prison experienced total isolation. They were expected to devote this time to a deep examination of their bad decisions in life. While isolated, reformers tried to restore the offenders' morality by forcing them to listen to "reproach of conscience" and "expostulation of religious" (p. 85). In the second phase of rehabilitation, the Pennsylvania reformers aimed to cure idleness by allowing offenders daily work in their cells. Such activity, they assumed, would instill habits of order and regularity. In the last phase of the process, the reformers' schema allowed individual treatment for inmates, rewarding inmate's good behavior with books and visitors.

Reformers in New York developed an alternative approach to organizing the prison. As opposed to the separated system in Pennsylvania, inmates in New York were not totally isolated, which is why their model was called the "congregate system". Prisoners were allowed to eat, work, and exercise together during the day. According to the reformers' theoretical principles, such lack of absolute isolation was a substantial threat to rehabilitation. Because inmates had contact with one another, the possibility of criminal contamination could not be precluded. To overcome the risk posed by daily contact with other offenders, the "congregate" system in New York enforced a strict code of silence—often with the lash. The reformers bolstered their rehabilitative discipline through rules that prohibited "all talking and even the exchanges of glances" (Morris & Rothman, 1995, p. 106). In addition, the reformers secured the rehabilitative process by compelling inmates to spend the night in individual cells and isolating them from contact with relatives and friends. Another substantial aspect that reformers in New York addressed was offenders' idleness. In the congregate system, reformers tried to instill good habits to inmates through a daily routine of hard labor in prison workshops.

During the 1820s and 1830s, Americans considered the prison to be "the pride of the nation," a place that would both reform offenders in a humanitarian way and stabilize the social order (Rothman, 1971, p. 79). During this optimistic period, the reformative models in New York and Pennsylvania spread throughout the country and trumpeted the correctional doctrines of separation, obedience, and steady labor. A few decades later, however, it was clear that the reformers' early expectations were unrealistic and increasingly irrelevant. The typical image of prisons in the post–Civil War era is of disorderly places filled with chronic offenders, lower-class citizens, and immigrants. In addition, ongoing stories from incarcerated offenders exposed the effects of prison overcrowding and the brutality used by officials to impose discipline. This reality blurred the appeal of the prison as a humanitarian enterprise, and undermined the notion that prison was a place where offenders should or could be rehabilitated.

By the 1860s, the arrangements in prisons no longer reflected the theoretical blueprint of the penitentiary reform movement (Rothman, 1971). First, prisons were overcrowded. As a consequence, it was no longer possible to isolate offenders from social communication. Second, prison wardens stopped focusing on rehabilitation and relied on obedience and harsh discipline to enforce order. Administrational convenience, not offender treatment, thus became wardens' primary concern. Finally, officials allowed the leasing of inmate labor to the private sector. This new practice signaled that wardens no longer believed they had special expertise in administering inmates' routines. Overall, the reformative enthusiasm gradually declined, and the regulation of chronic and dangerous offenders in overcrowded prisons became more and more brutal. It was clear, observed Rothman (1971), that the "all important task of administration was to safeguard the peace of the prison" (p. 246).

During the 1860s, it was evident that the internal regimen of incarceration alone could not accomplish reform. That is, prison in and of itself had no therapeutic power. Prisons failed to maintain the reformers' theoretical framework, and gradually, the commitment to rehabilitate offenders was replaced by a custodial operation. Outside prison, politicians and the public supported custody as a ready-to-use instrument to restrain immigrants and low-class citizens. The tendency was to view inmates as persons "whose behavior might be explained in terms of social Darwinism" (Cullen, 2013, p. 311). In prison, wardens grew comfortable with focusing on simply guarding offenders rather than dealing with any high expectations of reformation. Therefore, subjecting inmates to aimless punishment became an acceptable and standard practice within the penal system. According to Rothman (1971), "this was not a good time to counter the appeal of custody" (p. 257).

Nevertheless, in the mid-1860s, Enoch C. Wines and Theodore Dwight, members of the New York Prison Discipline Association, investigated the penal system and proposed a plan to reorganize of prisons. Their comprehensive report on the *Prisons and Reformatories of the United States and Canada* (1867) analyzed prison systems in Canada and 17 states within the United States. The ie report presented scholarly evidence that the reformative approach of both Pennsylvania and New York penal systems had become irrelevant, and that rehabilitation was no longer the primary goal of the prison systems in the United States. In addition, the authors outlined a scheme for new directions to approach prison's organization and discipline. Three years later, their recommendations became the theoretical base of a national consensus that reaffirmed rehabilitation.

Enoch C. Wines was the architect of the first National Congress on Penitentiary and Reformatory Discipline (1870a). In October 1870, more than 250 wardens, chaplains, judges, governors, and humanitarians from 24 states, Canada, and South America convened in Cincinnati, Ohio. (Other penologists from England, France, Italy, and Denmark sent papers to enrich the congress with their knowledge and experience.) The best thinkers and practitioners of the era discussed the next necessary changes in the American penal system, and eventually adopted the "Declaration of Principles." Four members composed a paper outlining the principles of organization and discipline, which were eventually condensed to the 37 principles of the declaration (Pisciotta, 1994): Dr. Enoch Wines, Rutherford B. Hayes (then the Ohio Governor and, between 1877 and 1881, the 19th president of the United States), Zebulon Brockway (the superintendent of the Detroit House of Correction), and Franklin Sanborn (the secretary of the Massachusetts Board of State Charities). This document presented a "new penology" for the American penal system. The declaration coalesced ideas of new direction in penology into "a coherent correctional philosophy" (Cullen & Gilbert, 1982, p. 68).

The Declaration of Principles reestablished rehabilitation as the supreme goal of public punishment. The congress stated unanimously that criminals are capable of reformation, and that "the treatment of criminals by society is for protection of society" (Wines, 1870a, p. 541). This goal rejected the practice of inflicting aimless punishment on inmates and the administration of a merely custodial operation. The declaration also stated a clear utilitarian goal for imprisonment: to reform criminals for protecting the society. In addition, the congress rejected the use of disciplinary punishment to deter offenders. Such practice was perceived as a strategy that inflicts unnecessary pain or humiliation on offenders, and therefore would have destructive effects. Zebulon Brockway, for example, claimed that the purpose of deterrence reflects social regression, a practice that drags the society "backward to the pillory, the whipping post, the gallows, the stake; to corporal violence and extermination!" (p. 42).

Importantly, the congress took another step toward reestablishing rehabilitation as the primary philosophy of punishment. As opposed to the reformers of the first half of the 19th century, the Declaration of Principles argued that the severity of crime should not dictate the nature of the punishment offenders should receive. That is, reformers subjected the retributive principle of ensuring the proportionality between sentence length and offense to the ultimate goal of rehabilitation. For example, to ensure society's protection, the congress suggested that habitual offenders, who resisted reform, might serve longer sentences because of the danger they posed—even if this sanction exceeded the pain they had caused. Most importantly, in this new approach, traditional fixed sentences should be replaced by sentences of indeterminate length. The length of all sentences, in that sense, should be limited "only by satisfactory proof of reformation" (pp. 541–542). Rehabilitation thus became the ultimate philosophical justification for the state's legitimacy to impose punishment through the criminal justice system.

The acclaimed Declaration of Principles not only reaffirmed rehabilitation as the correctional goal of the penal system, but also provided a theoretical blueprint for achieving the reforms. This theoretical outline influenced the organization of the correctional system throughout the 20th century and therefore merits close examination. In this context, the declaration reflected several correctional principles that the congress aimed to promote. The first was the essential role of the prison in the rehabilitation efforts. According to the declaration, imprisonment must be continued until reformation is accomplished. As with the reformers before them, the commitment of the congress to reform through imprisonment remained stable. The reformers still "looked primarily, indeed inclusively, to the penitentiary, its internal organization and routine, to effect rehabilitation" (Rothman, 1980, p. 32). However, as subsequent correctional principles show, the congress intended to achieve reformation with a different type of prison. As opposed to their predecessors, the reformers of 1870 did not design prison to serve as an example for society. Rather, the new penology organized prison as a "community" that should be a "faithful replication" of the outside environment (p. 118).

The second correctional principle is the introduction of human service. The causes of crime should be addressed through human and social service rather than through deterrence or vindictive retribution. According to the declaration, "the prisoner's self-respect should be cultivated to the utmost, and every effort made give back to him his manhood" (Wines, 1870a, p. 542). The new penology thus rejected the use of penal discipline and stated that the object of discipline was "being to make upright and industrious free men, rather than orderly and obedient prisoners" (p. 543). This new perspective of discipline aimed to stand side-by-side with the inmate "against opposing forces, whether in the form of inward propensity or outward temptation" (p. 554).

The third and the fourth correctional principles were adopted from penal administrations in Australia and Ireland. These are the progressive classification and the mark system that were carried out in 1840 by Alexander Machonochie in an Australian colony, and in 1854 by Walter Crofton in Ireland (Morris & Rothman, 1995). According to the principle of progressive classification, rehabilitation in prison is achieved through an intentional process rather than through exposure to the mere regimen of confinement. During a sentence, imprisonment was designed as a series of grades that inmates could progress through until they achieved reformation and then liberty. This promotion toward release is not an automatic process; rather, inmates "earn such promotion, gaining, at each advance, increased privilege and comport" (Wines, 1870b, p. 19).

The fourth correctional principle is the use of a "system of rewards" as a stimulus for inmates to engage in desirable behavior and, eventually, achieve reformation. An underlying assumption of this strategy was that hope is a powerful agent in facilitating rehabilitation. In this regard, hope is maintained when inmates constantly believe in their ability to perform expected actions and be rewarded. Another assumption of this principle was that behavior can be regulated through the manipulation of self-interests.

According to the new penologists, the operationalization of a well-devised system of rewards includes two dimensions. One dimension presents of concrete incentives to catch inmates' self-interest. Such rewards "should consist of: 1. A diminution of sentence. 2. A participation by prisoners in their earnings. 3. A gradual withdrawal of prison restrains. 4. Constantly increasing privileges, as they shall be earn by good conduct" (p. 549). The second dimension is the use of "well adjust mark system" as a technique to measure and modify behavior. This technique was designed to motivate inmates to perform desirable behaviors and to cease undesirable behaviors. The inmates can earn marks for "good conduct, industry, and attention to learning," and, with a sufficient amount of marks, they can earn more privileges (p. 549). By the same token, prison misconduct is resulted in subtracting marks, losing some privileges, and even reverse the progress toward liberty. Overall the new penologists designed a prison that placed inmates' destiny "in their own hands."

The fifth correctional principle is the use of a "probationary stage of imprisonment." This last stage in the reformative confinement was designed to test the "moral soundness" of inmates who "were judged to be reformed" (p. 549). The purpose of this strategy was to make sure that each inmate could be trusted as a free honest person with respect to the law. Under the probationary stage, officials should examine inmates' reformation in a more natural environment. That is, inmates are in a state between imprisonment and freedom. However, the authors of the declaration adopted this idea without providing a specific outline about the nature of this "natural environment." In the Irish system, for example, the concept of an "intermediate prison" allowed inmates the liberty to work outside the prison without supervision, errands in the city, and more education (Wines & Dwight, 1867/1973).

The sixth principle is the use of different reformatory disciplines for different offender populations. The reason for classification was to design prisons that specifically match offenders' "reception and treatment" (Wines & Dwight, 1867/1973, p. 115). The declaration thus suggested different prisons for first-time prisoners, young, women, misdemeanants, male felons, and incorrigible offenders.

The seventh correctional principle in the new penology is the important role of prison officers. According to the declaration, prison officers have a crucial role in achieving a successful process. Because prison officers were in charge of the therapeutic process, the new penology required them to be committed to the goal of reform. Indeed, prison officers were expected to be much more than guardians. According to the authors of the declaration, officers should be well trained and perform "entire self-devotion, a calm and cautions judgment, great firmness of purpose and steadiness of action, large experience, a true sympathy, and morality above suspicion" (Wines, 1870a, p. 551).

The eighth principle of reformation stretches the state's responsibility beyond the prison walls. According to the declaration, the state has to follow inmates after being released, and make sure that offenders are morally reintegrated, possess the desire to advance themselves, and have the capacity for industrial labor. The advocates of the new penology understood the difficulties that prisoners faced when they reentered the community after a long imprisonment. This principle thus required that released inmates be provided real opportunities to reintegrate into society.

The ninth principle drawn from the declaration relates to the role of religion, education, and labor in inmate rehabilitation. Prisons should provide inmates with industrial employment, education, and moral training (religion). The reformers perceived that religion was the key to changing the "human heart and life," and was the only way to deal with the incorrigible offenders. In this regard, the authors of the declaration claimed that they "have profound conviction of the inefficacy of all measures of reformation, except such as are based on religion, pervaded by its spirit, and vivified by its power" (p. 551). The new penologists also believed in the benefits of addressing offenders' education. Education was seen as a useful reformation tool for offenders "who have generally sinned through some form of ignorance, conjoined with vice" (p. 552). Regarding employment, the declaration stated that the basis of all reformation discipline should be "steady, active, honorable labor" (p. 543). In addition, the new penologists supported the development of a variety of industrial training for inmates. They believed that a variety of training would promote inmates' inner motivation for labor. The expectation was that training in prison would place the inmate "out of the reach of want; it is to make him master of the great art of self-help" (p. 555).

Ultimately, the first National Congress on Penitentiary and Reformatory Discipline (1870) presented a new theoretical framework of the penal system—known as the "new penology." Once again, the goal of changing the offender was established as the prime justification of the penal sanction. However, for the first time, the target of this effort also included the offenders' well-being and satisfaction. In other words, according to the new penology, the penal system should be directed and designed to reduce offenders' risk through principles that may also improve other aspects of their lives.

The first national congress also contributed to the view that crime was caused by a variety of factors. Influenced by emphasis on secular causes advanced by emerging social sciences, the Declaration of Principles explained that the way to eradicate crime is to address its psychological and environmental sources. Crime was no longer seen as a product of a single factor (e.g., a sinful soul, free will and hedonism, or disordered society). Rather, the new penologists adopted the view, advanced by the positivist school of criminology, that crime is caused by multiple factors. The new penologists thus argued that crime is caused by factors both within individuals (the mind or heredity) and external to individuals (social and economic circumstances). Later, in the beginning of the 20th century, this extension of behavioral science would build on the views embraced by the new penologists, proposing that offender rehabilitation must involve more than mere prison management. By this time, reformers were ready to investigate sources of criminal involvement identified by the emerging fields of psychology and sociology.

Indeed, reformers at the closing decades of the 19th century created a new vision. In this regard, Cullen and Gendreau (2000) observe that "the marriage of the 'new penology' and 'positivist criminology' resulted in the creation of the 'rehabilitative ideal'—a correctional paradigm that would reign supreme for nearly seven decades into the 20th century" (p. 116). The power of this correctional paradigm was the broad consensus that the improvement of offenders through rehabilitation should be the primary goal of corrections.

The Dominance of the Rehabilitative Ideal

The United States began the 20th century with a powerful liberal spirit of reform. Known as "Progressives," the reformists of that time sought to change economic and social inequality (Rothman, 1980). Their endeavors to humanize the industrial society led them to ask for assistance from the state. In doing so, they believed that the state could be trusted and perceived government power as a source of support that would help solve social problems. During the Progressive Era—the first decades of the century—reforms thus launched the creation of a welfare state (Cullen & Gilbert, 1982).

In this context, Progressives approached the crime problem and chose to reaffirm the vitality of the rehabilitative ideal by translating its core ideas into concrete policy reforms. As did their predecessors in the 19th century, they supported rehabilitation over other justifications for punishment and believed in providing human services to offenders. In addition, Progressives adopted the new penology ideas presented at the 1870 Cincinnati Congress as their rational blueprint of how to approach criminals.

During the Progressive Era, thus, Progressives designed reforms to realize the idea that rehabilitation should be individualized. The goals of programs of individualized treatment, they argued, should be both to improve the lives of offenders and to protect society. Such treatment ought to begin with a comprehensive investigation of the life story of each offender to identify the precise causes of crime. Then, on a case-by-case basis, the details of what led an individual into crime would be diagnosed. In turn, a particular curative program would be developed to change the unique criminogenic aspects of the offender. Critically, Progressives endorsed the administration of this individualized treatment with a maximum of flexibility and discretion. In this regard, they expected that state agents would use their unbridled discretion "to fit the punishment to the criminal rather to the crime" (Cullen & Gilbert, 1982, p. 76). Such an attitude reflected confidence in the state's commitment to the rehabilitative ideal as well as in the therapeutic qualification of its representatives (Rothman, 1980).

At the opening of the 20th century, the rehabilitative ideal shaped the development of a new correctional system reflecting the Progressives' line of thinking. A major characteristic of their enterprise was the implementation of alternatives to incarceration. Indeed, unlike the penologists in the 19th century, Progressives expanded their rehabilitative efforts beyond the prison walls. They perceived the exclusive use of prison as a uniform, inflexible, and therefore ineffective reaction to criminality. Their goal was to provide new sentencing options for individuals who needed to be rehabilitated in more natural settings.

Within the Progressives' correctional system, the individualization of treatment began in court (Rothman, 1980). Once the offender was pronounced guilty, the judge appointed a probation officer to conduct a presentence investigation and submit a presentence report. This report informed judges about the convicted offender's personal history, education and early life, family and neighborhood, home life, work history, and personality. Judges had wide discretion whether offenders would be rehabilitated in the community or in prison. In this regard, "the personal characteristics of the offender, not the actual crime, were to guide the decision" (p. 63).

Convicted offenders released into the community under "probation," a supervision that limited their liberty. A probation officer carried out this supervision with wide discretion, but was expected to act both as "counselor and policeman" (Cullen & Gilbert, 1982, p. 78). This job required a sensitive understanding of the offender's unique problems, a genuine response to particular needs, and firm action to protect the public safety by "sending the unreformed to prison for more intensive intervention" (Cullen & Gendreau, 2000, p. 117). The practice of probation became common between 1900 and 1920, and by 1930 "the federal government and thirty-six states had adult probation laws" (Rothman, 1980, p. 83).

For offenders who were sent to prison, Progressives supported a policy that replaced fixed sentences with sentences of indeterminate length. Like the new penologists, Progressives expected inmates to earn their release through rehabilitation. In that sense, confinement was essential because "many offenders required the restrictions of the prison and the experience of the intermediate sentence to be rehabilitated" (Cullen & Gilbert, 1982, p. 77). During this time, Progressives also created parole boards to determine the timing of the release and the conditions of post-release supervision. Similar to probation officers, parole officers conducted an investigation to provide the parole board with knowledge of an offender's criminality. Parole officers also supervised the released offenders, both to help them and police them. According to Rothman (1980), "by 1923, almost half of all inmates sentenced to state prisons were under an indeterminate sentence, and a little over half of all releases were under parole" (p. 44).

Among the various correctional reforms that transformed the abstract notion of the rehabilitative ideal into practice, the innovation of a separate juvenile justice system resembled the purest embodiment of the ideal. Within this system, ensuring the proper physical, mental, and moral development of each child by a wide state's discretionary authority had a solid sense. In this regard, juvenile court was created as a mechanism for individualized treatment administrated under "the most flexible procedures" and aimed to "save" the wayward youth from a life of crime (Rothman, 1980, p. 213). Unlike the adult system, juvenile court was not concerned with the severity of a specific charge or even with the question of guilt. Instead, the court was operated in a nonadversarial fashion to serve the best interests of the child. Overall the juvenile court "seemed to represent a significant victory for humanity and progress" (p. 215). The first juvenile court opened in 1899, and by 1920 "all but three states had a special court for hearing juvenile cases, and every state permitted probation for youths" (Cullen & Jonson, 2012, p. 31).

According to Rothman (1980), however, salient discrepancies between the ideal and its implantation followed the development of the "new" correctional system. The main reasons for this inconsistency were the lack of knowledge about what caused an individual's criminality and of how to translate the correctional principles into programs that would change the criminal behavior (Cullen & Gilbert, 1982). Nevertheless, reformers commonly attributed the inability to produce effective programs to organizational factors such as "the lack of resources and trained staff" (Cullen & Gendreau, 2000, p. 118). According to Cullen and Gendreau (2001), such reaction to the programs' failures reflected the criminologists' professional ideology. That is, their ideological commitment to rehabilitation drew their attention away from considering the whole progressives' enterprise.

Despite the difficulties, reformers were very optimistic about the future of correctional rehabilitation and continued to develop the correctional system (Cullen & Gilbert, 1982). In 1954, for example, the "American Prison Association" pledged the rehabilitative ideal by changing its name to the "American Correctional Association." This commitment to correct offenders made a concrete impact when the variations of correctional programs in prison were extended. "Correctional institutions" provided inmates with individual and group counseling, therapeutic milieu, work release and furloughs, collage education, and psychological classification systems (Cullen & Gilbert, 1982). In addition, creative experiments in rehabilitation spread beyond the prison walls. During the 1960s, the correctional field sought to professionalize the practice of community-based treatment programs and called for reintegrating offenders into the community (Cullen & Gendreau, 2000).

During the 1950s to the late 1960s rehabilitation "remained unchallenged as the dominant correctional ideology" (Cullen & Gilbert, 1982, p. 82). Allen (1981) ascribed the rehabilitative ideal remaining a persuasive paradigm to the vitality of two cultural factors. One was the common faith in an ability to change criminal behavior. This faith reflected a confidence in the capacity of the social institutions to transform offenders into law-abiding citizens "in good faith." The second cultural factor that allowed the rehabilitative ideal to remain dominant was the existence of common values. Individuals and the state shared a consensus about the goals of rehabilitation and the way to achieve them.

As American society entered the late 1960s, consensus over many social issues started to crack. Within the correctional system, confidence in the model of individualized treatment collapsed and the legitimacy of the rehabilitative ideal suffered a sudden decline. Within a few years, the support for rehabilitative efforts rapidly diminished to a level that "it had become common to ask, is rehabilitation dead?" (Cullen, 2013, p. 314). The next section will delineate how this crisis in the philosophy of rehabilitation became real.

The Decline of the Rehabilitative Ideal

From the mid-1960s to the mid-1970s, the philosophy of rehabilitation experienced a sudden decline in legitimacy, "moving from decades-long ideological hegemony to complete disrepute" (Cullen, 2013, p. 305). This decline is often linked to "cataclysmic changes" that transpired in the American society at that time (Cullen & Gilbert, 1982; Allen, 1981; Cullen & Gendreau, 2000). According to Cullen and Jonson (2012), America was thrown into turbulence, "marked by the Civil Rights Movement, urban riots, the Vietnam War and accompanying protest, the shooting at Kent State and Attica, Watergate and related political scandals, and escalating crime rates" (p. 33).

This ongoing social unrest troubled those on both the left and right political wings of American society. More and more citizens came to question the legitimacy of the prevailing social order and the methods that the government used to maintain it. As the 1970s progressed, the United States faced a radical loss of confidence in its political and social institutions. Indeed, this was a legitimacy crisis, "a confidence gap between the public and the government" (Cullen & Gendreau, 2001, p. 323). For many citizens, the ongoing events caused them to question whether the state could be trusted to govern American society. Significantly, conservatives and liberals interpreted the crisis in different ways.

Conservative and Liberal Attacks

Citizens who held a conservative perspective viewed the events and saw social disorder—a breakdown of law and order. Conservatives watched how numerous political protests throughout the nation often became a stage for direct confrontation with state authority. In addition, they perceived a deep erosion of traditional American moral values, especially those that related to obedience to authority, education, and family. During this period, "crime" became a real threat in the life of many citizens and was perceived as "a codebook for all that was wrong with American society" (Cullen & Gilbert, 1982, p. 93). In this regard, conservatives displayed a keen sensitivity to the public's fears of increasing crime.

Conservatives mistrusted the welfare state and perceived its ideology as the source of society's disruption. In the area of crime policy, they blamed the ideology and practice of rehabilitation for allowing lawlessness to flourish. First, conservatives argued that rehabilitation encouraged criminals to externalize responsibility. They contended that advocates of rehabilitation assumed that the causes of crime have social or innate sources and thus enabled offenders to neutralize their irresponsible choices (i.e., offenders' belief that their criminal acts were the result of circumstances beyond their control). Second, conservatives blamed the ideology of rehabilitation for the leniency of the correctional system. They stated that one of the major obstacles to maintaining the social order was the due process of legislation that protected the rights of suspects, defendants, and inmates. According to conservatives, this legislation sent a dangerous message to offenders: whatever you did wrong, the law would be on your side. Moreover, they argued that the therapeutic approach of the correctional system signaled to offenders that future convictions would result in a lenient reaction. That is, judges and parole boards would focus on offenders' needs and use their discretion to release them back into the community.

Conservatives generally opposed the notion of rehabilitating offenders and perceived it as an illegitimate practice. In the therapeutic state, they asserted, crime had become a rational choice— "crime paid"—because it brought rewards and posed little few risk of punishment (Cullen & Gilbert, 1982). Conservatives thus contended that the best way to stop the chaos was to implement laws that "severely limit[ed] the discretion exercised by judges and liberal parole boards" (p. 97). Specifically, they proposed replacing indeterminate sentences with determinate sentences. Judges, then, would no longer have the discretion to impose lenient sentences. Instead, they would have to impose sentences mandated by laws. Conservative legislators could pass laws to inflict harsh sentences on offenders for the crimes they committed.

As an alternative to the leniency of the "therapeutic state," conservatives argued that the solution to the crime problem was to "get tough" with offenders. This demand rested on their assumption that engaging in crime was a rational choice. Conservatives assumed that a conscious assessment of costs and benefits determined whether a person would choose to commit a crime. Crime, in their view, resulted from the perception that the benefits (satisfaction) from the illegal act outweighed its cost (punishment).

Conservatives believed that punitive policies would solve the crime problem—it would turn criminality into an irrational choice. Their suggestion was to inflict harsh sentences to deter both active criminals (i.e., specific deterrence) and potential criminals (i.e., general deterrence). In addition, conservatives advocated for sentencing policies that would send hardened offenders for lengthy prison terms. Thus, they supported laws that would impose prison terms on all criminals who committed serious offenses (i.e., collective incapacitation) or those who were chronic offenders (i.e., specific incapacitation).

Liberals, on the other side of the political spectrum, perceived the social turbulence in different terms than conservatives. While conservatives traditionally believed that rehabilitation was a false premise and were eager to demolish its dominancy, liberals experienced the events as a continuing disenchantment with their own ideology. During the late 1960s and the 1970s liberals could no longer maintain their faith in a state that no longer seemed to reflect the liberal reaction to crime. During this time, they detached themselves from the hope of a welfare state that promised to do good, and came to "doubted both the willingness and capacity of the government to achieve an equitable and human society" (Cullen & Gilbert, 1982, p. 104).

Moreover, liberals suddenly realized that the problems in the correctional system stemmed not from "the *absence* of a genuine commitment to treatment" but from "the *very presence* of rehabilitative ideology and practice" (p. 111, emphasis in original). That is, rehabilitation was no longer viewed as a humane ideal. Instead, liberals asserted that rehabilitation became a "dangerous myth that has long been used by the state to justify the unconscionable victimization of offenders" (Cullen & Gilbert, 1982, p. 125).

For the first time, liberals started to question the fundamental assumptions that lead the development of the therapeutic state for one-and-a-half centuries. Indeed, for liberals, the idea that "the rehabilitative ideal was not flawed and fixable but rotten to the core" was a paradigmatic shift (Cullen, 2013, p. 316). In this sense, liberals abandoned their own social welfare ideology.

According to Cullen and Gilbert (1982), liberals rejected rehabilitation for three reasons: the theory of rehabilitation was flawed and thus futile; the therapeutic system inflicted an excessive punishment on offenders; and the administration of individualized treatment was unjust. This liberal criticism of rehabilitation led to the decline of the rehabilitative ideal and therefore merits closer examination.

The first type of criticism was directed toward inherent *problems in the theory of rehabilitation.* These problems, liberals argued, indicated that "rehabilitation efforts are futile and wasteful" ("nothing works") (Garland, 2001, p. 70). One problematic issue was the reliance of correctional rehabilitation on positivistic criminology. That is, liberals advocated against the notion that the rehabilitative process required a change in offenders' criminogenic conditions. Instead, they contended that the roots of crime lay in the "structural features of an unjust society" (p. 113). Moreover, similar to conservatives, liberals in the 1970s followed the classical school of criminology and concluded that crime was the outcome of rational decisions. For liberals, however, crime was a rational reaction of people who had to make decisions in harsh and unjust social circumstances.

Another problem in the theory of rehabilitation, liberals argued, was the assumption that the way inmates behaved in prison would predict their behavior after release. According to liberal scholars, this assumption was flawed because prison officials did not have the scientific expertise to predict inmates' future behavior. That is, correctional rehabilitation had no capacity to identify inmates' criminogenic propensities and deliver effective intervention. Therefore, they concluded, this problematic assumption led to an inaccurate prediction of which inmates were or were not judged "rehabilitated." In addition, liberals argued firmly against the notion of enforced therapy, considering it a theoretical flaw. They argued that the practice was ineffective because "people cannot be reformed against their will" (Cullen & Gilbert, 1982, p. 116). Lastly, liberals dismissed the premise that rehabilitation could be achieved in prison. The corruptive nature of confinement, they asserted, is antithetical to any environment that aims to change offenders for the better.

The second type of liberal critique accused correctional rehabilitation of *doing harm* to offenders. That is, "rehabilitation makes offenders worse not better" ("everything backfires") (Garland, 2001, p. 70). Liberals claimed that, in practice, "the system is using the mask of benevolence to do considerable harm" (Cullen & Gilbert, 1982, p. 119). Liberals, for example, perceived sentences of indeterminate length "as a ruthless weapon to coerce inmate conformity" (p. 120). Their argument was that under the policy of indeterminate prison terms, the original condition of release was distorted. That is, the power to grant release was not used to promote inmates' reintegration into society but rather to serve custodial goals—the need to maintain order and to prevent escapes (Cullen, 2013). Therefore, they claimed that inmates experienced coercion, not correction. Rothman (1980) described the mechanism of this therapeutic endeavor and concluded that, "In the end, when conscience and convenience met, convenience won. When treatment and coercion met, coercion won" (p. 10).

Liberals thus were convinced that correctional rehabilitation in prison would inevitably be corrupted and harmful. They regarded the uncertainty of release under an indeterminate prison term as another harmful aspect of correctional rehabilitation. Liberals also criticized the nature of therapeutic techniques as a harmful aspect of rehabilitation. They asserted that under the cloak of a benevolent scientific approach, the correctional system used inhuman behavioral techniques such as electroshock therapy, sterilization, and psychosurgery. Liberals also claimed that the use of positive and negative reinforcement in institutions had been corrupted in order to achieve compliance.

The third type of liberal criticism was that rehabilitation should be rejected because it allowed the *administration of injustice*. Liberals contended that rehabilitation "undermined fundamental values such as moral autonomy, the rights of the individual, due process and the rule of law" ("justice is in jeopardy") (Garland, 2001, p. 70). They stated that the administration of individualized treatment created official decisions that were both "excessively arbitrary and capricious" and "blatantly discriminatory" (Cullen & Gilbert, 1982, p. 124).

Specifically, liberals argued that judges had no expertise to decide how each offender should be rehabilitated, and thus the decision-making in court relied on personal tendencies. Such subjective decisions, liberals asserted, led to different in punishments for crimes committed under identical circumstances. Moreover, liberals accused, subjectivity in court discriminated against poor and minority offenders. That is, "racial stereotypes shaped sentencing and subsequence decisions" (Cullen, 2013, p. 316). In addition, as mentioned above, liberals also argued against the harmful way prison officials administered their unfettered discretion to abuse inmates.

Taken together, these three reasons to reject rehabilitation reflected the cognitive shift that liberals experienced during the 1970s. In essence, for these liberals, these fundamental critiques "render[ed] the treatment enterprise fully illegitimate" (Cullen, 2013, p. 317). By 1975, liberals generally mistrusted the welfare state and agreed that the correctional system should abandon "the false hopes for a criminal justice system that would do good" (Cullen & Gilbert, 1982, p. 125). As an alternative to the rehabilitative ideal, liberal scholars proposed a model that would reflect their perception of justice—the "justice model" of corrections.

The justice model consisted of several assumptions that, together, aimed to reorganize the correctional process (Cullen & Gilbert, 1982; Cullen & Jonson, 2012). First, sanctions should be based on "just deserts" and not on individualized treatment. That is, punishment would fit the crime and not the criminal, and the abusive link between rehabilitation and liberty would be eliminated. Secondly, laws should narrow the range of punishment that judges can impose for each criminal offense. Liberals hoped to eliminate the disparity and discrimination in sentencing by creating clear sentencing guidelines. Thirdly, indeterminate sentences must be replaced by determinate sentences. Liberals perceived this change as a fundamental factor to protect offenders from being abused by state officials.

The fourth assumption of the justice model required the abolition of parole boards and parole release. Under determinate sentencing, and without the link between treatment progress and release, parole boards would no longer be needed. Fifth, prison terms should be short and "reserved for only the most serious crimes" (Cullen & Jonson, 2012, p. 58). This liberal assumption aimed to minimize both the deprivation of liberty and the criminogenic impact of prison. Sixth, prisons should become safe and just places. This liberals' image of prison involved prison officials who treat offenders in a non abusive manner, inmates who have access to civil rights, penalties that would be regulated according to due process principles, and inmates who would practice self-governance. Liberals thus wanted to ensure that, beyond the loss of liberty, inmates would not suffer additional pain. Seventh, participation in treatment programs should be voluntary. This assumption was intended to eliminate the harmful consequences of enforced therapy. Liberals believed that voluntary participation in treatment programs would create an authentic motivation to change.

From the mid-1960s to the mid-1970s, conservatives and liberals joined forces to solve what they perceived as the failure of American criminal justice. Indeed, although conservatives and liberals had different motivations, they called for similar policies: to abandon the therapeutic ideology and indeterminate sentences, and to replace them with "the principles of just desert and determinacy" (Cullen & Gilbert, 1982, p. 91).

Martinson and the Nothing Works Doctrine

In the spring of 1974, advocates of rehabilitation experienced a devastating strike that ended up the case against its legitimacy. In that year, Robert Martinson published the results of the most extensive evaluation study that ever conducted on the effectiveness of correctional treatment (Cullen & Gilbert, 1982; Allen, 1981). Martinson (1974) drew his findings from a larger project that was initiated in 1966 by New York State, completed in 1970, and fully published in 1975 (see Lipton, Martinson, & Wilks, 1975). This project was designated to provide an answer to the general question: Does rehabilitation work?

Martinson and his colleagues used "rigorous standards to select and analyze" 231 controlled studies, conducted from 1945 to 1967 (Cullen, 2013, p. 326). In his article, Martinson (1974) reviewed the effectiveness of several "treatment methods": education and vocational training, individual counseling, group counseling, milieu therapy, psychotherapy, imprisonment (sentence length and degree of security), medical treatment, "decarceration," probation, and parole. His analysis of these approaches led him to report that "With few and isolated exceptions the rehabilitative efforts that have been reported so far have had no appreciable effect on recidivism" (p. 25). Martinson then moved beyond his findings to stated a conclusion that reflected a pessimistic attitude toward rehabilitation. In the final section of his chapter, Martinson raised the possibility that efforts to rehabilitate offenders were futile due to an inherent theoretical flaw. That is, "education at its best, or that psychotherapy at its best, cannot overcome, or even appreciably reduce, the powerful tendency for offenders to continue in criminal behavior" (p. 49).

This notion that "nothing works" to reform offenders became a doctrine that had a tremendous impact on policy makers and criminologists. However, the appeal of this doctrine stemmed more from its historical context than from the scientific aspects of Martinson's evaluation. That is, by the time Martinson published his study "many criminologists—and other commentators on corrections—had already decided that rehabilitation was a failed enterprise" (Cullen & Gendreau, 2000, p. 122). In the mid-1970s, Martinson (1974) provided the final scientific proof to those who argued for a correctional system that should reject the existing social welfare approach and therapeutic principles in favor of either the justice model (advocated by liberals) or the get-tough crime-control model (advocated by conservatives) (Cullen & Gilbert, 2013).

In this regard, Cullen (2013) details three considerations that ascribe the popularity of Martinson's "nothing works" doctrine in an historical context. First, Martinson was not the first to show the ineffectiveness of correctional interventions (Cullen & Gendreau, 2000). In the 1950s and 1960s, scholars conducted reviews of empirical studies and presented negative results. However, those reviews emphasized the need for treatment integrity and did not present estimations that undermined the theoretical aspects of rehabilitation. Second, in 1979, Martinson published another evaluation that analyzed 555 studies and, in fact, renounced his nothing works claim (Martinson, 1979). However, this new evidence did not convince others "to follow Martinson in reconsidering their rejection of rehabilitation," and "was largely ignored" (Cullen, 2013, p. 328).

The third consideration that shows how the influence of Martinson (1974) related to the social context of that time is the way it was accepted by criminologists. In the 1970s, criminologists did not approach Martinson's doctrine with a critical examination of his report or try to address methodological flaws that could challenge the pessimistic conclusion. Instead, criminologists approached Martinson (1974) with an attitude that "sought to show that 'nothing works' when 'state control' is exercised" and to argue "that larger social justice is the solution to crime" (Cullen & Gendreau, 2001, p. 333). In other words, the "nothing works" doctrine, accepting became part of the field's "professional ideology" (Cullen & Gendreau, 2001). Criminologists in the 1970s welcomed Martinson's "nothing works" doctrine, accepting it "uncritically, abandoning the core norm of science that scholars subject empirical claims to organized skepticism" (Cullen, 2013, p. 328).

So, by mid 1970s, the legitimacy of the rehabilitative ideal had reached rock bottom—Martinson's study seemed to end the debate on the potential merits of rehabilitation. His article symbolized a solid "proof that rehabilitation was a failed and thus indefensible enterprise." Martinson's "nothing works" doctrine thus "quickly became accepted as a criminological fact—both within academia and among policy makers" (Cullen & Gilbert, 2013, p. 200).

In retrospect, Martinson's study actually reframed the debate on rehabilitation, establishing a silver lining that enabled to reaffirm its legitimacy. Martinson (1974) transformed the debate "from a broad and complex critique of the welfare state into the narrower and simpler issue of effectiveness" (Cullen, 2013, p. 329). The argument over which correctional theory should take precedence in guiding the correctional system's policies and practices increasingly became seen as a matter of evidence (Cullen & Gilbert, 2013). Ironically, Martinson paved the one way for advocates of offender treatment to restore the legitimacy of rehabilitative ideas: accumulate sufficient empirical evidence to show that treatment programs reduced recidivism. In other words, they needed to show, empirically, that the nothing works doctrine was wrong and that rehabilitation did in fact work.

Conclusion

This chapter has followed the impact of the rehabilitative ideal on the U.S. correctional system through three historical periods. The development of the rehabilitative ideal inspired a correctional paradigm that survived one-and-a-half centuries. During the first period, in the early 1800s, this paradigm was built on a broad consensus that the correctional system had the capacity to reform offenders through a sincere and honest human intention. This confidence in rehabilitation reflected the common belief in the curative power of the prison. However, by the mid–1800s, it became clear that this correctional design was unrealistic and doomed to failure. Therefore, the rehabilitative ideal had to change. The correctional system chose the model of individualized treatment to lead their rehabilitative efforts.

The second historical period lasted seven decades. During that time, the consensus around rehabilitation was virtually hegemonic. Rehabilitating offenders became the near-exclusive goal of the correctional system and justified the establishment of the therapeutic state (section two). However, in the late 1960s, the third historical period impacted the American correctional system (section three). For a decade, criminologists and politicians harshly criticized the correctional design and were eager to change its foundations. In essence, the collapse of the model of individualized treatment sent the rehabilitative ideal into a sudden decline. This decline in legitimacy followed a rejection of the social welfare approach in corrections and existing therapeutic orientation.

Instead of correctional rehabilitation, punitive penal policies started to govern the correctional system.

The next chapter will complete the rehabilitative ideal's historical context with a discussion of the latest historical period. This began in the late 1970s, when advocates of rehabilitation struggled to reaffirm the legitimacy of rehabilitation as a major correctional goal. As will be described in Chapter 2, during the last four decades, the legitimacy for rehabilitation has been transformed from "nothing works" to "what works" to "best practice." In essence, the restoration of the rehabilitative ideal was a long process that ultimately relied on a quantitative, evidence-based approach to corrections. By the early 21st century, the issue of how to do effective interventions became a central challenge in corrections. This book is an attempt to address this challenge and delineate a preferable guiding paradigm for rehabilitation.

The chapters to come examine two models of treatment intervention. Part II of this book, (Chapters 3 and 4) will discuss the Risk-Need-Responsivity (RNR) model, which emerged as the dominant approach to undertaking rehabilitation. Since the 1990s, this model has evolved into "a coherent treatment paradigm that both articulated how to rehabilitate offenders effectively and supplied the technology to undertake the task" (Cullen, 2012, p. 98; see also Andrews & Bonta, 1994, 1998, 2003, 2006, 2010; Bonta & Andrews, 2017). Importantly, the legitimacy of this model was established because its inventors were able to distill the scientific information into a package of principles that directs practitioners toward effective interventions. Specifically, Chapter 3 will discuss the development of the RNR model, including its underlying, and Chapter 4 will discuss the RNR model's core principles, and the technology of treatment that translated the ideas into practice. Taken together, Chapters 3 and 4 will present the evidence that led the RNR model to be considered as the only empirical validated guide for correctional intervention to reduce offender recidivism.

Part III (Chapters 5 and 6) will introduce a second model of intervention—the Good Lives Model (GLM). Since the early 2000s, this model has been suggested as an alternative overarching theoretical framework of correctional rehabilitation. Essentially, advocates of the GLM seek to preserve the merits of the RNR model "whilst actively engaging participants in the rehabilitation process and promoting desistance from crime" (Willis & Ward, 2013, p. 305; see also Ward & Maruna, 2007). The GLM challenges the RNR model and suggests another legitimate way to implement scientific information in correctional interventions. In this regard, Chapter 5 will cover the underlying theory of the GLM, and Chapter 6 will elaborate the correctional direction the GLM proposes and the evidence that supports its assumptions and practice.

In Part IV, Chapter 7 will describe the nature of the debate between the RNR model and the GLM and probe the extent to which these models are compatible or incompatible approaches to offender treatment. This debate, which followed the emergence of the GLM, revolves around the purpose of correctional rehabilitation and the legitimate ways to practice rehabilitation within the correctional system. The discussion focuses on how best to achieve an adequate balance between strengthening the social defense against criminality (e.g., reducing recidivism) and contributing to the welfare and satisfaction of others (e.g., improving an offender's life). This chapter will also evaluate whether the GLM can be considered as the pathway that will save the evidence-based orientation to rehabilitation from hitting "a kind of effective practice 'glass ceiling'" (Porporino, 2010, p. 63).

Finally, Chapter 8 will take the analysis beyond the current RNR-GLM debate. This chapter will discuss two possible futures of offender rehabilitation. One envisions the RNR model and the GLM as fundamentally incompatible models that should remain independent treatment paradigms which continue to compete with one another. The other future sees the value of both models and seeks to integrate them. In essence, the goal of Chapter 8 is to open up new promising ways to do effective treatments that reflect the spirit of both RNR and GLM. In this regard, Chapter 8 presents a specific integrated models with a correctional framework that aims to promote the legitimacy of rehabilitation in intervention programs while assisting offenders to build a healthier identity.

References

Allen, F. A. (1981). *The decline of the rehabilitative ideal: Penal policy and social purpose.* New Haven, CT: Yale University Press.

Andrews, D. A., & Bonta, J. (1994). *The psychology of criminal conduct.* Cincinnati, OH: Anderson.

Andrews, D. A., & Bonta, J. (1998). *The psychology of criminal conduct* (2nd ed.). Cincinnati, OH: Anderson.

Andrews, D. A., & Bonta, J. (2003). *The psychology of criminal conduct* (3rd ed.). Cincinnati, OH: Anderson.

Andrews, D. A., & Bonta, J. (2006). *The psychology of criminal conduct* (4th ed.). New Providence, NJ: Anderson/LexisNexis.

Andrews, D. A., & Bonta, J. (2010). *The psychology of criminal conduct* (5th ed.). New Providence, NJ: Anderson/LexisNexis.

Bonta, J., & Andrews, D. A. (2017). *The psychology of criminal conduct* (6th ed.). New York, NY: Routledge.

Cullen, F. T. (2005). The twelve people who saved rehabilitation: How the science of criminology made a difference. *Criminology, 43,* 1–42.

Cullen, F. T. (2012). Taking rehabilitation seriously: Creativity, science, and the challenge of offender change. *Punishment & Society, 14,* 94–114.

Cullen, F. T. (2013). Rehabilitation: Beyond nothing works. In M. Tonry (Ed.), *Crime and justice in America, 1975 to 2025—crime and justice: A review of research* (Vol. 42, pp. 299–376). Chicago, IL: University of Chicago Press.

Cullen, F. T., & Gendreau, P. (2000). Assessing correctional rehabilitation: Policy, practice, and prospects. In J. Horney (Ed.), *Policies, processes, and decisions of the criminal justice system: Criminal justice 2000* (Vol. 3, pp. 109–175). Washington, DC: U.S. Department of Justice, National Institute of Justice.

Cullen, F. T., & Gendreau, P. (2001). From nothing works to what works: Changing professional ideology in the 21st century. *The Prison Journal, 81,* 313–338.

Cullen, F. T., & Gilbert, K. E. (1982). *Reaffirming rehabilitation.* Cincinnati, OH: Anderson Pub. Co.

Cullen, F. T., & Gilbert, K. E. (2013). *Reaffirming rehabilitation* (2nd ed., 30th Anniversary ed.). Waltham, MA: Anderson/Elsevier.

Cullen, F. T., & Jonson, C. L. (2012). *Correctional theory: Context and consequences.* Thousand Oaks, CA: Sage.

Garland, D. (2001). *The culture of control: Crime and social order in contemporary society.* Chicago, IL: University of Chicago Press.

Lipton, D., Martinson, R., & Wilks, J. (1975). *The effectiveness of correctional treatment: A survey of treatment evaluation studies.* New York, NY: Praeger.

Martinson, R. (1974). What works?—questions and answers about prison reform. *Public Interest, 35*(2), 22–54.

Martinson, R. (1979). New findings, new views: A note of caution regarding sentencing reform. *Hofstra Law Review, 7*(Winter), 243–258.

Morris, N., & Rothman, D. J. (1995). *The Oxford history of the prison: The practice of punishment in western society.* New York, NY: Oxford University Press.

Ogloff, J. R. P., & Davis, M. R. (2004). Advances in offender assessment and rehabilitation: Contributions of the risk-needs-responsivity approach. *Psychology, Crime and Law, 10,* 229–242.

Pisciotta, A. W. (1994). *Benevolent repression: Social control and the American reformatory-prison movement.* New York, NY: New York University Press.

Porporino, F. J. (2010). Bringing sense and sensitivity to corrections: From programmes to 'fix' offenders to services to support desistence. In J. Brayford, F. Cowe, & J. Deering (Eds.), *What else works? Creative work with offenders* (pp. 61–85). Cullompton, Devon: Willan.

Rothman, D. J. (1971). *The discovery of the asylum: Social order and disorder in the new republic.* Boston, MA: Little, Brown.

Rothman, D. J. (1980). *Conscience and convenience: The asylum and its alternatives in progressive America.* Boston, MA: Little, Brown.

Ward, T., & Maruna, S. (2007). *Rehabilitation: Beyond the risk paradigm.* New York, NY: Routledge.

Willis, G. M., & Ward, T. (2013). The good lives model: Does it work? Preliminary evidence. In L. Craig, L. Dixon, & T. Gannon (Eds.), *What works in offender rehabilitation: An evidence-based approach to assessment and treatment* (pp. 305–317). London: Wiley-Blackwell.

Wines, E. C. (1870a). The present outlook of prison discipline in the United State. In E. C. Wines (Ed.), *Transactions of the national congress on penitentiary and reformatory discipline* (pp. 15–20). Retrieved from http://babel.hathitrust.org/cgi/pt?id=nyp. 33433075942023;view=1up;seq=7.

Wines, E. C. (Ed.). (1870b). *Transactions of the national congress on penitentiary and reformatory discipline.* Retrieved from http://babel.hathitrust.org/cgi/pt?id=nyp.3343 3075942023;view=1up;seq=7.

Wines, E. C., & Dwight, T. W. (1867/1973). *Report on the prisons and reformatories of the United States and Canada.* Albany, NY: AMS Press.

2

REAFFIRMING REHABILITATION

The previous chapter described how the rehabilitative ideal was discovered during the 1800s, dominated the correctional system throughout the 1900s, and declined in the 1970s. At that point in the mid-1970s, Martinson's (1974) publication seemed to sound the death knell for the policy and practice of offender treatment. Rehabilitation became a deserted ideology that struggled defenselessly against policy makers, academicians, and practitioners trumpeting the "nothing works doctrine." After all, "If Martinson was right, then it made little sense to continue any conversation about the value of rehabilitation" (Cullen & Gilbert, 2013, p. 200).

However, the full tale of the rehabilitative ideal within American corrections includes another historical period—its reaffirmation. Over the final two decades of the 1900s—which has continued to this day—a countermovement developed to challenge the nothing works doctrine. This chapter thus describes how advocates of rehabilitation reacted to this doctrine by showing empirically that offender treatment programs did, in fact, reduce reoffending. They began by amassing literature reviews in which they assessed the extant evaluation literature. Eventually, they used an emergent statistical technique—meta-analysis—to quantitatively synthesize the growing body of program evaluations. The results proved favorable to the treatment enterprise and largely undermined the legitimacy of the nothing works doctrine.

Thus, at the core of this effort to reaffirm rehabilitation was the compilation of empirical evidence—both through narrative reviews and then through meta-analyses—demonstrating that correctional programs were effective in reducing recidivism. A key finding of this research was that interventions have heterogeneous effects, with some increasing recidivism and others decreasing recidivism. This chapter ends with the conclusion that the challenge ahead is to continue to develop even more effective treatment approaches. This book is devoted to this task.

Narrative Reviews

Palmer's Reanalysis

In 1975, the legitimacy of correctional rehabilitation made the first step toward restoration. Ted Palmer, a researcher psychologist, doubted the empirical validity of Martinson's conclusion and thus examined "whether this conclusion takes account of the facts that were presented" (Palmer, 1975, p. 133). Palmer (1975) analyzed Martinson (1974) and developed a "systematic rebuttal of Martinson's 'nothing works' conclusion" (Cullen, 2005, p. 9). According to Cullen (2005), his study presented three important conclusions. The first was the empirical refutation of Martinson's statement that his study contained "only 'few and isolated' instances of treatment effectiveness" (p. 9). In his article, Palmer broke down 82 individuals studies, cited in Martinson (1974), into four categories that indicated different degrees of effectiveness.[1] Then he counted how many studies presented outcomes that reflected either the "positive," "partly positive," "ambiguous," or "negative" effect on recidivism. The findings showed that 39 studies of 82 had either a positive or partly positive effect on recidivism. In other words, rehabilitation efforts worked 48% of the studies in Martinson (1974).

The second important conclusion that could be drawn from Palmer (1975) was that Martinson's methodology links to his conclusion that nothing worked. Palmer noted that Martinson and his colleagues set a rigorous criterion for "success." That is, only a "treatment method" that always worked was considered as a "successful treatment." Therefore, when Martinson found that within each treatment method some programs were effective and some were not (i.e., inconsistent effect), he jumped to the conclusion that we cannot expect that any treatment program would be reliable enough to reduce recidivism through rehabilitation.

Martinson's qualitative judgment thus affected his interpretation. In fact, while Martinson interpreted the negative results in each treatment method as evidence of failure, Palmer interpreted the positive results in each method as evidence of success. Within the social context of the 1970s, however, Martinson's analytic framework could not be considered as an innocent perspective or an "inaccurate description of individual studies" (Palmer, 1975, p. 150). Indeed, Martinson's criterion of success might have reflected a "confirmation bias" in his work—a deliberately searched for evidence that would confirm his belief that nothing works to reform offenders (see Cullen & Gendreau, 2001; Kahneman, 2011).

The third conclusion was that Martinson expected each treatment method to have the same effect "for all or nearly all offenders" (Palmer, 1975, p. 150). That is, Palmer pointed at the fact that Martinson ignored the possibility that "some methods are nevertheless of value to at least *some* offenders" (p. 149, emphasis in original). Palmer (1975) then suggested an alternative perspective on the observed effects. He proposed that the findings reflected a pattern that was influenced by other intervening factors such as offender characteristics, type of treatment setting, and type of worker or service provider. Thus, Palmer (1975) called to researchers to move from searching methods of treatment that hold a "answer" for all offenders to research that focuses on "which methods work best for *which* types of offenders, and under *what* conditions or in what types of setting" (p. 150, emphasis in original).

In the 1970s, Palmer's work refuted Martinson's article but did not inspire the correctional field to question the underlying premises of the "nothing works doctrine." Indeed, in times when this doctrine became "a matter of almost religious faith" a single narrative review could be easily ignored (Cullen, 2013, p. 329). Martinson (1974) thus remained the "final word" for many criminologists, an essay that coincided conveniently "empirical reality and their ideological preferences" (Cullen & Gendreau, 2000, p. 131).

Gendreau and Ross's Two Reviews

In 1979, Paul Gendreau and Robert Ross joined Palmer in challenging Martinson's doctrine. They stated that those who embraced Martinson's conclusion not only ignored critical literature but also seemed indifferent to the fact that Martinson's research team relied on research published before 1967. Gendreau and Ross (1979) thus presented an extensive narrative review of the literature on correctional treatment—95 studies published between 1973 and 1978. Their review presented clear evidence of success in correctional rehabilitation and emphasized the important advances in rehabilitation ignored by Martinson. Cullen and Gendreau (2000) drew three major conclusions from this article.

First, Gendreau and Ross (1979) argued for a consensus among behavioral scientists that criminal behavior is learned. They claimed that Martinson incorrectly premised that "criminal offenders are incapable of relearning or of acquiring new behaviors" (pp. 465–466). Their review presented how behaviorally oriented programs successfully changed offenders' behavior in various situations and services. Specifically, they found reduction in recidivism in treatment programs that prompted and maintained behavior through a manipulation of rewards or reinforcements (*direct learning*—e.g., behavioral contract, token economy) and in programs that also focused on offenders' observation and imitation (*vicarious learning*—e.g., role modeling, peer group interaction). In addition, the review showed better results for programs that employed a combination of treatment methods (i.e., multimodal approach) rather than relying on a single method. The authors concluded that this finding reflected different learning styles among individuals and thus the importance of matching an individual's learning ability and the delivered service.

Second, Gendreau and Ross (1979) followed Palmer (1975) and emphasized the importance of the interactions between individual differences, type of treatment, and setting. Their review found that such an interaction increased "dramatically" the success of treatment methods (for example, in interventions that employed diversion, behavioral contracts, family interaction, contingency management, probation, or counseling) (Gendreau & Ross, 1979, p. 486).

Third, Gendreau and Ross (1979) considered lack of therapeutic integrity as a major cause of a program's failure (Cullen & Gendreau, 2000). Their review thus called on researchers to pay attention to the link between the original theoretical plan of the program and the actual way that it was eventually carried out. Specifically, they emphasized the following questions: "To what extent do treatment personnel actually adhere to the principles and employ the techniques of the therapy they purport to provide? To what extent are the treatment staff competent? How hard do they work? How much is treatment diluted in the correctional environment so that it becomes treatment in name only?" (Gendreau & Ross, 1979, p. 467).

In 1987, Gendreau and Ross continued to challenge the nothing works doctrine and to encourage the correctional field "to uncover what it is about programs that work that distinguishes them from programs that do not work" (Cullen & Gendreau, 2000, p. 129). They conducted another extensive narrative review of 130 studies published between 1981 and 1987. Their report analyzed the findings in various types of correctional interventions (e.g., biomedical, diversion, early/family intervention, education, getting tough, individual differences, parole/probation, restitution, and work) and offender populations (e.g., sex offenders, substance abusers, and violent offenders).

The findings in Gendreau and Ross (1987) presented updated support of correctional rehabilitation. In addition, the review indicated that the ability of correctional intervention programs to reform offenders relied on "principles underlying effective rehabilitation" (p. 395). Although the review did not provide a structured guidance, an effort to evolve principles of effective correctional intervention could be drawn from their analysis.

First, as in the 1979 review, Gendreau and Ross (1987) continue to demonstrate that effective programs relied on learning theories. Moreover, the updated review clearly showed the progress that occurred during the 1980s in this field of knowledge. That is, effective treatment programs designed to change both observed behavior and the way in which offenders think (i.e., offenders' cognitive process and skills). Specifically, the review indicated several successful programs that designed to enhance offenders' problem-solving skills and to redirect their beliefs, values, and attitudes (i.e., cognitive restructuring).

Second, Gendreau and Ross (1987) continued to advocate the interaction of individual differences, type of treatment, and settings as a factor that influenced the results. This review thus investigated this premise by examining only treatment programs "in which a component of individual difference was the primary concern" (p. 371). One type of findings indicated that an offender's personality or cognitive reasoning structure links to antisocial behavior. Another type of findings demonstrated the importance of the match between an offender's learning ability and the level of functioning required in a program (e.g., taking into account the offender's low cognitive functioning). The last type of findings was the connection between the offender's level of risk (to recidivate) and the effectiveness treatment programs. This pattern of results reflected a potential "to be the most potent individual-difference factor" (p. 373). Specifically, the review showed difference in recidivism "depending on whether high-risk cases received intensive services" and whether low-risk cases received "relatively minimal attention" (p. 373).

Third, Gendreau and Ross (1987) noted that the challenge for the correctional field would be to implement and maintain the scientific knowledge within "the social service delivery systems provided *routinely* by government and private agencies"—the real world—"that is what doesn't work!" (p. 395, emphasis in original). In this regard, they recommended on using risk assessment tools that would be represented by dynamic "personal needs" (e.g., degree of substance abuse, criminal thinking). In addition, they recommended on assigning high-risk offenders to programs that would be tailored "to fit their abilities and learning style" (p. 374).

Overall, Gendreau and Ross (1987) showed that by the late 1980s, many practitioners and researchers took rehabilitation seriously and focused on the developing methods, strategies, and approaches that resulted in effective treatment programs. Nevertheless, in those days, the significant advances in the correctional rehabilitation field only scratched the deeply entrenched "nothing works doctrine." That is, many criminologists and policy makers already decided that treatment was ineffective and tended to dismiss the reviews as biased studies (Cullen, 2005). They accused, thus, that authors of reviews presented selective studies, employed subjective interpretation, presented the findings in a misleading way, and ignored other study characteristics that might provide alternative explanations to the results (Cullen & Gendreau, 2000).

These charges were well known to Gendreau and Ross (1987). In their review, they also assessed the evolving field of a quantitative approach to literature evaluation. They noted that the correctional field was about to experience a significant methodological leap. That is, "the development of statistical syntheses of evaluation literature, particularly the technique known as meta-analysis . . . [was] considered in some quarters to represent a methodological breakthrough" (Gendreau & Ross, 1987, p. 391).

Meta-Analyses

By the end of the 1980s, there were already more than 400 controlled evaluations of intervention with offenders, and at least 40% of the better controlled studies "reported positive effects" (Andrews, Zinger, Lab, & Whitehead, 1990, p. 374). According to Palmer (1992), this ongoing research effort reflected a developing consensus that rehabilitation might be useful after all. However, the accumulating number of studies made it more and more difficult to conduct large narrative reviews that would reflect the findings from all the available research. Such an effort was important because narrative reviews of only a subset of studies could not overcome the alleged flaws that the conclusions were contaminated by a subjective selection and interpretation (Whitehead & Lab, 1989).

Gaining more legitimacy for rehabilitation thus required a new systematic way of addressing the findings from a large body of literature. That is, a reliable way was needed to overcome Martinson's (1974, p. 22) observation that "we have able to draw very little on any systematic empirical knowledge about the success or failure that we have met when we have tried to rehabilitate offenders, with various treatments and in various institutional and non-institutional settings." Fortunately, in the 1980s, a new method of assessing extant studies emerged: the technique of meta-analysis (Gendreau & Ross, 1987; Lipsey, 1992; Lösel, 1995; Palmer, 1992). Meta-analysis was used by scholars to provide a quantitative answer to the issues of what works in correctional rehabilitation.

In a nutshell, meta-analysis is a statistical method to summarize the findings of multiple independent research studies, which can run into the hundreds, on the same topic. Lipsey and Wilson (2001) define meta-analysis as a "form of survey research in which research reports, rather than people, are surveyed" (p. 1). In practice, meta-analysis is conducted through the following steps (Lipsey & Wilson, 2001): researchers (1) form a research question, (2) search for all the potential relevant research studies, (3) apply a criterion to maximize the inclusion of only relevant studies, and (4) establish coding form to identify explanatory, outcome, and moderator variables. Then, they (5) "interview" each research study according to the coding form and (6) calculate the precise effect size between each study and the outcome variables. In the last steps of the assessment, (7) the effects are statistically analyzed to provide the distribution of effect sizes and make statistical inferences. In addition, researchers may also (8) conduct a multivariate analysis to determine the degree to which the values of a moderating variables influence the relationship between the independent variable and the outcome variable.

In analyzing correctional rehabilitation studies, the outcome variable is often recidivism. In this regard, the effect sizes from the meta-analysis indicate that, on average, the intervention increased (positive effect size), had no effect (zero effect), or decreased recidivism (negative effect size). This effect size often reflects the effect of the treatment as a whole on recidivism (the "overall effect size"), but it can also reflect how other factors in the research study relate to recidivism. The salient contribution of the meta-analytic technique thus is the ability to measure these effect sizes while minimizing the opportunities for biased interpretation. That is, by using the meta-analytic technique, researchers can estimate empirically the impact of moderating variables in categories such as individual characteristics, study methods, type of intervention, settings, and the quantity and quality of treatment provided.

Within the field of corrections, the quantitative nature of the meta-analytic technique was crucial in changing skeptical views about the efficacy of interventions. In contrast to the narrative reviews, the interpretation of findings in the meta-analyses was short and clear. That is, the outcome in those reviews was simply a number—the effect size of the defined categories. Indeed, the quantitative nature of meta-analysis produced an outcome that was not only simple to grasp but also allowed more objective interpretation of the findings. Skeptical scholars thus could use the code form and the criteria for the inclusion of studies to replicate the decision-making that led to particular conclusions.

In addition, the meta-analytic technique was established as a better alternative to the vote-counting method. That is, while the vote-counting method summarized the knowledge by counting the number of studies that found a positive effect on recidivism, the meta-analytic technique provided a much more sophisticated tool to assess the data. Overall, thus, the meta-analytic technique offered a reliable methodology to face the general question: Can offenders be rehabilitated? Moreover, it could also clarify the pattern of results and thus answer the more specific questions: What does not work? What does work? And what factors moderate the outcome in correctional interventions?

Since the publication of the first meta-analysis research review that focused on treatment of offenders (Garrett, 1985), approximately 100 meta-analyses were used to assess the effectiveness of correctional treatment (Andrews & Bonta, 2010a; Lipsey & Cullen, 2007; Lösel, 1995; McGuire, 2004, 2013). Those reviews covered various areas such as juvenile offenders, offense type or offender classification (e.g., sex offenders, violent offenders, drink-driving, personality disorder), types of punitive sanctions, and specific types of interventions (e.g., education and vocation, sociotherapeutic prison, cognitive-behavioral, family-based, school-based, substance abuse, restorative justice) (McGuire, 2004). In addition, reviews have been designed to test specific hypotheses (e.g., the differential impact of gender, ethnic minority, age group, or adherence to certain correctional principles). Overall, these meta-analyses provided two key findings that challenged Martinson's "nothing works" doctrine. First, across all types of interventions, the average effect size showed a reduction in recidivism. The second key finding was the considerable heterogeneity of effect sizes across the interventions.

Overall Effect Size

The purpose of estimating the overall effect size across all types of correctional interventions is to know whether rehabilitation works in general. In fact, such assessment of the average effect size covers a broad spectrum of interventions without making any distinction by type of programs. That is, the estimation of the overall effect size reflects a broad perspective of society's correctional efforts that consist of the wide range of strategies, programs, policies, and interventions that are in use in corrections. Essentially, such efforts include not only programs that aim to alter the behavior, attitude, or the emotional state of offenders in a supportive and constructive process (Mackenzie, 2006) but also programs with primarily punitive orientation (i.e., deterrence-oriented correctional interventions), and community restraints (e.g., surveillance, supervision).

Lösel (1995) faced this task and assessed the outcomes in 13 meta-analyses published between 1985 and 1995. This review covered a total of more than 500 evaluation studies that were conducted with both adults and juveniles in community-based and residential correctional interventions. Lösel indicated that the treatment effect sizes in the literature varied between 0.05 (Lipsey, 1992) and 0.18 (Garrett, 1985). Then, he estimated the overall effect size of correctional interventions after considering the studies' sample sizes and potential methodological biases (e.g., variation in the study designed, publication bias, juveniles versus adults). Lösel's (1995) conclusion was that "the mean effect of all assessed studies probably has a size of about 0.10" (p. 89). This correlation of 0.10 means that the average percentage points of recidivism rate for the treatment group, across all intervention studies, was 10 percentage points lower than the recidivism rate for the control group.

During the last two decades, the estimation that the overall effect size of correctional interventions is approximately 0.10 was endorsed by several studies conducted by diverse scholars (Andrews & Bonta, 2010a; Cullen & Jonson, 2012; Lipsey & Cullen, 2007; McGuire, 2004; Redondo, Sanchez-Meca, & Garrido, 1999). These scholars shared a consensus about three interrelated aspects of this general estimation. One agreed-upon aspect is that the overall effect size is modest but not inconsequential. On the one hand, thus, broad classification of effect sizes leads to a conclusion that the general impact of correctional interventions on recidivism was small (Cohen, 1992). On the other hand, scholars agreed that this value is not without practical significance. This perspective relies mainly on practical reasons—"better alternatives are not available" and such reduction is potentially cost effective (Lösel, 1995, p. 91). In practical words, the overall effect size on recidivism cannot be overlooked, "especially when dealing with high-risk offenders" (Cullen, 2013, p. 338).

The second agreed-upon aspect is that the overall effect size shows a reliable positive impact of correctional intervention programs on recidivism. That is, rehabilitation programs worked. This positive effect, thus, reflects solid evidence that refutes a fundamental premise of Martinson's "nothing works" doctrine—offenders can be reformed by intentional correctional interventions. For example, this interpretation of the findings was so clear to Lipsey (1995) that he concluded that "It is no longer constructive for researchers, practitioners and policymakers to argue about whether delinquency treatment and related rehabilitative approaches 'work' as if that were a question that could be answered with simple 'yes' or 'no.' As a generality, treatment clearly works" (p. 78).

The third consensual aspect is the fact that the pattern of the data in rehabilitation treatment is much more informative than the overall effect size. Indeed, researchers stated that "the most general and striking findings of research on this topic is the great variability of the recidivism effects across different treatments and different studies" (Lipsey & Cullen, 2007, p. 306). That is, some programs were more effective than others. As will be discussed next, the positive overall effect size provided researchers a solid ground to move on for identifying and investigating the sources of this variability.

Heterogeneity in Effect Size

The second key finding from the meta-analyses literature was that treatment effect across studies was heterogeneous, not homogeneous. That is, meta-analyses found a spectrum of treatment effect sizes that stretched from studies with a negative effect value (increased recidivism) to studies that showed a positive value (up to 30 percentage points reduction in recidivism). Essentially, this consistent phenomenon refutes Martinson's conclusion that the treatment effect is uniformly weak across all type of interventions.

Since the early 1990s, researchers in corrections conducted meta-analyses to investigate the variation in treatment effect across studies and provide more reliable answers to "what works best, for whom, under what circumstances, and why" (Lipsey & Cullen, 2007, p. 307). These researchers adopted one of the two research strategies to investigate what works in correctional rehabilitation (Andrews & Bonta, 2010a; Lipsey, 2009; Lipsey & Cullen, 2007; Lipsey, Howell, Kelly, Chapman, & Carver, 2010).

The first type of research strategy was to conduct meta-analyses that focused on one type of program or program area (e.g., boot camps, cognitive-behavioral therapy [CBT], family therapy), on one type of offender (e.g., substance abuse), or on a particular program (e.g., multisystemic therapy, functional family therapy). This strategy, which was used in most of the reviews, produced reliable information about the effectiveness of particular topics and generally confirmed the effectiveness of rehabilitation. However, those studies revealed only a limited aspect of treatment effectiveness. That is, it was "difficult to piece such meta-analyses together into an overall picture of current knowledge about the nature of the most effective programs" (Lipsey et al., 2010, p. 21).

The alternative type of research strategy to conduct meta-analyses addresses this limitation. This strategy involved a comprehensive research review that investigated the entire body of literature. Researchers then were able to examine the relative effectiveness of different program types and approaches. Moreover, they could identify the general factors that correlated with effective programs and draw reliable conclusions about "what works" best in correctional rehabilitation. The next section will present the findings from such comprehensive meta-analyses. Specifically, this section will elaborate the two approaches that researchers used for this task—Lipsey's inductive approach and the Canadians' theoretical approach. Taken together, the conclusions from these research approaches serve as the foundation of evidence-based corrections.

Two Approaches to Knowing What Works

As described in the previous section, the development of meta-analyses provided a reliable conclusion that rehabilitation works. In addition, this systematic quantitative approach to evaluate correctional interventions enabled one to investigate their sources of variation and draw conclusions about what works and what works best.

In this regard, the meta-analysis literature presents two approaches to conduct a comprehensive research into correctional interventions. One approach is presented in Mark Lipsey's work (Lipsey, 1992, 2009; Lipsey & Wilson, 1998). This approach adopted an atheoretical and descriptive approach to investigate the variability of the effects on recidivism. The second approach is presented in the meta-analyses conducted by Don Andrews and his colleagues (Andrews & Bonta, 2006; Andrews, Zinger et al., 1990; Bonta & Andrews, 2017). Their approach "test[ed] the hypothesis that interventions adhering to certain principles . . . would yield higher effect sizes than other types of work" (McGuire, 2004, p. 143). These two ways of conducting comprehensive meta-analysis outlined what "works" and what "does not work" in correctional rehabilitation and therefore merits close examination. Thus, the first part of this section presents the findings from Lipsey's approach to meta-analyses and the second part discusses the findings from the Canadians' approach. The third part of this section summarizes the conclusions on what works.

Lipsey's Inductive Approach

Mark Lipsey conducted a series of comprehensive meta-analyses that focused on the effects of intervention with juvenile offenders (Lipsey, 1992, 1995, 1999, 2009; Lipsey & Wilson, 1998). As mentioned above, Lipsey's approach to research was atheoretical and essentially inductive. That is, "his analyses are not associated with theories of crime or even with theoretical positions in regard to the processes of behavioral influence and behavioral change" (Andrews & Bonta, 2010a, p. 375). Instead, Lipsey's work focused on the best way to measure the effect size after minimizing the opportunities for biased interpretation. For this task, Lipsey sorted studies into five categories: sample characteristics, study methodology, type of intervention (including the amount and quality of service), level of supervision and control, and publication bias. His conclusions thus were based on high-quality research that assessed the relative contribution of numerous treatment variables after controlling for methodological variables.

In 2009, Lipsey presented the findings from his most updated database. This comprehensive study covered 361 primary research reports (with 548 independent study samples) conducted between 1958 and 2002. The findings in this study reconfirmed the conclusions from Lipsey's previous work. In general, Lipsey (2009) found that treatment efforts result in a significant effect on recidivism even when the effects of the methodological variables and other nontreatment variables were controlled. Specifically, Lipsey's research strategy presented three factors that were "found to be most relevant when considering what works best for reducing subsequent offense rates" (Lipsey et al., 2010, p. 23; Lipsey, 2009).

The first most relevant factor was the risk level of juveniles. In Lipsey (2009), this factor was most strongly and consistently related to the effect of recidivism ($r = .42$). That is, "interventions applied to juveniles with higher levels of delinquency risk were more effective, though that effect was offset somewhat if the juveniles had aggressive/violent histories" (pp. 143–144). This relationship between offenders' level of risk and the effect size on recidivism echoed Lipsey's previous comprehensive meta-analyses. Lipsey (1992) reported that "there was a slight tendency for studies of juveniles with higher risk level" (p. 121). In addition, Lipsey and Wilson (1998) supported the practice of targeting high-risk offenders "over the view that serious delinquents cannot be helped to reduce offending" (p. 338). Lipsey (2014) thus concluded that the risk level of the juvenile participants was revealed as "a strong predictor of positive effects on subsequent offense rates . . . All else equal, effective programs produce larger effects for higher risk than lower risk juveniles" (p. 8).

The second most relevant factor found in Lipsey (2009) was the distinction between two broad types of interventions. That is, interventions that relied on "therapeutic" philosophy (categorized as counseling, skill training, restorative, and multiple services) had a stronger impact on recidivism than interventions that adapted "strategies of control or coercion" (surveillance, deterrence, and discipline). Indeed, this broad pattern across studies was also found in Lipsey (1992) and in Lipsey and Wilson (1998). In the later study, for example, consistent evidence of positive effects was found for treatments that were service oriented (e.g., individual counseling, interpersonal skills, behavioral program) whereas interventions that focused on punitive orientation (e.g., "wilderness challenge" programs, deterrence programs) produced weak or zero effect.

The third important factor indicated in Lipsey (2009) was the consistent relationship between the high quality of program implementation and reduction in recidivism. That is, the extent to which the program did what it intended to do affected the outcome. Specifically, the effect in this study was measured by "a composite variable that combined two correlated features" (p. 136). One is the existence of any problem with implementation (e.g., high dropout rates, staff turnover, poorly trained personnel) and the other is the degree of researcher's involvement in the delivery of the intervention. In essence, Lipsey (2009) confirmed the findings found in his previous work. That is, "treatments that were delivered by the researcher, or in which the researcher had a considerable influence, showed larger effect sizes" than treatments in which the evaluator was not part of the program team (Lipsey, 1992, p. 122). In addition, Lipsey and Wilson (1998) also indicated that in noninstitutional settings, "the less involved the researcher was in the design, planning, and delivery of treatment, the smaller the effect size" (pp. 321–322). In respect of institutional settings, "studies in which there was indication of high monitoring yielded larger effects than those in which implementation integrity was rated as low" (p. 327).

Beyond these three most relevant factors reported by Lipsey (2009), another important finding related to what was not found as distinguishing factors. In this regard, the study could not distinguish between the relative impacts of the particular types of treatment. In addition, the study found that the level of juvenile justice supervision and control (settings) and the amount of service (measured by the variation in the duration and total hours of service) were not generally related to recidivism in intervention programs for juveniles. Moreover, interventions were equally effective for younger and older juveniles, for males and females, and for whites and minorities.

Overall, since the early 1990s, Lipsey's studies have had an enormous impact on the correctional field, mainly due to the high quality of his research. The fact that he was not "identified as a rehabilitation activists" (unlike other researchers who argued against the "nothing works" doctrine) also enhanced the reliability of his work (Cullen, 2005, p. 19). Nevertheless, Lipsey's atheoretical approach to research has a problematic aspect. That is, Lipsey's practice to sort the studies into predefined types of treatment can be problematic when the analysis cannot statistically distinguish between the relative effect sizes of brand-name programs or generic type of programs (Lipsey & Cullen, 2007). In particular, Lipsey's strategy has limited informative value because the data often revealed high within-category variations in effect sizes. For example, the effect sizes in generic program type (e.g., counseling or vocational training) were found as "vary from provider to provider." In addition, "treatment elements are often mixed and combined in varied ways (e.g., drug-education classes combined with individual counseling and vocational training)" (p. 307). Therefore, without more details about what was actually done in the program, Lipsey's atheoretical approach "can, at best, provide only general guidance for effective programs" (p. 309).

The Canadians' Theoretical Approach

As mentioned above, in the early 1990s, Donald Andrews and his colleagues established an alternative approach to conduct a comprehensive meta-analysis (Andrews, Zinger et al., 1990; Andrews & Bonta, 2006, 2010a; Gendreau, 1996). As opposed to Lipsey's atheoretical approach, they relied on the criminological and psychological literature. Essentially, they used the meta-analytic technique to test and develop their theoretical model of correctional assessment and rehabilitation. The premise of this model was that adherence to certain principles would result in the single strongest correlation of effect size.

In 1990, Andrews and his colleagues conducted the first meta-analysis that tested their model—the Risk–Need–Responsivity approach (the RNR model). The presumption of this study was that rehabilitation works, and the "evidence of effective treatment was there from the earliest reviews" (Andrews, Zinger et al., 1990, p. 371). In addition, they relied on the thesis that "the effectiveness of correctional treatment is dependent upon what is delivered to whom in particular settings" (p. 372; see also Gendreau & Ross, 1979, 1987; Palmer, 1975). In that sense, Andrews, Zinger et al. (1990) assumed that the major sources of variation in correctional interventions were "the main and interaction effects of (a) preservice characteristics of offenders, (b) characteristics of correctional workers, (c) specifics of content and process of services planned and delivered, and (d) intermediate changes in the person and circumstances of individual offenders" (p. 372).

Thus, with very limited empirical and theoretical guidance, Andrews, Zinger et al. (1990) suggested the risk, need, and responsivity principles as three general characteristics of intervention that would explain the variability found in treatment effect. Moreover, their theoretical model suggested that adherence to these three principles would maximize the capacity of treatment to reduce recidivism. The next chapter will provide a broad discussion of the theoretical and empirical development of the principles that formulate the RNR model. For the purpose of this section, however, these principles will be discussed in brief and in relation to findings from the meta-analyses.

In short, the *risk principle* indicates *who* should be treated. This principle suggests that "higher levels of service are best reserved for higher risk cases and that low–risk cases are best assigned to minimal service" (Andrews, Zinger et al., 1990, p. 374). That is, the risk principle directs the correctional interventions to deliver treatment programs to higher risk cases rather than lower risk cases.

The *need principle* describes *what* should be treated. This principle "makes a distinction between criminogenic and noncriminogenic needs" (Andrews & Bonta, 2010b, p. 45). That is, the need principle suggests that correctional interventions should target criminogenic needs—"dynamic risk factors that, when changed, are associated with *subsequent* variation in the chances of criminal conduct" (Andrews, Zinger et al., 1990, p. 374; emphasis in original). In parallel, correctional intervention should avoid addressing noncriminogenic need because a change in these needs will not be efficient to reduce recidivism. In Andrews, Zinger et al. (1990), the criminogenic needs were clustered under the domains of "antisocial attitude and associations," "antisocial personality pattern," family (parent characteristics, family structure, family cohesiveness), "chemical dependency," and social achievement. In contrast, noncriminogenic needs included self-esteem, "increasing cohesiveness of antisocial peer groups," and personal distress. Overall, therefore, the criminogenic needs were a "subset of risk factors" that was initially drawn from the theoretical perspective of general personality and cognitive social learning, as well as from the early studies that focused on prediction of risk (Andrews, Bonta, & Hoge, 1990, p. 31) (see the next chapter for further discussion).

The *responsivity* principle addresses the *how* of intervention. That is, it identifies the styles and modes of service that is generally capable of influencing the criminogenic needs ("general responsivity"). Another aspect of the responsivity principle directs the rehabilitative effort to provide service that appropriately matched the learning style and the characteristic of the offenders ("specific responsivity"). Such individualized treatment takes into account the "strengths, ability, motivation, personality, and bio-demographic characteristics such as gender, ethnicity, and age" (Andrews & Bonta, 2010b, p. 47). In 1990, Andrews and his colleague viewed "appropriate correctional service" as a structured approach that "involve the use of behavioral and social learning principles of inter-personal influence, skill enhancement, and cognitive change" (Andrews, Zinger et al., 1990, p. 375). In their meta-analyses, they focused solely on "general responsivity" that was coded as any social learning or cognitive-behavioral programs that used modeling, role-play, problem-solving, and graduate practice.

Specifically, Andrews, Zinger et al. (1990) assessed 80 studies that yielded 154 effect size estimates that tested the relationship between the level of adherence to the RNR principles and reduction in recidivism. To this end, they examined the effectiveness of three categories of treatments that represented the level of adherence to the RNR principles ("inappropriate," "appropriate," and "unspecified" correctional services). Another category ("criminal sanctions") represented the effect of judicial process without any deliberate rehabilitative service. The analysis of the differential effect of these categories revealed that the average effect of programs that followed the RNR principles was significantly higher than unspecified treatment, inappropriate programs, and criminal processing (effect size of .30 versus .13, -.06, and -.07, respectively).

In the 2000s, Andrews and Bonta (2006, 2010a) continued to test the RNR model in a com-prehensive meta-analysis. They presented an updated set of 374 tests that examined their model through six hypotheses. The following are the findings that relate to each hypothesis. First, the analysis found that the mean effect size of programs that delivered human service was significantly higher than the mean effect size of programs that focused on criminal sanction (.12 versus −.03). Second, correctional treatment that adhered to all of the three RNR principles had a larger effect size than services that adhered to only two of these principles (.26 versus .18) or to one of the three principles (.26 versus .02). In addition, the study examined the independent effect of each principle. In this regard, significant differences were found between correctional treatments that followed the principles of risk (.10), need (.19), or responsivity (.23) compared to treatments that did not fol-low the particular principle (.03, −.01, or .04, respectively). Notably, this effect of adherence to the RNR model survived statistical controls for the effect of integrity and implementation, age, gender, and ethnicity.

The third finding from Andrews and Bonta (2006, 2010a) was the impact of community-based/residential-based intervention on recidivism. That is, the effect size of full adherence to the RNR model was larger in the community setting than in the residential setting (.35 versus .17). The fourth finding relates to therapists' skills and qualities ("core correctional practice"). The results showed that both indicators of high-quality relationship (e.g., relationship skills, effective modeling) and structuring indicators (e.g., structuring skills, effective reinforcement, effective disproval, structured skill learning, problem-solving, effective authority) were associated with improving effect size.

The fifth finding showed that indicators of integrity of implementation and service delivery increased the effect size (e.g., staff selected for relationship skills, staff trained, clinical supervision of staff, number of hours of service, printed manual, specific model, new program, small sample, involved evaluator). The sixth finding from Andrews and Bonta (2006, 2010a) showed that once the RNR principles were controlled, only four variables increased the effect of treatment service on recidivism: "an evaluator involved in the design and/or delivery of service," "community based setting," "nonjustice ownership of program," and "referral to program by a justice person" (p. 397). When three or four of the above characteristics were presented, adherence to the RNR model yielded the strongest effect size (.38).

Overall, the hypotheses in Andrews and Bonta (2010a) allowed researchers to produce constructive knowledge that Lipsey's inductive approach was incapable of generating. That is, the assessment of program efficacy in terms of treatment principles, rather than in terms of treatment types, seems to be "more consistent with the nature of the variability found in treatment effects" (Lipsey & Cullen, 2007, p. 310). Nevertheless, the comprehensive meta-analysis of Andrews and Bonta (2010a) is limited in its ability to provide good empirical guides to effective program principles. As with Lipsey's comprehensive studies, the studies of Andrews and his colleagues suffered from the fact that "many evaluations do not describe or measure the intervention with enough specificity to know what exactly was done" (Cullen & Jonson, 2011, p. 304).

Drawing Conclusions on What Works

As described above, meta-analytic reviews helped to uncover the general pattern of findings embedded within hundreds of studies. Through a systematic quantitative approach, researchers of various studies provided reliable leads regarding "what works" and "what does not work" in correctional rehabilitation. Taken together, the meta-analysis literature produced five general conclusions. The first three conclusions present the evidence found in the two approaches to conduct comprehensive meta-analyses (Andrews & Bonta, 2006, 2010a; Andrews, Zinger et al., 1990; Lipsey, 1992, 1999, 2009) and were also supported by more specific meta-analyses. The fourth and the fifth conclusions are based only on evidence from the comprehensive meta-analysis of Andrews, Zinger et al. (1990) and Andrews and Bonta (2006, 2010a), and the support from other meta-analyses that assessed studies of specific treatment or approaches.

The first conclusion that can be drawn from the meta-analyses literature is the distinction between correctional interventions that provide rehabilitative service and interventions that relied on correctional sanctions. Lipsey and Cullen (2007) indicated two clear patterns in the data. One showed the ineffectiveness of the punitive approach of changing criminal behavior. That is, evaluation studies that assessed "greater versus less, or no sanctions ha[d] found, at best, modest mean recidivism reductions for the greater sanctions and, at worst, increased recidivism for that condition" (p. 314; see also Jonson, 2010). Another pattern in the data showed that rehabilitation-oriented interventions produced a mean reduction of recidivism that varied between 10% and 38%. In fact, overview of the effect sizes revealed that "the least of those mean reduction is greater than the largest mean reduction reported by any meta-analysis of sanctions" (p. 314).

Indeed, meta-analysis reviews clearly supported the capability of correctional rehabilitation to reduce offender recidivism and the incapability of correctional sanction to achieve this goal. In this regard, the impact of rehabilitation-oriented treatments remained positive across categories of age, gender, and ethnicity (Lipsey, 1992, 2009; Andrews & Bonta, 2010a). Therefore, this pattern of findings across studies considers as "sufficiently sound general conclusion, bordering on beyond a reasonable doubt" (Lipsey & Cullen, 2007, p. 314).

The second general conclusion that can be drawn from the meta-analysis reviews is the salient impact of the quality of program integrity on recidivism. That is, meta-analyses consistently showed a larger effect size in correctional programs that were implemented as planned (Andrews & Bonta, 2010a; Cullen & Gendreau, 2000; Lipsey, 1992, 1995, 1999, 2009; Lipsey & Cullen, 2007; Lipsey & Wilson, 1998; McGuire, 2004). Specifically, the comprehensive meta-analyses indicated the positive impact of interventions that were constructed for demonstration or research purposes. In such projects, the involvement of evaluator in program was a dominant variable that increased the effect size on recidivism (Andrews & Bonta, 2010a; Lipsey, 1999, 2009). Further support to this conclusion was achieved from meta-analyses that were specifically designed to examine the relationship between program integrity and the effect size on recidivism. Those studies found that the involvement of the evaluator in the program setting produced a larger effect size (Petrosino & Soydan, 2005; Andrews & Dowden, 2005). Overall, however, due to lack of details about the implementation process, it is difficult to determine the relative impact of the various indicators of integrity (Lipsey & Cullen, 2007).

The third sound conclusion that can be drawn from the meta-analyses is the relationship between the level of risk and recidivism. As mentioned above, this relationship was supported in the comprehensive meta-analyses. In addition, the stability of risk effect on recidivism was also seen in meta-analyses that specifically examined the "risk principle" (Dowden & Andrews, 1999a, 1999b, 2003; Landenberger & Lipsey, 2005). Overall, there is sufficient evidence to make a general conclusion that planned intervention that targeted higher risk offenders produced a larger positive effect size than programs that did not consider offenders' risk. Nevertheless, this advice should be taken with caution because the mean effect sizes in meta-analyses that assessed the effect of risk in treatment programs measured risk in different ways. Indeed, studies that assessed the effect of risk on recidivism presented mean effect size with relatively wide confidence intervals. According to Smith, Gendreau, and Swartz (2009), this pattern of the effect size is "likely attributable, at least in part, to the fact that definitions of risk level can be wildly inconsistent when cumulating risk scores across studies" (p. 160).

The fourth conclusion relates to the intermediate targets that influence the effect size of treatments. That is, treatment programs that addressed certain dynamic intermediate targets yielded a larger effect on recidivism than interventions that avoided those targets. Notably, the relationship between changes in intermediate targets and recidivism was tested by Andrews and his colleagues but was absent from Lipsey's analyses. Since 1990, Andrews and his colleagues systematically distinguished between various personal and interpersonal domains according to the extent they functionally related to criminal behavior. As noted above, they found that treatment programs that targeted more criminogenic needs than noncriminogenic needs produced a greater effect on recidivism than programs that did not follow this scheme (i.e., the need principle) (Andrews & Bonta, 2006, 2010a; Andrews, Bonta et al., 1990).

In addition, several meta-analyses that specifically tested the hypotheses of the RNR model supported the efficacy of the adherence to criminogenic needs. Those studies found that treatment programs that followed the need principle produced a larger effect size in treatment programs for female offenders (Dowden & Andrews, 1999a), young offenders (Dowden & Andrews, 1999b), and sex offenders (Hanson, Bourgon, Helmus, & Hodgson, 2009). Furthermore, targeting criminogenic needs over noncriminogenic needs also yield a larger effect size in family intervention programs (Dowden & Andrews, 2003), in programs that used the relapse prevention model (Dowden, Antonowicz, & Andrews, 2003), and in correctional treatment programs on violent reoffending (Dowden & Andrews, 2000).

Overall, meta-analyses that investigated the relationship between potential predictor variables and recidivism (prediction studies) assisted researchers to map the effect found in treatment studies. Andrews and Bonta (2006) presented a quantitative summary of eight meta-analyses that assessed risk factors. They found that the grand mean predictive validity (r) of the four most dominant risk factors—criminal history, procriminal attitude, antisocial personality, and procriminal associations—was 0.26. In addition, they found that the grand mean of the other four risk/need factors that are considered part of the criminogenic needs—social achievement, family/marital issues, substance abuse, and lack of prosocial pursuit—was 0.17. Their summary also found that factors such as personal emotional distress/psychopathology, lower class origins, fear of official punishment, and low verbal intelligence had a grand mean predictive validity of 0.03 (Andrews & Bonta, 2010a). Those studies used to cluster variables in the general categories of criminogenic and noncriminogenic needs and therefore produced essential evidence-based knowledge of what to target in treatment programs.

The fifth conclusion that was supported by the meta-analyses reviews relates to the therapeutic strategies and the treatment components needed to change criminality—that is, the most efficient way to treat offenders. As mentioned above, due to within-type-of-treatment variations in effect sizes, Lipsey (2009) could only distinguish between "therapeutic philosophies" (i.e., counseling, skill training, restorative, and multiple services) and "non-therapeutic philosophies" (i.e., surveillance, deterrence, and discipline). In this regard, meta-analyses showed that categorizing studies by therapeutic strategies produced more informative knowledge. That is, Andrews, Zinger et al. (1990) found that treatment programs that used behavioral, cognitive-behavioral, and cognitive social learning strategies had a larger effect size than programs that used other strategies.

In addition, several specific meta-analyses that used exactly the same way of coding as Andrews, Zinger et al. (1990) found the same results (Dowden & Andrews, 1999a, 1999b, 2000; Dowden & Andrews, 2003; Dowden et al., 2003). Moreover, since the early 1990s, many other meta-analyses consistently showed that the general category of behavioral or cognitive-behavior programs were more effective than other approaches (Garrett, 1985; Hanson et al., 2009; Izzo & Ross, 1990; Landenberger & Lipsey, 2005; Lipsey & Wilson, 2001; MacKenzie, 2006; McGuire, 2004; Pearson, Lipton, Cleland, & Yee, 2002; Redondo et al., 1999; Smith et al., 2009; Wilson, Bouffard, & MacKenzie, 2005).

In brief, this general category of behavioral/cognitive-behavior intervention consists of two subcategories. One subcategory is behavioral therapy that aims to change criminal behavior through contingencies of positive reinforcement in order to develop and maintain appropriate patterns of behavior (Pearson et al., 2002). Within this therapeutic approach, two common procedures that are used with offenders include contingency contracting and token economy. The second subcategory is CBT. Although CBT includes a variety of clinical interventions, the therapies share an underling principle—what and how a person thinks control his/her behavior (Glick, 2006). In general, CBTs are designed to "help clients become aware of thought processes that lead to maladaptive behavioral responses and to actively change those processes in a positive way" (Wilson et al., 2005, p. 173). The goal of programs that use CBT in correctional settings is to have the offenders "return to their natural environment with new repertoires of skills so they can obtain reinforcement in socially acceptable ways instead of illegal means" (Pearson et al., 2002, p. 493). In essence, CBTs applied to offenders have been conceptualized as either cognitive restructuring therapies (aim to change the content of thinking) or coping skills programs (aim to change the structure of thinking). Moreover, CBTs are often considered as highly structured programs (as opposed to the nondirective treatment approach) (Landenberger & Lipsey, 2005).

Due to this consistent evidence that behavioral and cognitive-behavioral programs yielded the best effect on recidivism, meta-analyses also investigated the relative effect of the generic types of those programs. However, no specific type of either behavioral program or CBT produced an effect size that significantly outperformed the mean of all the other types (Landenberger & Lipsey, 2005; Pearson et al., 2002; Wilson et al., 2005). Therefore, rather than coding the types of CBT, meta-analyses tried to code the specific treatment element of this therapy (e.g., cognitive skills, cognitive restructuring, interpersonal problem-solving, social skills, anger control, moral reasoning, victim impact, substance abuse, relapse prevention, individual attention). In this regard, CBTs that included interpersonal problem-solving and anger control were associated with a larger effect size on recidivism, whereas programs with elements such as victim impact and behavioral modification produced a negative effect (Landenberger & Lipsey, 2005). Overall, thus, meta-analyses that assessed the offender treatment literature "have consistently favored cognitive-behavioral interventions over other treatment modalities" (Smith et al., 2009, p. 155). However, these systematic reviews did not produce much knowledge that specified the "elements or combination of elements that are critical in producing positive effect on offender's behavior" (Wilson et al., 2005, p. 200).

In sum, the above evidence from the various meta-analyses described the nature and the directions of the quantitative data now existed. In essence, meta-analyses played a crucial role in changing views about the effectiveness of correctional rehabilitation. In fact, accumulating knowledge clearly falsified the "nothing works doctrine." That is, "those who had long relished the apparent ineffectiveness of rehabilitation were now on the wrong side of science. The evidence was incontrovertible" (Cullen & Gilbert, 2013, p. 202). Moreover, the evidence that mapped the heterogeneity of the effect size provided researchers promising leads to maximize the effect of correctional intervention on recidivism.

Conclusion

This chapter examined the historical period that allowed rehabilitation to regain its credibility as a correctional theory that can shape policy and practice. Since the late 1970s, scholars have worked on building a scientific foundation for the rehabilitative enterprise and for implementing its premises in correctional systems. Specifically, they worked diligently through their research to confirm that criminality can be changed through planned correctional intervention.

During the last four decades, these scholars transformed the status of rehabilitation from "nothing works" to "what works" to "best practice." As described in length, ongoing empirical findings that showed clear correctional success played a primary role in reaffirming the treatment's legitimacy. In fact, the empirical findings were so convincing that the rehabilitative ideal rebuilt itself as a "core cultural belief" that first emerged in, and then survived since, the early 1800s (Cullen, 2005).

The effort to reaffirm rehabilitation continues to this day. In the opening decades of the 21st century, the challenge for advocates of rehabilitation is to maintain and promote the legitimacy of correctional rehabilitation. Accordingly, the issue of how to undertake effective intervention is now a central challenge in corrections. Overall, this book is an attempt to face this challenge and to delineate the preferable guiding paradigm of rehabilitation. Thus, the next part of this book (Chapters 3 and 4) will elaborate how the RNR model was developed for that purpose. In essence, this model followed the empirical reality that suggested the need for a theory—a set of principles—that could explain why rehabilitation programs either worked or did not work.

Note

1. Due to selection bias, Palmer (1975) excluded studies that discussed the effect of sentence length or the degree of security on recidivism (those studies were considered by Palmer as inevitably leading to a positive effect; see fn. 10 in that article).

References

Andrews, D. A., & Bonta, J. (2006). *The psychology of criminal conduct* (4th ed.). New Providence, NJ: Anderson/LexisNexis.

Andrews, D. A., & Bonta, J. (2010a). *The psychology of criminal conduct* (5th ed.). New Providence, NJ: Anderson/LexisNexis.

Andrews, D. A., & Bonta, J. (2010b). Rehabilitating criminal justice policy and practice. *Psychology, Public Policy, and Law, 16,* 39–55.

Andrews, D. A., Bonta, J., & Hoge, R. D. (1990). Classification for effective rehabilitation: Rediscovering psychology. *Criminal Justice and Behavior, 17,* 19–52.

Andrews, D. A., & Dowden, C. (2005). Managing correctional treatment for reduced recidivism: A meta-analytic review of programme integrity. *Legal and Criminological Psychology, 10,* 173–187.

Andrews, D. A., Zinger, I., Lab, S. P., & Whitehead, J. T. (1990). Does correctional treatment work? A clinically relevant and psychologically informed meta-analysis. *Criminology, 28,* 369–404.

Bonta, J., & Andrews, D. A. (2017). *The psychology of criminal conduct* (6th ed.). New York, NY: Routledge.

Cohen, J. (1992). Statistical power analysis. *Current Directions in Psychological Science, 1,* 98–101.

Cullen, F. T. (2005). The twelve people who saved rehabilitation: How the science of criminology made a difference. *Criminology, 43,* 1–42.

Cullen, F. T. (2013). Rehabilitation: Beyond nothing works. In M. Tonry (Ed.), *Crime and justice in America, 1975 to 2025—crime and justice: A review of research* (Vol. 42, pp. 299–376). Chicago, IL: University of Chicago Press.

Cullen, F. T., & Gendreau, P. (2000). Assessing correctional rehabilitation: Policy, practice, and prospects. In J. Horney (Ed.), *Policies, processes, and decisions of the criminal justice system: Criminal justice 2000* (Vol. 3, pp. 109–175). Washington, DC: U.S. Department of Justice, National Institute of Justice.

Cullen, F. T., & Gendreau, P. (2001). From nothing works to what works: Changing professional ideology in the 21st century. *The Prison Journal, 81,* 313–338.

Cullen, F. T., & Gilbert, K. E. (2013). *Reaffirming rehabilitation* (2nd ed., 30th Anniversary ed.). Waltham, MA: Anderson/Elsevier.

Cullen, F. T., & Jonson, C. L. (2011). Rehabilitation and treatment programs. In J. Q. Wilson & J. Petersilia (Eds.), *Crime and public policy* (pp. 293–344). New York, NY: Oxford University Press.

Cullen, F. T., & Jonson, C. L. (2012). *Correctional theory: Context and consequences.* Thousand Oaks, CA: Sage.

Dowden, C., & Andrews, D. A. (1999a). What works for female offenders: A meta-analytic review. *Crime and Delinquency, 45,* 438–452.

Dowden, C., & Andrews, D. A. (1999b). What works in young offender treatment: A meta-analysis. *Forum on Corrections Research, 11,* 21–24.

Dowden, C., & Andrews, D. A. (2000). Effective correctional treatment and violent reoffending: A meta-analysis. *Canadian Journal of Criminology, 42,* 449–467.

Dowden, C., & Andrews, D. A. (2003). Does family intervention work for delinquents? Results of a meta-analysis. *Canadian Journal of Criminology and Criminal Justice, 45,* 327–342.

Dowden, C., Antonowicz, D., & Andrews, D. A. (2003). The effectiveness of relapse prevention with offenders: A meta-analysis. *International Journal of Offender Therapy and Comparative Criminology, 47,* 516–528.

Garrett, C. J. (1985). Effects of residential treatment on adjudicated delinquents: A meta-analysis. *Journal of Research in Crime and Delinquency, 22,* 287–308.

Gendreau, P. (1996). The principles of effective intervention with offenders. In A. T. Harland (Ed.), *Choosing correctional interventions that work: Defining the demand and evaluating the supply* (pp. 117–130). Thousand Oaks, CA: Sage.

Gendreau, P., & Ross, B. (1979). Effective correctional treatment: Bibliotherapy for cynics. *Crime and Delinquency, 25*, 463–489.

Gendreau, P., & Ross, B. (1987). Revivification of rehabilitation: Evidence from the 1980s. *Justice Quarterly, 4*, 349–407.

Glick, B. (2006). History and development of cognitive behavioral interventions. In B. Glick (Ed.), *Cognitive behavioral interventions for at-risk youth* (pp. 1-1–1-16). Kingston, NJ: Civic Research Institute.

Hanson, R. K., Bourgon, G., Helmus, L., & Hodgson, S. (2009). The principles of effective correctional treatment also apply to sexual offenders: A meta-analysis. *Criminal Justice and Behavior, 36*, 865–891.

Izzo, R. L., & Ross, R. R. (1990). Meta-analysis of rehabilitation programs for juvenile delinquents: A brief report. *Criminal Justice and Behavior, 17*, 134–142.

Jonson, C. L. (2010). *The impact of imprisonment on reoffending: A meta-analysis.* Unpublished doctoral dissertation, University of Cincinnati, Cincinnati.

Kahneman, D. (2011). *Thinking, fast and slow.* New York, NY: Farrar, Straus and Giroux.

Landenberger, N. A., & Lipsey, M. W. (2005). The positive effects of cognitive-behavioral programs for offenders: A meta-analysis of factors associated with effective treatment. *Journal of Experimental Criminology, 1*, 451–476.

Lipsey, M. W. (1992). Juvenile delinquent treatment: A meta-analytic treatment inquiry into the variability of effects. In T. D. Cook, H. Cooper, D. S. Cordray, H. Hartmann, L. V. Hedges, R. J. Light, T. A. Lewis, & F. Mosteller (Eds.), *Meta-analysis for explanation: A casebook* (pp. 83–127). New York, NY: Russell Sage Foundation.

Lipsey, M. W. (1995). What do we learn from 400 research studies on the effectiveness of treatment with juvenile delinquency? In J. McGuire (Ed.), *What works: Reducing reoffending—guidelines from research and practice* (pp. 63–78). New York, NY: John Wiley.

Lipsey, M. W. (1999). Can intervention rehabilitate serious delinquents? *Annals of the American Academy of Political and Social Science, 564*, 142–166.

Lipsey, M. W. (2009). The primary factors that characterize effective interventions with juvenile offenders: A meta-analytic overview. *Victims and Offenders, 4*, 124–147.

Lipsey, M. W. (2014). Interventions for juvenile offenders: A serendipitous journey. *Criminology and Public Policy, 13*, 1–14.

Lipsey, M. W., & Cullen, F. T. (2007). The effectiveness of correctional rehabilitation: A review of systematic reviews. *Annual Review of Law and Social Science, 3*, 297–320.

Lipsey, M. W., Howell, J. C., Kelly, M. R., Chapman, G., & Carver, D. (2010). *Improving the effectiveness of juvenile justice programs: A new perspective on evidence-based programs.* Washington, DC: Center for Juvenile Justice Reform, Georgetown University.

Lipsey, M. W., & Wilson, D. B. (1998). Effective interventions for serious juvenile offenders: A synthesis of research. In R. Loeber & D. P. Farrington (Eds.), *Serious and violent juvenile offenders: Risk factors and successful interventions* (pp. 313–345). Thousand Oaks, CA: Sage.

Lipsey, M. W., & Wilson, D. B. (2001). *Practical meta-analysis.* Thousand Oaks, CA: Sage.

Lösel, F. (1995). The efficacy of correctional treatment: A review and synthesis of meta-evaluations. In J. McGuire (Ed.), *What works: Reducing reoffending—guidelines from research and practice* (pp. 79–111). New York, NY: John Wiley.

MacKenzie, D. L. (2006). *What works in corrections: Reducing the criminal activities of offenders and delinquents.* New York, NY: Cambridge University Press.

Martinson, R. (1974). What works?—questions and answers about prison reform. *Public Interest, 35*(2), 22–54.

Martinson, R. (1979). New findings, new views: A note of caution regarding sentencing reform. *Hofstra Law Review, 7*(Winter), 243–258.

McGuire, J. (2004). *Understanding psychology and crime: Perspectives on theory and action.* New York, NY: Open University Press.

McGuire, J. (2013). 'What works' to reduce re-offending: 18 years on. In L. Craig, L. Dixon, & T. Gannon (Eds.), *What works in offender rehabilitation: An evidence-based approach to assessment and treatment* (pp. 20–49). London, UK: Wiley-Blackwell.

Palmer, T. (1975). Martinson revisited. *Journal of Research in Crime and Delinquency, 12,* 133–152.

Palmer, T. (1992). *The re-emergence of correctional intervention.* Newbury Park, CA: Sage.

Pearson, F. S., Lipton, D. S., Cleland, C. M., & Yee, D. S. (2002). The effects of behavioral/cognitive-behavioral programs on recidivism. *Crime and Delinquency, 48,* 476–496.

Petrosino, A., & Soydan, H. (2005). The impact of program developers as evaluators on criminal recidivism: Results from meta-analyses of experimental and quasi-experimental research. *Journal of Experimental Criminology, 1,* 435–450.

Redondo, S., Sanchez-meca, J., & Garrido, V. (1999). The influence of treatment programmes on the recidivism of juvenile and adult offenders: An European meta-analytic review. *Psychology, Crime and Law, 5,* 251–278.

Smith, P., Gendreau, P., & Swartz, K. (2009). Validating the principles of effective intervention: A systematic review of the contributions of meta-analysis in the field of corrections. *Victims and Offenders, 4,* 148–169.

Whitehead, J. T., & Lab, S. P. (1989). A meta-analysis of juvenile correctional treatment. *Journal of Research in Crime and Delinquency, 26,* 276–295.

Wilson, D. B., Bouffard, L. A., & Mackenzie, D. L. (2005). A quantitative review of structured, group-oriented, cognitive-behavioral programs for offenders. *Criminal Justice and Behavior, 32,* 172–204.

PART II

The Risk-Need-Responsivity Model

3

THE THEORETICAL FOUNDATION OF THE RNR MODEL

The Risk–Need–Responsivity (RNR) model is an approach to correctional assessment and treatment that is based on the current theoretical and empirical understanding of criminal behavior. In general, this model presents "principles of effective intervention" that instruct practitioners in the correctional system how to rehabilitate offenders. Those principles reflect the applied value of the knowledge that was accumulated in the correctional system.

In brief, the chronology of the development of the RNR model can be traced back to the mid-1970s. As described in Chapter 1, it was not a propitious time to advocate for increasing the rehabilitative efforts in corrections. Within the correctional system in the United States, the individualized model was under attack and many individualized rehabilitation programs were being criticized, if not abandoned. The correctional system thus shifted away from service-oriented programs toward a reliance on punitive programs to deal with crime. In essence, during that time, proponents of rehabilitation had to face a radical loss of confidence in the capacity of correctional interventions to achieve beneficial direction to criminal behavior. Overall, across the United States, the "nothing works doctrine" prevailed among academics and policy makers.

Across the border, Donald Andrews joined with a number of colleagues to pursue a more effective approach to correctional treatment. This group, which will be referred to as "Andrews et al.," included in particular James Bonta and Paul Gendreau who would work closely with Andrews across subsequent decades. Other colleagues were Jerry Kiessling, Robert Hog, Robert Ross, and Stephen Wormith. These scholars tended to work in the Canadian correctional system and therefore were less affected by the changes occurring in the U.S. system. Moreover, Andrew et al. were PhD trained psychologists who were trained according to a "scientific–practitioner model." Accordingly, they were "well-grounded in, and strongly influenced by, learning theory" and believed that "the pre-eminent professional role within this model was to implement, administer and evaluate offender assessment and treatment programs" (Gendreau, Smith, & French, 2006, p. 420, 422). The evolution of the RNR model thus was carried out by psychologists who believed in rehabilitation and tried to promote both science and applied science.

During the 1970s, Donald Andrews and his colleagues started to translate crime theories into effective correctional service practices. They used systematic program evaluations to expand knowledge that served to predict, influence, and explain criminal behavior. In the 1980s, their efforts led to a unique perspective on human behavior that could also integrate criminology and social psychology. In 1990, the first version of the RNR model was published (Andrews, Bonta, & Hoge, 1990). This early version consisted of four "principles of classification for effective rehabilitation"—Risk, Need, Responsivity, and Professional override.

In 1994, the RNR model was published in a comprehensive book, authored by D. A. Andrews and James Bonta that explained its scientific basis—*The Psychology of Criminal Conduct* (Andrews & Bonta, 1994). Including the three core principles (Risk, Need, and Responsivity), the early version of the RNR model consisted of a total of 16 principles that constitute its theoretical and empirical support (Andrews, 1995; Gendreau, 1996). Since then, the model continued to be developed and revised (Andrews & Bonta, 1998, 2003, 2006, 2010a; Bonta & Andrews, 2017). In the second decade of the 21st century, the RNR model consists of 15 principals and is commonly presented as a comprehensive and interdisciplinary synthesis of empirical research and theory of criminal behavior (Cullen, 2013).

The purpose of Chapters 3 and 4 is to explore the "black box" of the RNR model—its theoretical foundation (Chapter 3) and correctional applications (Chapter 4). Chapter 3 elaborates the theoretical evolution of the RNR model and describes how this knowledge was narrowed into the RNR model's correctional principles. Specifically, this chapter delineates the evolution of the RNR model in five sections.

The first section will introduce the paradigmatic framework of the RNR model—the particular "psychology of criminal conduct" (PCC). Andrews and his colleagues chose this scientific-professional framework to accommodate their perspective on both human behavior and research products. The second section will discuss the general personality, the social learning, and the social cognitive perspective on human behavior. This will begin with the development of general learning and behavior theories. In addition, this section will describe the general personality perspective and its integration with the cognitive social learning perspective to human behavior.

The third and fourth sections of this chapter elaborate the criminological component of the RNR model. These sections will examine how Andrews and his collaborators articulated "a theory that explains why people offend, which then leads logically to how best to change the conduct" (Cullen, 2013, p. 341). Specifically, the third section describes how they translated the general personality and social psychology perspective on human behavior from the existing criminological theories. In the late 1980s, this theoretical effort led to their General Personality and Cognitive Social Learning (GPCSL) perspective on human behavior. The fourth section of this chapter will examine the particular version that Andrews et al. developed for their general personality and social psychology perspective. This version—the Personal, Interpersonal, and Community-Reinforcement (PIC-R)—was chosen to explain the occurrence of criminality in the immediate situation (i.e., the mechanism that led to criminality in a particular situation).

The last section of this chapter provides an introduction to the RNR principles. In essence, this is a description of how Andrews et al.'s PCC and GPCSL were developed against mainstream criminology, how Andrews et al. systematically explored and mapped the sources of variability in recidivism, and how this overall knowledge was distilled into the core RNR principles.

The Psychology of Criminal Conduct (PCC)

As described above, the combination between professional and scientific interests was a key factor in the evolution of the RNR model. Essentially, Andrews and his colleagues recognized the need to bridge the gap between theory and practice and focused on the importance of using scientific knowledge for serving practical purposes. Thus, in the late 1970s, they claimed that practitioners conduct treatment programs that "have often been based on incomplete theory and woeful lack of descriptive data or demonstrated poor integration of theory with treatment methods" (Gendreau & Ross, 1979, p. 466). In addition, they argued that theorists should "recognize the potential of rigorous program evaluation as a means of testing the causal significant of theoretical principles" (Andrews, 1980, p. 460). In this regard, the centrality of this combination between professional and scientific interests was explicitly constituted as the working definition of the PCC—and therefore of the RNR model. According to Bonta and Andrews (2017, p. 4):

> As a science, the psychology of criminal conduct is an approach to understanding the criminal behavior of individuals through: (a) the ethical and humane application of systematic empirical methods of investigation, and (b) the construction of rational explanatory systems.
>
> Professionally, a psychology of criminal conduct involves the ethical application of psychological knowledge and methods to the practical tasks of predicting and influencing the likelihood of criminal behavior, and to the reduction of the human and social costs associated with crime and criminal justice processing.

Notably, beyond emphasizing the roles of science and profession, this definition also illuminates the core of the PCC: the "PCC" sought *to account* for variation in the criminal behavior of individuals (Andrews, 1995; Bonta & Andrews, 2017). In the 1970s, such a framework "was required because sociological criminology and forensic mental health simply could not account for variation in the criminal behavior of individuals" (Andrews, Bonta, & Wormith, 2011, p. 747). Importantly, their focus on variation in behavior reflected a respect for human diversity, the complexity of human behavior, and the empirical evidence that showed unequal engagement in criminal activity (Andrews & Bonta, 2010a). According to the PCC, people differ "in the number, type, and variety of criminal acts in which they engage" (i.e., interindividual variation), and in when and under what circumstances they act in harmful ways or reduce (or even refrain from) their antisocial activity (i.e., intraindividual variation) (p. 8).

In this regard, according to Andrews and Bonta (2010a), the core value of the PCC lays in its ability to *describe* such variation. Beyond description, they expected the PCC to produce knowledge that would assist in *predicting* future criminality of individuals (a better framework) and would suggest "deliberate interventions that will reduce future crime and to offer warnings regarding actions that may increase crime" (a very good framework) (p. 3). In addition, as theorists of human behavior, Andrews and Bonta also wanted to explain the occurrence of criminal behavior in theoretical terms. The objective of the PCC thus was to achieve a rational and empirical understanding of the variation in criminal behavior of individuals. This objective consists of three interrelated aspects of variation in criminal behavior among people—empirical, theoretical, and practical understanding. These three aspects compose the conceptual basic of the RNR model and therefore merit close examination.

An *empirical understanding* of variation in criminal behavior seeks knowledge of the covariates of the particular variations. This understanding is the key to PCC because empirical explanations consist of both "knowledge of the observable facts regarding the nature and the extant of individual variation in criminal conduct" and "knowledge of the biological, personal, interpersonal, situational, and social variables associated with or correlated with criminal behavior" (p. 13). In other words, the PCC seeks knowledge of any covariate of variation that can be observed systematically. With such knowledge, the PCC classifies the covariates into three types: *correlates* (knowledge that comes from "observations of individuals known to differ in their criminal activity," p. 24); *predictors* of risk (knowledge that comes from "observations conducted within a longitudinal study," p. 26); and *causal (functional)* variables that account for the effects of deliberate interventions (knowledge that comes from experimental studies). In sum, the empirical understanding of variation not only describes the particular variables that are associated with criminality but also indicates their relative single or combined strength.

A *theoretical understanding* of variation in criminal behavior focuses on providing predictive explanations. Within the PCC, the most important aspect of theoretical understanding is to provide "empirically defensible" predictions—theoretical predictions that can be validated by findings of systematic research. In this regard, the PCC states "four major empirical tests of the adequacy of a theoretical understanding of criminal behavior" (Andrews & Bonta, 2010a, pp. 16–17): one empirical test examines "how the various risk factors are associated with each other." The second empirical test examines "the ability to predict accurately variation in criminal behavior." The third test assesses the "potential to influence criminal activity by way of deliberate interventions that focus on the causal variables suggested by the theory." The fourth empirical test of theoretical adequacy examines "the accuracy of prediction and the effects of intervention with different types of people under different circumstances."

According to the PCC, a *practical understanding* of variation in criminal behavior is expected to drive from a sound empirical and theoretical understanding of criminal behavior. In such sound understanding, the PCC assumes high practical value "because knowledge of predictors and causes brings with it the potential . . . to influence the occurrence of criminal behavior" (p. 19). In turn, this practical aspect of understanding directs the search for the other two aspects of understanding to lean on "theories and empirical investigations that show the greatest practical potential" (Andrews & Bonta, 2010a, p. 20).

In sum, the objective of PCC is to establish an empirical, theoretical, and practical understanding of criminality that will serve practical (predict and influence criminality) and theoretical (test explanations of criminality) goals. This psychological perspective of criminal conduct has respect for quantitative evidence and rigorous methodology (rational empiricism approach to knowledge), human diversity and complexity of behavior (interdisciplinary informed approach), and ethical and human practice, including respect for personal autonomy ("a key aspect of ethical practice") (Andrews & Bonta, 2010a, p. 6).

In the aftermath of Martinson's article, Andrews and his collaborators believed that the PCC would be the most efficacious way to overcome the tarnished legitimacy of the rehabilitation ideal caused by the radical loss of confidence in America's political and social institutions. The PCC was thus designed to follow the only avenue that would enable rehabilitation to be reaffirmed: doing rehabilitation according to evidence-based corrections. In regard to the correctional system, advocates of the PCC assumed that "systematic program evaluation provides the tools—and the opportunity—for a bridging of the gaps between general sociology and general psychology and between social science and social service" (Andrews, 1980, p. 448). In addition, they believed that the correctional system, "like any other area of human and social service, must be concerned with fairness and efficiency, as well as participant and public satisfaction with its efforts" (Andrews, 1982b, p. 1). In this regard, Andrews (1982b) stated that, compared to other human and social agencies, "what makes the correctional system unique is its focus upon the management of a court-imposed sentence and the public mandate to reduce the likelihood of recidivism during the period of sentence" (p. 9). Since the mid-1970s, thus, the focus of Andrews and his colleagues on variation in recidivism reframed the evolution of the RNR model as an attempt to construct "a theory of recidivism" (Cullen, 2013, p. 342).

Understanding Human Behavior: The GPCSL Perspective

Andrews and his collaborators were strongly influenced by the social psychology approach to human behavior and, in particular, by social learning theory. As psychologists who worked in the correctional system, they were "well versed in learning theory and related behavioral treatment, [and] operated under the assumption that criminal behavior, like almost all forms of social behavior, was largely learned, thereby modifiable through the application of schedule of ethnically appropriate contingent reward and punishment" (Gendreau et al., 2006, p. 420). This theoretical and practical influence guided these scholars to develop a unique perspective on human behavior—the General Personality and Cognitive Social Learning perspective (GPCSL). The following paragraphs elaborate how these perspectives explain the human behavior. Specifically, this review starts with the historical background of Bandura's (1977) social learning theory and continues with Bandura's (1986, 1997, 2001) social cognitive theory. The integration between the general personality model and the cognitive social learning perspective will be discussed later.

Historically, social learning theory was developed from the three general learning theories that influenced psychologists during the first half of the 20th century: Guthrie's (1935) contiguity theory, Hull's (1943) systematic behavior theory, and Tolman's (1932) purposive theory. These theories, which were embedded in the neobehaviorism tradition, postulated that a behavioral response is learned and that the "rate, frequency of occurrence, or form of behavior (response) [is] a function of environmental events and stimuli" (Schunk, Meece, & Pintrich, 2014, p. 21).[1] In addition to these three "big" theories, a radical perspective of behaviorism was presented by Skinner's (1953) operant conditioning theory.

Like other "radical" behaviorists, Skinner assumed that "environmental or external stimuli are the primary—if not the sole—determinants of all behavior" (Bartol & Bartol, 2011, pp. 87–88). In other words, his theory posits that "internal processes that accompany responding (e.g., needs, drives, cognitions, emotions) are not necessary to explain behavior" (Schunk et al., 2014, p. 25). People, in that sense, respond to environmental stimuli to receive rewards (reinforcement) and avoid punishment. Skinner thus believed that environmental stimuli, observable behavior, and reward could explain the development of human behavior. His operant conditioning (or operant learning) theory posits that a person "make or withhold a particular response because of its consequences" (Bartol & Bartol, 2011, p. 89). Skinner's principles of operant conditioning suggested that a person might be motivated to continue a specific behavior because it was socially rewarded or enabled to remove (or avoid) unpleasant stimuli.

During the first half of the 20th century, behaviorism "became one of the major schools of psychological thought" (McGuire, 2004, p. 50). Accordingly, the concept of reinforcement (reward for behavior) became "one of the most soundly established principles in psychology" (Bartol & Bartol, 2011, p. 91).

However, according to McGuire (2004), findings from behavioral research began to show that Skinner's perspective of human behavior overemphasizes the impact of environment on behavior and therefore overlooks additional factors that can explain behavior. Thus, in the 1970s, a convergence between behaviorism and cognitive psychology—"two previously separate strands of research and theorizing"—broadened the behavioral perspective (p. 49). Specifically, cognitive psychologists argued that mental processes are crucial to understand observed behavior. In this regard, McGuire (2004) indicates that two major developments led behaviorist researchers to accept that "events that were not directly observed, but were indirectly inferred or reported, could nevertheless be important factors in explaining learning and other forms of behavioral change" (p. 51). One major development was the research that showed how a step-by-step learning process could lead individuals to replace their negative emotions with positive emotions. This new way to change emotions was important because it increased the possibility of behavioral change. The second development was fostered when behavioral researchers examined "the process of self-regulation of behavior." These behavioral researchers found that "actions are governed by cognitive events that occur automatically, without deliberate reflection and outside conscious awareness" (p. 51).

Thus, during the 1970s, behaviorists came closer to cognitive psychologists who investigated the development of thinking, memory, reasoning, the role of language in thought, and other aspects of cognition (e.g., Beck, 1963; Ellis, 1962; Meichenbaum, 1977). They moved toward "more vibrant and flexible behaviorism that embraced social learning and cognitive conceptualization of behavior" (Gendreau et al., 2006, p. 422). These changes in perspectives on human behavior led Albert Bandura to develop his social learning theory. According to Bandura (1977), "in the social learning view, people are neither driven by inner forces nor buffeted by environmental stimuli. Rather, psychological functioning is explained in terms of a continuous reciprocal interaction of personal and environment determinants. Within this approach, symbolic, vicarious, and self-regulatory processes assume a prominent role" (pp. 11–12). This theory thus posits that "most human behavior is learned observationally through modeling: from observing others one forms an idea of how new behaviors are performed, and on later occasions this coded information serves as a guide for action" (p. 22).

In 1986, Bandura renamed his social learning theory as "social cognitive theory." This development brought more attention to the internal state of the individual that intervenes between the stimulus (the external event or condition) and the response (the behavioral reaction). Specifically, social cognitive theory emphasizes the major role of cognition in encoding and performing behaviors (Bandura, 1986, 2001). According to this theory, "internal personal factors in the form of cognitive, affective, and biological events, behavior, and environmental events all operate as interacting determinants that influence one another bidirectionally" (Bandura, 2000, p. 331). Within this transactional view of self and society, social cognitive theory "assigns a central role to cognitive, vicarious, self-regulatory, and self-reflective processes in human development and functioning" (p. 331). In other words, humans learn behavior either deliberately or unintentionally and regulate and guide their behavior by observing what others do and the consequences for them. This theory provides an explanation of "how people acquire knowledge, rules, skills, strategies, beliefs, and emotions through their interaction with and observation of others" (Schunk et al., 2014, p. 168).

As mentioned above, Andrews and his colleagues considered not only the social learning and social cognitive approaches but also the general personality perspective on human behavior. According to Andrews and Bonta (2010a), all three approaches "recognize that there are fundamental dimensions of personality on which most if not all human beings may be located" (p. 36). In that sense, personality refers to "characteristic pattern of thinking, feeling, and acting" (p. 172). Accordingly, the fundamental dimensions of personality include five patterns of responding that are common to all humans. These normal aspects of personality are neuroticism, extraversion, openness to experience, agreeableness, and conscientiousness (the "Big Five"). Andrews and Bonta (2010a) stated that these five fundamental dimensions of personality "have biological underpinnings, and several are heavily influence [*sic*] by heredity" (p. 36). Moreover, they assumed that "as the human being develops from infant to young adult through old age, biological potentials are shaped through interactions with environment" (p. 36).

Thus, according to the cognitive social learning framework, "personality is no longer just a study of stable personality traits but also the study of the dynamic psychological processes that are the mediators between traits and the situation of action" (p. 198). In other words, the essence of the cognitive social learning approach to personality is that even a relatively stable behavioral pattern should not be considered a fixed trait. Rather, such a behavioral pattern is viewed to "consist of relative continuities in 'processing dynamics,' or recurring patterns in the ways in which individuals perceive and respond to situations" (McGuire, 2004, pp. 62–63).

Overall, thus, the GPCSL approaches provide a unique integrated perspective on human behavior—biological factors lie at the base of the behavior and the cognitions of the individual are the cause of behavior. These approaches thus posit that all human beings share the same constellation of personality dimensions and the same way of behavioral learning. In that sense, offenders and nonoffenders are the same. Where they differ, however, is in where they lie on these personality dimensions and in their basic cognitive capabilities. The following section will show how Andrew et al. tied these human psychology approaches to the field of criminology.

Bringing in Criminology to the GPCSL Perspective

As mentioned above, Andrews and his collaborators directed their efforts to describe and assess "empirical, theoretical, and practical status of the psychology of criminal conduct (PCC)" (Andrews & Bonta, 2010a, p. 131). In the mid-1970s, however, assessment of the practical value of the PCC was a distant goal (see the next chapter). In addition, only in the early 1990s these scholars were able to provide data that consistently supported their empirical understanding of criminality. During the 1970s, they focused on establishing their theoretical understanding of the PCC. Specifically, they sought ways to establish what causal factors identified by existing criminological theories were empirically supported and to extend their knowledge of the predictive validity of correlates of individual criminal conduct. Such efforts were essential for building a predictive understanding of criminal conduct and demonstrating causal significant.

Andrews and his colleagues thus chose the GPCSL perspective as an approach "that is linked with a general psychology of human behavior that has demonstrated functional value" (Andrews & Bonta, 2010a, p. 155). Then, they emphasized the general personality and the social psychology perspectives in criminological theories and research. Specifically, these scholars uncovered how the "psychodynamic, social bonding, differential association, and strain theoretical perspectives are converging on general personality and cognitive social learning perspective" (p. 129).

As described below, Andrews and Bonta (2010a) sought to bring these four theoretical perspectives under the framework of the GPCSL perspective. They believed that this approach revealed which aspects of these theories were empirically supported and was more explicit in showing why individuals engage in criminal behavior in the immediate situation of action. In addition, Andrews and Bonta's (2010a) theoretical framework led them to propose that four key variables influence human behavior. These "Big Four" variables are (1) "cognitions supportive of a particular behavior"; (2) "a history of engaging the particular behavior"; (3) "association with others who approve of the behavior"; (4) "temperament or personality predisposition for the behavior" (p. 36). They stated that "the most empirical defensible theories will be those that assign causal significant to at least two of the four" (p. 132). Thus, beyond the general impact of these factors on human behavior, the Big Four are considered "the major causal variables in the analysis of criminal behavior of individuals" (p. 55). Overall, the identification of these causal factors allows the GPCSL perspective to predict not only the immediate situation but also moderate or long-term criminality.

Differential Association Theory

Andrews and his colleagues initiated their research enterprise with a series of systematic program evaluations that investigated the "causal and, hence, practical significant of certain principles of differential association theory" (Andrews, 1980, p. 449). Differential association theory eventually developed into social learning theory, which earned considerable empirical support. This perspective and research helped to shape the development of the RNR model by Andrews and Bonta. These issues are explored below.

Edwin Sutherland presented the original statements of differential association theory in the 1939 edition of his *Principles of Criminology*. He adopted a perspective that "social organization—the context in which individuals are embedded—regulates criminal involvement" (Lilly, Cullen, & Ball, 2011, p. 47). His theory posits that criminal behavior is learned through social interactions and criminals differ from noncriminals in the content of what they have learned. In a list of principles, Sutherland (1947) proposed that the learning process includes techniques of committing crime and specific direction of motives, drives, rationalizations, and attitudes. In this regard, he stated that "a person becomes delinquent because of an excess of definitions favorable to violation of law over definitions unfavorable to violation of law" (Sutherland, 1947)—this is the principle of differential association. However, within this context, Sutherland rejected individualistic explanation of crime and was critical of theories that "linked crime not to general social process—like differential association—but to a range of variables, with individual differences being prominent among them" (Cullen, Wright, Gendreau, & Andrews, 2003, p. 340). Overall, Sutherland was not against the notion of rehabilitation but his theory did not provide any direction to correctional intervention (Cullen et al., 2003).

Notably, Donald Cressey (1955) explicitly linked the principles of differential association to correctional intervention programs (Cullen et al., 2003; Wormith, 1984). Similar to Sutherland, Cressey (1955) assumed that criminals' characteristics "depend upon the groups to which the criminals belong" (pp. 117–118). Specifically, he suggested that "the focus of the programs should be the attitude, values, and beliefs of groups rather than of individuals" (Andrews, 1980, p. 449). Cressey also advocated for experimental studies in corrections that would be designed to test the impact of a group's cohesiveness or attitude on criminality. According to Cressey (1955), these studies would assess the validity of the differential association as a theory of crime causation.

During the 1960s, Burgess and Akers (1966) further revised Sutherland's theory. Their revision integrated between the differential association theory and Skinner's radical behavior framework. Specifically, Burgess and Akers (1966) integrated "the basic elements of operant conditioning with Sutherland's nine theoretical propositions" (Cullen & Wilcox, 2010, p. 124). This behavioral reformulation—called "differential association-reinforcement" theory—enhanced the practical values of the differential association theory in two major ways. First, this theory specified the primary learning mechanism in acquiring criminal behavior. By doing so, the theory made Sutherland's theory less ambiguous. Second, this theory followed the most updated knowledge in the social psychology perspective on human behavior (i.e., the principles of operant conditioning). Their behavioral reformulation thus opened the theoretical concept of differential association "in such a way that it becomes more amenable to empirical testing" (Burgess & Akers, 1966, p. 129). In addition, this behavioral reformulation allowed a substantial change in the causal chain in Sutherland's theory. From a causal sequence of antisocial associates that results in acquisition of antisocial attitudes and then to antisocial behavior, the behavioral reformulation allowed antisocial attitudes to play a causal role in criminality (Lilly et al., 2011).

During the 1970s, Ronald Akers continued to develop the behavioral reformulation of differential association theory (Akers, 1973, 1977). He elaborated the differential association-reinforcement theory to establish his "social learning theory" of deviant behavior. Specifically, "Akers had tempered social learning theory with principles more consistent with the cognitive learning approach advocated by Albert Bandura" (Cullen & Wilcox, 2010, p. 23). The result was a mechanism of learning that consists of both behavioral learning principles (e.g., operant conditioning, differential reinforcement, and discriminative stimuli) and cognitive learning principles (e.g., imitation, anticipated reinforcement, and self-reinforcement). However, although Akers's social learning theory includes cognitive principles, the sources of criminality in his theory remain social in nature. Thus, within this theory, role models or group dynamics are considered the source of both the individual's definitions of behavior and the balance between reinforcement and punishment of the behavior.

Notably, the reformulated differential association theory was extensively tested by criminologists. In this context, Andrew et al. used a series of experimental studies that tested the behavioral reformulation of the principles of differential association theory (for a review of those studies, see Andrews, 1980). Importantly, this research strategy allowed Andrews and his collaborators to draw conclusions not only on the applicability of behavioral principles and techniques to corrections but also on the causal significant of the differential association principles. These scholars thus found "strong and consistent evidence that the contingency and relationships principles of DA [differential association] have causal significant with reference to both criminal attitude and criminal behavior" (Andrews, 1980, p. 459). More specifically, the meaning of finding support for the "contingency principle" was that "criminal learning occurs by way of association with criminal pattern and relative isolation from anticriminal pattern" (p. 450). In behavioral terms, this finding indicates that the chance of criminal influence increases with the exposure to patterns of criminal modeling and reinforcement. Accordingly, the meaning of finding support for the "relationship principle" was that "part of learning occurs within intimate personal groups" (p. 451). In behavioral terms, this finding showed that the quality role models increase the influence on behavior (i.e., high quality relationship had an impact).

Along with other empirical evidence, these findings supported both Akers's social learning theory and the predictive factors suggested by differential association theory. This pattern of findings has remained consistent over the years (Pratt et al., 2010). Indeed, "the research is supportive of this perspective, including studies in which social learning theory was tested against competing explanations of crime" (Lilly et al., 2011, p. 57). Furthermore, evaluations of correctional rehabilitation showed that this perspective consists of two of the strongest causes of criminal conduct—antisocial attitudes and antisocial associates. In this regard, "when antisocial attitudes, thinking, and associations are targeted and do in fact change, offenders decrease their participation in criminal behavior" (Cullen et al., 2003, p. 354). Research into differential association theory thus lends support to the GPCSL perspective. Within the PCC, differential association theory not only highlighted two strong validated correlates of criminality but also "directs attention to the powerful influence strategies of modeling and reinforcement in the context of prevention and treatment" (Andrews & Bonta, 2010a, p. 125).

Psychodynamic Theory

In addition to differential association theory, Andrews and his colleagues endorsed psychodynamic theory as a human psychology that could serve the purposes of the PCC. According to Andrews and Bonta (2010a), they "were favorably disposed to early psychodynamic thought," especially as a theory of action—a theory that was "based on the person in immediate situations" (pp. 121, 123; see also Andrews & Wormith, 1989). In this regard, the Freudian model of human behavior posits that "human beings seek pleasure and avoid pain, and that pursuit is governed by the demands, constraints, and opportunities of the immediate situation and by the internal controls that are developed through socialization experiences" (pp. 94–95). According to the early psychodynamic perspective, "the most obvious routes [to persistent criminal behavior] are weak internal controls . . . which in Freudian theory are directly linked to family process and parenting" (p. 110).

Within the criminological context, Andrews and Bonta appreciated the empirical research undertaken by Sheldon and Eleanor Glueck ("the Gluecks") and the way they reformulated the psychodynamic theory. They considered this reformulation as one of "the best validated of all predictive models of criminal behavior" (Andrews & Bonta, 2010a, p. 95). Specifically, the Gluecks conducted a three-wave study of criminal behavior over a 25-year period (1940–1965), comparing 500 delinquent boys and 500 nondelinquent boys. In general, their empirical analysis found that changes in criminal behavior could not be ascribed solely to external environment factors. In addition, Glueck and Glueck (1950) found that "among the forces that count most in whether or not a boy will be conditioned to antisocial is the home atmosphere, and especially the intimate relationships of the parent and child and their psychological deposits in the personality and character of the boy" (p. 287).

Based on these findings, the Gluecks stated a causal formula of antisocial behavior that reflected the Freudian theory. This reformulation of the psychodynamic theory "emphasized weak internal control . . . resulting from poor parenting practices and parental modeling, and temperamental/ constitutional predispositions toward the expression of aggressive energy and the pursuit of self-interest" (Andrews & Bonta, 2010a, pp. 95–96). In other words, the Gluecks concluded that "within particular social arrangements, person-based variables will account for variation in behavior" (Andrews & Wormith, 1989, p. 298). They relied on the person-based variables found in their empirical study and relate to antisocial attitude and antisocial personality pattern.

In addition to the Gluecks, Andrews and Bonta (2010a) found another point of convergence between psychodynamic and cognitive social learning approach. First, they recognized a theoretical link between the "Freudian concepts [and] the methods and concepts of an emerging behavioral perspective on human behavior" (p. 111). Specifically, they followed Dollard, Doob, Miller, Mowrer, and Sears (1939), who hypothesized that "all aggression is preceded by frustration, and frustration is always followed by some form of aggression" (p. 111). The Freudian perspective thus was "influenced by radical theory and the conditioning models" (p. 134). Next, Andrews and Bonta (2010a) recognized how other scholars revised this frustration-aggression hypothesis. Specifically, they endorsed the developments presented by Berkowitz (1962) and Buss (1966), who incorporated the principles of observational learning and cognitive models of self-control. In other words, these scholars viewed the person as an active individual who "had learned to interpret a wide variety of persons and situations as threatening or frustrating and has learned habits of aggression to these cues" (Andrews & Bonta, 2010a, p. 112). According to Andrews and Bonta (2010a), this integrated perspective is often called "social learning or social cognition theory" (p. 134). Within the GPCSL perspective, this integration emphasized the notion of aggression and criminality as a "complex function of facilitators, inhibitors, prior learning, and the immediate situation" (p. 112). Moreover, it allowed to link psychodynamic perspectives in criminological theories to causal explanations of antisocial associates.

Social Bond Theory

Hirschi's social bond theory was "based on the assumption that humans are naturally self-interested and thus need no special motivation to break the law" (Lilly et al., 2011, p. 119). According to Hirschi (1969), all individuals are equally motivated to commit crimes and four "social bonds"—attachment, commitment, involvement, and belief—explain the "variation in the extent to which people engage in crime" (Lilly et al., 2011, p. 114). Although this theory reflects a sociological perspective of the causes of delinquency, Andrews and Bonta found converging points between the social bond theory and the GPCSL perspective.

First, Andrews and Bonta translated the social bonds into a psychodynamic perspective to reveal their social psychological aspects. Within the GPCSL perspective, this strategy focused on the social bond of "attachment." According to Hirschi (1969), attachment represents "the emotional closeness that youths have with adults, with parents typically being the most important . . . When close to their parents, youngsters care about their opinions and do not wish to disappoint them" (Lilly et al., 2011, p. 119). The parent, in that case, "is psychologically present when temptation to commit crime appears" (Hirschi, 1969, p. 88). According to Andrews and Bonta (2010a), such indirect control reflects a social psychology explanation of criminality. In addition, they stated that Hirschi "maintained the causal status of antisocial attitudes" by linking "weak attachment to conventional others, institutions, and pursuits" (p. 110).

Second, Andrews and Bonta (2010a, p. 106) found "strikingly similar findings" between Hirschi's (1969) empirical study and the study conducted by the Gluecks. The image of delinquents in these two studies was of "energetic and easily bored, monomorphic, below average in verbal aptitude, lacking in self-control, exhibiting a generalized violation of age-based norms, and having dislike for school, poor family relations, poor parental supervision, procriminal and antiauthority attitude, weak conventional ambitions, and delinquent associates" (p. 105).

General Strain Theory (GST)

In addition to the psychodynamic perspective, social bond theory, and differential association theory, Andrews and Bonta (2010a) found points of convergence between Agnew's general strain theory (GST) and the general personality and social psychological perspective. In short, Agnew's (1992) theory suggested three types of strain that are conductive to crime in the immediate situation. Those types of strain can be induced by (1) being blocked "from any positively valued goal . . . (2) actual or anticipated removal (loss) of positively valued stimuli from individual . . . [or] (3) actual or anticipated presentation of negative or noxious stimuli" (Lilly et al., 2011, p. 75). In this regard, Andrews and Bonta (2010a) claim that the GST is a "general psychology [theory] of criminal behavior with a particular interest in negative emotionality" (p. 116). Therefore, they continued, the general personality and social learning perspective may benefit from studies that examined the general psychology of aggression. They also noted that, "studies of recidivism from correctional psychology . . . forensic mental health . . . and youth services . . . are revealing that acute dynamic indicators of negative emotionality may enhance the predictability of criminal recidivism" (p. 116).

Summing up the GPCSL perspective on criminal behavior, Andrews and Bonta (2010a) created a theoretical framework that has predictive power, reflects interdisciplinary criminology, and is flexible enough to "incorporate new conceptions and strategies" (p. 53). As detailed above, the theoretical understanding of criminal behavior relied on criminological theories that could be revised as empirical defensible theories. Such revisions added a practical value of prediction and prevention through an integration of radical behavior theory with criminological perspectives. The result of these efforts at theoretical integration was to show how criminological perspectives converged under the GPCSL perspective on criminal behavior. As will be described later in this chapter, Andrews and his colleagues went a step further and, in the early 1980s, provided more specific theory that would explain the immediate psychology of action in the GPCSL perspective—the personal, interpersonal, community-reinforcement (PIC-R) (Andrews, 1982a).

During the 1980s, these scholars continued to extend their empirical understanding of criminality. However, it was not until the early 1990s that they could demonstrate consistent empirical support to the theoretical framework suggested by the GPCSL. At that time, the development of the meta-analyses reviews enabled systematic identification of empirically validated predictors of recidivism. This development thus enhanced the predictive validity of the GPCSL perspective on criminal behavior.

Specifically, according to the GPSCL, "if you want to predict [criminal] behavior in the immediate situation of action, you must understand the situation in psychological terms"—through the general personality, social learning and social cognitive theoretical perspectives (Andrews & Bonta, 2010a, p. 36). Accordingly, "if you want to predict behavior over the moderate or longer term," the "Big Four" are "the best-established risk factors for criminal conduct within almost any sample" (pp. 36, 131). In addition, research into the predictive validity of the GPCSL perspective found four other risk factors that are moderately correlated with criminal behavior. These "Moderate Four" risk/need factors relate to the individuals' (1) "quality of relationships" and "behavioral expectations" within their family of origins and marital circumstances, (2) "interpersonal relation-ships" within school and/or work, (3) "problems with alcohol and/or drugs," and (4) their level "of involvement and satisfaction in prosocial leisure pursuits" (Bonta & Andrews, 2017, pp. 45–46). Taken together, within the GPSCL, the Big Four and the Moderate Four comprise the "Central Eight" risk/need factors that predict criminal behavior.

However, it should be noted that Bonta and Andrews (2017) have recently qualified the clear distinction previously made between the Big Four and Moderate Four factors. They have noted that recent research has not consistently found a difference in the predictive power between the risk/need factors comprising these two categories. Because meta-analyses regularly show that all these factors are related to reoffending, Bonta and Andrews have suggested that it might be more appropriate to use the more omnibus term of the "Central Eight Risk/Need Factors" (2017, pp. 44–45).[2]

The PIC-R Perspective: Criminality in the Immediate Situation

In the early 1980s, Donald Andrews presented the Personal, Interpersonal, and Community-Reinforcement (PIC-R) as a specific perspective on deviant behavior (Andrews, 1982a). During that time, this perspective was considered "a variant of the general social-learning perspective" (p. 1). In more recent terms, the PIC-R—as it is commonly referred to—is described as a "broad cognitive social learning perspective on human conduct" (Andrews & Bonta, 2010a, p. 141) and as "one example of the general personality and social psychological approach" to account for deviant behavior (Andrews & Bonta, 2003, p. 165). Overall, although some modifications have been made, the essence of the PIC-R remains similar to the one presented in the early 1980s. In its most recent version, the PIC-R perspective consists of 13 principles (Andrews & Bonta, 2010a).

Essentially, this theoretical perspective was constructed to explain variations in the probability of the occurrence of criminal behavior in the immediate situation. Compared to the GPCSL perspective, the PIC-R is considered as a "more specific theory of the central mechanisms of criminal conduct" (Polaschek, 2012, p. 3). Thus, the PIC-R provides principles that describe how behavior is operated, why behavior is directed toward criminality, and what affects the strength of this direction. Overall, the theoretical construct of the PIC-R underlies the RNR model and its principles.

The PIC-R relies on behavioral and cognitive social learning principles. Andrews et al. endorsed these kind of theoretical principles due to their potential to achieve the goals of the PCC. In essence, the value of behavioral and cognitive social learning principles resides in "their demonstrated functional power in applied settings" (Andrews & Bonta, 2010a, p. 141). Specifically, the PIC-R reflects the theoretical principle of radical behaviorism that "variation in the immediate contingencies of action is responsible for the acquisition, maintenance, and modification" of criminal behavior (p. 142). Accordingly, with cognitive social learning principles, the PIC-R reflects a theoretical framework of human behavior that accounts for the correlates and predictors of crime, incorporates personality, and demonstrates clinical applicability.

As a perspective that drives from the PCC and the GPCSL, the PIC-R is open to incorporating factors from any discipline that assists in accounting for individual differences in criminal behavior. According to Andrews and Bonta, "theoretical reasons" directed them to constitute the PIC-R around the Big Four factors. In this regard, they noticed that the most empirically defensible theories explain the cause of crime through at least two of these four factors. Thus, in the PIC-R, the Big Four are part of the causal mechanism of behavior and, in turn, the principles of the PIC-R explain their predictive power. In this regard, Andrews and Bonta (2010a) emphasize the fact that these theoretical statements "preceded the explosion of meta-analytic evidence," which enabled the empirical validity of these four factors (p. 132).

This section thus describes the PIC-R perspective through four parts. The first part introduces the PIC-R perspective on basic operation of behavior. The second part explains what increase or decrease the probability of a criminal behavior (i.e., the expected direction of response) and what affect the strength of this probability. The third part presents other general principles of the PIC-R. The fourth part describes the potential of the PIC-R to assist correctional interventions in prediction of future criminality and in direction of effective correctional services.

Basic Operations of Behavior

According to the PIC-R, "the factors responsible for variation in human conduct are found in the immediate situation of action" (Andrews & Bonta, 2010a, p. 143). Within the immediate situation, the behavioral response is under the control of many factors that vary in their importance both inter- and intraindividually. Specifically, the PIC-R distinguishes between two types of events that control the occurrence of deviant and nondeviant behavior: "antecedent control" and "consequent control" (principle 1).

Antecedent control implies stimulus events that precede the behavior and may influence the probability of behavior occurring ("antecedent stimuli"). Such stimuli "gain control over behavior" through the processes of "classical conditioning" (i.e., relatively automatic stimulus–response relationship), "vicarious learning" (i.e., observations on models), and "discrimination learning" (i.e., reliance on information from previous behavioral performances) (Andrews & Bonta, 2010a, p. 144). The second type of control—*consequence control*—is based on the operant conditioning theory. Accordingly, consequence control implies that "behavior produces changes in the environment and the changes it produces (its consequences) may influence the chances of that behavior recurring" (Andrews, 1982a, p. 3).

Such consequent influences may increase the chance of behavior recurring ("rewards" or "reinforcers"), decrease such chance ("costs" or "punishers"), or has no influence on future behavior ("neutral stimuli"). According to the PIC-R, "inter- and intraindividual variations in the probability of occurrence of a given class of behavior (deviant or nondeviant) are due to variations in the signaled reward and costs for that class of behavior" (principle 2) (Andrews & Bonta, 2010a, p. 139). In addition, the PIC-R indicates that rewards and costs, and the antecedents that signal their delivery, fall into "two major types" of environmental events: "additive events" and "subtracting events" (principle 4). In this regard, "additive events" add something to the environment and "subtracting events" subtract something from the environment. Note that additions to the environment may increase or decrease the chance of behavior recurring (i.e., can signal either rewards or costs). Accordingly, subtraction from the environment may also increase or decrease the chance of behavior recurring.

Overall, the concepts of antecedent and consequent control allow the PIC-R to use knowledge from a variety of sources and integrate it in the study of deviant behavior (principle 3). In this regard, the PIC-R stressed "the inter-disciplinary nature of the analysis of deviant behavior" and enables linkages among the biophysical, psychological, sociocultural, and political-economic level of analysis (Andrews, 1982a, p. 1). In addition, the PIC-R permits "a ready classification of the classical but narrower perspective on deviance" (p. 1). In other words, the PCI-R incorporates the explanatory power of the major social psychological theories of deviance. In brief, motivational theories of deviance, which emphasize the potential rewards for deviant behavior, explain the criminogenic effect of rewards in the immediate situation of action. Accordingly, control theories of deviance, which emphasize "the potential costs of—or factors that deter—deviance," explain the criminogenic effect of costs in the immediate situation (Andrews & Bonta, 2010a, p. 151).

The Direction and Magnitude of Effects on Behavior

The PIC-R explains what increase or decrease the probability of an act (i.e., the direction of effects on behavior) and "how much of an increase or decrease is observed" (i.e., the magnitude of effects on behavior) (Andrews, 1982a, p. 23). Within the immediate situation, variation in the probability of the occurrence of a given class of behavior (deviant or nondeviant) is a function of the *density* of reward and costs (principle 5).[3] In that sense, the chance to observe deviant behavior increases with the density of the rewards for deviant behavior and decreases with the density of the costs for deviant behavior. Importantly, "criminal behavior reflects not just particular motivations or particular constraints but the density of signaled rewards and costs" (Andrews & Bonta, 2010a, p. 155). The PIC-R thus explains a criminal act through "shifts in the balance of signaled rewards and costs for criminal acts and noncriminal alternatives" (p. 135).

According to the PIC-R, three major sources of antecedents and consequences influence the direction and strength of the signaled rewards and costs: (1) the actor, (2) other persons, and (3) the act itself. This perspective on the immediate situation of action implies that rewards and costs, and the antecedents that signal their delivery, may be personally mediated, interpersonally mediated, or nonmediated (principle 6).

Personally mediated events arise from the actor. In the PIC-R, the strength of personal mediated events increases "with a general predisposition toward high personal constraint, the availability of specific self-management skills such as problem-solving and self-control skills, and when personal cognitions deviate from the neutral" (Andrews & Bonta, 2010a, p. 139). The direction of this influence "depends upon the procriminal versus anticriminal nature of cognitions" (p. 139). In other words, it depends on whether "personal attitude, values, beliefs, rationalizations, identities, and cognitive-emotional states" support criminal or noncriminal behavior (p. 139).

Interpersonally mediated events arise from the influence of other persons. In the PIC-R, the strength of interpersonal mediated influence "increases with adherence to the relationship principle" (Andrews & Bonta, 2010a, p. 140). That is, "interpersonal influence by antecedent and consequent processes is greater in situations characterized by open, warm, enthusiastic, and nonblaming communication, and by collaboration, mutual respect, liking and interest" (p. 381). In the PIC-R, the direction of interpersonally mediated influence is "determined by the structuring principle"—"the nature of the behavior patterns that are modeled, rehearsed, and subject to reinforcement and punishment contingencies" (pp. 140, 381).

Nonmediated events arise from the act itself. Such influences "are relatively automatic as a function of the act itself and primarily reflect a history of reinforcement for the target behavior" (p. 140). That is, habitual and automatic events control the behavior (p. 147).

Importantly, through these three major sources of antecedents and consequences, the PIC-R explains the predictive power of the Big Four and other factors that were found as correlates of criminality. First, these sources highlight that "the construct of *antisocial attitude* has a crucial role in PIC–R" (Andrews & Bonta, 2010a, p. 154, emphasis in original). Specifically, factors that relate to cognitions "contribute to the standard of conduct that determine whether personally mediated control favors criminal over noncriminal choices. They also represent the pool of justifications and exonerating statements that the person has available in any particular situation" (p. 154). Second, these sources also indicate that the role of the construct of *antisocial associations* is "very important" in the PIC–R. Specifically, antisocial associates "influence the procriminal versus anticriminal nature of modeling in the situation of action as well as govern the rules by which rewards and costs are signaled and delivered" (i.e., direct influence) (p. 154). In addition, "antisocial significant others also impact on antisocial attitude, which in turn may influence personally mediated control even in the absence of others" (i.e., indirect influence) (p. 154).

Third, these three major sources of antecedents and consequences also reflect that "the construct of *history of antisocial behavior* is also theoretically relevant" (Andrews & Bonta, 2010a, p. 154, emphasis in original). In the PIC–R, the history of behavior "increases self-efficacy beliefs with regard to being able to complete the act successfully and serves as a measure of habit strength in the tradition of behaviorism" (p. 154). Fourth, these sources of events accommodate the *personality* correlates of criminality. Specifically, correlates such as "impulsivity and weak self-control are explained through personality mediated control" (p. 153). In addition, the PIC–R explains antisocial behavior through the interactions of personality attributes with certain attitudes or associates. Such interactions may increase motivation toward criminality or decrease personal and social control that facilitates criminality.

Fifth, the PIC–R makes "theoretical sense" in the Moderate Four. According to the PIC–R, factors such as (1) family, (2) school/work, and (3) leisure/recreation "represent major behavioral settings, and the contingencies within those settings may have a great impact on the overall density of rewards and costs for criminal behavior" (p. 154). In addition, the PIC–R explains the moderate impact of (4) substance abuse. This factor might be illegal by definition and also "can lead to criminal activity through a variety of routes including disruption of personally mediated control both automatic and effortful" (p. 155). According to Andrews and Bonta (2010a), the Central Eight (the Big Four and the Moderate Four risk factors) and other "relatively minor personal risk/need factors [that] may also be operative within PIC–R" (e.g., measures of psychological discomfort) ("strength/protective factors") are "closely linked with the PIC–R model of criminal conduct" (pp. 154, 380).

The PIC–R provides more specific explanation about the magnitude of the probability of an act (principles 7 and 8). In this regard, the magnitude of the effects of rewards and costs is expected to be "interdependence and indeed interactive in their impact on behavior" (Andrews & Bonta, 2010a, p. 147). According to the PIC–R, "the magnitude of the effect of any one signaled reward for any class of behaviors depends upon the signaled density of other rewards for that class of behaviors" (p. 140). In addition, "variation in the signaled reward and costs for one class of behavior (deviant or nondeviant) may produce variations in the probability of occurrence in another class of behavior" (p. 140).

Relatedly, the PIC–R suggests the behavioral mechanism that operates the magnitude of the effect. This mechanism emphasizes the importance of building up rewards for noncriminal behavior. Specifically, it suggests that "the rewards for non-deviant behavior approach their maximum impact on the chance of deviant behavior under three conditions" (Andrews & Bonta, 2010a, p. 140): first, delivering rewards for noncriminal behavior that are similar to the rewards delivered by deviant behavior; second, increasing the overall density of the rewards for nondeviant behavior; and third, delivering rewards for behaviors that are incompatible with deviance.

Other General Issues Suggested by the PIC-R

Beyond explanations of the general operation of behavior and the probability of behavioral occurrence, the PIC-R provides other general propositions. First, the PIC-R discusses how to analyze the effect of political and sociocultural systems on behavior (principles 10 and 11). In other words, the PIC-R suggests an analytic approach to situations in which "variations in the contingencies may be described as structure inequalities in the distribution of resources and power" (Andrews, 1982a, p. 34). In this regard, the PIC-R directs to examine "all systems of which the individual is part" (p. 40). Then, the PIC-R suggests analyzing the situation in terms of "what is being modeled, what is reinforced, and what is punished" (Andrews & Bonta, 2010a, p. 148). Second, the principles of the PIC-R provide a "reminder of the practical value of individualized understanding of the reward-cost contingencies in effect" (p. 149) (principle 12). Third, the principles of the PIC-R also provide a "reminder that research and practice proceed in a [*sic*] ethical, humane, and just manner" (p. 148) (principle 13).

PIC-R and Offender Assessment

As detailed above, the PIC-R was constituted not only to explain the occurrence of criminal behavior but also as theory with a potential to provide meaningful assistance in assessments of future criminality. In the early 1980s, Andrews (1982a) provided directions how to assess the chance that persons in the immediate situation would choose a criminal response. He suggested that indicators of reward and cost in effect or signaled for criminal behavior ("ties to crime") may be found in a comprehensive examination of the followings attributes of persons and their situation: "(a) prior (and rewarded) involvement in deviant behavior; (b) possession of prerequisite skills for deviance; (c) personal endorsement of sentiments supportive of deviance in general and specific deviant act in particular; (d) value placed on outcomes which are more readily obtained by deviant than by nondeviant behaviors; (e) social support for deviance (including necessary resources, models, association with others involved in deviance, affective ties to such others)" (p. 47).

Accordingly, a complementary set of indicators is needed to assess the density of the rewards and costs in effect for nondeviant behavior ("ties to convention norms"). In this regard, a comprehensive assessment of the factors that tie to conventional norms can lead to a mirror image of the indicators of "ties to crime" (Andrews, 1982a). According to Andrews (1983), such assessment "samples the density of the reward and satisfactions associated with a variety of noncriminal pursuits, especially those that occur in the company of anticriminal others and within anticriminal settings such as the home, school, work, recreation, neighborhood, and other social settings such as the church and unions" (p. 183).

These early suggestions led to the development of specific (and more sophisticated) assessment tools to predict criminality (see the next chapter). In general, the PIC-R provides a theoretical guidance for criminal assessment that serves two clinical purposes: effective prediction of future risk and targeting interventions. In this regard, Andrews and Bonta (2010a) indicate that the PIC-R offers four "lessons" for the clinical development of offenders' assessment. The first lesson is to "sample multiple domains of criminal conduct" (p. 307). This lesson is based on the principle that criminal behavior is under the control of many factors. In other words, the rewards and costs for both criminal and noncriminal behavior arise from multiple sources.

The second lesson is to "assess the dynamic as well as the static covariates of criminal conduct" (p. 308). In this regard, Andrews and his colleagues were aware of the fact that several static measures might yield the maximum amount of variance. Nevertheless, they emphasized the practical value of the inclusion of dynamic measures. They stated that prediction of criminal behavior "rarely is the primary concern of practitioners (or theorists)" (Andrews, 1982a, p. 46). Rather, they claimed, "their concern is with those attributes of persons and their situations which are reasonably and ethically amenable to influence and whose influence would in turn be associated with variations in the chances of deviant activity" (p. 46). In other words, dynamic predictors are potential targets for interventions and therefore have to be part of the assessment of criminal behavior.

The third lesson that the PIC-R can offer for offender assessment is that "offender assessment can guide the intensity of treatment" (Andrews & Bonta, 2010a, p. 308). According to this lesson, offender assessments have to provide a clear distinction between low-, moderate-, and high-risk offenders. In this regard, Andrews (1982a) claimed that correctional intervention may make low-risk offenders worse. He explained that "when the density of the rewards for deviant is low and the density of the costs is high," the probability of future criminality is low (p. 52). In such case, he stated, interventions may produce shifts in the density of rewards and costs that "can only be in the prodeviant direction" (p. 52). As opposed to low-risk offenders, moderate and high-risk offenders "need and may profit from agency efforts" (p. 52). Therefore, PIC-R directs assessments to provide knowledge about "how much treatment is needed to reduce an offender's risk" (Andrews & Bonta, 2010a, p. 308).

The fourth lesson from PIC-R is that "offender assessment can guide how we provide treatment" (Andrews & Bonta, 2010a, p. 308). According to this lesson, assessments should provide information about "personal-cognitive-emotional factors" that interfere with personally or interpersonally mediated control. Such information is important because these factors (e.g., low intelligence or low levels of interpersonal skills) may render offenders' ability to learn from the environment. Thus, treatment may be interested in assessment of individual characteristics "that may not be predictors of criminal behavior but are still relevant for the delivery of services" (p. 308). In that sense, matching delivery of service to an individual's learning ability may facilitate new prosocial cognitions.

PIC-R and Crime Prevention

In addition to providing assistance in prediction of future criminality, the clinical value of the PIC-R resides in its ability to explain effective design and delivery of correctional services. Recall that reduction of future criminality is the ultimate goal of the PCC, and the RNR model is expected to carry on this goal. PIC-R thus contributes to this effort by providing theoretical explanation about the causes of stability and change in criminal behavior.

As mentioned above, the premise of the PIC-R is that "offenders, being human, seek pleasure and try to avoid pain" (Andrews & Bonta, 2010a, p. 390). Based on this premise, the PIC-R explains that the behavior "is influenced by the immediate contingencies of action that are situationally induced and personally and interpersonally mediated" (p. 390). Essentially, the PIC-R uses these contingencies to explain stability and change in criminal behavior. According to the PIC-R, "stability in human behavior is evident because these contingencies are maintained by such personal variables as personality, attitudes, competencies, and incompetencies, and by important others such as partners and peers" (p. 390). In this regard, stability in criminal behavior reflects a relatively stable balance between signaled rewards and costs that favor deviant behavior over signaled rewards and costs that favor nondeviant alternatives.

Accordingly, change in these contingencies of action may produce behavioral change. Specifically, such changes create shifts in "the density of the incentives [i.e., rewards] and disincentives [i.e., costs] for criminal acts and noncriminal acts" (Andrews & Bonta, 2010a, p. 390). Thus, behavioral change depends on whether these shifts result in a new balance between density of signaled rewards and costs that favor one behavior over an alternative behavior. In relation to criminal behavior, shifts in the density of the incentives and disincentives may change this balance from favoring deviant response to less favoring such response or favoring nondeviant alternative responses.

In clinical practice, thus, "without alteration of the personal, interpersonal, and community sources of rewards and costs, long-term behavior change is unlikely" (Andrews & Bonta, 2010a, p. 143). According to the PIC–R, the focus of correctional intervention should be on rewarding nondeviant alternative behaviors. This emphasis on reinforcement—the process of rewarding—reflects an underlying assumption that rewarding nondeviant alternative serves two proposes: reduction in motivation for deviance and increase in the subtractive costs of crime (i.e., there is more to lose).

Introduction to the Risk-Need-Responsivity Principles

During the 1980s, the PCC was developed against the political and criminological mainstream. As described in previous chapters, the notion of correctional rehabilitation was devaluated by policy makers and academicians, and "getting tough" on criminals became the major criminal justice policy to deal with offenders. Within this broad context, the objectives and assumptions of PCC contrasted those endorsed by mainstream criminologists. Nevertheless, Andrews and his collaborators continue to use the theoretical perspective for conducting systematic research to explore the variability of recidivism among correctional intervention. Essentially, the theoretical and empirical knowledge that was available in the early 1990s led them to suggest Risk, Need, Responsivity, and Professional override as four "principles of classification for effective rehabilitation" (Andrews et al., 1990).

Beyond Mainstream Criminology

In this regard, Andrews et al. (1990) indicated four major differences between PCC and mainstream criminology. The first difference was the perused objectives. While the PCC sought to understand the variation in criminal conduct of individuals, "mainstream criminology [was] preoccupied with interpreting aggregated crime rates, law and order, and with overcoming structured inequality in the distribution of societal wealth and power" (p. 21). The second difference was their scope of inquiry. While the PCC was open to covariates from any discipline of knowledge that may assist in accounting the variation in criminal conduct of individuals, mainstream criminology devaluated individual differences and personality explanation (Andrews & Wormith, 1989). Instead, mainstream criminologists emphasized the "structural 'root causes' of crime" (Cullen & Gendreau, 2001, p. 326).

The third fundamental difference between PCC and mainstream criminology was their attitude toward clinical criminology. While the PCC sought for both theoretical and practical understanding of human service, mainstream criminology believed "that clinical service is ineffective, perhaps 'evil,' and certainly not as powerful or as dignified as punishment" (Andrews et al., 1990, p. 21). The fourth difference resided in the professional ideology of Andrews and his colleagues and mainstream criminologists. While the PCC used science as "a way of knowing the world and changing it for the better" (i.e., endorsed "knowledge construction"), mainstream criminologists adopted professional ideology of "knowledge destruction" (Cullen & Gendreau, 2001, p. 331). That is, mainstream criminologists concentrated on showing what does not work in corrections (Andrews & Wormith, 1989).

As mentioned above, despite the anti-rehabilitation environment, Andrews and his collaborators adhered to their rational empirical psychology of crime. Specifically, they consistently sought ways to promote the empirical, theoretical, and practical understanding of variation in criminal conduct of individuals. As described above, their early empirical research provided the core criminological component for the PCC (Andrews, 1980). In this regard, their experimental studies demonstrated how criminological theory (the differential association theory) could affect the practical outcome with offenders. In the early 1980s, this important finding led Don Andrews to constitute the PIC-R (Andrews, 1982a). Essentially, the PIC-R established a new bridge between criminology and rehabilitation research—a bridge that was made by converging key aspects of several criminological theories around the cognitive social learning perspective of human behavior.

Searching for Factors That Matter in Offender Rehabilitation

During the 1980s, Andrews and his collaborators developed a broad methodological framework that intended to enhance the practical understanding of variation in correctional rehabilitation. Their broad framework—the "model of direct intervention"—was designed to address issues in respect of the general social service, including correctional services (Hoge & Andrews, 1986). Hoge and Andrews (1986) presented the model "as a framework for understanding the dynamics of the process as it operates in these settings and as guide for research on the process" (p. 334). In essence, this model endorsed an underlying assumption that followed the premises of PIC-R: "most human problems have their sources within the individual, the family group, or the immediate situation" (p. 332). Accordingly, the direct intervention strategy directed treatments "at the personal, interpersonal and immediate situation" (p. 332).

Importantly, Andrews and his colleagues endorsed a "functional perspective" to their framework— the relative value of elements in the intervention process would be examined in relation to the goal that the agency was trying to achieve (Andrews, 1982b). Accordingly, within the correctional context, they chose recidivism as the ultimate outcome of correctional agencies. In that sense, "it may be worse than useless to select factors within a given set to meet some presumed ideal which bears no obvious relation to recidivism" (p. 10).

The goal of this model thus was to identify factors, and relationships between factors, that are relevant to recidivism and can optimize treatment effects. In this regard, Andrews and his collaborators mapped six major categories—sets of factors—that represent independent source of variability in recidivism: (1) offender factors; (2) correctional worker factors; (3) counseling process factors; (4) program-level factors; (5) intermediate outcomes; and (6) setting factors. The general assumption of the model of direct intervention was that offender, worker, practice, programs, and setting "operate as main effects in the determination of outcomes" (Hoge & Andrews, 1986, p. 338). In addition, it postulated that "these variables sometimes interact with one another and impact in that fashion on outcomes" (p. 338). Overall, research into these factors and their interactions on recidivism influenced and directed the articulation of the principles of effective intervention. Therefore, the set of factors are described below.

Preservice Characteristics of Offenders

Andrew et al. considered the characteristics of offenders as "the most important class of factors" because recidivism—the ultimate outcome measure—"ties directly to the criminality of individuals" (Andrews, 1982b, p. 14). In this regard, they also relied on the theoretical perspective of PIC-R and the early empirical studies that demonstrated the role of offender variables in the intervention process (e.g., Andrews, 1980; Andrews & Kiessling, 1980). Specifically, attributes of clients and their situations include biophysical functioning and states, conventional attitude, personality, compatibilities, social and historical elements, and "structural and cultural aspects of social system or groups of which the client is or has been a member" (Andrews, 1982b, p. 13).

During the 1980s, Andrews and his colleagues suggested that the investigation of this category should focus on specific problems that brought the offenders into the correctional system and on measures that would assess the levels of risk/need for service and the level of readiness for intervention services. Overall thus, this category set the stage for "the development of operational definitions of these concepts and of practical measures" (Hoge & Andrews, 1986, p. 336). Specifically, future investigations of this category were expected to assist in (1) designing risk-assessment instruments; (2) developing strategies that would match offenders to "the most appropriate type of workers, practices, programs, and surrounding conditions;" and (3) panning interventions that would focus on the dynamic individual factors as "intermediate targets" (i.e., targets that when changed would associate with subsequent reduction in recidivism) (pp. 14–15; see also Andrews, 1983).

Characteristics of Correctional Workers

This category followed the PIC-R that interpersonally mediated events arise from the influence of other persons (e.g., the relationship principle). In addition, empirical studies supported the potential impact of correctional workers' factors on recidivism. First, studies in literature in the general human service provided "ample evidence that therapists and counselor variables have direct and indirect bearing on the outcomes of therapy" (Hoge & Andrews, 1986, p. 337). Second, studies in corrections that examined the impact of therapist characteristics found promising results (Andrews, 1982b; see also Andrews & Kiessling, 1980). Within the model of direct intervention, the variables that relate to the characteristic of correctional workers were conceptualized in four sets: (1) "demographic," (2) "training/experience," (3) "relationship style," and (4) "practice preferences" (Hoge & Andrews, 1986, p. 337).

Practice Factors

Measures of the content and process of services reflect "the nature and quality of the interactions between [correctional] workers and clients" (Andrews, 1982b, p. 16). According to the model of direct intervention, there was a general agreement that the use of "global construct" to describe treatment (e.g., psychotherapy, client–center, or behavioristic) was "of little utility" (Hoge & Andrews, 1986, p. 337). Instead, this model focused on four "specific aspects of the counselor-client interaction": (1) "ongoing contracting" (i.e., records of thoughts and reactions), (2) "message content (i.e., the topics of discussion), (3) "relationship style," and (4) "number, duration, and density of contacts" (p. 337). Overall, by setting this category, Andrews (1982b) expected that "intervention practices may correlate with measures of worker and client factors . . . [and] may make independent contributions to the ability to predict and control recidivism" (p. 16).

Program Factors

This category referred to factors that "operate at the level of the agency or institution in which the counseling is provided" (Hoge & Andrews, 1986, p. 337). According to Andrews (1982b), "systematic empirical investigations of the relation of these factors to recidivism are almost totally lacking" (p. 44). Nevertheless, the model of direct intervention presented three sets of variables that may relate to recidivism "independently of characteristics of workers, client, and practice" (p. 17). These sets of variables are (1) agency philosophy, (2) prescribed programs, and (3) agency resources.

Setting Factors

This category refers "to attributes of the broader community or systems of which any given program is part" (Andrews, 1982b, p. 18). General examples of setting factors would include "levels of unemployment, attitudes toward unemployment, availability of housing, and size of community" (Hoge & Andrews, 1986, p. 336). By definition, setting factors may account only for between-setting variation in recidivism (i.e., different political-economic situations). In the early 1980s, Andrews and his colleagues were not "aware of *any* empirical evidence that variations in recidivism rates may be attributed to broader setting factors, except of course, where *client* factors such as age, socio-economic status, or ethnic background are misrepresented as setting factors" (p. 48, emphasis in original; see also Andrews & Wormith, 1989).

Intermediate Outcomes

Intermediate outcome refers to goals, which, if achieved, would be associated with changes in an ultimate outcome (e.g., recidivism). From the PIC-C perspective, "the overall intermediate target is to alter the density of the rewards and the density of the costs for criminal and noncriminal behaviors such that the noncriminal are favored" (Andrews, 1982b, p. 34). In the model of direct intervention, general measures of intermediate outcomes may include "indices of changes in [1] client problems, [2] movement on risk/need factors, and [3] client satisfaction" (Hoge & Andrews, 1986, p. 337). As mentioned above, Andrews and his collaborators expected that intermediate outcomes in the correctional system would link the intervention process with recidivism. In the early 1980s, "the number of factors with some documented dynamic validity [was] very small. In fact, if we were to demand utterly convincing empirical evidence regarding dynamic validity, the list of factors would be an empty set" (Andrews, 1982b, p. 33).

Overall, in the mid-1980s, Andrews and his colleagues presented frameworks for searching the theoretical (PIC-R), empirical (Central Eight), and practical (the model of direct intervention) understanding of variation in recidivism. However, during that time, the correctional filed had very little sound empirical data to validate these types of understanding. For example, the model of direct intervention might be considered an unrealistic guidance because it seemed "impossible to assess complex interactions among the large set of variables involved" (Hoge & Andrews, 1986, pp. 338–339). Thus, further developments in the predictability of recidivism in corrections depended on the ability to use new and more powerful statistical techniques.

As described in the previous chapter, the development of meta-analytic technique was considered as a "methodological breakthrough" in corrections (Gendreau & Ross, 1987). Since the mid-1980s, this statistical tool enabled systematic assessment that would present the relative impact of a set of variables and their interactions on recidivism. Overall, thus, the meta-analytic technique provided a systematic quantitative approach to understand the variation in recidivism. Essentially, with the criminological and psychological foundations of GPCSL and PIC-R, this approach allowed rehabilitation to fulfill its potential to become empirically defensible practice in criminal justice. In other words, the developments of PCC and meta-analytic technique "began to consolidate the conclusion that treatment can be effective in reducing recidivism and significantly so" (Andrews & Bonta, 2010b, p. 44).

In the early 1990s, these developments led Andrews and his colleagues to present two related publications that constituted the core of the RNR model. One paper suggested four principles of classification for effective rehabilitation—risk, need, responsivity, and professional override (Andrews et al., 1990). These four principles were designed to "provide reasonable guides to service and research in rehabilitation" (p. 45). The other paper presented findings from a comprehensive meta-analysis that examined the effect of these principles on recidivism (Andrews, Zinger, Lab, & Whitehead, 1990) (see the previous chapter for more details on this study). Together, these publications represent the early version of the RNR model—the introduction of a set of testable principles that, "if followed, were said to have meaningful treatment effect" (Cullen, 2005, p. 17).

The suggested risk (R), need (N), and responsivity (R) principles became the three core principles in the "RNR model." The fourth principle—professional override—reflected the idea that "decisions regarding rehabilitative service are a joint function of risk, need, and responsivity consideration . . . [and] rehabilitation professional will always be called upon to beyond extant knowledge in their decision making" (Andrews et al., 1990, p. 44). The next chapter will discuss these principles in length as well as the essence of the other principles in the RNR model. In brief, during the early 1990s, Andrews and his colleagues offered guidance that covered three clinical key concerns: (1) *who* should be treated; (2) *what* should be treated; (3) *how* to intervene.

The *Risk principle* guides "whom we offer intensive correctional treatment services" (Andrews, 1995, p. 41). In this regard, the risk principle stated that "higher levels of service are reserved for higher risk cases" (Andrews et al., 1990, p. 20). The *Need principle* guides "what do we target if an ultimate objective is reduced recidivism" (Andrews, 1995, p. 41). According to this principle, "targets of service are matched with the criminogenic needs of offenders. Such needs are case characteristics that, when influenced, are associated with changes in the chance of recidivism" (Andrews et al., 1990, p. 20). The *Responsivity principle* guides "what modes and styles of treatment service do we employ if we target the criminogenic needs of those at risk for criminal conduct" (Andrews, 1995, p. 41). The responsivity principle thus suggested that "styles and modes of service are matched to the learning styles and ability of offenders" (Andrews et al., 1990, p. 20). Importantly, such matching should be applied to both criminogenic needs and "attributes and circumstances of cases that render cases likely to profit from that particular type of service" (p. 20).

Conclusion

This chapter followed the theoretical development of the RNR from the mid-1970s to the present day. During this period, Andrews and his colleagues established a theoretical framework that reaffirmed the legitimacy of rehabilitation within the correctional system. As discussed in this chapter, these scholars demarcated theoretical, empirical, and practical bases for understanding the variation in criminal conduct of individuals in correctional interventions. Against the mainstream ideas of how to approach criminality, they developed a theoretical enterprise that equipped the philosophy of rehabilitation with a solid framework to describe (PCC), predict (GPCSL), and affect (PIC-R) this variability.

This section elaborated the research strategy that followed these theoretical ideas and, eventually, that resulted in a theoretical leap in correctional rehabilitation. In the early 1990s, Andrews and his colleagues used their theoretical framework to distill the accumulated empirical findings into core correctional principles—the RNR principles. Essentially, their assumption was that if correctional interventions adhere to these principles, then offenders' recidivism will be reduced.

Accordingly, the next chapter will examine the current correctional framework of the RNR model. In this regard, the latest versions of the RNR model include 15 principles (Andrews & Bonta, 2010a; Bonta & Andrews, 2017). Importantly, this discussion reveals how the principles in the RNR model reflect the PCC, the GPCSL perspective on human behavior, and the PIC-R perspective on deviant behavior. It also becomes clear that the RNR model "remains a work-in-progress"—a model that allows future developments to "enhance the multiple contributions of psychology to the understanding and management of criminal offending" (Andrews & Bonta, 2010b, p. 51).

Notes

1. Neobehaviorism was the second phase of behaviorism. The first phase of behaviorism translated the Darwinian outlook into psychology, "assuming that most kinds of human action were the result of biologically innate urges or drives: the instincts" (McGuire, 2004, p. 49).
2. For an illustration of this change in the long-standing distinction between the Big and Moderate Four risk factors, compare Figure 1 in Bonta, Blais, and Wilson (2014, p. 280) with Figure 3.1 in Bonta and Andrews (2017, p. 44).
3. "Density" refers to "the number, variety, quality, and magnitude of rewards [/costs] as well as the immediacy, frequency, and regularity with which they are delivered" (Andrews & Bonta, 2010a, p. 147; see also Andrews, 1982a).

References

Agnew, R. (1992). Foundation for a general strain theory of crime and delinquency. *Criminology, 30*, 47–88.

Akers, R. L. (1973). *Deviant behavior: A social learning approach.* Belmont, CA: Wadsworth.

Akers, R. L. (1977). *Deviant behavior: A social learning approach* (2nd ed.). Belmont, CA: Wadsworth.

Andrews, D. A. (1980). Some experimental investigations of the principles of differential association through deliberate manipulations of the structure of service systems. *American Sociological Review, 45*, 448–462.

Andrews, D. A. (1982a). *A personal, interpersonal and community-reinforcement perspective on deviant behavior (PIC-R).* Toronto, ON: Ministry of Correctional Services.

Andrews, D. A. (1982b). *The supervision of offenders: Identifying and gaining control over the factors that make a difference.* Program Branch User Report. Ottawa, ON: Solicitor General of Canada.

Andrews, D. A. (1983). The assessment of outcome in correctional samples. In M. L. Lambert, E. R. Christensen, & S. S. DeJulio (Eds.), *The measurement of psychotherapy outcome in research and evaluation* (pp. 160–201). New York, NY: Wiley.

Andrews, D. A. (1995). The psychology of criminal conduct and effective treatment. In J. McGuire (Ed.), *What works: Reducing reoffending—guidelines from research and practice* (pp. 35–62). New York, NY: John Wiley.

Andrews, D. A., & Bonta, J. (1994). *The psychology of criminal conduct.* Cincinnati, OH: Anderson.

Andrews, D. A., & Bonta, J. (1998). *The psychology of criminal conduct* (2nd ed.). Cincinnati, OH: Anderson.

Andrews, D. A., & Bonta, J. (2003). *The psychology of criminal conduct* (3rd ed.). Cincinnati, OH: Anderson.

Andrews, D. A., & Bonta, J. (2006). *The psychology of criminal conduct* (4th ed.). New Providence, NJ: Anderson/LexisNexis.

Andrews, D. A., & Bonta, J. (2010a). *The psychology of criminal conduct* (5th ed.). New Providence, NJ: Anderson/LexisNexis.

Andrews, D. A., & Bonta, J. (2010b). Rehabilitating criminal justice policy and practice. *Psychology, Public Policy, and Law, 16,* 39–55.

Andrews, D. A., Bonta, J., & Hoge, R. D. (1990). Classification for effective rehabilitation: Rediscovering psychology. *Criminal Justice and Behavior, 17,* 19–52.

Andrews, D. A., Bonta, J., & Wormith, J. S. (2011). The risk-need-responsivity (RNR) model: Does adding the good lives model contribute to effective crime prevention? *Criminal Justice and Behavior, 38,* 735–755.

Andrews, D. A., & Kiessling, J. J. (1980). Program structure and effective correctional practices: A summary of the CaVIC research. In R. R. Ross & P. Gendreau (Eds.), *Effective correctional treatment* (pp. 441–463). Toronto, TR: Butterworth.

Andrews, D. A., & Wormith, J. S. (1989). Personality and crime: Knowledge, destruction and construction in criminology. *Justice Quarterly, 6,* 289–309.

Andrews, D. A., Zinger, I., Lab, S. P., & Whitehead, J. T. (1990). Does correctional treatment work? A clinically relevant and psychologically informed meta-analysis. *Criminology, 28,* 369–404.

Bandura, A. (1977). *Social learning theory.* Englewood Cliffs, NJ: Prentice Hall.

Bandura, A. (1986). *Social foundations of thought and action: A social cognitive theory.* Englewood Cliffs, NJ: Prentice Hall.

Bandura, A. (1997). *Self-efficacy: The exercise of control.* New York, NY: Freeman.

Bandura, A. (2000). Social cognitive theory. In A. E. Kazdin (Ed.), *Encyclopedia of psychology* (pp. 329–332). New York, NY: Oxford University Press.

Bandura, A. (2001). Social cognitive theory: An agentic perspective. *Annual Review of Psychology, 52,* 1–26.

Bartol, C. R., & Bartol, A. M. (2011). *Criminal behavior: A psychological approach.* Upper Saddle River, NJ: Pearson Education/Prentice Hall.

Beck, A. T. (1963). Thinking and depression: I. Idiosyncratic content and cognitive distortions. *Archives of General Psychiatry, 9,* 324–333.

Berkowitz, L. (1962). *Aggression: A social psychological analysis.* New York, NY: McGraw-Hill.

Bonta, J., & Andrews, D. A. (2017). *The psychology of criminal conduct* (6th ed.). New York, NY: Routledge.

Bonta, J., Blais, J., & Wilson, H. A. (2014). A theoretical informed meta-analysis of the risk for general and violent recidivism for mentally disordered offenders. *Aggression and Violent Behavior, 19,* 278–287.

Burgess, R. L., & Akers, R. L. (1966). A differential association-reinforcement theory of criminal behavior. *Social Problems, 14,* 128–147.

Buss, A. H. (1966). *Psychopathology.* New York, NY: Wiley.

Cressey, D. R. (1955). Changing criminals: The application of the theory of differential association. *American Journal of Sociology, 61,* 116–120.

Cullen, F. T. (2005). The twelve people who saved rehabilitation: How the science of criminology made a difference. *Criminology, 43,* 1–42.

Cullen, F. T. (2013). Rehabilitation: Beyond nothing works. In M. Tonry (Ed.), *Crime and justice in America, 1975 to 2025—crime and justice: A review of research* (Vol. 42, pp. 299–376). Chicago, IL: University of Chicago Press.

Cullen, F. T., & Gendreau, P. (2001). From nothing works to what works: Changing professional ideology in the 21st century. *The Prison Journal, 81*, 313–338.

Cullen, F. T., & Wilcox, P. (Eds.). (2010). *Encyclopedia of criminological theory.* Thousand Oaks, CA: Sage.

Cullen, F. T., Wright, J. P., Gendreau, P., & Andrews, D. A. (2003). What correctional treatment can tell us about criminological theory: Implications for social learning theory. In R. L. Akers & G. F. Jensen (Eds.), *Social learning theory and the explanation of crime: A guide for the new century: Advances in criminological theory* (Vol. 11, pp. 339–362). New Brunswick, NJ: Transaction.

Dollard, J., Doob, L., Miller, N., Mowrer, O., & Sears, R. (1939). *Frustration and aggression.* New Haven, CT: Yale University Press.

Ellis, A. (1962). *Reason and emotion in psychotherapy.* Secaucus, NJ: Lyle Stuart.

Gendreau, P. (1996). The principles of effective intervention with offenders. In A. T. Harland (Ed.), *Choosing correctional interventions that work: Defining the demand and evaluating the supply* (pp. 117–130). Thousand Oaks, CA: Sage.

Gendreau, P., & Ross, B. (1979). Effective correctional treatment: Bibliotherapy for cynics. *Crime and Delinquency, 25*, 463–489.

Gendreau, P., & Ross, B. (1987). Revivification of rehabilitation: Evidence from the 1980s. *Justice Quarterly, 4*, 349–407.

Gendreau, P., Smith, P., & French, S. (2006). The theory of effective correctional intervention: Empirical status and future directions. In F. T. Cullen, J. P. Wright, & K. R. Blevins (Eds.), *Taking stock: The status of criminological theory: Advances in criminological theory* (Vol. 15, pp. 419–446). New Brunswick, NJ: Transaction.

Glueck, S., & Glueck, E. T. (1950). *Unravelling juvenile delinquency.* Cambridge, MA: Harvard University Press.

Guthrie, E. R. (1935). *The psychology of learning.* New York, NY: Harper.

Hirschi, T. (1969). *Causes of delinquency.* Berkeley: University of California Press.

Hoge, R. D., & Andrews, D. A. (1986). A model for conceptualizing interventions in social service agencies. *Canadian Psychology, 27*, 332–341.

Hoge, R. D., & Andrews, D. A. (1996). *Assessing the youthful offender: Issues and techniques.* New York, NY: Plenum Press.

Hull, C. L. (1943). *Principles of behavior: An introduction to behavior theory.* New York, NY: Appleton-Century.

Lilly, J. R., Cullen, F. T., & Ball, R. A. (2011). *Criminological theory: Context and consequences.* Thousand Oaks, CA: Sage.

McGuire, J. (2004). *Understanding psychology and crime: Perspectives on theory and action.* New York, NY: Open University Press.

Meichenbaum, D. (1977). *Cognitive-behavior modification: An integrative approach.* New York, NY: Plenum Press.

Polaschek, D. L. L. (2012). An appraisal of the risk–need–responsivity (RNR) model of offender rehabilitation and its application in correctional treatment. *Legal and Criminological Psychology, 17*, 1–17.

Pratt, T. C., Cullen, F. T., Sellers, C. S., Winfree, L. T., Jr., Madensen, T. D., Daigle, L. E., Fearn, N. E., & Gau, J. M. (2010). The empirical status of social learning theory: A meta-analysis. *Justice Quarterly, 27*, 765–802.

Schunk, D. H., Meece, J. L., & Pintrich, P. R. (2014). *Motivation in education: Theory, research, and applications* (4th ed.). Boston, MA: Pearson.

Skinner, B. F. (1953). *Science and human behavior.* New York, NY: Macmillan.

Sutherland, E. H. (1947). *Principles of criminology* (4th ed.). Philadelphia, PA: J. B. Lippincott.

Tolman, E. C. (1932). *Purposive behavior in animals and men.* New York, NT: Century.

Wormith, J. S. (1984). Attitude and behavior change of correctional clientele: A three year follow-up. *Criminology, 22*, 595–618.

4

THE PRINCIPLES OF EFFECTIVE CORRECTIONAL TREATMENT

Theory and Technology

In the early 1990s, Andrews et al. published two studies that demonstrated the science of criminal behavior (Andrews, Bonta, & Hoge, 1990; Andrews, Zinger, Lab, & Whitehead, 1990). These studies presented a theoretical perspective that was empirically defensible and reflected their psychology of criminal conduct. In essence, Andrews et al. (1990) introduced their rational empirical psychology of crime as a perspective that "provides a stimulating and facilitative home for the analysis and development of rehabilitation" (p. 20). Accordingly, in the following years, empirical evidence continued to support their perspective that gained more attention due to "its ability to predict criminal activity, to influence criminal activity, and to explain criminal activity" (Andrews, 1995, p. 36). Essentially, they accumulated and assessed these two publications during a time when the correctional rehabilitation field was starting to regain its legitimation to search for effective correctional intervention (Palmer, 1992).

In 1994, Donald Andrews and James Bonta published a book named after their perspective: *The Psychology of Criminal Conduct* (PCC). This book covered the knowledge base of their perspective (i.e., the PCC's goals and objectives, and the theoretical frameworks and the research related to the GPCSL and the PIC-R). Based on this knowledge, Andrews (1995) expanded the principles suggested in Andrews et al. (1990) to a total of 16 "principles of effective prevention and correctional treatment" (pp. 42–43). Together, these principles were designed to translate the accumulating knowledge into a form that would provide clear guidance regarding how to engage in effective correctional intervention. In the mid-1990s, this expanded set of principals was presented as hypotheses. However, according to Andrews (1995), "they [were] hypotheses with rational and empirical support sufficient to suggest that they may be used to guide evaluated policy and practice that is concerned with the reduction of criminal conduct" (p. 41).

This chapter thus discusses the correctional framework of the RNR model in two sections. The first section examines the RNR model's principles of correctional assessment and treatment. Specifically, this section evaluates each of the 15 principles as presented in Andrews and Bonta (2010a) and Bonta and Andrews (2017). These latest editions of *The Psychology of Criminal Conduct* present the most updated version of those principles. The second section will examine the practical implication of these principles. Specifically, this section will introduce structured assessment tools that are in use in the correctional system. Those tools assist the correctional system in predicting the likelihood of individuals to reoffend (e.g., LSI-R) and the likelihood of correctional intervention to influence criminal behavior of individuals (e.g., CPAI).

The RNR Model of Correctional Assessment and Treatment

Since first presented, Andrews and Bonta continued to develop and modify the principles of effective intervention. They did so in six editions of *The Psychology of Criminal Conduct* (Andrews & Bonta, 1994, 1998, 2003, 2006, 2010a; Bonta & Andrews, 2017) and in a series of articles (Andrews, 1995, 2001; Andrews & Bonta, 2010b; Bonta & Andrews, 2007; Gendreau, 1996). Indeed, this ongoing effort represents the development of the RNR model.

In essence, the RNR model is the correctional component of the PCC—the "blueprint for intervening with offenders . . . that is conveyed through the principles of effective correctional treatment" (Cullen, 2013, p. 341). In this regard, according to Cullen (2005), the decision to set forth the existing knowledge in "propositional form" and organize it around principles of effective intervention was "of immense *strategic* value" (p. 16, emphasis in original). First, "by developing principles, Andrews and Bonta succeeded in placing knowledge about treatment effectiveness in a form in which it could be transferred to practitioners . . . Second, the statement of principles made their theory testable and thus of potential scientific value" (p. 17).

As mentioned above, this section discusses the full RNR model as presented in the latest (fifth and sixth) editions of *The Psychology of Criminal Conduct*. Within these editions, Andrews and Bonta outlined 15 principles that represent the "Risk–Need–Responsivity (RNR) Model of Offender Assessment and Treatment" (Bonta & Andrews, 2017, pp. 176; see also Andrews & Bonta, 2010a, pp. 46). The authors divided their 15 principles into three parts: (1) Overarching principles; (2) core RNR principles and key clinical issues; (3) organizational principles: setting, staffing, and management. In this regard, the discussion of the principles that follows will be divided to correspond with these three parts. Note that the 15 principles as set forth by Bonta and Andrews (2017) will be reprinted in their original form in Tables 4.1, 4.2, and 4.3—one table to correspond to each of the three parts.

TABLE 4.1 RNR model's overarching principles

---

1. **Respect for the Person and the Normative Context:** Services are delivered with respect for the person, including respect for personal autonomy, being humane, ethical, just, legal, decent, and being otherwise normative. Some norms may vary with the agencies or the particular settings within which services are delivered. For example, agencies working with young offenders may be expected to show exceptional attention to education issues and to child protection. Mental health agencies may attend to issues of personal well-being. Some agencies working with female offenders may place a premium on attending to trauma and/or to parenting concerns.

2. **Psychological Theory:** Base programs on an empirically solid psychological theory (e.g., General Personality and Cognitive Social Learning).

3. **General Enhancement of Crime Prevention Services:** The reduction of criminal victimization may be viewed as a legitimate objective of service agencies, including agencies within and outside of justice and corrections.

Source: Reprinted with permission from Bonta & Andrews, *The Psychology of Criminal Conduct*, 6th Edition.

In brief, Table 4.1 includes three overarching principles that "restate and underscore the importance of the theoretical and normative issues" (Andrews, 2001). In brief, principle 1 links the RNR model to the public mandate to intervene in the life of offenders. Thus, this principle underscores that correctional interventions have to consider the context appropriate to local and surrounding conditions. Principle 2 links the RNR to its underlying theory. In this regard, this principle states that the GPCSL is more effective in correctional settings than any alternative perspective of human behavior. Principle 3 states the RNR model can enhance the effectiveness of crime prevention efforts "in the locally appropriate context child welfare, family services, mental health, community development etc." (Andrews, 2001).

Table 4.2 includes the core RNR principles and other principles that address key clinical issues (principles 4–12). Principle 4 highlights the use of human service strategy over services based on retribution, restorative justice, deterrence, or incapacitation. Principles 5–8 present the RNR principles. These principles remain at the core of the model since it was first presented and "have exerted a considerable influence on correctional theory, practice, and policy" (Andrews, Bonta, & Wormith, 2011, p. 736). Principle 9 suggests targeting a number of criminogenic needs, especially in interventions that deal with high-risk offenders. Principles 10–12 direct correctional interventions in assessment of offenders. Specifically, these principles underscore strength factors (principle 10), the use of structured assessment (principle 11), and the ability of professionals to deviate from the RNR principles and its assessments (principle 12).

The organizational principles are presented in Table 4.3. These principles were designed to direct correctional interventions through the challenges faced by treatment in the real world. These principles reflect the fact that "it requires major efforts on the part of managers and staff for adherence [to the RNR principles] to be accomplished" (Andrews & Bonta, 2010a, p. 505). Specifically, principle 13 directs that community-based services facilitate better levels of adherence to the RNR principles. Accordingly, principles 14 and 15 underscore the importance of "staff establishing collaborative and respectful working relationships with clients and correctional agencies and managers providing policies and leadership that facilitate and enable effective interventions" (Bonta & Andrews, 2007, p. 1).

Principle 1: Respect for the Person and the Normative Context

As noted, the first three principles of the RNR model are the overarching principles. They are listed in Table 4.1. Importantly, as psychologists, Andrews and Bonta recognized that any correctional intervention must be ethical and thus follow norms that ensure offenders are treated appropriately. Thus, principle 1 establishes the normative contexts of the RNR model. First, this principle calls for respect for the person. Within the RNR model, such respect reflects an awareness to the punitive nature of the correctional system. In this regard, Andrews and Bonta (2010a) highlighted the respect for the personal autonomy in correctional interventions because this practice field tends to emphasize "structure, discipline, accountability, and state-sanctioned imposition of restrictions and punishment" (p. 7). Thus, according to their perspective, the respect for personal autonomy is "a key aspect of ethical practice" (p. 6).

Second, principle 1 also underscores the importance of respect for the normative context in which the service is provided. According to Andrews and Bonta (2010a), any agency that provides human service should "respect the norms of the broader and narrower communities of which it is a part" because "all forms of human, social, and clinical services are subjective to evaluations in regard to ethically, legality, and some other norms" (p. 52). Essentially, this principle guides those delivering an intervention to respect ethical norms even in conditions when the compliance of norms has only a weak connection with reduction of recidivism (e.g., respect to sentences that were imposed "according to criminal law and the principle of specific deterrence") (Andrews, 2001). In addition, correctional interventions are expected to take into consideration that norms can be different in different settings for different offender populations.

Principle 2: Psychological Theory

Principle 2 reflects the focus of the RNR model on the reduction in recidivism as the major goal of correctional intervention. First, interventions that aim to influence the behavior of offenders should be based on psychological theory. Specifically, this principle recommends using theories of criminal behavior that focuses on individual differences. According to Bonta and Andrews (2017), such theories are capable of identifying variables and strategies that provide better assistance in reduction reoffending. Thus, principle 2 distinguishes the recommended psychological theory from other theories that do not focus on individual differences of criminals as their ultimate outcome (e.g., biological, behavioral, sociological, humanistic, judicial or legal perspective on justice, social equality, or aggregated crime rates) (Andrews, 2001).

Second, principle 2 follows the PCC and requires that the underling psychological theory will be empirically defensible. Specifically, the RNR model argues that the GPCSL is the most effective theoretical perspective on human behavior. The previous section explained the merits of the GPCSL perspective in length. In a nutshell, the power of the GPCSL has been summarized in four major aspects: (1) the GPCSL has a general effective applicability. In other words, this perspective on human behavior identifies effective "clinical practices and interpersonal influence strategy" that can be applied across age, gender, race/ethnicity, and social class (Andrews & Bonta, 2010a, p. 53). (2) The GPCSL perspective seeks to identify causal factors that have an immediate personal and interpersonal influence on criminality. Accordingly, this perspective informs the correctional intervention field with knowledge about the most relevant factors that can assist in prediction and influence criminality. In addition, the use of the GPCSL perspective leads to factors that facilitate the learning of alternative noncriminal behavior. (3) The GPCSL perspective allows the integration of theoretical elements and findings from other perspectives such as biological/neuropsychological perspectives and broader social structure and cultural perspective. (4) The GPCSL perspective has the flexibility "to incorporate new conceptions and strategies (such as motivational interviewing)" (Bonta & Andrews, 2017, p. 178).

Principle 3: General Enhancement of Crime Prevention Services

Principle 3 is the final overarching principle. This principle expands the RNR model to include the treatment of at-risk individuals by "health and other agencies outside of justice and corrections" (Bonta & Andrews, 2017, p. 178). For example, agencies may deal with young individuals who are not yet involved in criminality but are at high risk of offending because they "confront a life of increasing *cumulative disadvantage*" (Cullen & Jonson, 2012, p. 172; emphasis in original). In this regard, knowledge of the RNR model can help the staff in these agencies identify increasing criminogenic risk and to use effective strategies that will reduce youths' entry into crime. In addition, this principle may be relevant to the mental health agencies. According to Andrews and Bonta (2010a), the principles of effective intervention can be useful to staff in these agencies because they "may be threatened by the very presence of criminal" (p. 400). Therefore, these agencies "must bring their counseling staff to think in RNR terms" (p. 400).

Principle 4: Introduce Human Service

Table 4.2 lists the core RNR principles and various clinical issues that are related to these principles. In Bonta and Andrews's (2017) articulation of their perspective, this part covers principles 4 to 12.

Principle 4 highlights the idea that correctional interventions that provide human services are more effective than correctional sanctions. According to Bonta and Andrews (2017), this recommendation is based on the empirical research showing that "the typical legal and judicial principles of deterrence, restoration, just desert, and due process have little to do with the major risk/need factors" (p. 178). Instead, principle 4 proposes that "it is through human, clinical, and social services that the major causes of crime may be addressed" (p. 178).

This perspective on the nature of correctional intervention has historical roots. Recall that in the 19th century, the first National Congress on Penitentiary and Reformatory Discipline (1870) embraced the notion that the causes of crime should be addressed through human and social service rather than deterrence or vindictive retribution (see Chapter 1). In addition, strong and clear support for principle 4 can be found in the ample empirical studies. In this regard, a series of meta-analyses reported strong and consistent support to the capability of correctional services to reduce reoffending compared to correctional interventions that tried to change criminality through sanctions (see Chapter 2). Indeed, in empirical terms, principle 4 was confirmed "beyond a reasonable doubt" (Lipsey & Cullen, 2007, p. 314).

This pattern in the data can also be explained by the theoretical principles of the PIC-R and the literature of behavioral therapy (Spiegler & Guevremont, 2010). In general, a "sanction" is imposed as a consequence to a behavior and intends to decelerate undesired behavior from reoccurring (this is also called "punishment"). In PIC-R terms, punishment can be experienced through adding costs or by subtraction of rewards for a particular behavior. Indeed, theoretically, punishment can be effective in reducing the probability of criminality. However, according to Andrews and Bonta (2010a), it seems that "the necessary conditions for effective punishment are virtually impossible to meet for the criminal justice system" (p. 451).

Specifically, Andrews and Bonta (2010a) illustrate several difficulties to achieving effective punishment in the criminal justice system. First, it is difficult to respond to every criminal act with *maximum intensity*. In this regard, the criminal justice system reacts to a crime with sentences that are based on "legal factors" such as the type and severity of offense and prior criminal history. Indeed, sentences that ignore these factors may be considered as a reaction to criminality that "offends our sense of justice and fairness" (p. 444). However, the inclusion of these factors as guideline for punishment may mitigate the intensity of punishment (e.g., the punishment for first conviction will be less intense than punishment that will be inflicted on chronic offenders). Second, for punishment to be effective, the sanction should be inflicted *immediately* after the criminal activity is performed. However, in criminal cases, offenders are often released before being convicted and punished. Therefore, instead of immediate response to criminality, "there are opportunities for the [criminal] behavior to be reinforced prior to the delivery of punishment" (p. 444). Third, effective punishment requires that "the undesired behavior [will be] punished every time it occurs" (p. 444). However, such *certainty* in punishment rarely occurs in the criminal justice system because offenders are not caught every time they commit a criminal act. Therefore, criminals have more opportunities "to engage in other unwanted behavior that may be rewarded" (p. 445). Fourth, due to a "variety of person factors (e.g., biological, cognitive, state conditions)," people may vary in their reaction to the same punishment (p. 447). Therefore, imposing effective punishment requires *matching* between sanction and the characteristics of the offender. However, within the criminal justice system, such matching is often considered as "extra-legal" considerations in sentencing that "violate the principle of fairness" (p. 447).

Beyond practical difficulties to applying punishment effectively in the criminal justice system, imposing punishment can also lead to "unintended and undesirable behaviors" (Andrews & Bonta, 2010a, p. 448). First, these "side effects" include situations when punishment "is coupled with a situation in which there is no escape," which may lead offenders to develop depression and "poor coping with stress" (p. 448).

In this regard, when offenders perceive punishment as an inevitable consequence, they tend to minimize their willingness to take responsibility for their undesired behavior. In correctional intervention, this mental state may negatively affect the ability to change their criminality. Another side effect of punishment appears when punishment leads to "anger and hate toward the punisher or feelings of rejections" (p. 448). In correctional interventions, such negative emotions can hinder the attempts to influence the behavior. Finally, when correctional interventions use punishment as a response, they signal offenders that inflicting pain or harm on others is a rewarded practice. Accordingly, offenders who witness such practice may use it more frequently as a solution to their problems.

Therefore, the RNR model focuses on the process of rewarding nondeviant alternative behaviors rather than punishing deviant behaviors. Recall that the underlying assumption of the PIC-R is that the process of rewarding (reinforcement) is expected to reduce the motivation for deviance and increase the costs for future criminality. Specifically, according to Andrews and Bonta (2010a), interventions that use reinforcement have two important advantages over interventions that concentrate on punitive sanctions. First, "only reinforcement can shape new behaviors; punishment only suppresses existing behavior" (p. 450). In other words, the RNR model recommends using reinforcement because this is the only way to change the behavior of those with limited prosocial skills (see also Spiegler & Guevremont, 2010). Second, "reinforcement procedures avoid the obvious ethical and professional dilemmas associated with purposefully inflicting pain" (Andrews & Bonta, 2010a, p. 451).

TABLE 4.2 Core RNR principles and key clinical issues

---

4. **Introduce Human Service:** Introduce human service into the justice context. Do not rely on the sanction to bring about reduced offending. Do not rely on deterrence, restoration, or other principles of justice.

5. **Risk:** Match intensity of service with risk level of cases. Work with moderate and higher-risk cases. Generally, avoid creating interactions of low-risk cases with higher risk cases.

6. **Need:** Target criminogenic needs predominately. Move criminogenic needs in the direction of becoming strengths.

7. **General Responsivity:** Employ behavioral, social learning, and cognitive-behavioral influence and skill building strategies.

8. **Specific Responsivity:** Adapt the style and mode of service according to the setting of service and to relevant characteristics of individual offenders, such as their strengths, motivations, preferences, personality, age, gender, ethnicity, cultural identifications, and other factors. The evidence in regard to specific responsivity is generally favorable but very scattered, and it has yet to be subjected to a comprehensive meta-analysis. Some examples of specific responsivity considerations follow:
   a) When working with the weakly motivated:
      - build on strengths;
      - reduce personal and situational barriers to full participation in treatment;
      - establish high-quality relationships; and
      - deliver early and often on matters of personal interest.
   b) Attend to the evidence in regard to age, gender, and culturally responsive services.
   c) Attend to the evidence in regard to differential treatment according to interpersonal maturity, interpersonal anxiety, cognitive skill level, and the responsivity aspects of psychopathy.
   d) Consider the targeting of noncriminogenic needs for purposes of enhancing motivation, the reduction of distracting factors, and for reasons having to do with humanitarian and entitlement issues.

9. **Breadth (or Multimodal):** Target a number of criminogenic needs relative to noncriminogenic needs.

10. **Strength:** Assess strengths to enhance prediction and specific responsivity effects.

11. **Structured Assessment:**
    a) Assessments of Strengths and Risk-Need-Specific Responsivity Factors: Employ structured and validated assessment instruments.
    b) Integrated Assessment and Intervention: Every intervention and contact should be informed by the assessment.

12. **Professional Discretion:** Deviate from recommendations only for very specific reasons. For example, functional analysis may suggest that emotional distress is a risk/need factor for *this* person.

Source: Reprinted with permission from Bonta & Andrews, *The Psychology of Criminal Conduct*, 6th Edition.

Principle 5: Risk

The risk principle is one of the three notable principles of the RNR model in that it represents the first "R" in this now-famous acronym. The risk principle has two components: prediction of criminal behavior and the "*matching levels of treatment services to the risk level of offender*" (Bonta & Andrews, 2017, p. 178, emphasis in original). The first component—prediction of recidivism—emphasizes the assessment of risk factors. In essence, this component highlights the individual differences that exist in criminal conduct and therefore the challenge of finding the risk factors that account for this variation (Andrews, 1995). According to Andrews et al. (1990), these risk factors "refer to personal attributes and circumstances that are assessable prior to service and are predictive of future criminal behavior" (p. 24).

As described in the previous chapter, the factors that increase the probability for later offending can be conceptualized through the PIC-R. In this regard, the PIC-R assists researchers to identify the particular attributes of persons and their situations that may tie them to either crime or conventional norms. Then, these attributes can be operationalized for empirical research and be examined through longitudinal analysis. This examination enables researchers to validate the power of particular variables to predict future offending (see the next section for more details on the development of effective risk assessments of offenders).

The second component—the matching of service to offender risk—is "the essence of the risk principle and is the bridge between assessment and effective treatment" (Bonta & Andrews, 2017, p. 178). In this regard, offenders are considered high/moderate/low risk in relation to the number and strength of the risk factors that they possess. Thus, the risk principle states that "as risk level increases then the amount of treatment needed to reduce recidivism also increase" (Bonta & Andrews, 2007, p. 9). In other words, higher risk cases require more intensive human services and low-risk cases require minimal or even no service.

As indicated in the previous chapter, the interaction between the level of risk and treatment can also be explained by the PIC-R (Andrews, 1982a; Andrews & Bonta, 2010a). Thus, high-risk offenders have a high density of rewards and a low density of costs for criminal behavior. Accordingly, low-risk offenders have a low density of rewards and a high density of costs for criminality. Therefore, the PIC-R supports the use of risk assessment as guidance for adequate intensity of treatment.

While higher risk offenders need more service simply because there is more to change about them, the reasons why agencies should avoid intensive treatment for lower risk offenders are less intuitive. One reason for such concern is the potential interaction that can occur between low-risk offenders and high-risk offenders. According to the social learning theory and the social cognitive theory, such interaction may lead to a learning process that increases the likelihood that low-risk offenders will learn antisocial attitudes (Bandura, 1977, 1986; see also Andrews, 1980). Thus, within the mixed group of offenders, the high-risk offenders may become antisocial role models for the lower risk offenders. Importantly, within a correctional program, such concern is mostly relevant when the lower risk offenders have low intellectual functioning and lack of maturity (i.e., can be manipulated more easily by other offenders) (Lovins, Lowenkamp, & Latessa, 2009; Lowenkamp, Latessa, & Holsinger, 2006).

Another reason for minimum treatment efforts for low-risk offenders is that overtreatment may increase the likelihood of reoffending (Bonta & Andrews, 2017; Cullen & Jonson, 2012). When interventions provide more treatment than needed, they may have iatrogenic effects. The cause for such negative effects may be the impact of a structured, intrusive intervention on low-risk offenders. Such intensive intervention tends to isolate the low-risk offenders from conventional aspects in their life (e.g., steady work, supportive family). As a result, individual attributes that may have kept low-risk offenders out of crime may lose their influence and be changed for the worst. In such cases, the intensive intervention may facilitate the creation of new risk factors that increase the likelihood of criminality.

Empirical support for the risk principle has been growing since the 1970s. Andrews, Robinson, and Balla (1986) indicated that seven "reasonably well-controlled experimental studies of prevention and correctional programs [had] reported significant Risk × Treatment interactions (Andrews & Kiessling, 1980; Andrews & Robinson, 1984; Baird, Heinz, & Bemus, 1979; Byles & Maurice, 1982; Hackler & Hagan, 1975; Jeffery & Woolport, 1974; O'Donnell, Lydgate, & Fo, 1971)" (p. 203).

Recently, more studies of individual research supported the impact of this interaction on recidivism (Bonta, Rugge, Scott, Bourgon, & Yessine, 2008; Lowenkamp & Latessa, 2002).

In addition, as detailed in Chapter 2, studies that conducted meta-analyses strongly supported the relationship between the level of risk and recidivism (Andrews, Zinger et al., 1990; Andrews & Bonta, 2006, 2010a; Lipsey, 1992, 2009, 2014). Moreover, meta-analyses also provided direct support for the conclusion that the risk principle is related to recidivism (Dowden & Andrews, 1999a, 1999b, 2003; Landenberger & Lipsey, 2005). According to Andrews (2001), the empirical support for the risk principle depends on whether other principles of effective intervention are incorporated into the intervention. That is, the effect of the risk principle becomes stronger "as you move up from studies of the effects of sanctions through studies of human service in general to studies of human service that is consistent with the need and general responsivity principles" (Andrews, 2001).

Principle 6: Need

The need principle—the "N" in the RNR model—proposes that correctional interventions should focus on a particular subset of risk factors as intermediate targets. Specifically, these risk factors should be "dynamic attributes of offenders and their circumstances that, when changed, are associated with changes in the chances of recidivism" (Andrews et al., 1990, p. 31). In essence, the need factor distinguishes between static risk factors that cannot be changed (e.g., criminal history), dynamic risk factors that can be changed only naturally (e.g., age), and dynamic risk factors that can be changed through a deliberate intervention that aim to reduce recidivism ("criminogenic needs").

In addition, the need principle distinguishes between "criminogenic needs" and "noncriminogenic needs." As opposed to criminogenic needs, noncriminogenic needs represent dynamic and changeable attributes of offenders that "have a very minor or no causal relationship to criminal behavior" (Andrews & Bonta, 2010b, p. 45). In other words, "addressing noncriminogenic needs is unlikely to alter future recidivism significantly unless doing so indirectly impacts on criminogenic needs" (Bonta & Andrews, 2017, p. 180). Thus, according to Andrews and Bonta (2010a), the need principle is also called *"criminogenic need principle"* (p. 49, emphasis in original).

The search for criminogenic needs is a search for "a functional links among variation in service, changes on intermediate targets, and recidivism" (Andrews et al., 1990, p. 32). Such needs can be drawn from the criminological theories (e.g., differential association theory, control theories, general strain theory). For empirical validation, a strict process to determine criminogenic need requires a multiwave longitudinal study that shows three related conditions: "(1) deliberate interventions produce changes on the potential need factor, (2) deliberate interventions produce changes in criminal conduct, and (3) the magnitude of the associations between intervention and criminal behavior may be reduced through the introduction of statistical controls for change on the potential need factor" (p. 31).

Bonta and Andrews (2017) present seven criminogenic need domains: antisocial cognition, antisocial personality pattern, antisocial associates, dysfunctional family relationships, dysfunctional relationships within school/work, noninvolvement in conventional organized leisure-time activities, and problems relates to substance abuse. Indeed, the research found that together with criminal history (a static predictor), these seven criminogenic needs are represented by the "Central Eight." In this regard, the Central Eight are part of the GPCSL perspective of human behavior and can be explained by the PIC-R (see the previous chapter).

Recall that Chapter 2 showed that meta-analyses reviews supported the predictive validity and functional validity of criminogenic needs (see also Andrews & Bonta, 2010a). In this regard, correctional interventions that targeted criminogenic needs presented larger effect on recidivism than interventions that ignored these intermediate targets. In addition, the meta-analyses reviews found a wide support for the need principle. Specifically, studies showed that when correctional intervention targeted more criminogenic needs than noncriminogenic needs, they were more effective in reducing recidivism than interventions that did not prioritize criminogenic needs.

Principle 7: General Responsivity

The responsivity principle—the last "R" in the RNR model—involves two aspects that address "the how of intervention": the "general" and "specific" responsivity (Andrews & Bonta, 2010b, p. 46). Principles 7 covers the "general responsivity" and principle 8 discusses the "specific responsivity." The general responsivity principle suggests that correctional interventions have to consider "the responsivity of offenders to different styles and modes of service" (Andrews et al., 1990, p. 35).

According to Bonta and Andrews (2017), "the *general responsivity principle* is quite straightforward: Offenders are human beings, and the most powerful influence strategies available are cognitive-behavioral and cognitive social learning strategies" (pp. 181–182, emphasis in original). Theoretically, this principle reflects strategies and behavioral change approaches that are drawn directly from the GPCSL perspectives on human behavior. As mentioned in the previous section, Andrews and his colleagues focused on the GPCSL perspective due to its demonstrated ability to change human behavior and to explain this change through criminological theories.

Based on the GPCSL perspectives, Bonta and Andrews (2017) specify general responsivity practices that provide the most effective way to teach people new prosocial behaviors. These "powerful influence strategies include modeling, reinforcement, role-playing, skill building, modification of thoughts and emotions through cognitive restructuring, and practicing new, low-risk alternative behaviors over and over again in a variety of high-risk situations until one gets very good at it" (p. 182). According to McGuire (2013), these strategies have "clear, concrete objectives, their contents are structured and there is a focus on the activity and the acquisition of skills" (p. 32) (see also Cullen & Gendreau, 2000). In this regard, the success of the responsivity principle also relates to the ability of correctional workers to follow the relationship principle (i.e., how to promote learning) and the structuring principle (i.e., how to direct learning) (see principle 14, Core Correctional Staff Practice).

As described in length in Chapter 2, the meta-analyses literature provides support to the impact of the general responsivity principle on recidivism (Andrews & Bonta, 2006, 2010a; Andrews, Zinger et al., 1990; Dowden & Andrews, 1999a, 1999b, 2000; Dowden & Andrews, 2003; Dowden, Antonowicz, & Andrews, 2003). In particular, meta-analyses consistently demonstrated that the general category of behavioral or cognitive-behavior programs was more effective than other treatment approaches (Smith, Gendreau, & Swartz, 2009).

Principle 8: Specific Responsivity

The specific responsivity principle is the second aspect of considering responsivity in correctional interventions. This principle "is rooted in the notion that there can be potent interactions between the characteristics of individuals and their settings or situations" (Gendreau, 1996, p. 122). In this regard, Bonta and Andrews (2017) highlight the importance of using "differential treatment" in correctional interventions—an approach that seeks how "a certain treatment strategy and/or certain therapist are matched to the characteristics of offender" (p. 182).

The literature on the RNR model highlighted some potential responsivity variables such as verbal skills, motivation to engage in treatment, level of anxiety, level of impulsiveness, psychiatric problems, level of interpersonal sensitivity, level of interpersonal and cognitive maturity, intelligence, gender, age, and/or ethnicity (Andrews, 1995; Gendreau, 1996; Andrews & Bonta, 2010a). In essence, "rather than ignoring these important individual differences, the specific responsivity principle demands that we attend to these differences" (Andrews et al., 2011, p. 747). Overall, hypotheses related to the specific responsivity principle often consider the matching between treatment, offender type, and therapist's style (Gendreau, 1996). Specifically, when working with offenders, specific responsivity is the matching of (1) "the treatment approach with the learning style and personality of the offender"; (2) "the characteristics of the offender with those of the therapist"; and (3) "the skills of the therapist with type of program" (p. 123).

The RNR literature presents several specific hypotheses about the most effective matching in correctional interventions. However, none of the hypotheses were supported by the results from a comprehensive meta-analysis, and only some were studied in any detail. In this regard, this section will follow the four substantive examples of specific responsivity considerations that are presented in principle 8. These substantive examples are motivation, biodemographic characteristics (e.g., age, gender, and culture), personality and cognitive styles, and the role of noncriminogenic needs as legitimate targets (Andrews & Bonta, 2010a). Although promising, systematic studies are needed to examine these general hypotheses in the context of correctional treatment.

First, Andrews and Bonta (2010a) mention "the issue of *amenability or motivation* to treatment [as] an important area of research" (p. 51, emphasis added). In general, enhancing motivation in correctional interventions has a potential to engage offenders in treatment (i.e., motivation for service), effect their behavioral change, or do both. In this regard, Bonta and Andrews (2017) often refer to the principles of "motivational interviewing" (MI) as a model that is relevant in the field of corrections.

In brief, the MI model "describes clients as being at different stages in their readiness to change. These stages range from just thinking about the possibility of having a problem to actually doing something about it" (Bonta & Andrews, 2017, pp. 167–168; see also Miller & Rollnick, 2002, 2013). According to Miller and Rollnick (2012), the MI is a "'bottom-up' model that emerged from practical experience in the field of alcohol treatment. The original description of MI suggested some links to social psychological theories, but focused on an intuitive approach in treating alcohol problems" (p. 1). Nowadays, the MI model is presented as "a form of collaborative conversation for strengthening a person's own motivation and commitment to change. It is a person-centered counseling style for addressing the common problem of ambivalence about change by paying particular attention to the language of change" (www.motivationalinterviewing.org).

According to Bonta and Andrews (2017), the MI model is an example of a model that can serve the purposes of the specific responsivity principle in relation to motivation. First, the MI is "often a preparatory first step to more formal, structure treatment and relapse prevention treatment" (p. 168). Specifically, the MI model also recognizes the external interests of offenders to participate in treatment and then matches the treatment program to the offender's level of motivation. Such matching is expected to reduce personal barriers to engagement in treatment that follows the general responsivity principle. Second, as a counseling technique, the MI model adjusts "the therapist's style of intervention . . . to the client's cognitive and affective characteristics at a particular point in time" (Andrews & Bonta, 2010a, p. 290).

Meta-analytic reviews that examined the impact of MI in treatments for nonoffender populations (e.g., medical patients, gamblers, addictions) found a positive effect. In treatment for offenders, McMurran (2009) conducted a systematic review that examined 19 evaluated applications of MI. She concluded that due to "the variation among these studies in treatment populations . . . and the variation in treatment targets . . . no overall definitive conclusion about the effectiveness of MI with offenders can be drawn" (p. 95). In addition, according to Alexander, Lowenkamp, and Robinson (2012), recent studies show mix results: "some studies showing MI interventions can reduce reconviction rates for male offenders (Anstiss et al., 2011) while others have found no effect on probationer outcome (Walters et al., 2010)" (Ch. 14, Section 2, Para 2). Moreover, the quality of the MI interventions in many of these studies is unknown, and therefore "it is difficult to determine the fidelity of the intervention, which is critical to the evaluation of its impact" (Ch. 14, Section 2, Para 3; see also McMurran, 2009).

Overall, according to Andrews and Bonta (2010a), the MI is a model that "promise[s] [a] major behavior change through miniscule interventions [and therefore] is too attractive to ignore" (p. 508). Nevertheless, so far, the evidence that MI approaches are able to reduce recidivism is slim. Therefore, the MI model cannot be expected "to have an impact on criminal recidivism. MI is basically a responsivity technique to increase motivation to attend and adhere to treatment" (p. 291).

The second substantive example of specific responsivity in principle 8 recommends considering *biodemographic profiles* such as age, gender, and culture. These characteristics of offenders are considered a specific responsivity because the evidence has shown that "the impact of RNR adherence and breadth on future offending varies with age, race, or gender" (Andrews & Bonta, 2010a, p. 512). In other words, aspects of age, gender, and culture contribute to our understanding of how best to change criminogenic needs. In this regard, differences in age, gender, social class, and ethnicity may reflect how offenders may respond differently to services in relation to meaning, contexts, associated norms, and traditions.

For example, according to Van Voorhis and Salisbury (2014), "women tend to do better in groups that take their relationships into consideration" (p. 350). Another example relates to the potential of cultural issues to affect participation in treatment program. On the one hand, cultural identity may encourage participation in treatment when it reflects "strong levels of family and community support and spiritual strength" (p. 350). On the other hand, cultural issues such as "differences in language, communication style, use of body language, or verbal skills" may result in misunderstanding and therefore discourage engagement in therapy (p. 350).

Third, Andrews and Bonta (2010a) emphasize the importance of considering *personality and cognitive styles* as a specific responsivity issue in correctional intervention. Such consideration aims to enhance the effectiveness of treatment programs by specifying the use of structured and unstructured approaches to therapy, counseling, and casework. In this regard, the default decision is guided by the principle of general responsivity: correctional interventions should use structured approaches. Within the RNR model, the term "structured approaches" means that the counselors use "direct training procedure such as behavioral rehearsal, systematic conditioning (classical or operant), role-laying, or coaching" (Andrews & Bonta, 2010a, p. 383). This is as opposed to "unstructured" approaches that do not make use of these procedures but "rely heavily upon 'talk,' 'emotional support,' and 'therapist-client relationships' in group or individual therapy" (p. 383).

In essence, the principle of specific responsivity presents several hypotheses that highlight the idea that "offenders with interpersonal and cognitive problems require particularly structured services, but the more mature offender may respond to less structured styles of service" (Andrews & Hoge, 1995). For example, as presented in principle 8, this approach suggests that correctional interventions will avoid "highly confrontational therapy with anxious, and in particular interpersonally anxious, individuals" (Andrews, 1995, p. 57). In addition, Bonta and Andrews (2017) advise that "style and services that are verbally and interpersonally demanding and depend upon cognitive skills and interpersonal sensitivity [should] be avoided with all offenders but the very high functioning ones" (p. 346). Accordingly, they recommend that correctional interventions will consider the interpersonal skill level and cognitive maturity of individuals (e.g., combinations of "empathy, interpersonal maturity, self-regulation skills, verbal intelligence") (p. 345).

Another hypothesis that relates to the personality and cognitive styles of offenders proposes that a different approach to delivering treatment be taken when working with individuals diagnosed as psychopaths (i.e., offenders who present low anxiety, low empathy, shallow emotion, and manipulation). In this regard, Andrews (1995) warned that negative effects could occur if psychopaths were given "evocative, peer-assisted and anti-behavioral programming" (p. 57). Relatedly, Andrews and Bonta (2010a) recommended the use of highly structured programs with psychopaths. They also advised that to know when psychopaths were attempting to manipulate staff, those working with these clients have to communicate with one another. Overall, this hypothesis, as well as the other hypotheses in this example, should be examined in systematic studies in the context of correctional treatment.

The fourth example in principle 8 discusses the *role of noncriminogenic needs* as another important aspect of the specific responsivity principle. As mentioned in principle 6 (the need principle), non-criminogenic needs are attributes of offenders that have insignificant causal relationship to criminal behavior. Therefore, in general, correctional interventions should avoid targeting noncriminogenic needs. However, Andrews and Bonta (2010a) suggest an exception to this core principle of the RNR model. They argue that "the normative and specific responsivity principles of RNR stress the value of a concern with noncriminogenic needs for humanitarian and motivational purposes" (p. 513).

Specifically, Bonta and Andrews (2017) suggest that "noncriminogenic needs may be set as intermediate targets for humanitarian and entitlement reasons in accordance with the normative principle. Additionally, collaborative treatment planning may establish the motivational value of targeting selected noncriminogenic needs for particular offenders" (p. 346). In this regard, Ogloff and Davis (2004) indicated that "non-criminogenic needs affect responsivity when they occur to such an extent that the individual cannot, does not, or will not focus on treatment to reduce criminogenic needs. Similarly, responsivity factors can impede longer-term rehabilitation of offenders. While not directly related to recidivism per se, they moderate the efficacy of treatment" (p. 233). For example, providing childcare services in a community-based program may allow parents to participate in treatment. Another example is to address mental health issues in programs and the development of aftercare services designed for mentally disordered offenders.

However, according to Bonta and Andrews (2017), the evidence that these responsivity variables may lead to a reduction in recidivism is "generally favorable but very scattered" (p. 176). Moreover, "theories of personality and crime suggest a host of possibilities that have barely been considered by researchers on corrections" (Andrews & Bonta, 2010a, p. 51). In this regard, according to Andrews (2011), "the lack of a cumulative summary of the extant evidence in regard to specific responsivity concern is a weakness in the RNR approach (and for the differential treatment movement generally)" (p. 13).

Principle 9: Breadth (or Multimodal)

In principle 9, Bonta and Andrews (2017) note that it is important to "target a number of criminogenic needs relative to noncriminogenic needs" (p. 177). Essentially, this principle "highlights the importance of targeting multiple criminogenic needs when working with high-risk cases" (p. 182).

This is a clinical issue because treatment programs are expected to focus on offenders who possess multiple needs (high-risk offenders). Thus, targeting only a single criminogenic need will have a minimal effect in reducing the recidivism of high-risk offenders. The reason is that such interventions will not address other criminogenic needs that any given offender is likely to possess.

Therefore, according to the breadth principle, effective intervention with high-risk offenders requires programs that use a combination of targets and well-established methods ("multimodal programs") (Glick, 2006; McGuire, 2004; Palmer, 1992). In other words, this principle prefers programs that "have broad objectives and wide spectrum of treatment targets" over programs that "have a very precise focus on a single problem area" (McGuire, 2001).

Several meta-analyses lend support to the breadth principle (Dowden et al., 2003; Dowden & Andrews, 1999a, 1999b, 2000, 2003). Specifically, these studies show the effectiveness of correctional interventions that targeted for change criminogenic needs over noncriminogenic needs. Importantly, within these studies, this definition of the breadth principle was used to operationalize the need principle.

Principle 10: Strength

Another clinical issue in the RNR model is the assessment of strengths. According to Bonta and Andrews (2017), this principle argues that it is important to assess an individual's strengths because such strengths have "implication for both accurate prediction of recidivism and for specific responsivity" (p. 183). They define strength factors as "characteristics of people and their circumstances that are associated with reduced chances of criminal activity" (Andrews & Bonta, 2010a, p. 22). For example, high school achievement is often considered as a factor that predicts low probability of offending (Farrington, Loeber, & Ttofi, 2012).

Note that within the RNR model, a strength factor is not merely the opposite end on a scale that has a risk factor at the other end. For example, the fact that poor parental supervision is a risk factor does not mean that good parental supervision might be a protective factor (Farrington et al., 2012). In addition, within the RNR model, a strength factor is not considered as a factor that interacts with the risk factor to minimize its effect. In other words, the impact of the strength factor is not revealed only with the presence of a risk factor but exerts an impact as an independent factor.[1] According to Andrews et al. (2011), the "RNR is about building on strengths and rewarding noncriminal alternatives to the risk factors that are favoring criminal activity" (p. 743). For example, a correctional intervention that identifies an offender with high IQ (a strength) may facilitate an environment that provides an academic achievement. Thus, overall, "a focus on strengths is already part of RNR-based assessment and treatment" (p. 751).

Similar to risk factors, strength factors are considered as components in assessment that make an independent contribution to the prediction of recidivism (for a description of how researchers disentangle risk and protective effects, see Stouthamer-Loeber, Loeber, Wei, Farrington, & Wikström, 2002). Therefore, in the prediction of future offending, RNR-based assessment tools (e.g., LS/CMI, ORAS) include systematic surveys of strengths. In this regard, based on two prospective longitudinal surveys of offending that examined potential strength factors, Farrington et al. (2012, p. 2) present several conclusions: (1) "the most important factors that should be targeted in intervention are impulsiveness, school achievement, child-rearing methods, young mothers, child abuse, parental conflict, disrupted families, poverty, delinquent peers, and deprived neighborhoods." (2) "However, little is known about whether these variables operate primarily as risk or promotive factors or both." In addition, (3) "little is known about whether these variables act as causes or what are the important causal mechanism linking these factors with outcomes such as offending." Similarly, (4) "little is known about what factors protect children from different types of risky backgrounds against becoming offenders."

Overall, more research is needed to determine whether the inclusion of protective factors in assessment tools will improve the prediction of recidivism. Accordingly, without much empirical knowledge, Andrews et al. (2011) state that in order to reduce recidivism, it is necessary to change the major criminogenic factors not only "in a direction away from risk" but also "in the direction of becoming strengths" (p. 742). In this regard, principle 10 provides general direction that correctional interventions will assess strength factors as part of the assessment of specific responsivity principle. As mentioned above, this principle encourages "treatment planners to build on strengths and consider removal of any barriers to full participation in service, issues particularly important to minority cultural groups . . . and women" (Andrews & Bonta, 2010b, p. 47). Thus, Andrews (2011) advise researchers to find more solid evidence through replications of "strength-by-practice interactions" (p. 13).

Principle 11: Structured Assessment

Principle 11 presents another clinical issue that provides guidance when offenders are being assessed. This principle indicates that correctional interventions should follow a structured assessment when assessing strengths and RNR factors. In this regard, Bonta and Andrews (2017) provide two directions for such assessment: (1) employ "structured and validated assessment instruments," and (2) integrate the finding from such assessments into the particular intervention (p. 177). In essence, these general directions recommend that correctional interventions will use the most recent RNR-based assessment tools.

First, and most important, Bonta and Andrews (2017) argue that existing empirical evidence demonstrates that "the validity of structured assessments greatly exceeds that of unstructured professional judgment" (p. 183) (see also Andrews, Bonta, & Wormith, 2006). As a result, their RNR model is based on the use of an actuarial-based assessment—a highly structured assessment approach that asks offenders "the same empirically based questions," organize the information "into a quantitative mode and interpret it in a uniform manner" (Bonta & Wormith, 2013, p. 72).

By contrast, they argue against the use of an unstructured approach to offender assessment. Unstructured assessments of offenders refer to "correctional staff (i.e., probation officers and prison staff) and clinical professionals (i.e., psychologists, psychiatrists and social workers)" who use unstructured interviews to make decisions about the risks posed by and treatment needs of offenders (Bonta & Andrews, 2007, p. 3). In other words, "the key feature of [this] clinical approach is that the reasons for the decision are subjective, sometimes intuitive, and guided by 'gut feelings'—they are not empirically validated" (Bonta & Andrews, 2017, p. 193).

In addition to avoiding the use of unstructured assessments, the RNR model distinguishes between the recommended highly structured assessment and an alternative approach that uses "structured professional (or clinical) judgment" (SPJ). This less structured approach, which is used mainly in forensic mental health settings, differs from both unstructured and highly structured assessment approaches. According to Bonta and Wormith (2013), "SPJ differs from unstructured clinical judgment in that it requires the assessor to consider a preset list of risk factors, most or all of which have been derived from the same empirical literature as statistically measures of offender risk. However, SPJ differs from statistically based approaches in that it does not include a numerical scoring of items or predetermined rules to convert the number and degree of risk present to descriptive risk score or level" (p. 79).

Studies that examined the predictive validity of assessment tools that rely on the SPJ approach showed its ability to predict recidivism among sex offenders and offenders who engage in general violent recidivism. However, according to Bonta and Wormith (2013), there is "very little research that has shown dynamic predictive validity . . . and provide directions for subsequent intervention which are related to actual reduction in offender risk" (p. 80). In sum, the RNR model prefers an actuarial approach to assessment that uses formal observable criteria for making decisions.

Second, principle 11 directs correctional interventions to use assessment approach that links offender assessment to treatment intervention. In other words, this principle underscores that the primary concern of correctional interventions is to influence criminality. In that sense, useful assessment tools include dynamic risk factors as indicators of potential intermediate targets in interventions. This is as opposed to alternative actuarial assessment tools that rely solely (or mainly) on static factors. Such "static" assessment tools predict recidivism but cannot assist in the building of individualized treatment plans because its predictors cannot be changed. Overall, principle 11 highlights that, according to the RNR model, the main concern of correctional intervention is to influence criminality rather than merely providing prediction of release decision and supervision classification.

Third, according to principle 11, effective assessment requires more than an actuarial-based assessment approach that relies on dynamic risk factors. An assessment approach that follows the RNR model is also expected to translate the knowledge of risk assessment to practice. Specifically, such assessment tools may assist in "allocating supervision resources appropriately (risk principle) and targeting intervention (need principle)" (Bonta & Andrews, 2017, p. 197).

According to Andrews (2011), the evidence that effective programs should adopt structured assessment approach over alternative assessment system is "limited" due to lack of studies that compared between different assessment systems. In this regard, principle 11 had not been subjected to meta-analysis. Therefore, although "the predictive validity of risk/need assessment instruments is well-established through multiple validation studies . . . the inability to find strong evidence in support of the principle of structured assessment is a serious gap in the evidential base of the RNR" (pp. 9–10).

Principle 12: Professional Discretion

Principle 12 is a key clinical issue that explains the recommended balance between professional discretion and the RNR model. In general, principle 12 reflects a strong belief in the theoretical, empirical, and practical foundations of the RNR model. According to Bonta and Andrews (2017), professionals should deviate from a "structured decision making" only on rare occasions with specific documented reasons (p. 183). Still, Andrews and his colleagues consistently argue that "rehabilitation professionals will always be called upon to step beyond extant knowledge in their decision making" (Andrews et al., 1990, p. 44; see also Andrews & Bonta, 1994). Thus, principle 12 highlights several essential aspects of the role of professional discretion in the RNR model.

First, the inclusion of the ability to override structured assessments, or any other principle of the RNR model, reflects a general understanding that the empirical knowledge is limited. Specifically, Andrews and Bonta (2010a, pp. 131–132) indicated four issues that demonstrate the gap in the existing knowledge: (1) "The specific moderators of the covariates of criminal conduct . . . remain an issue." (2) "The impact of broader social arrangements on individual criminal conduct is poorly documented." (3) Particular constructs are limited in their impact "because of choice of research design or because of errors of measurements and/or conceptualization." (4) "Empirical knowledge can reflect only the findings of studies that have already been conducted and reported upon." Due to these inherent limitations, the RNR model considers the fact that empirical knowledge "is not only relative, political, socially constructed, but it also partial and incomplete" (p. 132). In other words, Andrews and Bonta (2010a) explicitly recognize that professional discretion will always be an integrated part of the correctional rehabilitation field. Yet, according to the RNR model, the challenge is to maintain a "systematic monitoring and follow-up of the consequences of these overrides" (Andrews et al., 1990, p. 44). That is, to use the function of professional override "as an opportunity to improve our assessments" (Andrews & Bonta, 1994, p. 178).

Second, the RNR model also acknowledges that the management of an offender population may require professional decisions that are not supported empirically. According to Bonta and Wormith (2013), there are "other socially, clinically or legally 'valid' reasons for exercising the override function" (p. 81). In this regard, "the information justifying an override could be of a personal, historical, clinical or even environmental/situational nature" (p. 81). Notably, during the development of the RNR model, this contextual aspect of professional discretion became a separated overarching principle (see principle 1: Respect for the person and the normative context) (see also Andrews, 1995).

Nowadays, it seems that the main purpose of principle 12 is to emphasize the importance of adhering to the principles of the RNR model, and in particular to the assessments that follow this model. This importance was clearly demonstrated in empirical studies that showed how adherence to the core principles of the RNR model (the RNR principles) increased the likelihood of correctional interventions to reduce recidivism (see Chapter 2). Additional support was found in evaluations of structured assessment tools that are based on the principle of effective intervention and aim to predict offenders' risk/needs (e.g., LSI-R, ORAS) or the effectiveness of a particular intervention (e.g., CPAI-2000, CPC) (see the next section). Moreover, studies that examined the use of professional override showed "a slight decrement in predictive validity after the override option [was] made available to assessors" (Bonta & Wormith, 2013, p. 81).

Principle 13: Community-Based

Principle 13 is an organizational principle that underscores community-based services as the preferable setting in which to intervene with offenders when using the RNR model. As mentioned in the previous chapter, the attitude toward the therapeutic power of institutional settings was changed since prison became a setting of punishment. In the early 1800s, prisons were considered to be a place that protected offenders from the corruption and disorder that prevailed in the community. However, by the end of the 1800s, this perspective had changed dramatically, and the therapeutic environment in prison tried to replicate the outside environment. Thus, during the 20th century, the options for community-based interventions were developed and professionalized. In the early 1990s, when the RNR model was first presented, Andrews (1995) expected that the effectiveness of correctional intervention would increase "when the total agency and community surround is supportive of treatment process, goals, and outcomes" (Andrews, 1995, p. 58).

A community-based approach has theoretical basis. According to the PIC-R perspective on criminal behavior, "without alteration of the personal, interpersonal, and community sources of rewards and costs, long-term behavior change is unlikely" (Andrews & Bonta, 2010a, p. 143). Accordingly, within the RNR model, a community-based approach in clinical practice directs correctional interventions to focus on the acquisition and maintenance of new alternative skills that may maximize their chance of offenders to attain prosocial rewards and assist to avoid high-risk situations. Relatedly, the RNR model prefers community-based settings because the impact of such learning is assumed to be more effective in the offenders' natural environment than in custody. In this regard, Andrews (2001) suggests that "home and school-base services rather than agency-based services" will be the most effective settings (see also McGuire, 2004).

Importantly, the expectation that community-based services will result with greater reduction in recidivism than custody-based services also reflects a therapeutic approach that prisons should be the "last resort" for offenders. In this regard, Andrews and his collaborators conducted a comprehensive meta-analysis that supported the notion that community settings are more likely to adhere to the RNR model than residential settings (Andrews, Zinger et al., 1990; Andrews & Bonta, 2006; Bonta & Andrews, 2017). In addition, Andrews (2011) indicates that some of the findings in Lipsey (2009) supported the hypothesis of "the RNR principle favouring community-based service delivery" (p. 13). As a result, he concluded that, "in terms of meta-analytic evidence, a sound conclusion to date is that community settings are preferred over institutional settings" (p. 13). Accordingly, the RNR model directs interventions in residential or custodial placement to use "community-oriented services"—"services facilitating return to the community and facilitating appropriate service delivery in the community" (e.g., relapse prevention) (Andrews, 2001).

TABLE 4.3 RNR model's organizational principles: settings, staffing, and management

---

13. **Community-Based:** Community-based services are preferred but the principles of RNR also apply within residential and institutional settings.

14. **GPCSL–Based Staff Practices:** Effectiveness of interventions is enhanced when delivered by therapists and staff with *high-quality relationship skills* in combination with *high-quality structuring skills*. Quality relationships are characterized as respectful, caring, enthusiastic, collaborative, valuing personal autonomy, and using motivational interviewing to engage the client in treatment. Structuring practices include prosocial modeling, effective reinforcement and disapproval, skill building, cognitive restructuring, problem-solving, effective use of authority, and advocacy/brokerage.

15. **Management:** Promote the selection, training, and clinical supervision of staff according to RNR and introduce monitoring, feedback, and adjustment systems. Build systems and cultures supportive of effective practice and continuity of care. Some additional specific indicators of integrity include having program manuals available, monitoring of service process and intermediate changes, adequate dosage, and involving researchers in the design and delivery of service.

Source: Reprinted with permission from Bonta & Andrews, *The Psychology of Criminal Conduct*, 6th Edition.

Principle 14: Core Correctional Staff Practices

Another organizational principle in the RNR model was designed to highlight the role of the correctional worker. In general, within the RNR model, correctional staff should serve "as an anticriminal model for clients and as a source of reinforcement for their anticriminal expressions and efforts" (Andrews & Bonta, 2010a, p. 407). Specifically, according to principle 14, "staff with *high quality relationship skills* in combination with *high-quality structuring skills*" enhance the effectiveness of interventions (Bonta & Andrews, 2017, p. 177; emphasis in original; see also Andrews & Kiessling, 1980; Andrews et al., 1990). Importantly, this principle reflects the overarching principle that recommend the GPCSL approach (principle 2) and the general responsivity principle (principle 7) that specifies the effective strategies to address criminality. In this regard, Andrews and Bonta (2010a) suggest four characteristics of effective correctional workers.

First, effective correctional workers establish *high-quality relationship* with their clients. In essence, this is the "relationship principle" that underscores the notion of high-quality interpersonal relationship as a factor that "creates a setting in which modeling and reinforcement can more easily take place" (Andrews & Bonta, 2010a, p. 410). In this regard, recall that the PIC-R provides a theoretical explanation for this principle (other person influent interpersonally mediated events) (see the previous chapter). In brief, according to Andrews (2001), "indicators of relationship skills include some combination of the following: being respectful, open, warm (not cold, hostile, indifferent), caring, non-blaming, flexible, reflective, self-confident, mature, enthusiastic, understanding, genuine (real), bright and verbal, and other indicators including elements of motivational interviewing strategies (express empathy, avoid argumentation, roll with resistance)" (see also Andrews, 1982c; Bonta & Andrews, 2017; Andrews & Kiessling, 1980).

Second, effective correctional workers demonstrate *effective modeling*. This is the interpersonal influence of the "structuring principle" that recommend anticriminal expressions over procriminal expressions. According to Andrews (2001), "anticriminal modeling" include the following: providing "alternatives to procriminal attitudes, values, beliefs, rationalizations, thoughts, feelings and behavioural patterns; anticriminal differential reinforcement; cognitive restructuring; structured learning skills; the practice and training of problem-solving skills; core advocacy/brokerage activity; and effective use of authority. More generally expressed, some indicators are being directive, solution focused, contingency based and, from motivational interviewing, developing discrepancy and supporting beliefs that the person can change his or behaviour (supporting prosocial self-efficacy)" (see also Andrews & Bonta, 2010a; Van Voorhis & Salisbury, 2014).

Third, effective correctional workers maintain *high-level reinforcement* in an interpersonal situation. According to Andrews and Bonta (2010a, p. 411), the elements of such reinforcement include the following: (1) "strong, emphatic, and immediate statement of approval, support, and agreement with regard to what the probationer has said or done"; (2) "Elaboration of the reason why agreement and approval are being offered"; (3) "Expression of support should be sufficiently intense to distinguish it from the back ground level of support, concern, and interest that you normally offer"; (4) "worker's feedback should at least match the probationer's statement in emotional intensity . . ., and his or her elaboration of the reason for support should involve some self-disclosure."

Fourth, effective correctional workers also use their high-quality interpersonal relationship to express *effective disapproval*. According to Andrews and Bonta (2010a, p. 412), such disapproval is characterized by the following: (1) "strong, emphatic, and immediate statement of disapproval, non-support, and disagreement with what the client has said or done"; (2) "Elaboration of the reason why disagree and disapprove"; (3) "Expression of disapprove stand in stark contrast to the level of interest, concern, and warmth previously offered the probationer"; (4) "The level of disapproval should be immediately reduced and approval introduced when the probationer begins to express or approximate anticriminal behavior."

Overall, it is important not to overuse reinforcement. That is because such practice "results in a satiation effect and the reward begins to lose its power—it is no longer potent" (Latessa, Listwan, & Koetzle, 2013, p. 72). Therefore, advocates of the RNR model often recommend correctional interventions to achieve a 4:1 ratio of rewards to punishments (Bonta & Andrews, 2017; Gendreau, 1996). In this regard, Wodahl, Garland, Culhane, and McCarty (2011) found that "the probability of completing ISP [Intensive Supervision Probation] increases substantially as the rewards-to-punishments ratio grows until a 4:1 ratio is achieved. At this point, increases in the probability of completion sharply diminish" (p. 400).

Principle 15: Management

The last organizational principle is the role of effective management. According to principle 15, managers in the correctional rehabilitation field are responsible for implementing the core RNR principles, maintaining integrity, and promoting the intervention outside the agency. Regarding the staff, Bonta and Andrews (2017, pp. 248–249) state that managers should have three "key management functions": (1) "select your staff on the basis of their possession of the relationship and structuring skills required in the program where they will be working"; (2) "provide preservice and in-service training in those skills"; (3) "provide high-quality clinical supervision to the workers." Other managerial responsibilities include the availability of quality program manual, decisions regarding sample size, treatment dosage, and the degree of involvement of the program's evaluator.

In sum, this section presented the RNR model and its 15 principles. In essence, these principles delineate a blueprint for effective intervening with offenders. Indeed, "the importance of the risk-need-responsivity (RNR) principles is evident in the domains of both offender assessment and treatment" (Andrews et al., 2011, p. 735). In this regard, the next section will present the technology component of the RNR model that was designed to implement the principles. Specifically, that section will elaborate the RNR-based treatment tools that assist practitioners to assess offenders (e.g., LSI-R) and treatment programs (e.g., CPAI-2000).

RNR-Based Technology of Treatment

This section presents the technological component of the RNR model. In general, this component was designed to face the challenge of "technology transfer" in the human service field—"the transmission of scientific knowledge from the producers to the potential consumers of this intervention" (Cullen & Jonson, 2011, p. 324). Within the RNR model, the technology of correctional interventions reflects approaches to rehabilitation that are "theoretically informed, evidence-based, and practical" (Cullen, 2012, p. 108). In other words, the technological component of the RNR model applies the theoretical, empirical, and practical understanding of the variation in criminal behavior of individuals. In essence, this application translates the principles of effective intervention into practice. As a result, correctional programs are equipped with RNR-based assessment tools that are expected to maximize their impact on recidivism.

During the evolution of the RNR model, Andrews and his colleagues developed two types of RNR-based assessment tools: the Level of Service Inventory-Revised (LSI-R) and the Correctional Program Assessment Inventory (CPAI). The former was designed to assess offenders, and the latter was designed to assess correctional programs. Specifically, the LSI-R is a "theoretically based risk/

need offender assessment" (Bonta & Andrews, 2017, p. 195). In practice, this instrument is expected to predict the level of risk of individuals, to identify their needs, and to assist in planning and delivering rehabilitation programs. The CPAI is a "measure of RNR adherence" (Andrews & Bonta, 2010a, p. 404). This assessment tool evaluates the likelihood that a particular rehabilitative program will produce optimal results in terms of rehabilitating offenders.

This section introduces these practical applications of the RNR model in two parts. The first part discusses the treatment technology that was designed to predict criminal behavior and classify offenders. This section focuses on the Level of Service instruments (LS). The second part of this section discusses the treatment technology designed to predict the quality of correctional programs. Specifically, this section focuses on the CPAI and the way it was designed to convey the components of the ideal correctional program and then measure the extent to which real-world programs approximated this ideal.

RNR-Based Assessment Tools to Predict Criminal Behavior and Classify Offenders

The Importance of Assessment

The assessment and classification of offenders is a fundamental activity in the modern criminal justice system. First, an assessment of future criminal behavior "guides police officers, judges, prison officials, and parole boards in their decision-making" (Bonta & Andrews, 2017, p. 185). Second, the routine management of correctional agencies, institutions, or programs includes classification of offenders for security, custody, and treatment purposes.

Within this broad context of assessment and classification, this section discusses the purposes of correctional treatment and counseling. According to Van Voorhis and Salisbury (2014), the Risk, Need, and Responsivity principles "are the most important" purposes of classification (p. 139). First, the purpose of the risk principle is to distinguish between offenders who possess different levels of risk (high-, medium, and low-risk offenders). The reason is to match the intensity of treatment to the level of risk and to prevent interpersonal relationships between low-risk and high-risk offenders. Second, the purpose of the need principle is to identify and target criminogenic needs. This reflects a priority to focus on needs that not only relate to future offending (i.e., future risk), but also are amenable to change with deliberate intervention. Third, the purpose of the principle of specific responsivity is to identify and respond to individual differences that enhance the ability of offenders to respond to treatment (treatment amenability). In this regard, correctional services are expected to maximize the impact of treatment by providing services that match the learning style and the characteristic of offenders.

Thus, the purposes of the RNR principles direct practitioners to advocate the use of structured risk/need offender assessment tools (see principle 11 in the previous section). Notably, these risk/need assessment instruments are also called "the third generation" of offender assessment approaches (Bonta, 1996). This "generation" of assessment differs from the other offender assessments that rely on professional judgment or on actuarial risk scales that consist of solely (or mainly) static risk factors.[2]

In essence, the risk/need assessment instruments enable to show whether chances in the total score of an assessment are associated with changes in reoffending (i.e., to test the predictive validity of the tool). Moreover, such assessment instruments provide correctional staff "with information as to what needs should be targeted in their interventions" (Bonta & Andrews, 2007, p. 4). In order to meet these purposes, Andrews and his colleagues developed and promoted the use of the Level of Service-Revised (LSI-R) as their preferred offender assessment instrument (Andrews & Bonta, 1995; Bonta & Andrews, 2017).

The Level of Service-Revised (LSI-R)

In brief, the LSI-R is a risk/need offender assessment that combines 54 items measuring dynamic and static risk factors into one instrument. These items cover a range of 10 domains: (1) criminal history, (2) education/employment, (3) financial, (4) family/marital, (5) accommodation, (6) leisure/ recreation, (7) companions, (8) alcohol/drug problem, (9) emotional/personal, and (10) attitude/ orientation. Indeed, the LSI-R reflects the empirical understanding of the variation in criminal behavior of individuals. In other words, the LSI-R consists of items measuring static and dynamic factors that the research found to be associated with criminality. Consistent with Andrews and Bonta's psychology of criminal conduct, most of the items across the domains assess the Central Eight factors.

Thus, the theoretical foundation of the LSI-R is the General Personality and Cognitive Social Learning (GPCSL) perspective on human behavior, and more specifically, the Personal, Interpersonal, Community-Reinforcement (PIC-R) perspective on deviant behavior (see the previous chapter). Relatedly, the LSI-R follows the four "lessons" that the PIC-R offers for offender assessment: (1) "sample multiple domains of criminal conduct," (2) includes "dynamic as well as the static covariates of criminal conduct," (3) "guide the intensity of treatment," and (4) "guide how to provide treatment" (see the previous section) (Andrews & Bonta, 2010a, pp. 307–308). In this regard, according to Van Voorhis and Salisbury (2014), the classification strategy of the LSI-R "best fits programs that are grounded in behavioral, social-learning, and cognitive-behavioral treatment strategies" (p. 147).

The origins of the LSI-R can be traced to the early 1980s when Andrews (1982b) first reported the validity of "the Level of Supervision Inventory" (LSI-VI).[3] Back then, the LSI-VI was developed to assist probation officers to adjust the level of attention or supervision they provided to probationers (Andrews & Bonta, 1994). In addition, Andrews, Robinson, and Hoge (1984) presented the Youth Level of Service Inventory (YLSI) as the youth version of the LSI. In the mid-1990s, the LSI was "identified as comprehensive, reliable, and valid [instrument] . . . with the best predicted validities" available (Gendreau, 1996, p. 122; see the literature review of the LSI in Andrews & Bonta, 1994, 1998).

In 1995, Andrews and Bonta (1995) revised the LSI and presented the LSI-R—the Level of Service Inventory-Revised. Accordingly, Hoge and Andrews (1994) developed the Youth Level of Service/Case Management Inventory (YLS/CMI) as an "adaptation of the Level of Service Inventory for children and adolescences" (Hoge & Andrews, 1996, p. 90). Since then, the Level of Service assessment tools (the LS) became a "family of instruments [that] represents the clearest products of RNR" (Andrews et al., 2011, p. 736). Specifically, within the LS "family," the LSI-R "assesses general risk level and criminogenic needs," the LS/CMI and the LS/RNR "have the added feature of assessing responsivity factors," and the YLS/CMI "extend the principles of LS, including responsivity, to juvenile offenders" (p. 736).

In recent years, the most notable development within the LS instruments is the Level of Service/Case Management Inventory (LS/CMI) (Andrews, Bonta, & Wormith, 2004, 2006). This tool was designed to link assessment to case management. This incremental function is often considered as "the fourth generation" of offender assessment (Andrews et al., 2006; Andrews & Bonta, 2010a; Bonta & Wormith, 2013; Bonta & Andrews, 2017). Specifically, compared to the LSI-R, the LS/CMI is also expected "to integrate the results of the risk/need assessment directly into the case plan process to ensure that agents of change target those criminogenic needs that are tied specifically to reoffending" (Latessa & Lovins, 2010, pp. 213–214). Moreover, the LS/CMI was designed to address broader areas of need. Thus, the LS/CMI is expected (1) to "acknowledge the role of personal strengths in building a prosocial orientation," (2) to facilitate "the assessment of special responsivity factors to maximize the benefits from treatment," and (3) to provide a "structured monitoring of the case from the beginning of supervision to the end" (Bonta & Andrews, 2017, p. 198). In other words, this instrument reflects the effort to design a structured assessment that "take on more holistic clinical perspective of the offender" (Bonta & Wormith, 2013, p. 79). This assessment approach directs treatment in addressing responsivity factors such as motivation, gender-specific, low intelligence, and antisocial personality/psychopathy. Moreover, this approach encourages correctional staff "to explore other potential responsivity variables" (Bonta & Andrews, 2017, p. 201).

The evidence shows that the LSI-R predicts criminality. For example, Andrews et al. (2006) estimated the predictive validity of the LSI-R and found an overall mean correlation (Pearson correlation coefficients) of .36 for general recidivism and .25 for violent recidivism. In addition, Vose, Cullen, and Smith (2008) examined the empirical status of the LSI-R across 47 studies conducted between 1982 and 2008. They concluded that the LSI-R "is a valid predictor of recidivism" across different groups of offenders (e.g., adults, juveniles, males, and females), "measures of recidivism," and "a variety of correctional settings and domestic and international offenders" (p. 26). Importantly, meta-analytic reviews supported these findings (Gendreau, Little, & Goggin, 1996; Campbell, French, & Gendreau, 2009; Smith, Cullen, & Latessa, 2009).

Overall, according to Andrews and Bonta (2006), "all of the comparisons showed the LSI-R to predict as well or better than the other instruments" (p. 289). Moreover, according to Andrews and Bonta (2010a), studies showed that "changes in LSI-R scores are related to recidivism" (i.e., the dynamic validity of the LSI-R) (p. 316). They also argue that the literature that examined the LS instruments has revealed its predictive validity "with mentally disorder offenders," "male batters," "sex offenders," "drug offenders," "long-term offenders," "frequently unemployment" offenders, and offenders who live "in high-crime neighborhoods" (p. 334).

However, other scholars continue to challenge the applicability of the LS instruments. Most notably, they argue for the need to develop *gender-specific* instruments for female offenders. According to this view, the LSI-R was not designed to reflect women's unique criminogenic pathways and needs and therefore cannot be considered a "gender-neutral" instrument (Hannah-Moffat, 2009; Wright, Salisbury, & Van Voorhis, 2007; Van Voorhis, Wright, Salisbury, & Bauman, 2010). In other words, these scholars recognize that the LSI-R predicts women's recidivism but indicate that "sources observe that [it is] not as relevant to the needs of women offenders as [it] should be" (Van Voorhis & Salisbury, 2014, p. 147). Specifically, "scholars note the absence of assessment scales pertaining to relationships, depression, parental issues, self-esteem, self-efficacy, trauma, and victimization" (Van Voorhis et al., 2010, p. 262). In this regard, they suggest that these gender-responsive factors "either (a) are not typically seen among men, (b) are typically seen among men but occur at a greater frequency among women, or (c) occur in equal frequency among men and women but affect women in uniquely personal and social ways that should be reflected in current correctional assessments" (p. 263).

This perspective on offender assessment differs from the theoretical position taken by Andrews and Bonta (2010a). From their perspective, the LSI-R is based upon a GPCSL and therefore, "would apply equally to men and women" (p. 329). In addition, they assert that "there is no evidence that male offenders do not follow very similar pathways to crime," and "the majority of indicators of 'gendered' pathways are actually well-known risk/need factors" (p. 331) (see also Andrews et al., 2012; Bonta & Andrews, 2017). Andrews and Bonta claim that the calls for "gender responsivity" are based on research that "studied female offenders exclusively and thus provides no direct information on gender similarities and gender differences in risk/need" (p. 331).

Thus, on one side of the argument, Andrews and his colleagues insist that gender responsiveness is an issue that can be addressed in two ways. First, modify the LS instruments to "give more attention to the substance abuse domain" (Bonta & Wormith, 2013, p. 85; see also Andrews et al., 2012). Second, address "gender-specific needs" within the principle of specific responsivity. On the other side of this dispute, advocates of gender-specific instruments argue for "gender-informed" risk/need instruments to adequately reflect the special needs of women offender population. Recently, Van Voorhis and her colleagues developed such an instrument—the Women Risk/Need Assessment (WRNA). This gender-specific assessment instrument was designed to integrate between the LSI-R and scales relevant to parenting, abuse, relationship issues, self-esteem, and self-efficacy (Van Voorhis et al., 2010). According to Van Voorhis and Salisbury (2014), the WRNA has been validated "on samples of women offenders and [has] been found to make statistically significant improvements to the earlier gender-neutral tools" (Van Voorhis & Salisbury, 2014, p. 147).

In addition to gender-responsive factors, another challenge in the offender assessment field is estimating the impact of *ethnicity and culture* on the prediction of recidivism. Indeed, as with the call for gender-specific instruments, there is "pressure" to validate risk/need assessment instruments "on the many cultural groups that are now found under correctional care" (Bonta & Wormith, 2013, p. 85). Accordingly, Bonta and Andrews (2017) continue to claim that, theoretically, the LS instruments should have similar impact across ethnic and cultural groups. Their reason is the general applicability of the GPCSL perspective on human behavior (which also includes the relevancy of the Central Eight factors on human behavior).

Bonta (1989) examined the impact of ethnicity in Canada and found evidence of the predictive validity of the LSI-R in Native offenders (see also Hogg, 2011). In addition, Gutierrez, Wilson, Rugge, and Bonta (2013) conducted a meta-analysis to examine the applicability of the Central Eight risk factors to Canadian Aboriginal offenders. This study found that "all of the Central Eight risk/need factors predicted general recidivism and seven of the eight (there was an insufficient number of studies for leisure/recreation) predicted violent recidivism for Aboriginal offenders" (p. 78). Notably, this study also reported that variables such as emotional problems and history of victimization "act as potential criminogenic needs for Aboriginal offenders" (p. 79). In the United States, studies that examined the predictive validity of the LS instrument among American Native, African American, and Latino offenders found "mixed" results (Bonta & Wormith, 2013, p. 85). Overall, Andrews and Bonta (2010a) assert that "further studies that can contribute to a meta-analysis are needed before reaching a more definitive conclusion" (pp. 333–334) (see also Bonta & Andrews, 2017).

In addition to gender and ethnicity, correctional practitioners and administrators face other issues that challenge the process of effective offender assessment. For example, agencies that apply the RNR-based assessment tools often struggle with *limited human and financial resources* (Bonta & Wormith, 2013). However, there are not enough "cost-benefit and cost-effective studies (e.g., Aos et al., 2011)" that "clearly demonstrate the fiscal soundness of offender assessments" (p. 82; see also Latessa & Lovins, 2010; Lowenkamp, Lemke, & Latessa, 2008).

Another challenging aspect about the applicability of effective offender assessment is whether a single assessment produces better outcome than the use of multiple assessments—*single versus multiple assessments* (Bonta & Wormith, 2013). Mills and Kroner (2006) examined the use of multiple assessment tools and found that the "predictive accuracy is threatened where there is discordance between risk estimates" (p. 16). Bonta and Wormith (2013) posit that a plausible explanation for such discordance in predictive accuracy is the different theoretical basis and methodological etiology among the assessment tools. That is, the assessor using multiple assessment should consider different scales that "may evaluate a particularly shared construct slightly differently (e.g., marital relationship)" (p. 83). Moreover, the assessor is required to reconcile "any differences in prognostication that may come from multiple instruments" (p. 83). Overall, beyond an exception for using two assessment tools to predict sexual recidivism (Static-99 and Stable-2007), Bonta and Wormith (2013) conclude that there is no evidence that using multiple instruments to predict the same outcome adds incremental validity.

Finally, Andrews and Bonta (2010a) sum up four obstacles to the use of empirically based risk assessment with offenders. First, psychologists tend to assess offenders with tests that are based on psychopathological models of criminal behavior. The predictive power of these tests has not been validated. Second, professionals are reluctant to abandon their clinical judgment in favor of empirical, actuarial assessment methods. Instead, professionals tend to embrace "structured clinical judgment" (SCJ) instruments that consist of relevant risk factors but do not have numerical scoring (i.e., are not actuarial instruments). Third, correctional agencies tend not to pay much attention to the integrity of assessment. Due to lack of training or inability to maintain an adequate level of competency, the staff often use assessment instruments in different ways than for which they were designed (see also Andrews et al., 2011). Fourth, many feminist scholars, critical criminologists, and legal experts express ongoing "skepticism to the application of offender risk instruments" (p. 339). Andrews and Bonta (2010a) believe that such skepticism becomes problematic when these scholars ignore information that has demonstrated empirically based risk prediction.

RNR-Based Assessment Tools to Predict the Quality of Correctional Programs

The Development of Assessment Tools

During the last decades, Andrews and his collaborators have developed an evidence-based instrument designed to assess correctional programs. This assessment tool—the CPAI—measures "the degree of adherence to the principles of RNR demonstrated by a program or correctional agency" (Andrews et al., 2006). As an RNR-based instrument, the CPAI design reflects the literature on what works in reducing recidivism. In this regard, empirical evidence specifically shows that adherence to the RNR principles is "associated with significant reduction in recidivism, whereas treatment that fails to follow the principles yields minimal reductions in recidivism and, in some cases even increase recidivism" (Andrews & Bonta, 2010b, p. 48; see also Andrews & Dowden, 2007).

The research efforts that evolved into the CPAI can be traced to the end of the 1970s. At that time, Gendreau and Andrews (1979) had started to map "the factors and characteristics that associated with program success and failure" (Wormith, 2011, p. 81). During the 1980s, Andrews and his colleagues continued to produce research that enhanced their understanding of variation in correctional rehabilitation. In 1986, Hoge and Andrews presented the "model of direct intervention" as a methodological framework that would direct the research into correctional human service (Hoge & Andrews, 1986). Their model suggested six major independent sources of variability in recidivism: offender factors, correctional worker factors, counseling process factors, program-level factors, intermediate outcomes, and setting factors (as discussed in the previous chapter). The model was designed to assist researchers in identifying factors and relationships between factors that had a potential to optimize treatment effects.

In 1989, Gendreau and Andrews developed an inventory of the principles of effective intervention—the Correctional Program Evaluation Inventory (CPEA) (Gendreau & Andrews, 1989). A few years later, Gendreau and Andrews (1994) presented their first version of the CPAI. This program assessment instrument contained 65 items across six domains of assessment: (1) Program Implementation, (2) Client Preservice Assessment, (3) Program Characteristics, (4) Characteristics of Practice and Staff, (5) Evaluation, and (6) Other.

In 2001, Gendreau and Andrews made substantial revisions with the CPAI-2000. This version expanded the CPAI to 131 items categorized into eight domains[4]: (1) organization culture, (2) program implementation and maintenance, (3) management/staff characteristics, (4) client risk/need practice, (5) program characteristics, (6) core correctional practice, (7) interagency communication, and (8) evaluation. In this revision, the major change in the CPAI was the inclusion of two new domains: Cultural Organization and Core Correctional Practice. More recently, Gendreau, Andrews, and Thériault (2010) presented the latest version of the CPAI—the CPAI-2010—which includes 133 items across eight domains.

Overall, the CPAI was the first instrument that provided a standardized way to bridge the research into effective intervention and practice. According to Van Voorhis and Brown (1996), program evaluations that preceded the CPIA examined only "whether a program has a well articulated target population and program objective" (p. 16). In other words, other evaluations assessed only the integrity of the program (i.e., how well correctional interventions delivered the services that were intended to be delivered) and the program's record-keeping function. By contrast, the CPAI was a unique program assessment because it included domains that also assessed the quality of treatment. That is, the CPAI reflected a theoretical and empirical basis that could reasonably evaluate "whether the program is targeting the individual problems most likely to reduce recidivism with the services found by previous research to be the most effective" (p. 16).

Importantly, the various versions of the CPAI assess two basic areas of assessment: the *capacity* to deliver human service and the *content* of such service. Thus, within the CPAI, *capacity* "refers to whether a correctional program has the capability to deliver evidence-based interventions and services for offenders" (Smith & Schweitzer, 2012, p. 9). This area includes five domains that "consider a number of organizational factors and contextual issues" (p. 9). *Content*, the second basic area of assessment, includes three domains that focus on the substance of assessment and treatment. This content reflects the purpose of the core RNR principles.

This integration of both capacity and content in one assessment tool reflects the notion that simply delivering expected services (i.e., integrity in program implementation and delivery) is not sufficient to reduce recidivism (Andrews & Dowden, 2005; Holsinger, 1999; Lowenkamp, Latessa, & Smith, 2006; Lowenkamp, Makarios, Latessa, Lemke, & Smith, 2010). Instead, "the effectiveness of interventions is maximized with RNR adherence in combination with integrity of service delivery" (Andrews, 2011, p. 20). In this regard, the eight domains of the CPAI-2000 are expected to constitute the ideal capacity and content of correctional programs and therefore merit close examination.

The Ideal Capacity of Correctional Programs

The CPAI contains five domains that assess the *capacity* of a program to deliver evidence-based interventions and services: (1) Organizational Culture, (2) Program Implementation and Maintenance, (3) Management and Staff Characteristics, (4) Interagency Communication, and (5) Evaluation and Quality Assurance.

First is the domain of *Organizational Culture*. Within the CPAI, the ideal of organizational culture is drawn from theories of general management and industrial organization (Smith & Schweitzer, 2012). In this regard, the ideal organization has "a culture that is receptive to implementing new ideas and has a code of ethics" (Gendreau, Smith, & French, 2006, p. 425). Culture is also reflected in "low staff turnover, frequent in-service training and within house sharing information" (Gendreau, French, & Gionet, 2004). An ideal organization should use a formal pilot period before implementing new initiatives in full scale. Overall, although promising, the domain of Organizational Culture has remained insufficiently studied and thus has scant empirical verification. That is, the validity of organizational culture "rests, so far, on the good common sense and clinical wisdom of practitioners" (p. 433).

The second domain to assess the capacity of correctional programs is *Program Implementation and Maintenance*. According to the CPAI-2000, the ideal implementation of program "occurs during a period when the organization does not face contentious issues (e.g., fiscal, staffing levels, stakeholder concerns) that might jeopardize the project" (Gendreau et al., 2004, p. 27). Moreover, programs should be implemented only when such service is required. Thus, the CPAI assesses the actual need for a particular service by comparing it with alternative and relevant services that may be more promising. For this task, "the program director and other key staff should conduct a thorough literature review and make evidence-based decisions accordingly" (Smith & Schweitzer, 2012, p. 13). According to Gendreau et al. (2006), the Program Implementation and Maintenance domain is "gaining empirical momentum" (p. 433). For example, Lowenkamp (2004) found that compared to the other domains, the average score of Program Implementation items in the CPAI was most strongly related to the measures of effectiveness (r =.54).

The third domain in the capacity area of assessment is *Management/Staff Characteristics*. Essentially, this domain assesses "the qualification and involvement of the program director" (Smith & Schweitzer, 2012, p. 13). Indeed, as described in principle 14 of the RNR model, the responsibility of program directors in the correctional rehabilitation field encompasses the implementation of RNR-based services and the maintenance of program integrity (Latessa et al., 2013). Program directors also ensure that the staff members have relevant education (e.g., related to human service), experience in working with offenders, adequate competency in delivering the particular services, and suitable qualities and skills to demonstrate the Core Correctional Practice (discussed in the

Content area of assessment). Overall, the relevance of the Management/Staff Characteristics domain is supported by "the general clinical psychology literature" and "the correctional treatment literature" (Gendreau et al., 2006, p. 433; see also Andrews & Bonta, 2010a; Bonta & Andrews, 2017; Van Voorhis & Salisbury, 2014).

The fourth domain assessing the capability of programs to deliver evidence-based services is *Interagency Communication*. This domain underscores the importance of "formal links with other agencies to ensure services are available to meet offenders' diverse needs" (Smith & Schweitzer, 2012, p. 14; see also Gendreau et al., 2006). Such communication is important to ensure the quality of advocacy brokerage and the other interests that might serve the offenders. However, currently, there is no empirical evidence to demonstrate the incremental impact of this communication on recidivism.

The last domain assessing the capacity area is *Evaluation*. According to the CPAI, an ideal program develops "both internal and external quality assurance processes" (Latessa et al., 2013, p. 231). These evaluations include monitoring offenders' treatment progress with "periodic, objective, standardized assessments of the client targeted behaviors" (Smith & Schweitzer, 2012, p. 14). In addition, ideal programs follow clients' outcomes and communicate the findings. Periodical evaluations also help maintain quality programs. Therefore, ideal correctional agencies should have "specialized unit or designated staff members for this purpose," or better, use external evaluators for this task (p. 14; see also Van Voorhis, 2006).

The Ideal Content of Correctional Programs

The CPAI evaluates the *content* of correctional programs in three domains: (1) Client Risk and Need Practices, (2) Program Characteristics, and (3) Core Correctional Practice. These domains reflect a "general consensus about which offender needs should be targeted, the best measures to use in this regard, and the most effective treatment strategies" (Smith & Schweitzer, 2012, p. 14). (The strong theoretical and empirical foundations of these treatment aspects are described in length throughout the previous section.) Here, these three domains will be discussed in terms of bridging research and practice.

The first domain is *Client Risk and Need Practices*. Within this domain, the ideal program should have a "clear admission and exclusionary criteria to define who (and who is not) appropriate for the intervention" (Smith & Schweitzer, 2012, p. 15). The program should use a valid offender assessment tool to identify both risk and need factors, and follow the risk principle, keeping high-risk and low-risk offenders in separate locations. In addition, the program should match the intensity of service to the level of risk. Accordingly, an ideal program should also assess the relevant criminogenic needs and other factors that might affect responsivity to treatment (see the previous section).

The second domain assessing the content of a correctional program is *Program Characteristics*. Within the CPAI, this domain underscores the need principle and therefore indicates whether the program targets criminogenic needs. Equally important in the CPAI is whether a program employs treatment strategies that follow the GPCSL perspective on human behavior (i.e., the general responsivity principle). Other items that assessed within this domain are whether the program has a detailed manual, an emphasis on acquiring prosocial skills, adequate ratio of rewards to punishment (at least 4:1), and clear completion criteria (Gendreau et al., 2004). Furthermore, an ideal program would prepare relapse prevention plans for participates and provide after care services.

The last domain is the use of *Core Correctional Practice*. This domain aims to put principle 14 of the RNR model (Core Correctional Staff Practices) into practice. According to this domain, the staff of an ideal program should practice high-quality relationship skills in combination with high-quality structuring skills. Specifically, program staff should demonstrate crucial competencies and skills related to service delivery, including anticriminal modeling, high-level reinforcement, effective disapproval, effective use of authority, skill building through structured learning (e.g., problem-solving, cognitive self-change), cognitive restructuring skills, and MI skills (Bonta & Andrews, 2017; Latessa et al., 2013) (see also the previous section).

According to Smith (2013), "the various versions of the instrument [i.e., CPAI] have been used to evaluate more than 700 correctional treatment programs . . . the majority (roughly 60 percent) of which failed to achieve a passing grade" (p. 77; see also Lowenkamp, 2004). Indeed, this number demonstrates "the chasm between research and practice" (p. 76).

To date, only a few studies have examined the predictive validity of the CPAI scores (i.e., the CPAI as a predictor of recidivism) (Gray, 1997; Holsinger, 1999; Nesovic, 2003; Lowenkamp, 2004; Lowenkamp et al., 2006). However, all of these studies reported moderate to strong correlations between the CPAI total score and reduction in recidivism. Still, several considerations prevent these studies from offering a full validation of the CPAI-2000. First, all of the studies used variations of the original version of the CPAI (i.e., not the CPAI-2000). Specifically, the number of CPAI items in these studies did not exceed 66, whereas the number of items in the CPAI-2000 is 131. Second, with the exception of Holsinger (1999), the above studies evaluated the programs with abbreviated versions of the CPAI. Third, with the exception of Lowenkamp (2004), the assessment of programs in these studies was not completed during the evaluation process. Rather, "the CPAI was simply used to structure data collection and the scoring of program characteristics" (Lowenkamp, Latessa, & Smith, p. 215). Last, as reviewed by Andrews (2006), "frankly, there is some inconsistency from study to study in findings at the item and subscale levels" (p. 596).

Recently, researchers at the Center for Criminal Justice Research at the University of Cincinnati developed an alternative to the CPAI—the Correctional Program Checklist (CPC). This program assessment tool shares the same theoretical and empirical knowledge as the CPAI, and is also designed to reflect the principle of the RNR model. However, as opposed to the CPAI, several different versions of the CPC were developed to evaluate the quality of correctional programs in different settings (e.g., in drug courts, mental health courts, community supervision, and treatment groups offered to offenders). Similar to the CPAI, the CPC focuses on two basic areas of assessment: capacity and content. Yet, the domains in the CPC are slightly different than those of the CPAI. The capacity area covers three domains: (1) Leadership and Development, (2) Staff, and (3) Quality Assurance. The content area consists of two domains: (1) Offender Assessment and (2) Treatment. The University of Cincinnati used the CPC to evaluate community-based programs (e.g., Latessa, Lovins, & Smith, 2010), institutional treatment programs (Latessa, Smith, Schweitzer, & Lovins, 2009), and juvenile drug courts (Latessa, Sullivan, Blair, Sullivan, & Smith, 2013). As a relatively new tool, the prediction validity of this instrument has not been validated.

In sum, the RNR-based technology of treatment is facing the "real world" of correction, where "weak adherence with RNR is the rule rather than the exception" (Andrews & Bonta, 2010a, p. 397). In this regard, research into the LSI-R and CPAI continues to build an important bridge between research and practice. Specifically, the LSI-R is an empirically validated tool and therefore constitutes a stable bridge. The main challenges in the offender assessment field remain bolstering its theoretical and practical foundations for a variety of offender populations and to ensure that correctional agencies use it appropriately. Regarding the CPAI, the challenge of the offender assessment research field is to produce more empirical evidence that support the domains that reflect the capacity of correctional program to deliver human service. Equally important is to validate the power of CPAI-2000 and/or the CPC to predict program outcomes.

Conclusion

This chapter presented the RNR model's correctional principles and the RNR-based technology of treatment. Indeed, this correctional framework is the major reason that the status of rehabilitation changed dramatically. Nowadays, rehabilitation is no longer considered as a futile theory or a practice that "does not work" with offenders. Essentially, the legitimacy of the rehabilitative ideal of rehabilitation has been reaffirmed and it now exerts increasing influence on correctional policy and practice. In this context, the RNR model has emerged in the correctional system as the dominant approach to undertaking rehabilitation.

Overall, the RNR model is best considered a paradigm comprised of three components. First, the criminological component, based on the PCC, identifies the factors that give rise to criminal involvement generally and, specifically, to recidivism (i.e., the Central Eight) (see the previous chapter). Second, the correctional component set forth 15 principles, with the RNR principles at its core, for how to effectively rehabilitate offenders. Third, the technology component provides the tools needed to assess offenders and to create an organizational context conducive to offender treatment. Taken together, these components constitute a treatment approach that is theoretically informed and evidence-based, that tells practitioners how to rehabilitate offenders, and that supplies the tools needed to apply these principles. No other existing model of rehabilitation achieves these goals.

Over the past decade, however, an alternative vision of offender rehabilitation has emerged: the Good Lives Model or the "GLM." The fifth and sixth chapters will present this approach in detail. According to its advocates, the GLM "was developed as an alternative overarching theoretical framework that seeks to preserve the merits of traditional approaches whilst actively engaging participants in the rehabilitation process and promoting desistance from crime" (Willis & Ward, 2013, p. 305). In other words, the GLM is a rehabilitation model that emphasizes the motivation of offenders to change their lives. In this regard, the GLM presents a systematic and promising approach to rehabilitation (Cullen, 2012). The next chapter will discuss the evolution of the GLM model, including its underlying theory. Accordingly, Chapter 6 will evaluate the GLM's correctional aspects and present the empirical evaluations of GLM-consistent interventions.

Notes

1. This definition of strength/protective factors was presented by Andrews and Bonta (2010a). Farrington et al. (2012) suggest alternative terminology that defines "promotive factors" as "variables that predict a low probability of offending," and "protective factors" as "variables that predict a low probability of offending among persons exposed to risk factors" (p. 2). In essence, strength/protective factors in Andrews and Bonta (2010a) is considered "promotive factors" in Farrington et al. (2012). This inconsistency might be due to the fact that, over the years, Andrews et al. changed their definition to protective factors. While Andrews (1995) provided a similar definition as Farrington et al. (2012), Andrews and Bonta (2010a) claim that such a definition cannot be operationalized. As a result, they chose different definitions of strength factors.

2. According to Bonta (1996), the first-generation assessments are characterized as being *"subjective assessment, professional judgment, intuition, and gut-feelings"* (p. 19) (emphasis in original). Furthermore, the second-generation assessment is empirically based risk assessment that consists of items that are "historical in nature" (i.e., static predictors) (p. 22) (see also Bonta, 2002).
3. According to Bonta and Wormith (2013), the Level of Supervision Inventory (LSI) "was introduced into probation in 1981" (p. 74).
4. As with the CPAI, the CPAI-2000 also includes an additional unscored domain of assessment: Program Demographics.

References

Alexander, M., Lowenkamp, C. T., & Robinson, C. R. (2012). A tale of two innovations: Motivational interviewing and core correctional practices in United States probation. In P. Ugwudike & P. Rynor (Eds.), *What works in offender compliance* (pp. 242–255). New York, NY: Palgrave Macmillan.

Andrews, D. A. (1980). Some experimental investigations of the principles of differential association through deliberate manipulations of the structure of service systems. *American Sociological Review, 45,* 448–462.

Andrews, D. A. (1982a). *A personal, interpersonal and community-reinforcement perspective on deviant behavior (PIC-R).* Toronto, ON: Ministry of Correctional Services.

Andrews, D. A. (1982b). *The Level of Supervision Inventory (LSI-VI).* Toronto, ON: Ministry of Correctional Services.

Andrews, D. A. (1982c). *The supervision of offenders: Identifying and gaining control over the factors that make a difference.* Program Branch User Report. Ottawa, ON: Solicitor General of Canada.

Andrews, D. A. (1995). The psychology of criminal conduct and effective treatment. In J. McGuire (Ed.), *What works: Reducing reoffending—guidelines from research and practice* (pp. 35–62). New York, NY: John Wiley.

Andrews, D. A. (2001). Principles of effective correctional programs. In L. L. Motiuk & R. C. Serin (Eds.), *Compendium 2000 on effective correctional programming* (pp. 9–17). Ottawa, ON: Correctional Service Canada.

Andrews, D. A. (2006). Enhancing adherence to risk-need-responsivity: Making quality a matter of policy. *Criminology & Public Policy, 5,* 595–602.

Andrews, D. A. (2011). The impact of nonprogrammatic factors on criminal-justice interventions. *Legal and Criminological Psychology, 16,* 1–23.

Andrews, D. A., & Bonta, J. (1994). *The psychology of criminal conduct.* Cincinnati, OH: Anderson.

Andrews, D. A., & Bonta, J. (1995). *The Level of Service Inventory–Revised.* Toronto, Canada: Multi-Health Systems.

Andrews, D. A., & Bonta, J. (1998). *The psychology of criminal conduct* (2nd ed.). Cincinnati, OH: Anderson.

Andrews, D. A., & Bonta, J. (2003). *The psychology of criminal conduct* (3rd ed.). Cincinnati, OH: Anderson.

Andrews, D. A., & Bonta, J. (2006). *The psychology of criminal conduct* (4th ed.). New Providence, NJ: Anderson/LexisNexis.

Andrews, D. A., & Bonta, J. (2010a). *The psychology of criminal conduct* (5th ed.). New Providence, NJ: Anderson/LexisNexis.

Andrews, D. A., & Bonta, J. (2010b). Rehabilitating criminal justice policy and practice. *Psychology, Public Policy, and Law, 16,* 39–55.

Andrews, D. A., Bonta, J., & Hoge, R. D. (1990). Classification for effective rehabilitation: Rediscovering psychology. *Criminal Justice and Behavior, 17,* 19–52.

Andrews, D. A., Bonta, J., & Wormith, S. J. (2004). *The Level of Service/Case Management Inventory (LS/CMI).* Toronto, Canada: Multi-Health Systems.

Andrews, D. A., Bonta, J., & Wormith, J. S. (2006). The recent past and near future of risk and/or need assessment. *Crime and Delinquency, 52,* 7–27.

Andrews, D. A., Bonta, J., & Wormith, J. S. (2011). The risk-need-responsivity (RNR) model: Does adding the good lives model contribute to effective crime prevention? *Criminal Justice and Behavior, 38,* 735–755.

Andrews, D. A., & Dowden, C. (2005). Managing correctional treatment for reduced recidivism: A meta-analytic review of programme integrity. *Legal and Criminological Psychology, 10,* 173–187.

Andrews, D. A., & Dowden, C. (2007). The risk–need–responsivity model of assessment and human service in prevention and corrections: Crime-prevention jurisprudence. *Canadian Journal of Criminology and Criminal Justice, 49,* 439–464.

Andrews, D. A., Guzzo, L., Raynor, P., Rowe, R. C., Rettinger, L. J., Brews, A., & Wormith, J. S. (2012). Are the major risk/need factors predictive of both female and male reoffending? A test with the eight domains of the level of service/case management inventory. *International Journal of Offender Therapy and Comparative Criminology, 56,* 113–133.

Andrews, D. A., & Hoge, R. D. (1995). Psychology of criminal conduct and principles of effective prevention and rehabilitation. *Forum of Corrections Research,* 7, 34–36. Retrieved from www.csc-scc.gc.ca/research/forum/special/spe_b_e.pdf.

Andrews, D. A., & Kiessling, J. J. (1980). Program structure and effective correctional practices: A summary of the CaVIC research. In R. R. Ross & P. Gendreau (Eds.), *Effective correctional treatment* (pp. 441–463). Toronto, TR: Butterworth.

Andrews, D. A., Robinson, D., & Balla, M. (1986). Risk principle of case classification and the prevention of residential placements: An outcome evaluation of the share the parenting program. *Journal of Consulting and Clinical Psychology, 54,* 203–207.

Andrews, D. A., Robinson, D., & Hoge. R. D. (1984). *Coding manual for the Youth Level of Supervision Inventory (YLSI).* Ottawa, ON: Carleton University.

Andrews, D. A., Zinger, I., Lab, S. P., & Whitehead, J. T. (1990). Does correctional treatment work? A clinically relevant and psychologically informed meta-analysis. *Criminology, 28,* 369–404.

Anstiss, A., Polaschek, D. L. L., & Wilson, M. J. (2011). A brief motivational interviewing intervention with prisoners: When you lead a horse to water, can it drink for itself? *Psychology, Crime, and Law, 17,* 689–710.

Aos, S., Lee, S., Drake, E. *et al.* (2011). Return on investment: Evidence-based options to improve statewide outcomes, Document no. 11-07-1201, Washington State Institute for Public Policy, Olympia.

Baird, S. C., Heinz, R. C., & Bemns, B. J. (1979). *The Wisconsin case classification and staff development project: A two-year follow-up report.* Madison, WI: Division of Corrections.

Bandura, A. (1977). *Social learning theory.* Englewood Cliffs, NJ: Prentice Hall.

Bandura, A. (1986). *Social foundations of thought and action: A social cognitive theory.* Englewood Cliffs, NJ: Prentice Hall.

Bonta, J. (1989). Native inmates: Institutional response, risk, and needs. *Canadian Journal of Criminology, 31,* 49.

Bonta, J. (1996). Risk, needs, assessment and treatment. In A. Harland (Ed.), *Choosing correctional options that work: Defining the demand and evaluating the supply* (pp. 18–32). Thousand Oaks, CA: Sage.

Bonta, J. (2002). Offender risk assessment: Guidelines for selection and use. *Criminal Justice and Behavior, 29,* 355–379.

Bonta, J., & Andrews, D. A. (2007). *Risk-need-responsivity model for offender assessment and rehabilitation.* User Report 2007–06. Ottawa, ON: Public Safety Canada.

Bonta, J., & Andrews, D. A. (2017). *The psychology of criminal conduct* (6th ed.). New York, NY: Routledge.

Bonta, J., Rugge, T., Scott, T., Bourgon, G., & Yessine, A. K. (2008). Exploring the black box of community supervision. *Journal of Offender Rehabilitation, 47,* 248–270.

Bonta, J., & Wormith, S. J. (2013). Applying the risk-need-responsivity principles to offender assessment. In L. Craig, L. Dixon, & T. Gannon (Eds.), *What works in offender rehabilitation: An evidence-based approach to assessment and treatment* (pp. 71–93). London: Wiley-Blackwell.

Byles, J. A., & Maurice, A. (1982). The juvenile services project: A n experiment in delinquency control. *Canadian Journal of Criminology, 24,* 155–165.

Campbell, M. A., French, S., & Gendreau, P. (2009). The prediction of violence in adult offenders: A meta-analytic comparison of instruments and methods of assessment. *Criminal Justice and Behavior, 36,* 567–590.

Cullen, F. T. (2005). The twelve people who saved rehabilitation: How the science of criminology made a difference. *Criminology, 43,* 1–42.

Cullen, F. T. (2012). Taking rehabilitation seriously: Creativity, science, and the challenge of offender change. *Punishment & Society, 14,* 94–114.

Cullen, F. T. (2013). Rehabilitation: Beyond nothing works. In M. Tonry (Ed.), *Crime and justice in America, 1975 to 2025—crime and justice: A review of research* (Vol. 42, pp. 299–376). Chicago, IL: University of Chicago Press.

Cullen, F. T., & Gendreau, P. (2000). Assessing correctional rehabilitation: Policy, practice, and prospects. In J. Horney (Ed.), *Policies, processes, and decisions of the criminal justice system: Criminal justice 2000* (Vol. 3, pp. 109–175). Washington, DC: U.S. Department of Justice, National Institute of Justice.

Cullen, F. T., & Jonson, C. L. (2011). Rehabilitation and treatment programs. In J. Q. Wilson & J. Petersilia (Eds.), *Crime and public policy* (pp. 293–344). New York, NY: Oxford University Press.

Cullen, F. T., & Jonson, C. L. (2012). *Correctional theory: Context and consequences.* Thousand Oaks, CA: Sage.

Dowden, C., & Andrews, D. A. (1999a). What works for female offenders: A meta-analytic review. *Crime and Delinquency, 45,* 438–452.

Dowden, C., & Andrews, D. A. (1999b). What works in young offender treatment: A meta-analysis. *Forum on Corrections Research, 11,* 21–24.

Dowden, C., & Andrews, D. A. (2000). Effective correctional treatment and violent reoffending: A meta-analysis. *Canadian Journal of Criminology, 42,* 449–467.

Dowden, C., & Andrews, D. A. (2003). Does family intervention work for delinquents? Results of a meta-analysis. *Canadian Journal of Criminology and Criminal Justice, 45,* 327–342.

Dowden, C., Antonowicz, D., & Andrews, D. A. (2003). The effectiveness of relapse prevention with offenders: A meta-analysis. *International Journal of Offender Therapy and Comparative Criminology, 47,* 516–528.

Farrington, D. P., Loeber, R., & Ttofi, M. M. (2012). Risk and protective factors for offending. In D. P. Farrington & B. C. Welsh (Eds.), *The Oxford handbook of crime prevention* (pp. 46–69). Oxford: Oxford University.

Gendreau, P. (1996). The principles of effective intervention with offenders. In A. T. Harland (Ed.), *Choosing correctional interventions that work: Defining the demand and evaluating the supply* (pp. 117–130). Thousand Oaks, CA: Sage.

Gendreau, P., & Andrews, D. A. (1979). Psychological consultation in correctional agencies: Case studies and general issues. In J. J. Platt & R. J. Wicks (Eds.), *The psychological consultant* (pp. 177–212). New York, NY: Grune & Stratton.

Gendreau, P., & Andrews, D. A. (1989). *The correctional program assessment inventory.* St. Johns, NB: University of New Brunswick.

Gendreau, P., & Andrews, D. A. (1994). *Correctional program assessment inventory* (4th ed.). St. John, NB: University of New Brunswick.

Gendreau, P., Andrews, D. A., & Thériault, Y. (2010). *Correctional program assessment inventory-2010.* St. John, NB: University of New Brunswick.

Gendreau, P., French, S. A., & Gionet, A. (2004). What works (what doesn't work): The principles of effective correctional treatment. *Journal of Community Corrections, 13,* 4–30.

Gendreau, P., Little, T., & Goggin, C. (1996). A meta-analysis of the predictors of adult offender recidivism: What works! *Criminology, 34,* 575–607.

Gendreau, P., Smith, P., & French, S. (2006). The theory of effective correctional intervention: Empirical status and future directions. In F. T. Cullen, J. P. Wright, & K. R. Blevins (Eds.), *Taking stock: The status of criminological theory: Advances in criminological theory* (Vol. 15, pp. 419–446). New Brunswick, NJ: Transaction.

Glick, B. (2006). Multimodal interventions. In B. Glick (Ed.), *Cognitive behavioral interventions for at-risk youth* (pp. 4-1–4-8). Kingston, NJ: Civic Research Institute.

Gray, G. (1997). *Does coercion play a significant role in community treatment programs that reduce offender recidivism?* Unpublished master dissertation, University of New Brunswick, New Brunswick.

Gutierrez, L., Wilson, H. A., Rugge, T., & Bonta, J. (2013). The prediction of recidivism with aboriginal offenders: A theoretically informed meta-analysis. *Canadian Journal of Criminology and Criminal Justice, 55,* 55–99.

Hackler, J. C., & Hagan, J. L. (1975). Work and teaching machines as delinquency prevention tools: A four-year follow-up. *Social Services Review, 49,* 92–106.

Hannah-Moffat, K. (2009). Gridlock or mutability: Reconsidering "gender" and risk assessment. *Criminology & Public Policy, 8,* 209–219.

Hoge, R. D., & Andrews, D. A. (1986). A model for conceptualizing interventions in social service agencies. *Canadian Psychology, 27,* 332–341.

Hoge, R. D., & Andrews, D. A. (1994). *The youth level of service/case management inventory and manual.* Ottawa, ON: Department of Psychology, Carleton University.

Hoge, R. D., & Andrews, D. A. (1996). *Assessing the youthful offender: Issues and techniques.* New York, NY: Plenum Press.

Hogg, S. M. (2011). *The level of service inventory (Ontario revision) scale validation for gender and ethnicity: Addressing reliability and predictive validity.* Unpublished master's dissertation, University of Saskatchewan, Saskatoon.

Holsinger, A. M. (1999). *Opening the 'black box': Assessing the relationship between program integrity and recidivism.* Unpublished doctoral dissertation, University of Cincinnati, Cincinnati.

Jeffery, R., & Woolport, S. (1974). Work furlough as an alternative to incarceration: An assessment of its effects on recidivism and social *cost. Journal of Criminal Law and Criminology, 65,* 404–415.

Landenberger, N. A., & Lipsey, M. W. (2005). The positive effects of cognitive-behavioral programs for offenders: A meta-analysis of factors associated with effective treatment. *Journal of Experimental Criminology, 1,* 451–476.

Latessa, E. J., Listwan, S. J., & Koetzle, D. (2013). *What works (and doesn't) in reducing recidivism.* Waltham, MA: Anderson.

Latessa, E. J., & Lovins, B. (2010). The role of offender risk assessment: A policy maker guide. *Victims and Offenders, 5,* 203–219.

Latessa, E. J., Lovins, L. B., & Smith, P. (2010). *Follow-up evaluation of Ohio's community based correctional facility and halfway house programs: Outcome study.* Cincinnati, OH: Division of Criminal Justice, Center for Criminal Justice Research, University of Cincinnati.

Latessa, E. J., Smith, P., Schweitzer, M., & Lovins, L. (2009). *Evaluation of selected institutional offender treatment programs for the Pennsylvania department of corrections.* Cincinnati, OH: Division of Criminal Justice, Center for Criminal Justice Research, University of Cincinnati.

Latessa, E. J., Sullivan, C., Blair, L., Sullivan, C. J., & Smith, P. (2013). *Outcome and process evaluation of juvenile drug courts: Final report.* Cincinnati, OH: Division of Criminal Justice, Center for Criminal Justice Research, University of Cincinnati.

Lipsey, M. W. (1992). Juvenile delinquent treatment: A meta-analytic treatment inquiry into the variability of effects. In T. D. Cook, H. Cooper, D. S. Cordray, H. Hartmann, L. V. Hedges, R. J. Light, T. A. Lewis, & F. Mosteller (Eds.), *Meta-analysis for explanation: A casebook* (pp. 83–127). New York, NY: Russell Sage Foundation.

Lipsey, M. W. (2009). The primary factors that characterize effective interventions with juvenile offenders: A meta-analytic overview. *Victims and Offenders, 4,* 124–147.

Lipsey, M. W. (2014). Interventions for juvenile offenders: A serendipitous journey. *Criminology and Public Policy, 13,* 1–14.

Lipsey, M. W., & Cullen, F. T. (2007). The effectiveness of correctional rehabilitation: A review of systematic reviews. *Annual Review of Law and Social Science, 3,* 297–320.

Lovins, B., Lowenkamp, C. T., & Latessa, E. J. (2009). Applying the risk principle to sex offenders: Can treatment make some sex offenders worse? *Prison Journal, 89,* 344–357.

Lowenkamp, C. T. (2004). *Correctional program integrity and treatment effectiveness: A multi-site program-level analysis.* Unpublished doctoral dissertation, University of Cincinnati, Cincinnati.

Lowenkamp, C. T., & Latessa, E. J. (2002). *Evaluation of Ohio's community based correctional facilities and halfway house programs.* Cincinnati, OH: Division of Criminal Justice, Center for Criminal Justice Research, University of Cincinnati.

Lowenkamp, C. T., Latessa, E. J., & Holsinger, A. M. (2006). The risk principle in action: What have we learned from 13,676 offenders and 97 correctional programs? *Crime and Delinquency, 52,* 77–93.

Lowenkamp, C. T., Latessa, E. J., & Smith, P. (2006). Does correctional program quality really matter? The impact of adhering to the principles of effective intervention. *Criminology & Public Policy, 5,* 575–594.

Lowenkamp, C. T., Lemke, R., & Latessa, E. J. (2008). The development and validation of a pretrial screening tool. *Federal Probation, 72*(3), 2–9.

Lowenkamp, C. T., Makarios, M. D., Latessa, E. J., Lemke, R., & Smith, P. (2010). Community corrections facilities for juvenile offenders in Ohio: An examination of treatment integrity and recidivism. *Criminal Justice and Behavior, 37,* 695–708.

McGuire, J. (2001). Defining correctional programs. In L. L. Mutiuk & R. C. Serin (Eds.), *Compendium 2000 on effective correctional programing.* Ottawa, ON: Correctional service Canada. Retrieved from www.cscscc.gc.ca/005/008/compendium /2000/chap_1-eng.shtml.

McGuire, J. (2004). *Understanding psychology and crime: Perspectives on theory and action.* New York, NY: Open University Press.

McGuire, J. (2013). 'What works' to reduce re-offending: 18 years on. In L. Craig, L. Dixon, & T. Gannon (Eds.), *What works in offender rehabilitation: An evidence-based approach to assessment and treatment* (pp. 20–49). London: Wiley-Blackwell.

McMurran, M. (2009). Motivational interviewing with offenders: A systematic review. *Legal and Criminological Psychology, 14,* 83–100.

Miller, W. R., & Rollnick, S. (2002). *Motivational interviewing: Preparing people for change* (2nd ed.). New York, NY: Guilford.

Miller, W. R., & Rollnick, S. (2012). Meeting in the middle: Motivational interviewing and self-determination theory. *The International Journal of Behavioral Nutrition and Physical Activity, 9*(1), 25–26.

Miller, W. R., & Rollnick, S. (2013). *Motivational interviewing: Helping people change* (3rd ed.). New York, NY: Guilford.

Mills, J. F., & Kroner, D. G. (2006). The effect of discordance among violence and general recidivism risk estimates on predictive accuracy. *Criminal Behaviour and Mental Health, 16,* 155–166.

Nesovic, A. (2003). *Psychometric evaluation of the correctional program assessment inventory (CPAI).* Unpublished doctoral dissertation, Carleton University, Ottawa.

O'Donnell, C. R., Lydgate, T., & Fo, W. S. O. (1971). The buddy system: Review and follow-up. *Child Behavior Therapy, 1,* 161–169.

Ogloff, J. R. P., & Davis, M. R. (2004). Advances in offender assessment and rehabilitation: Contributions of the risk-needs-responsivity approach. *Psychology, Crime and Law, 10,* 229–242.

Palmer, T. (1992). *The re-emergence of correctional intervention.* Newbury Park, CA: Sage.

Smith, P. (2013). The psychology of criminal conduct. In F. T. Cullen & P. Wilcox (Eds.), *The Oxford handbook of criminological theory* (pp. 69–88). New York: Oxford University Press.

Smith, P., Cullen, F. T., & Latessa, E. J. (2009). Can 14,737 women be wrong? A meta-analysis of the LSI-R and recidivism for female offenders. *Criminology & Public Policy, 8,* 183–208.

Smith, P., Gendreau, P., & Swartz, K. (2009). Validating the principles of effective intervention: A systematic review of the contributions of meta-analysis in the field of corrections. *Victims and Offenders, 4,* 148–169.

Smith, P., & Schweitzer, M. (2012). The therapeutic prison. *Journal of Contemporary Criminal Justice, 28,* 7–22.

Spiegler, M. D., & Guevremont, D. C. (2010). *Contemporary behavior therapy* (5th ed.). Belmont, CA: Wadsworth.

Stouthamer-Loeber, M., Loeber, R., Wei, E., Farrington, D. P., & Wikström, P.-O. H. (2002). Risk and promotive effects in the explanation of persistent serious delinquency in boys. *Journal of Consulting and Clinical Psychology, 70,* 111–123.

Van Voorhis, P. (2006). Comprehensive evaluation of cognitive behavioral programs in corrections: Guidelines and approaches. In B. Glick (Ed.), *Cognitive behavioral interventions for at-risk youth* (pp. 15-1–15-16). Kingston, NJ: Civic Research Institute.

Van Voorhis, P., & Brown, K. (1996). *Evaluability assessment: A tool for program development in corrections.* Washington, DC: National Institute of Corrections.

Van Voorhis, P., & Salisbury, E. (2014). *Correctional counseling and rehabilitation* (8th ed.). Cincinnati, OH: Elsevier/Anderson.

Van Voorhis, P., Wright, E. M., Salisbury, E., & Bauman, A. (2010). Women's risk factors and their contributions to existing risk/needs assessment: The current status of a gender-responsive supplement. *Criminal Justice and Behavior, 37,* 261–288.

Vose, B., Cullen, F. T., & Smith, P. (2008). The empirical status of the level of service inventory. *Federal Probation, 72*(3), 22–29.

Walters, S. T., Vader, A. M., Nguyen, N., Harris, T. R., & Eells, J. (2010). Motivational interviewing as a supervision strategy in probation: A randomized effectiveness trial. *Journal of Offender Rehabilitation, 49*(5), 309–323.

Willis, G. M., & Ward, T. (2013). The good lives model: Does it work? Preliminary evidence. In L. Craig, L. Dixon, & T. Gannon (Eds.), *What works in offender rehabilitation: An evidence-based approach to assessment and treatment* (pp. 305–317). London: Wiley-Blackwell.

Wodahl, E. J., Garland, B., Culhane, S. E., & McCarty, W. P. (2011). Utilizing behavioral interventions to improve supervision outcomes. *Criminal Justice and Behavior, 38*, 386–405.

Wormith, J. S. (2011). The legacy of D. A. Andrews in the field of criminal justice: How theory and research can change policy and practice. *International Journal of Forensic Mental Health, 10*, 78–82.

Wright, E., Salisbury, E., & Van Voorhis, P. (2007). Predicting the prison misconducts of women offenders: The importance of gender responsive needs. *Journal of Contemporary Criminal Justice, 23*, 310–340.

PART III

The Good Lives Model

5

THE THEORETICAL FOUNDATION
OF THE GOOD LIVES MODEL

The origins of the Good Lives Model (GLM) can be traced to the early 2000s. As noted, by that time, the accumulated empirical evidence showed the wisdom of employing rehabilitative as opposed to punitive correctional interventions (Gendreau, 1996; Lösel, 1995). Moreover, scholars endorsed the evidence-based approach to what works in corrections as the most reliable way to reaffirm rehabilitation (Cullen & Gendreau, 2000; Latessa, Cullen, & Gendreau, 2002; MacKenzie, 2000; McGuire, 2002). Within this scientific orientation to corrections, the RNR model became the dominant paradigm of offender rehabilitation.

However, not all of the scholars who supported rehabilitation fully embraced this scientific orientation. One of those scholars was Tony Ward, a New Zealander-PhD psychologist who was trained in the clinical and forensic field. In the opening of the 21st century, Ward was well aware that a growing amount of empirical evidence had enabled rehabilitation to regain its legitimacy. Nevertheless, he argued against using an approach to correctional rehabilitation that was strictly evidence based. In this regard, he asserted that "empirical adequacy on its own provides an overly thin measure of programme's value" (Ward, 2013b, p. xxii).

In Ward's view, the overreliance on science was problematic because it enmeshed the practice of rehabilitation in a framework of risk rather than a framework of welfare. He argued that the empirical knowledge that had been translated into practice overemphasized risk management. That is, "the primary aim of rehabilitating offenders is to avoid harm to the community" (Ward & Stewart, 2003, p. 126). In such practice, the actual satisfaction of offenders may be considered as a desired outcome but only as "a means to the end of reduced risk to the community" (p. 126). Therefore, Ward perceived the RNR model, which had emerged through evidence-based corrections, as a model of rehabilitation that gives priority not to the interests of offenders but to the interests of the non offending public. Thus, he concluded that a better model of offender rehabilitation is needed.

In contrast, Ward favored a vision of rehabilitation that underscores the role of clinical psychology models in correctional interventions. According to this vision, the primary aim of rehabilitation should be to enhance offenders' well-being and capabilities (Ward & Stewart, 2003). In general, the goal is thus to equip offenders with "capabilities to meet their needs, pursue their interests, and therefore live happy, fulfilling lives" (Ward & Maruna, 2007, p. 109). In this regard, Ward argued that the focus on offenders' lives is important because "every rehabilitation program presupposes conceptions of possible good lives for offenders and, associated with this, an understanding of the necessary internal and external conditions for living such lives" (Ward, 2002b, p. 513). Thus, the challenge of rehabilitation programs is to assist offenders in finding answers for a fundamental question in their change process: how offenders can live a different life (Porporino, 2010).

In 2003, Tony Ward and Claire Stewart introduced the GLM as a model of offender rehabilitation that reflected their ideas and served "as a complementary theory to RNR" (Ward & Maruna, 2007, p. 142). Ward and his collaborators tried to integrate the RNR model and the psychological research in positive psychology and strength-based practice (Laws & Ward, 2011; Ward, 2002a; Ward & Gannon, 2006; Ward & Maruna, 2007; Ward, Yates, & Long, 2006; Yates, Prescott, & Ward, 2010). The resulting GLM was intended to provide guidance to rehabilitation programs on how best to "equip clients with internal and external resources to live a good or better life—a life that is socially acceptable and personally meaningful" (Ward, Yates, & Willis, 2012, p. 95). These scholars expected that correctional interventions that would improve the quality of offenders' life would also maximize their ability to reduce recidivism.

Chapters 5 and 6 introduce the systematic perspective that the GLM offers to the study and practice of correctional rehabilitation. The overview of this model is based on the writings that Ward and his colleagues have published since the early 2000s.[1] These chapters also rely on a 2007 book published by Tony Ward and Shadd Maruna, *Rehabilitation: Beyond the Risk Paradigm*. This volume presents the GLM as a paradigm that has the potential to improve the quality of interventions throughout the correctional system. Essentially, Ward and Maruna (2007) provide the keys to understand the core ideas of the GLM and its further theoretical and practical developments. In this regard, the current chapter describes the theoretical framework of the GLM, whereas Chapter 6 discusses the GLM's correctional framework and evaluates its empirical status.

In brief, the GLM focuses on the promotion of two categories of goods: "primary human goods" and "secondary goods." Within this model, the *primary human goods* are goals held by all human beings, including offenders. In general terms, these goods are described as "states of mind, personal characteristics, or experiences that are intrinsically beneficial and sought for their own sake" (Ward et al., 2012, p. 95). The GLM demarcates 10 primary human goods that all humans seek in their life. The priority that individuals give to each of these primary good reflects their self-reflection and values.

The second category of goods is the *secondary (or instrumental) goods*. This category represents the specific and concrete activities or strategies that a person uses to obtain the primary human goods. The secondary goods can be appropriate or inappropriate. Appropriate secondary goods are personally meaningful activities or strategies that are used to achieve the primary human goods in a socially acceptable way. The GLM considers these goods as a person's strengths. As opposed to appropriate secondary goods, inappropriate secondary goods are considered flaws in an individual's ability to attain the desired primary goods.

This chapter discusses the GLM's theoretical framework in three sections. The first section introduces the three theoretical perspectives that informed the development of the GLM: humanistic psychology, positive psychology, and strength-based approach to offender rehabilitation. The second section then discusses the underlying assumptions of the GLM. The section presents the GLM's eight basic assumptions that reflect ideas about the purpose of offender rehabilitation and its essential components (Ward & Maruna, 2007). These basic assumptions concern the purpose of the

GLM as a rehabilitation model. The discussion of each assumption also includes an estimation of its empirical strength. The third section in this chapter explains the relationship between the GLM's basic assumptions and criminal behavior. This discussion follows what Ward and Maruna (2007) have referred as the "cognitive map or general overview of the broad causes of antisocial behavior" (p. 120). As with the basic assumptions, this section elaborates the theoretical and empirical aspects of these criminological explanations.

Beyond Deficits: Building on the Positive

The GLM takes a positive psychological approach to offender rehabilitation. In general, this means that the model "has its roots in the positive psychology and humanistic traditions" (Ward & Gannon, 2006, p. 78). However, according to Ward and Maruna (2007), the GLM "was developed independently of the positive psychology movement" (pp. 110–111). Indeed, Ward and his collaborators often discuss the theoretical aspects of positive psychology only through its shared core assumptions with the GLM (e.g., Ward, Mann, & Gannon, 2007). Therefore, the opening section of this chapter tries to fill this gap of knowledge with a brief introduction of humanistic and positive psychology. In addition, this section introduces the strength-based approach to offender rehabilitation. Such an introduction is important because the GLM is considered to be a strength-based rehabilitation framework that encourages intervention programs to focus on an offender's strengths and goals.

Humanistic Psychology

Humanistic psychology emphasizes the individual's capabilities and potentialities. Within the discipline of psychology, this perspective on behavior and mental processes stands alongside the two other major perspectives: psychoanalysis and behaviorism. In this regard, humanistic psychology "does not explain behavior in terms of unconscious, powerful inner forces and does not focus on environmental stimuli and responses as determinants of behavior" (Schunk, Meece, & Pintrich, 2014, p. 35). Instead, this psychology is "identified with the study and promotion of positive experience" (Duckworth, Steen, & Seligman, 2005, p. 632).

Schunk et al. (2014) identify three common assumptions of humanistic theories. One assumption is that the study of the human is holistic. That is, within humanistic theories, the study of behavior, thoughts, and feelings "emphasize individuals' *subjective* awareness of themselves and their situations" (p. 36, emphasis added). The second common assumption is the importance of concepts such as "human choices, creativity, and self-actualization" (p. 36). In general, this means that researchers should understand people through the study of their attempts "to be creative and maximize their capabilities and potential" (p. 36). The third common assumption among humanistic theories highlights "the importance of the problem" over the quality of methodology. According to this assumption, "it is better to study an important problem with less-refined methodology than a trivial problem with a complex methodology" (p. 36).

Carl Rogers and Abraham Maslow are considered the two "grandparents" of humanistic psychology (Duckworth et al., 2005, p. 632). Rogers (1959, 1961) developed client-centered therapy that underlies the "human process of personal growth or achieving wholeness"—the process of self-actualization (Schunk et al., p. 36). According to Rogers (1959), this process represents "the inherent tendency of the organism to develop all its capacities in ways which serve to maintain or enhance the person" (p. 196). Thus, Rogers's theory depicts people as "forever growing, unfolding their potentialities, and constantly changing in the process" (Ziegler, 2002, p. 86). Human beings are viewed as "basically rational and eminently capable of directing their behavior through reason" (p. 82). Relatedly, this perspective assumes that during the process of self-actualization, people become more aware of their own being and functioning. According to Rogers, this development of self-awareness also is affected by the person's environment because "experiences and interpretation of them foster or hinder our growth" (Schunk et al., p. 36).

Abraham Maslow, the second prominent humanistic psychologist, set forth a theory that explains "the process by which individuals could become self-actualized" (Duckworth et al., 2005, p. 632). In this regard, he classified all human needs into five groups that differ in their importance for human development. Within this hierarchy of needs, a state of self-actualization reflects the highest personality growth (Maslow, 1962). People who reach self-actualization have "access to the full range of their talents and strengths" (Duckworth et al., 2005, p. 632).

However, according to Maslow's theory, self-actualization cannot be achieved until the needs in the lower groups in the hierarchy (i.e., the "deficiency needs") will be satisfied. In this regard, physiological needs (e.g., food, water) are at the bottom of the hierarchy of needs, followed by safety needs (e.g., protection from pain, fear, order, anxiety), belongingness and love (e.g., affection, security, social acceptance, identity), esteem needs (e.g., gain approval, recognition), and self-actualization needs at the top of the hierarchy (Maslow, 1954). Maslow explained that an individual's life is directed toward self-actualization because "a need that is unsatisfied generates behavior designed to satisfy the need" (Schunk et al., p. 173). Similar to Rogers, Maslow states that the environment has an important role in the process toward self-actualization. That is, without opportunities for satisfaction of needs, the person's growth and development would not occur as desired.

Positive Psychology

The positive approach in psychology emerged as an alternative to the focus in clinical psychology and psychiatry on "medical-oriented psychology" (Jorgensen & Nafstad, 2004). Specifically, this growing scientific discipline presents an alternative to psychological approaches that emphasize disorders, pathologies, faults, and dysfunctions. Within clinical psychology, positive psychology serves as a conceptual framework for "researchers and practitioners interested in all aspects of optimal human functioning" (Linley & Joseph, 2004, p. 3). In this regard, Duckworth et al. (2005, p. 630) suggest a common belief among those who adapt the positive psychology approaches:

> We believe that persons who carry even the weightiest psychological burdens care about much more in their lives than just the relief of their suffering. Troubled persons want more satisfaction, contentment, and joy, not just less sadness and worry. They want to build their strengths, not just correct their weaknesses. And, they want lives imbued with meaning and purpose. These states do not come about automatically simply when suffering is removed. Furthermore, the fostering of positive emotion and the building of character may help—both directly and indirectly—to alleviate suffering and to undo its root causes.

This common belief reflects the basic assumption of the positive psychology approaches: "the human being has given potential for positive character or virtues" (Jorgensen & Nafstad, 2004,

p. 18). In that sense, all human beings are fundamentally social and moral rather than motivated primary by their self-interests. In other words, advocates of positive psychology assert that "goodness and morality thus do not come from outside the person. They do not arise from cultural sources nor from moral rules of society, but from the potentials of human being himself or herself" (p. 22).

The discipline of positive psychology focuses on the study of three domains: positive experiences, positive individual traits, and the institutions that facilitate the development of positive experience and traits. According to Seligman and his colleagues, each of these three domains is represented by a particular kind of human life (Duckworth et al., 2005; Seligman, 2002; Seligman & Csikszentmihalyi, 2000).

First is the *pleasant life* that is based on the person's positive experiences. During a pleasant life, the person is able to maximize positive emotions and minimize negative emotions. This is what Linley and Joseph (2004) call a "subjective well-being" (p. 5). According to positive psychology, the pleasant life is possible by developing positive emotion about the past, present, and future. In applied positive psychology, the study of this process includes the examination of subjective experiences such as "well-being, contentment, and satisfaction (in the past); hope and optimism (for the future); and flow and happiness (in the present)" (Seligman & Csikszentmihalyi, 2000, p. 5).

The second domain in positive psychology is represented by the *engaged life*. This reflects the desire for "psychological well-being"—the "engagement with and full participation in the challenges and opportunities of life" (Linley & Joseph, 2004, p. 5). Such engagement involves the use of individual traits that reflects "strengths of character"—"qualities considered virtuous across cultures and historical areas" (Duckworth et al., 2005, p. 635). Specifically, the desired individual traits include "the capacity for love and vocation, courage, interpersonal skill, aesthetic sensibility, perseverance, forgiveness, originality, future mindedness, spirituality, high talent, and wisdom" (Seligman & Csikszentmihalyi, 2000, p. 5).

The third domain in positive psychology is the *meaningful life*. This domain reflects the assumption that "meaning drives from belonging to and serving something larger than oneself" (Duckworth et al., 2005, p. 636). In applied positive psychology, scholars study the meaningful life through concepts that represent "the civic virtues and the institutions that move individuals toward better citizenship: responsibility, nurturance, altruism, civility, moderation, tolerance, and work ethic" (Seligman & Csikszentmihalyi, 2000, p. 5).

In the clinical field, positive psychology is considered "a strength-based approach in that it seeks to equip people with the capabilities to meet their needs, pursue their interests, and therefore live happy, fulfilling lives" (Ward & Maruna, 2007, p. 109). Thus, positive psychologists focus on people's strengths, capacities, and resources to promote optimal functioning. Their therapies aim to allow people "to survive, and in some cases flourish, despite the obstacles they have faced" (Linley & Joseph, 2004, p. 8).

According to Linley and Joseph (2004), the application of positive psychology consists of six points: First, it aims to *facilitate* optimal functioning in a way that helps people "to achieve their objectives," rather than dictating them toward specific objectives (p. 5). Second, the goal of facilitating *optimal functioning* refers to helping people in a broad range of psychological processes and outcomes. This includes "valued psychological processes" such as using positive traits and acting as a good citizen. This also includes "positive outcomes" such as individual and collective well-being (p. 5). The third point in applied positive psychology relates to the *value position* in phrases such as "good life," "good citizenship," "positive individual traits," and "valued subjective experiences" (p. 5). In this regard, applied positive psychology endorses a scientific approach to these phrases. This is achieved through an explicit statement of the valued positions of these phrases and by avoiding positions that dictate individuals toward "specific ways in which they should live their lives" (p. 5). The fourth point of applied positive psychology underscores its different *levels of application*. In practice, within various social and cultural contexts, positive psychology can be applied to "individuals, groups, organizations, communities, and societies" (Linley & Joseph, 2004, p. 5). The fifth point is the applicability of positive psychology to the *full range of human functioning*. This means an effort to "facilitate optimal functioning by moving [clients] *beyond* the zero point of psychopathology" (p. 6, emphasis in original). The last point of applied positive psychology is the creation of *collective identity* and common language for psychologists that have an interest in aspects of optimal human functioning.

Strength-Based Approach

Strength-based approaches to offender rehabilitation use individuals' core commitments and capabilities in the process of behavioral change. In this regard, the goal is to "elicit information from [individuals] about their strengths to build skills that will offset any deficits" (Serran & Marshall, 2010, p. 5). Enhancing individuals' capabilities is intended to allow them "to live meaningful, constructive, and ultimately satisfying lives" (Langlands, Ward, & Gilchrist, 2009, p. 119). Within the context of offender rehabilitation, the assumption is that strength-based interventions are the best way to reinforce desistance processes. This is "because of their sensitivity to offender commitments and social ecology" (Willis & Ward, 2013, p. 314; see also Langlands et al., 2009; Ward, 2011).

According to Ward and Maruna (2007), the GLM is "the most systematically developed theory in the strength-based domain" (p. 24). In this regard, the GLM is a strength-based approach in two respects. First, the GLM takes seriously offenders' personal preferences and values in the design of treatment programs. Then, the GLM draws on these personal core commitments "to motivate individuals to live better lives" (Whitehead, Ward, & Collie, 2007, p. 580). Second, within the GLM, "therapists seek to provide offenders with the competencies (internal conditions) and opportunities (external conditions) to implement treatment plans" based on the "things that matter most to them in the world" (p. 580; see also Thakker, Ward, & Chu, 2013; Ward & Fortune, 2013; Ward & Marshall, 2007).

The General Assumptions of the Good Lives Model

Ward and Maruna (2007) present eight general assumptions of the GLM. These assumptions concern the purpose of rehabilitation, and "specify the values and views that underlie rehabilitation practice and the kind of overall aims for which clinicians should be striving" (p. 34). Thus, this section introduces the GLM's eight general theoretical assumptions as was presented by Ward and his colleagues. In addition, this introduction also indicates the intellectual sources of these assumptions.

Assumption 1: As Human Beings, "Offenders Share the Same Inclinations and Basic Needs as Other People and Are Naturally Predisposed to Seek Certain Goals, or Primary Human Goods" (Ward & Maruna, 2007, p. 112)

At its core, this assumption reflects ideas from humanistic theories and the positive psychology. First, the GLM argues that offenders have similar needs and aspirations as nonoffenders. Second, the GLM assumes that individuals are self-motivated to seek their well-being; that is, their psychological processes are held to be self-directed toward optimal cognitive and emotional functioning. Third, the GLM proposes that there is a close link between the person's well-being and his/her social environment. In that sense, human beings are "fundamentally social creatures, driven to find meaning in their life through social interaction and individual achievement" (p. 143).

The theoretical source of this assumption can be traced to Self-Determination Theory (SDT). Ward and Stewart (2003, p. 135) consider this theory as "the most comprehensive psychological theory of needs currently available." According to the SDT, psychological needs are "innate psychological nutriments that are essential for ongoing psychological growth, integrity, and well-being" (Deci & Ryan, 2000, p. 229). In GLM's terms, the satisfaction of certain needs depends on humans' psychological growth, fulfillment, and optimal functioning. The basic assumption in the SDT is that "people are by nature active and self-motivated, curious and interested, vital and eager to succeed because success itself is personally satisfying and rewarding" (Deci & Ryan, 2008, p. 14). Accordingly, the GLM views all human beings as goal-directed organisms that are predisposed to seek certain goals (Ward et al., 2007). In addition, SDT and the GLM share the assumption that the social environment influences the conditions and processes that facilitate the development and persistence of human needs. According to this perspective, the social context can either support innate human nature or thwart it. In other words, certain social conditions can change the individuals' innate human nature from being self-motivated toward optimal functioning to individuals that are "alienated and mechanized, or passive and disaffected" (Deci & Ryan, 2008, p. 14).

SDT identifies three innate psychological needs—for autonomy, competence, and relatedness—that account for these outcomes. Specifically, the need for *competence* refers to the person's ability to "have an effect on the environment as well as to attain valued outcomes within it" (i.e., the need for mastery of the environment). The need for *relatedness* refers to "the desire to feel connected to others—to love and care, and to be loved and cared for" (i.e., the need to belong to a group). The need for *autonomy* refers to the person's experience of internal control or freedom of choices and actions. A person with autonomy reflects "the organismic desire to self-organize experience and behavior and to have activity be concordant with one's integrated sense of self" (Deci & Ryan, 2000, p. 231). According to SDT, a success to satisfy the need for competence, autonomous, and relatedness to others will result in the most effective human functioning (i.e., "optimal human development and well-being"). At the same time, a failure to satisfy even one of these needs will result in significant negative psychological consequences (i.e., "degradation and ill-being") (p. 229).

Advocates of the GLM agreed autonomy, competence, and relatedness as three basic human needs (Ward & Stewart, 2003). However, they argued that to explain fully the goals that people pursue, other needs would have to be identified. Thus, Ward and Maruna (2007) relied on disciplines such as "anthropology, social science, social policy, psychology, evolutionary theory, practical ethics and philosophical anthropology" to expand the number of human needs that are valued as ends to themselves (p. 145). They agreed upon basic human needs that represent "states of affairs, state of mind, personal characteristics, activities or experiences that are sought for their own sake and are likely to increase psychological well-being if achieved" (Ward & Maruna, 2007, p. 113; McMurran & Ward, 2004; Wilson & Yates, 2009). Within the GLM, these basic human needs are considered the *primary goods* of human life.

The advocates of the GLM identified 10 groups of primary goods that they argued all humans seek in their life (Yates et al., 2010, pp. 38–39): (1) life (healthy living and functioning—the basic need in life); (2) knowledge acquisition (desire for information and understanding about oneself and the world); (3) excellence in play and work (including mastering experiences); (4) excellence in agency (autonomy, independence and self-directedness); (5) inner peace (freedom from emotional turmoil and stress); (6) friendship (connections to others through intimate, romantic, familial, and other types of relationships); (7) community (a sense of belonging to a larger group of individuals with shared interests); (8) spirituality (i.e., a broad sense of finding meaning and purpose in life); (9) happiness (i.e., a state of being of overall contentedness in one's life; the experience of pleasure); and (10) creativity (i.e., to desire to have novelty or innovation in one's life). Notably, Ward and his colleagues stated that this list does not represent a definite set of primary goods[2] (Ward & Stewart, 2003; Ward & Maruna, 2007).

According to the GLM, people are self-motivated to seek out all the primary goods but vary in how they prioritize each good. Ward et al. (2012, p. 95) argue that "the weightings or priorities given to specific primary goods reflect an individual's particular values and life priorities." In addition, they explain that the individuals' specific cultural context account for variations in the way they value or rank the primary goods. Thus, overall, primary goods represent individuals' "interpretation of interpersonal and social events" (Ward & Maruna, 2007, p. 144) and reflect their sense of "who they are and what is really worth having in life" (Ward et al., 2012, p. 95).

In addition to the primary goods, the GLM asserts that a second category of goods exists: *secondary (or instrumental) goods*. According to the GLM, this category of goods provides the concrete means of securing the primary goods. That is, the secondary goods are "the specific roles, practices, and actions that provide routes to the primary goods" (Ward et al., 2012, p. 96). Therefore, in essence, the value of the secondary goods depends entirely on their contribution to achieve the primary goods. In this regard, the GLM distinguishes between two types of secondary goods: appropriate and inappropriate goods.

Appropriate secondary goods represent socially accepted means or strategies of securing primary goods. The assumption is that more adaptive behavior relates to higher levels of well-being. Thus, within the GLM, the use of secondary goods to achieve the primary goods in a socially acceptable way reflects a person's strengths. By contrast, inappropriate secondary goods are considered as socially unaccepted means or strategies to attain the primary goals. According to Ward et al., inappropriate secondary goods will not result in high levels of well-being. They explain this result in the expected unpleasant social sanction that follows the involvement in illegal activities. Thus, within the GLM, inappropriate secondary goods represent flaws in an individual's ability to fully secure their primary goods.

Note that Table 5.1 presents the 10 primary human goods, their common life goals, definition, and the possible secondary goods that can achieve them. This table was reprinted from Willis, Prescott, and Yates (2013).

Assumption 2: "Rehabilitation Is a Value-Laden Process and Involves a Variety of Different Types of Value" (Ward & Maruna, 2007, p. 116)

Within the GLM, *values* are considered as "fundamental commitments concerning what is worthwhile and best in life and as such underlie choices about how to behave" (Day & Ward, 2010, p. 289). Ward and Maruna (2007, p. 37) argue that "values play a significant role in rehabilitation theories as they serve to identify therapeutic goals and to constrain rehabilitative attempts" (Ward & Maruna, 2007, p. 37). In that sense, the rehabilitative process is designed to obtain certain valued

TABLE 5.1 Primary goods, common life goals, definitions, and possible secondary goods

Primary Good	Common Life Goal	Definition	Possible Secondary/Instrumental Goods
Life (healthy living and functioning)	Life: Living and Surviving	Looking after physical health, and/or staying alive and safe.	Pursuing a healthy diet, engaging in regular exercise, managing specific health problems, earning or stealing money to pay rent or to meet basic survival or safety needs.
Knowledge	Knowledge: Learning and Knowing	Seeking knowledge about oneself, other people, the environment, or specific subjects.	Attending school or training courses, self-study (e.g., reading), mentoring or coaching others, attending a treatment or rehabilitation program.
Excellence in Work and Play	Being Good at Work and Play	Striving for excellence and mastery in work, hobbies, or leisure activities.	Being employed or volunteering in meaningful work, advancing in one's career; participating in a sport, playing a musical instrument, arts and crafts.
Excellence in Agency (autonomy and self-directedness)	Personal Choice and Independence	Seeking independence and autonomy, making one's own way in life.	Developing and following through with life plans, being assertive, having control over other people, abusing or manipulating others.
Inner Peace (freedom from emotional turmoil and stress)	Peace of Mind	The experience of emotional equilibrium; freedom from emotional turmoil and stress.	Exercise, meditation, use of alcohol or other drugs, sex, and any other activities that help manage emotions and reduce stress.
Relatedness (intimate, romantic, and family relationships)	Relationships and Friendships	Sharing close and mutual bonds with other people, including relationships with intimate partners, family, and friends.	Spending time with family and/ or friends, having an intimate relationship with another person.
Community	Community: Being Part of a Group	Being part of, or belonging to, a group of people who share common interests, concerns of values.	Belonging to a service club, volunteer group, or sports team; being a member of a gang.
Spirituality (finding meaning and purpose in life)	Spirituality: Having Meaning in Life	Having meaning and purpose in life; being a part of a larger whole.	Participating in religious activities (e.g., going to church, prayer), participating in groups that share a common purpose (e.g., environmental groups).
Happiness	Happiness	The desire to experience happiness and pleasure.	Socializing with friends, watching movies, sex, thrill-seeking activities, drinking alcohol, taking drugs.
Creativity	Creativity	The desire to create some-thing, do things differently, or try new things.	Painting, photography, and other types of artistic expression; participating in new or novel activities.

Note: Reprinted with permission from Willis, Prescott, and Yates (2013).

outcomes, and those valued outcomes determine the necessary conditions to remove therapeutic obstacles or to facilitate need fulfillment. Specifically, the GLM identifies three different types of values: prudential, ethical, and cognitive values.

Prudential values are "synonymous with primary goods" (see above) (Ward & Marshall, 2007, p. 288). This type of values reflects the best interests of individual offenders (i.e., "the ultimate ends of correctional programs") (Ward & Maruna, 2007, p. 149). According to this perspective, the concept of prudential values establishes a link between certain valued goods and individuals' optimal functioning. In this regard, prudential values are particularly important for offender treatment because they motivate individuals "to engage in treatment and form the more adaptive narrative identity" (p. 149). Notably, the term "good" in the title "the Good Lives Model" refers to "prudential or self-regarding goods" rather than the other types of values (Ward & Fortune, 2013, p. 35).

Ethical values concern the "best interests of community" (Ward & Maruna, 2007, p. 149). Ethical values represent "foundational or core standards used to construct ways of living and behaving" (p. 36). In essence, the standards of good life and behavior emerged through an ethical judgment— the characterization of aspects of the community and other persons in terms of right or wrong, good or bad. Advocates of the GLM assert that "offender rehabilitation may be one of the only forms of treatment in existence that is explicitly intended for the benefit of others (the 'community') rather than for the person undergoing the counseling itself" (p. 17). Thus, they call attention to the "ethical tensions created between a need to protect the community (criminal justice values; normative code) and the requirement that practitioners act in ways that respect offenders' autonomy and seek to enhance their level of well-being" (Ward, 2013a, p. 99).

Cognitive (or epistemic) values reflect "our best-practice models and methods" (Ward & Maruna, 2007, p. 116). Thus, cognitive values inform decision-making during the rehabilitative process. Specifically, these knowledge-related values "help researchers and clinician identify effective interventions and ways of helping individuals to desist from further offending" (p. 149). In practice, cognitive values determine the standards that should be used when dealing with issues such as "research design, analytic strategies, and what kind of evidence is admissible when deciding on best practice" (p. 36).

Overall, within the GLM, "values are not only directly reflected in the goals offenders hold when committing offences and the ways in which they choose to live their lives but are also evident in the countless professional decisions made by forensic practitioners" (Day & Ward, 2010, p. 303). In other words, Day and Ward recognize values in offenders' primary goods, as well as in the way practitioners assess offenders, conduct treatment, and evaluate their efforts. In that sense, values "penetrate deeply into every facet of rehabilitative work" (p. 303).

Assumption 3: Correctional Interventions That Address Both Goods Promotion and Risk Reduction Will Produce Better Outcomes than Intervention That Neglect Either of These Aims

Within the GLM, this assumption is called the "dual aims" or the "twin focus" of correctional interventions. In general, the focus in the risk reduction approaches is on avoiding harm to the community ("avoidance goals"), whereas the focus in the good promotion approaches is to improve the quality of offenders' life ("approach goals") (Ward & Gannon, 2006).

According to Ward et al. (2007, p. 92), the major aim of treatment is to lead offenders to a different life. Their assumption is that offenders' new life consists of "the basic primary goods, and ways of effective securing them, built into it." Thus, the twin focus approach in therapy with offenders is expected to equip offenders with the necessary internal conditions (i.e., skills, values, beliefs) and external conditions (i.e., resources, social support, opportunities). Within the GLM, these conditions are necessary "for meeting [offenders'] needs in more adaptive way" (Ward & Stewart, 2003, p. 126).

Overall, Ward and Maruna (2007) argue that the twin focus is a realistic aim in correctional practice. They assert that this unique attention to both good promotion and risk reduction "enable the GLM to deal with issues of motivation, identity, and lifestyle" (p. 164). In other words, Ward and his colleagues assume that a rehabilitative treatment with a dual aim maximize the offenders' motivation to be engaged in their change process.

Assumption 4: The Process of Rehabilitation Requires a Construction of Adaptive Narrative (or Personal) Identity

This assumption is based on the view that the construction of a new personal identity is an essential part in the human behavior change process. Accordingly, Ward and Maruna (2007) assume that the reconstruction of identity is a crucial aspect of effective rehabilitation for offenders. In this regard, they define narrative identity as the "stories of past experience and sets of expectation about future experiences and lives . . . [that] both guide the actions of individuals and shape their experiences and lives" (Ward & Marshall, 2007, p. 288). In that sense, the rehabilitative process is considered an opportunity to develop personal stories about the self (Burnett & Maruna, 2006). Overall, Ward et al. (2007) expect that the new adaptive personal identity will promote offenders' sense of meaning and fulfillment, and will enable offenders to stop offending and to abstain from further criminality.

In general, advocates of the GLM perceive the development of an adaptive identity as "a dynamic, interpersonal process" that requires the offenders' commitment or engagement (Ward & Marshall, 2007, p. 295). In their view, such a process "requires the provision of both capabilities and environments that are able to facilitate and sustain offenders' attempts to fashion new lives, new selves" (p. 295). In essence, Ward and his collaborators assume that offenders develop their "new selves" through a self-reflection. That is, they expect that offenders' new adaptive identity will emerge "from the individual's understanding of where he or she is located within [their network of social, cultural and physical] relationships and what particular goals (goods) are most important to him or her" (Ward & Maruna, 2007, p. 163).

Thus, the GLM emphasizes the relationship between offenders' personal identity and their understanding of what establishes a good life. In this regard, "the weightings or priority allocated to specific primary goods is constitutive of an offender's personal identity and spells out the kind of life sought and, relatedly, the kind of person he or she would like to be" (Ward, 2002a, 519; see also McMurran & Ward, 2004). In other words, the concept of personal identity contains and represents the offenders' value commitments and the way these values are expressed in their daily activities and lifestyle (i.e., their deeply held beliefs that govern behavior) (Farmer, Beech, & Ward, 2012). Relatedly, Ward and his colleagues assert that the pursuit of primary goods in functional (or dysfunctional) ways relates to the offenders' adaptive (or maladaptive) narrative identities.

According to Ward and his collaborators, the construction of adaptive narrative identity during the rehabilitative process refers to the ideas of (1) understanding what really matters to offenders and (2) assisting them to resolve difficulties and create a new pro social self-image. In essence, Ward (2002a, p. 522) expects that the rehabilitative process will help offenders to make sense of their "earlier crimes and experience of adversity and [to] create a bridge between their undesirable life and the adoption of new ways of living." In this regard, Wilson and Yates (2009, p. 160) rely on Shadd Maruna's work as the criminological link between "the development of a new narrative of personal identity and desistance from crime among offenders." They consider Maruna's (2001) work as a "ground-breaking study" that influenced the development of the GLM (Ward, 2002a, p. 522; see also Ward & Maruna, 2007). Overall, Maruna's (2001) theoretical perspective is used to support "the utilization of the GLM in treatment" and therefore merits close examination (Wilson & Yates, 2009, p. 160).

In a nutshell, Maruna's theoretical perspective explains the desistance process through changes in individuals' subjective orientations. According to Maruna (2001), cognitive changes are represented by individuals' narrative identity, which consists of the stories that they construct "to account for what they do and why they did it" (p. 40). His assumption is that the self-narratives "act to shape and guide future behavior, as people act in ways that agree with the stories or myths they have created about themselves" (p. 40). Thus, Maruna conducted a study that examined the relationship between the "identity deconstruction" and behavioral change of criminals.

Maruna interviewed 20 offenders who continue to commit crimes ("persistent offenders") and 30 offenders who had long history of persistent criminality but were able to successfully maintain an abstinence from crime ("desistance offenders"[3]). Notably, according to Maruna (2001), persisting and desisting offenders "represent similar individuals in different stages of the process of change" (p. 74). In brief, Maruna concludes that "to desist from crime, ex-offenders need to develop a coherent, prosocial identity for themselves" (p. 8). Specifically, he suggests that the offenders reconstruct their new prosocial identity through the process of using a "redemption script." This script is a method that "allows the person to rewrite a shameful past into a necessary prelude to a productive and worthy life" (p. 87). As opposed to desistence offenders, persistent offenders live their lives according to a "condemnation script" that leads them to "a sense of being doomed or fated to their situation in life" (p. 11).

Maruna (2001) concluded that there are three essential characteristics of offenders' redemption scripts (i.e., of offenders' desisting identity narratives). The first key characteristic is *generative motivations*. This concept refers to the offender's "concern for, and commitment to, future generation" (Farmer et al., 2012, p. 933). In this regard, Maruna argued that offenders with a motivation to promote the well-being of others have a better chance of desisting from crime. That is, because generative motivation equips the offender with a sense of meaning and achievement, relieves their sense of guilt and shame, allows them to gain a legitimate role in society, and assists to maintain their reform efforts. The second characteristic of the redemption script is the notion of a *core-self* (or *real me*). This notion is "explicitly distinct from the party responsible for committing the bulk of crimes in the narrator's past" (Maruna, 2001, p. 131). In other words, the notion of the core-self allows the person to see the way out from the negative situation resulting from crime and to link between this way and a new meaning and purpose in life. The third characteristic of the redemption script is the person's *sense of agency*. This refers to the offender's "strong sense that he or she is in control of his or her destiny" (p. 147). In essence, offenders have a sense of agency when they "do not blame themselves for their problems but hold themselves responsible for the solution to their own problem" (p. 148).

Assumption 5: "Human Beings Are Multifaceted Beings Comprised of a Variety of Interconnected Biological, Social, Cultural and Psychological Systems, and Are Interdependent to a Significant Degree" (Ward & Maruna, 2007, p. 117)

This assumption presents the GLM as an ecological framework to offender rehabilitation. Ecological frameworks highlight the reciprocal relationship between human beings and the social, cultural, and physical contexts in which they live their lives. Specifically, it underscores the notion that "human beings are interdependent and rely on other people and social institutions to function" (Ward, Melser, & Yates, 2007, p. 224). From the GLM perspective, these social and ecological networks play a critical role in offending because they account for goals that individuals seek in life.

In this regard, Ward and Gannon (2006) argue that ecological factors such as social and cultural environment, personal circumstances, and physical environment explain why individuals offend. First, they argue that "early exposure to adverse ecological factors will compromise the basic internal strategies and resources" necessary to achieve primary human goods in acceptable ways (p. 85). Thus, an early exposure to adverse ecological factors results in the person's inability "to secure the primary goods needed for a good life, or secure these goods in an appropriate manner" (p. 85). Second, Ward and Gannon (2006) assert that the person's "current ecology or physical environment is also an important contributor to the etiology" of offending (p. 85). According to this view, the offenders' specific environmental contexts facilitated their way to victims and triggered their dynamic risk factors (Willis & Grace, 2009).

Thus, Ward and Maruna (2007) assert that any offender assessment and treatment that seeks to promote adaptive functioning has "to grasp the specific contexts in which individuals live and the unique challenges they face" (p. 118). They assume that this approach to offender rehabilitation "ensures that the treatment plan and expected outcomes are personally relevant to individual and the contexts in which they live, including the opportunities and limitations that will be present" (Ward et al., 2007, p. 97; see also Langlands et al., 2009; Thakker & Ward, 2010). Overall, thus, Ward and his collaborators argue that relevant, realistic, and successful offender interventions take into account the social, cultural, and physical contexts in which offenders are likely to be released into.

Assumption 6: Risk Is a Multifaceted and Contextualized Concept

This assumption follows the previous assumption. Simply, human beings are conceptualized as multifaceted beings, and, therefore, the risk that they impose on the society should also be viewed as a multifaceted concept. According to this perspective, risk contains "individual, social, physical (situational) and cultural components" (Ward & Maruna, 2007, p. 151). In essence, this perspective views that the meaning of any potential risk factor depends on its specific psychological, cultural and situational contexts.

According to Ward and Maruna (2007), the contextualized concept of risk has "clear etiological and practice implications" (p. 79). First, the GLM explains criminality through individual, social, situational, and cultural factors that block the attainment of primary goods or contribute to attain these goods through offending. These factors can be either dynamic or stable, including an individual's "relatively stable personality traits or feature" (p. 152).

Second, risk as a contextualized concept is assumed to bridge between the relevant risk factors and treatment considerations (Ward et al., 2007). Within the GLM, this means that any offender assessment should "always be contextually and temporally tagged" (Ward & Maruna, 2007, p. 152). In addition, therapists should incorporate the various aspects of risk in offenders' treatment plan.

Assumption 7: "A Treatment Plan Should Be Explicitly Constructed in the Form . . . [That] Take[s] Into Account Individuals' Strengths, Primary Goods and Relevant Environments, and Specify Exactly What Competencies and Resources Are Required to Achieve These Goods" (Ward & Maruna, 2007, p. 119)

This assumption emphasizes the commitment of the rehabilitative process to the offender's agency and autonomy. In general, it means that the therapist and the offender are expected to collaborate in deciding treatment options and in formulating the treatment goals as personally meaningful goals. Thus, within the GLM, such collaboration should lead to a translation of "each individual's preference for certain primary goods . . . into his or her daily routine" (p. 119).

According to Ward and Maruna (2007), "this assumption is both normative and pragmatic" (p. 119). This is a normative assumption because the GLM emphasizes a rehabilitative process that should work with the offenders on their goal achievement. In that sense, it is assumed that a transparent and sensitive rehabilitation process will lead offenders to choose personal change while they exercise their agency and autonomy. According to Ward and his colleagues, this assumption is also pragmatic because a collaborative approach increases the offenders' "interest and motivation to partake in the programme, and to enhance patients' understanding of how addressing treatment needs may be beneficial to them as individuals" (Gannon, King, Miles, Lockerbie, & Willis, 2011, p. 160; see also Ward & Maruna, 2007).

Assumption 8: Rehabilitative Efforts That Secure the Offenders' Human Dignity Are Protected and Promoted by Offenders' Human Rights

This assumption reflects a perspective that politicians, researchers, and other members in the public should secure offenders' right to "redeem themselves and to live worthwhile and better life" (Ward & Birgden, 2007, p. 629). In this regard, Ward and Maruna (2007) argue that the state has a moral and legal obligation "to provide [rehabilitation] to those who want to change their life" (p. 120). According to Ward (2011), this obligation is derived from the notion that every human being should live a dignified life—a life that is "characterized by personal choice and a certain level of well-being" (p. 108). In that sense, a correctional system that follows the notion of human rights should guarantee the access to goods that promote offenders' personal choice and well-being.

Specifically, Ward (2011) argues that the concept of human dignity consists of the "ethical heart of the human rights" (p. 111). This concept is represented by two components: well-being (also called constraint) and freedom (also called empowerment). The well-being component "emphasizes the basic conditions that must be met if people are to live dignity lives" (p. 106). The freedom component "stress the importance of uncoerced choice and freedom of movement for human beings as they go about their lives" (p. 106). Ward and Birgden (2007) argue that these two core components of human dignity can be unpacked into the five human rights objects. In this regard, the component of well-being incorporates the objects of personal security, material subsistence, and elemental equality. Accordingly, the component of freedom incorporates into personal freedom, and social recognition.

According to Ward (2011), the GLM is a rehabilitative model that applies the notion of human rights to offender rehabilitation. First, as a strength-based approach, the GLM "resonates strongly" with a human rights framework (Ward & Birgden, 2007, p. 637). This assertion is based on the assumption that "the acquisition of the capabilities to improve the quality of their own lives and to respect those of others will necessarily involve recognition of the freedom and well-being of other people" (Ward, 2011, p. 113). Second, Ward (2011) argues that the concept of human rights is intended "to safeguard the provision of the social, economic, environmental, and psychological goods necessary for a dignified human life" (p. 107). Therefore, within the GLM, offenders' human rights justify their entitlements to have an "access to primary goods" (p. 112).

Third, the notion of offenders as "simultaneously human rights-violators . . . and human rights holder" justifies the GLM's "dual aims" approach (Ward, 2011, p. 112). That is, the GLM focuses on both risk reduction and good promotion and therefore balances between the safety of the community and the offenders' human dignity (i.e., their well-being and freedom). Fourth, a rehabilitative effort that follows the core human rights values "helps practitioners evaluate all aspects of their work and to consider the ethical implication of rehabilitation" (p. 113). Within the GLM, this refers to offender assessment and treatment that secure offenders' well-being and freedom. Specifically, the practical application of human rights is assumed to facilitate the desired "value-laden process," "dual aims" approach, new personal identity, and collaborative treatment process (see the previous assumptions).

The Etiological Assumptions of the Good Lives Model

Ward and Maruna (2007) also present the etiological assumptions of the GLM. They argue that these assumptions "flow logically" from the above general assumptions and give practitioners and clients a general understanding of the "broad causes of antisocial behavior" (p. 120). In general, Ward and his colleagues do not use terminology of criminological theories to support their explanations of crime. Indeed, Ward and Maruna (2007) provided a rare statement that the GLM follows "the central premise of 'strain theory' . . . that crime might best be understood as the product of obstacles to the pursuit of legitimate goals" (p. 121). Nevertheless, this reliance on the criminological "strain theory" is absent from the other GLM's literature. Moreover, Ward et al. (2012) explicitly rejected "the suggestion that the GLM is a reformulation of the frustration-aggression hypothesis or criminological strain theory" (p. 102).

Overall, although Ward and his collaborators do not follow specific criminological theories, they suggest consistent explanation of the causes of crime. In Ward and Maruna (2007, p. 146), these explanations have roots in the GLM's naturalistic orientation.

> The etiological commitments of the GLM are *general* in form and stem from a naturalistic view of human beings as goal-seeking, culturally embedded animals who utilize a range of strategies to secure important goods from their environment. When the internal or external conditions necessary to achieve values outcomes are incomplete, individuals tend to become frustrated and may engage in antisocial behavior.
>
> *(Ward & Maruna, 2007, p. 124, emphasis in original)*

Specifically, advocates of the GLM present three etiological assumptions. These assumptions explain the relationship between primary goods and offending, the pathways toward primary goods that results in the onset of offending, and the essence of the factors that push individuals to seek their primary goods in socially unacceptable ways. The rest of this section elaborates these three assumptions.

Etiological Assumption 1: "Individuals Seek a Number of Primary Goods in Their Offending" (Ward & Maruna, 2007, p. 154)

According to the GLM, offending occurs when the person fails to obtain primary goods in an effective and non-harmful way. As described above, primary goods consist of 10 groups of self-motivated goals that all humans seek in their life. The GLM thus explains criminality through distortions in the attainment of these highly valued goals. In essence, the GLM's perspective of criminal behavior derives from its perspective of human behavior (Ward & Maruna, 2007).

In general, the GLM explains human behavior as a consequence of the interaction between the individual's biological processes, ecological factors, and psychological functioning (Ward & Gannon, 2006; Ward et al., 2007). According to this perspective, biological processes ("genetic inheritance and brain development") and ecological factors (i.e., "social, cultural, and personal circumstances") have "a significant impact" upon individuals' psychological functioning (Ward et al., 2007, p. 91). Specifically, biology and natural selection explain humans' inherent tendencies to seek out primary goods (Ward & Gannon, 2006). In addition, ecological variables explain the way in which individuals seek the primary goods. These ecological variables include "(a) the actual resources and opportunities available in their social and cultural environment . . . and (b) the set of skills and competencies formed through socialization in these contexts" (p. 85).

Essentially, the dynamic interaction between biological and ecological factors results in the establishment of the human psychological functioning (i.e., psychological processes and outcomes). According to the GLM, this functioning consists of three "interlocking neuropsychological systems: motivation/emotional, perception and memory, and action selection and control systems" (Ward et al., 2007, p. 91). Within the GLM, these three systems can be viewed as "underpinning human behavior and provide a scientific basis for understanding how and why people act as they do" (p. 91).

Accordingly, the GLM explains criminality through this psychological functioning of individuals. The etiological assumption is that "when individuals are unable to secure a number of primary human goods, constructing meaningful and purposeful lives is frustrated and wellbeing is compromised" (Langlands et al., 2009, p. 120). In such case, the attainment of primary goods in socially unaccepted ways (i.e., inappropriate secondary goods) will inevitably result in low levels of wellbeing. According to the GLM, this psychological outcome is expected because the consequence of the socially unaccepted activities will eventually be an unpleasant sanction.

Thus, according to the GLM, the causes of criminality do not reside in the primary goods but rather in the activities or strategies individuals use to obtain the primary goods (i.e., in the secondary goods). Within the GLM, these activities and strategies represent flaws in the way individuals live their life (daily activities, functioning, behaviors) or the way they plan to live their life (i.e., their life plan) (Purvis, Ward, & Willis, 2011). Specifically, the GLM suggests "four major types of problems that can be evident in the person's way of living or life plan: capacity, scope, means and coherence" (p. 8).

The first major type of problem occurs when the individual *lacks the capacity* to secure the primary goods (Ward & Maruna, 2007; Yates et al., 2010). This might be due to certain conditions in the individual's *internal* or *external* capacity (Ward & Stewart, 2003). Lack of internal capacity to secure goods refers to problems in the person's internal conditions such as lack of appropriate skills (or low level of such skills), lack of belief or motivation to attain goods, or lack of relevant knowledge for this task. Accordingly, lack of external capacity to secure primary goods refers to problems in the person's external conditions such as scarce social support, resources, or environmental opportunities.

The second major type of problems in the individuals' way of living and life plan is their *degree of scope*. These problems occur because important primary goods are neglected. Such lack of scope appears "when an individual's good life plan is too narrow, with important goods left out" (Yates et al., 2010, p. 41). According to Purvis et al. (2011), "problems in scope can simply be caused by a disinterest in some goods; however a lack of scope is usually caused by problems in capacity" (p. 9). The third major type of problems occurs when individuals use *inappropriate or harmful means* to secure the primary goods. In such cases, the use of counterproductive strategies results in failure to obtain the desired goods.

The fourth type of problems resides in the *coherence of goods*. This kind of problem occurs "when a conflict exists between two primary goods and/or the ways the individual goes about obtaining them" (Yates et al., 2010, p. 41). Ward and Maruna (2007) assume that individuals with a conflict "among the goods being sought . . . experience acute psychological stress and unhappiness" (p. 124). According to Purvis et al. (2011), there are two types of potential problems in the coherence of goods: a problem in the horizontal coherence and a problem in the vertical coherence (see also Ward & Fortune, 2013). A problem in the horizontal coherence refers to conflicts in "the extent to which goods are explicitly related to each other in a mutually consistent and enabling way" (p. 10). A problem in the vertical coherence refers to conflict in the hierarchical clarity among goods. That is, individuals do not understand "which goods are most important to them and have the most priority in their life" (p. 10). The problem arises because this understanding "should govern what activities the individual engages in on a daily basis" (p. 10).

Overall, criminological research affords "some (weak) support for the link between the attainment of each of the primary goods and criminal behavior" (Ward & Maruna, 2007, p. 156). In this regard, advocates of the GLM draw support for this etiological assumption from "the vast amount of work on human needs, subjective well-being, quality of life, and personal strivings" (p. 157). In essence, rooted in a scientific approach to human conduct, they argue that the literature on the non offender population "is clearly relevant" to offenders (p. 157). Ward and Maruna (2007) assert that this literature provides strong evidence that offenders' "levels of well-being and happiness are linked to personal goals and their achievement" (p. 158).

Etiological Assumption 2: Criminogenic Needs Are "Internal or External Obstacles That Frustrate and Block the Acquisition of Primary Human Goods" (Ward & Maruna, 2007, p. 123)

According to this etiological assumption, criminogenic needs explain the relationship between risk factors and primary human goods. Within the GLM, criminogenic needs are dynamic risk factors that signal the obstacles that exist while individuals aim to obtain primary goods (Ward & Maruna, 2007; Whitehead et al., 2007). These dynamic risk factors "are directly linked to basic needs distortion and the absence of the internal [(e.g., skills and capabilities)] and external [(e.g., opportunities and supports)] conditions necessary for a person to lead a fulfilling life" (Ward & Stewart, 2003, p. 138). Importantly, "criminogenic needs are not actually needs themselves" (p. 138). Rather, they are "symptoms or markers of ineffective or inappropriate strategies employed to achieve" the primary goods (Wilson & Yates, 2009, p. 159; see also Ward & Brown, 2004). In other words, within the broader strength-based framework, criminogenic needs are indicators of maladaptive functioning.

Thus, when a criminogenic need is detected, it means a flaw exists in an individual's attempts to secure primary human goods. Specifically, criminogenic needs "arise from frustrated basic human needs and involve the acquisition of proxy goals and their accompanying dysfunctional beliefs and behavioral strategies" (Ward & Stewart, 2003, p. 138). In this regard, the GLM hypothesizes that individuals commit criminal offenses because they "lack the capabilities to realize valued outcomes, in [their] environment, in personally fulfilling and socially acceptable ways" (Ward & Brown, 2004, p. 249; see also McMurran & Ward, 2004).

Overall, Ward and Maruna (2007, p. 160) suggest three advantages of the GLM's conceptualization of criminogenic needs. First, it explains "how human needs and other motivational constructs are related" to dynamic risk factors. Second, it accounts "for the relationship between various criminogenic needs." Third, it provides an understanding of "how criminogenic needs results in criminal activities."

Etiological Assumption 3: "There Are Different Routes to Offending, Direct and Indirect" (Ward & Maruna, 2007, p. 154)

Although the first two etiological assumptions concern goals in the context of attaining primary and secondary goods, this etiological assumption concerns goals in the context of offense progression (Yates et al., 2010). From the GLM perspective, offending occurs when an individual translates primary goods into concrete forms. At this translation point, the potential offender seeks human primary goods with means and strategies that are related to offending. Advocates of the GLM argue that when this occurs, there are "two routes to the onset of offending, direct and indirect" (Ward & Gannon, 2006, p. 86).

The individual follows a *direct route* to offending when he or she "seeks certain types of goods directly through criminal activity" (Ward & Maruna, 2007, p. 122). Specifically, a central flaw in the direct route is the use of inappropriate or harmful strategies to obtain a particular primary good or goods (Ward et al., 2012; Yates et al., 2010). For example, "an individual lacking the competencies to satisfy the good of intimacy with an adult might instead attempt to meet this good through sexual offending against a child" (Ward et al., 2012, p. 96).

According to the GLM, this direct route to offending can be either an explicit or an implicit way to achieve the human primary goods. That is, individuals might follow the direct route to offending without being aware that their actions are meant to attain the primary goods.

The second route to offending is the *indirect route*. The individual follows the indirect route to offending when he or she "does not have the direct intention to offend, but has problems in the pursuit of other goods which eventually culminate in an offence" (Willis & Ward, 2013, pp. 307–308). In this regard, Ward and Gannon (2006, p. 86) explain that "the pursuit of a good or set of goods is frustrated in some way . . . [and] this may create a ripple effect in the person's personal circumstances." Accordingly, "these unanticipated effects increase the chances to offend" (p. 86). For example, an individual can value both the primary goods of relatedness and excellence in work. However, long shifts in work can lead to a breakdown in the person's intimate relationship (the good of relatedness). Then, an indirect route to offending is evident when this breakdown leads to the use of alcohol to cope with emotions and, eventually, to a loss of control in certain situations, which might result in an offense.

According to Ward and Maruna (2007), the assumption that there are two distinctive routes to offending is based on the research on the offense process in sexual offending. In this regard, Ward and his colleagues developed the Self-Regulation Model (SRM) (Ward & Hudson, 1998, 2000; Ward, Louden, Hudson, & Marshall, 1995). In the general literature, the term *self-regulation* refers to "the process whereby [individuals] personally activate and sustain behaviors, cognitions, and affects that are systematically oriented toward the attainment of goals" (Schunk et al., 2014, p. 379). Accordingly, the SRM was developed "to account for the variety of offense pathways evident in sexual offenders and to provide therapists with a more comprehensive treatment model" (Ward & Maruna, 2007, p. 158).

In recent years, the Self-Regulation Model was revised (SRM-R) and explicitly incorporates elements from the GLM (Yates & Ward, 2008; Yates et al., 2010). The purpose of this integration was to situate the SRM within a rehabilitation theory. According to Yates et al. (2010), this combination presents "a comprehensive, integrated approach to the treatment and supervision of sexual offenders" (p. ix). In this regard, Ward and Gannon (2006, p. 87) provide two reasons why the GLM endorses the SRM. First, the SRM emphasizes the "role of agency and self-regulation in the offense process." Thus, similar to the GLM, the SRM promotes the idea that offenders seek to achieve specific goals and correspond "to the meaning of certain events in light of their values and knowledge." Second, similar to the GLM, the SRM is based on the assumption that "the offense process can only be adequately understood in light of the interaction between individuals and their relevant circumstance." Taken together, the integration between the GLM and SRM (SRM-R) aims to account for the causal mechanism associated with offenders' regulation strategies and therefore merits close examination.

The SRM-R posits four pathways to offending and 10 phases in the offense process[4] (Ward & Maruna, 2007; Yates et al., 2010). In essence, the SRM-R "describes the *offense progression* or the chain of events that occurs during a specific sexual offense or series of offenses, in order to identify the cognitive, behavioral, emotion, and situational factors that culminate in offending" (Yates et al., 2010, p. 44, emphasis in original). Basically, the SRM-R suggests that the onset of offending is composed of (1) the type of offense-related goals and (2) the particular strategy individuals use to achieve those goals.

First, the SRM-R suggests two types of *offense-related goals*: the avoidance orientation to offending (i.e., avoidance goals) and the approach orientation to offending (i.e., approach goals) (Ward & Gannon, 2006; Ward et al., 2007). The avoidance orientation to offending is represented by individuals who "define their targets in terms of situations they want to avoid or behavior they wish to cease enacting" (Mann, Webster, Schofield, & Marshall, 2004, p. 66). In this regard, the offense-related avoidance goals guide behavior "to avoid or prevent an undesired outcome, specifically with respect to sexual offending" (Yates et al., 2010, p. 47).

In contrast to the avoidance orientation, the approach orientation to offending is represented by individuals who "define their goals in terms of what they want to achieve" (Mann et al., 2004,

p. 66). This type of offense-related goals guides behavior "to achieve a desired state or outcome during the offense progression" (Yates et al., 2010, p. 47). Importantly, Ward and his collaborators propose that there is a close link between the GLM and these two types of offense-related goals. They argue that the approach orientation corresponds to the direct route to offending and the avoidance orientation corresponds to the indirect route to offending (Lindsay et al., 2007; Ward & Gannon, 2006; Ward et al., 2007).

Second, the SRM suggests that the *strategies* individuals select to achieve their goals relate to their self-regulation style and capacity. In brief, according to the SRM-R, individuals seek their goals with one of the three self-regulation styles: under-regulation, mis-regulation, and intact self-regulation. Under-regulation involves the failure of individuals "to control their behavior in the service of their goals" (Ward & Gannon, 2006, p. 88). Distinctively, mis-regulation involves "misguided or counter-productive" attempts to control behavior (i.e., an inappropriate selection of strategy to cause a failure in behavioral control) (Yates et al., 2010, p. 44). Last, the intact self-regulation style allows individuals to function as desired. That is, individuals who use this style are able to control their behavior in achieving desired goals.

In addition to these self-regulation styles, the SRM suggests that individuals vary in their self-regulation capacity (Ward & Gannon, 2006). That is, "individuals utilize either *passive* or *active* strategies in the offense progression in order to achieve an offense related goal" (Yates et al., 2010, p. 49, emphasis in original). The passive strategies "involve situations in which an individual fails to implement any strategies to prevent offending" (p. 49). Accordingly, the active strategies "are used in the offense progression to prevent an offense from occurring" (p. 49).

Overall, according to the SRM-R, the combinations of type of offense-related goals and self-regulation style and capacity create four distinctive pathways to offending. First, the *avoidant-passive* pathway combines the avoidance orientation to offending and the under-regulation style. Individuals who follow this pathway wish to refrain from offending (avoidance goals) but lack the necessary strategies to achieve this goal or, alternatively, employ insufficient strategies to prevent offending (under-regulation style). In this regard, the under-regulation style to prevent offending leads individuals to "ignore offense-related desires or urges" or refrain from using "any strategies in the situation" (passive strategies) (Yates et al., 2010, p. 49).

Second, the *avoidant-active* pathway combines the avoidance orientation to offending and the mis-regulation style. Individuals who follow this pathway wish to refrain from offending (avoidance goals) and try to employ strategies to prevent an offense from occurring (active strategies). However, individuals in this pathway use ineffective strategies that may increase the risk of offending (mis-regulation style).

Third, the SRM-R suggests the *approach-automatic* pathway that combines the approach orientation to offending and the under-regulation style. These individuals welcome the opportunity to offend (approach goals) but "fail to control their behavior during the offense progression" (under-regulation style) (Yates et al., 2010, p. 53). Within this pathway, triggers in a specific situation evoke relatively automatic response to engage in offending. However, this approach-automatic response involves an "unsophisticated and rudimentary" plan to offend and mostly relies on offenders' impulses (passive strategies) (Kingston, Yates, & Firestone, 2012, p. 216).

Fourth, the *approach-explicit pathway* combines the approach orientation to offending and the intact self-regulation style. Individuals who follow this pathway seek the opportunity to offend (approach goals) and "demonstrate few or no deficits in their ability to monitor, evaluate, and modify their behavior in order to achieve [this] goal (intact self-regulation style) (Yates et al., 2010, p. 54). Within this pathway, individuals "explicitly plan to offend and then implement strategies to achieve this goal" (active strategies) (p. 49).

As mentioned above, in addition to the four pathways to offending, the SRM-R identifies 10 distinctive phases in the offense process. In their book, Ward and Maruna (2007) mentioned the SRM's phases but did not elaborate them. In fact, within the GLM literature, these phases are discussed only in relation to sexual offending (e.g., Ward & Hudson, 1998, 2000; Webster, 2005; Yates et al., 2010). Therefore, it is unclear whether advocates of the GLM view this mechanism of offense as a feature that can be generalized to the broader offender population. Anyway, a complete discussion of the GLM requires an introduction of this mechanism. Thus, the following paragraphs provide a short description of the SRM-R's 10 phases as presented in Yates et al. (2010).

In brief, according to the SRM-R, an individual's background and predisposed factors influence the person's specific response to a life event (phase 1). In this pre-offense phase, an individual "evaluates or interprets [those factors] within the context of his own experience, cognitive schemas, and the like" (Yates et al., 2010, p. 56). At some point in the person's life, an event may trigger either a desire to respond through offending or a desire to achieve a particular primary good (phase 2). This event (and its subjective interpretation) triggers some type of desire (e.g., deviant, aggressive, or appropriate desire) (phase 3). Then, "once a life event triggers a desire, the individual will establish [pro social or offense-related] goals in response to the desire" (p. 57) (phase 4). If an offense-related goal was established, the type of goal (i.e., avoidant or approach goals) "determines the offense pathway followed during the commission of the offense, in conjunction with the strategies selected to achieve the goal [(i.e., passive or active strategies)]" (p. 58) (phase 5).

In the offense process, the particular offense pathway leads to an opportunity to achieve the desired goals (i.e., the primary human goods) (phase 6). When such opportunity occurs, "the individuals engage in specific behaviors that lead to offending" (p. 59) (phase 7). Next, "during the commission of the sexual offense, the individual achieves his offense-related goal of offending and may also attain non-offending good lives goals, albeit in harmful and maladaptive ways" (p. 59) (phase 8). Immediately after the commission of the offense, the individual experiences reinforcement contingencies that result in a self-evaluation of his behavior (phase 9). This evaluation leads the individual to "develop, refine, and formulate future intentions and expectations with respect to offending" (p. 60) (phase 10). In addition, the SRM-R posits that "individuals may also formulate future plans, intentions, and expectations with respect to achieving their good lives plans" (p. 61).

Overall, the empirical research that investigated the elements of the SRM focused exclusively on offenders who were convicted of a sexual offense (for a review of this literature, see Kingston et al., 2012; Webster, 2005). Moreover, these empirical evaluations have not directly tested the assumption that sexual offending is related "to inappropriate pursuit of human goods" (Ward & Maruna, 2007, p. 158). In this regard, Webster (2005) argues that this literature provides little evidence that the SRM "can be used to guide an offender's treatment" (p. 1177; see also Kingston et al., 2012). Thus, at present, the studies that have examined the SRM provide only evidence for "the relationship between approach goals and personal goals" (Ward & Maruna, 2007, pp. 158–159).

Regarding the assumption that there are direct and indirect routes to offending, advocates of the GLM rely on the empirical support provided by Purvis (2006, 2010) (Lindsay, Ward, Morgan, & Wilson, 2007; Ward & Maruna, 2007; Ward & Gannon, 2006). This empirical preliminary work examined this assumption by investigating 26 child molesters. Purvis's qualitative analysis showed that individuals achieve different primary goods in different ways. First, she concluded that "most participants showed a combination of the three types of means in their lives": (1) "means that were unrelated to offending," (2) "means that formed an indirect pathway to offending," and (3) "means that formed a direct pathway" (Purvis et al., p. 11). Then, she argued that understanding the person's "overall picture" can help to disentangle this combination of means and reveal whether he or she is in a direct or indirect route to offending (Ward & Maruna, 2007, p. 159). However, similar to other studies that examined the routes to offending, this study focused only on sex offenders and therefore "cannot be easily generalized to the wider offender population" (Ward & Maruna, 2007, p. 159). Thus, at this stage, the empirical support for the direct and indirect routes to offending is considered "weak and tentative" (p. 159).

Relatedly, Ward and his colleagues also refer to Mann et al. (2004) as an empirical study that supported the approach-goal orientation over avoidance-goal orientation (Ward & Maruna, 2007; Willis & Ward, 2013). In this study, Mann et al. (2004) compare a relapse prevention program with an approach-focused orientation (24 sex offenders) to a relapse prevention program with an avoidant-focused orientation (23 sex offenders). Notably, the same therapists delivered both programs. According to Mann et al. (2004), at the end of treatment, therapists used their clinical opinion to rate each participant "for how genuinely motivated he was to live in the future without offending" (p. 69). A statistical analysis of this rating revealed that the approach group was perceived to be more significantly motivated than the avoidance group. However, the therapists also reported that compared to participants in the avoidant-oriented group, participants in the approach-oriented group "may leave treatment not being clear about the nature of their individual risk factors" (p. 72).

Conclusion

This chapter followed the development of the GLM of offender rehabilitation from the early 2000s to the present day. During this period, the legitimacy of rehabilitation continued to be reaffirmed by the ongoing scientific evidence. As discussed in Chapters 3 and 4, the theoretical framework of the RNR model dominated correctional policy and practice. In this context, Ward and his colleagues developed the GLM as a comprehensive rehabilitative framework. Although admitting that their approached emerged "out of the RNR model of evidence-based correctional practice" (Ward & Maruna, 2007, p. 143), they constructed the GLM as an alternative (or at least supplement) approach to rehabilitation.

As described in the first section of this chapter, the GLM was influenced by humanistic perspectives and the research in applied positive psychology and strength-based practice. As noted, the GLM's theoretical foundation consists of two levels of assumptions: (1) eight general assumptions "that specify the values that underlie rehabilitation practice and the kind of overall aims that clinicians should be striving for"; and (2) three etiological assumptions "that serve to explain offending and identify its functions" (Ward & Maruna, 2007, p. 111).

Overall, the GLM is best considered a strength-based rehabilitation theory that emphasizes offender motivation. That is, the GLM is designed to be "responsive to offenders' particular interests, abilities and aspirations, and directs practitioners to develop intervention plans that assist offenders in acquiring the capabilities and accessing the relevant internal and external resources to achieve goals which are personally meaningful" (Casey, Day, Vess, & Ward, 2013, pp. 41–42).

The next chapter sets forth the correctional framework of the GLM. For this task, Ward and his colleagues translated the above general and etiological assumptions into practical implications. This discussion presents Ward and his colleagues' concrete suggestions for program aims and orientation, offender assessment, intervention planning, intervention content, and program delivery. In addition, the next chapter examines the empirical status of the GLM's correctional approach to offender rehabilitation.

Notes

1. The official website of the Good Lives Model (www.goodlivesmodel.com) consists of a list of 224 publications that researchers and scholars have produced on the GLM (last updated on 04.09.2017). According to this list, Tony Ward is the single or coauthor in 124 of the 224 publications.
2. In the early 2000s, when Ward and his colleagues introduced the GLM, they suggested only nine primary goods. According to Purvis et al. (2011), Purvis's work enabled them to expand this list. First, based on Purvis (2006), they were convinced to separate the goods of relatedness and community. Second, based on Purvis (2010), they argued that the good of excellence in play and work can also be presented as two independent goods.
3. In Maruna (2001), desistance offenders are those who reported an abstinence from crime for two to three years.
4. The original SRM posited a nine-phase process.

References

Burnett, R., & Maruna, S. (2006). The kindness of prisoners: Strengths-based resettlement in theory and in action. *Criminology & Criminal Justice*, *6*, 83–106.

Casey, S., Day, A., Vess, J., & Ward, T. (2013). *Foundations of offender rehabilitation*. New York, NY: Routledge.

Cullen, F. T., & Gendreau, P. (2000). Assessing correctional rehabilitation: Policy, practice, and prospects. In J. Horney (Ed.), *Policies, processes, and decisions of the criminal justice system: Criminal justice 2000* (Vol. 3, pp. 109–175). Washington, DC: U.S. Department of Justice, National Institute of Justice.

Day, A., & Ward, T. (2010). Offender rehabilitation as a value laden process. *International Journal of Offender Therapy and Comparative Criminology*, *54*, 289–306.

Deci, E. L., & Ryan, R. M. (2000). The "what" and "why" of goal pursuits: Human needs and the self-determination of behavior. *Psychological Inquiry*, *11*, 227–268.

Deci, E. L., & Ryan, R. M. (2008). Facilitating optimal motivation and psychological well-being across life's domains. *Canadian Psychology*, *49*, 14–23.

Duckworth, A. L., Steen, T. A., & Seligman, M. E. (2005). Positive psychology in clinical practice. *Annual Review of Clinical Psychology*, *1*, 629–651.

Farmer, M., Beech, A., & Ward, T. (2012). Assessing desistance in child molesters: A qualitative study. *Journal of Interpersonal Violence*, *27*, 930–950.

Gannon, T., King, T., Miles, H., Lockerbie, L., & Willis, G. M. (2011). Good lives sexual offender treatment for mentally disordered offenders. *British Journal of Forensic Practice*, *13*, 153–168.

Gendreau, P. (1996). The principles of effective intervention with offenders. In A. T. Harland (Ed.), *Choosing correctional interventions that work: Defining the demand and evaluating the supply* (pp. 117–130). Thousand Oaks, CA: Sage.

Jorgensen, I. S., & Nafstad, H. E. (2004). Positive psychology: Historical, philosophical, and epistemological perspectives. In P. A. Linley & S. Joseph (Eds.), *Positive psychology in practice* (pp. 15–34). Hoboken, NJ: John Wiley & Sons.

Kingston, D. A., Yates, P. M., & Firestone, P. (2012). The self-regulation model of sexual offender treatment: Relationship to risk and need. *Law and Human Behavior*, *36*, 215–224.

Langlands, R., Ward, T., & Gilchrist, L. (2009). Applying the good lives model to male perpetrators of domestic violence. *Behaviour Change, 26,* 113–129.

Latessa, E. J., Cullen, F. T., & Gendreau, P. (2002). Beyond correctional quackery: Professionalism and the possibility of effective treatment. *Federal Probation,* 66, 43–49.

Laws, D. R., & Ward, T. (2011). *Desistance from sexual offending: Alternatives to throwing away the keys.* New York, NY: Guilford Press.

Lindsay, W., Ward, T., Morgan, T., & Wilson, I. (2007). Self-regulation of sex offending, future pathways and the good lives model: Applications and problems. *Journal of Sexual Aggression, 13,* 37–50.

Linley, P. A., & Joseph, S. (2004). Applied positive psychology: A new perspective for professional practice. In P. A. Linley & S. Joseph (Eds.), *Positive psychology in practice* (pp. 3–12). Hoboken, NJ: John Wiley & Sons.

Lösel, F. (1995). The efficacy of correctional treatment: A review and synthesis of meta-evaluations. In J. McGuire (Ed.), *What works: Reducing reoffending—guidelines from research and practice* (pp. 79–111). New York, NY: John Wiley.

MacKenzie, D. L. (2000). Evidence-based corrections: Identifying what works. *Crime and Delinquency, 4,* 457–471.

Mann, R. E., Webster, S. D., Schofield, C., & Marshall, W. L. (2004). Approach versus avoidance goals in relapse prevention with sexual offenders. *Sexual Abuse: A Journal of Research and Treatment, 16,* 65–75.

Maruna, S. (2001). *Making good: How ex-convicts reform and rebuild their lives.* Washington, DC: American Psychological Association.

Maslow, A. H. (1954). *Motivation and personality.* New York, NY: Harper & Row.

Maslow, A. H. (1962). *Toward a psychology of being.* New York, NY: Van Nostrand-Reinhold.

McGuire, J. (2002). Integrating findings from research reviews. In J. McGuire (Ed.), *Offender rehabilitation and treatment: Effective programmes and policies to reduce re-offending* (pp. 4–38). Chichester: Wiley.

McMurran, M., & Ward, T. (2004). Motivating offenders to change in therapy: An organizing framework. *Legal and Criminological Psychology, 9,* 295–311.

Porporino, F. J. (2010). Bringing sense and sensitivity to corrections: From programmes to "fix" offenders to services to support desistence. In J. Brayford, F. Cowe, & J. Deering (Eds.), *What else works? Creative work with offenders* (pp. 61–85). Cullompton, Devon: Willan.

Purvis, M. (2006). *Good lives plans and sexual offending: A preliminary study.* Unpublished doctoral dissertation, University of Melbourne, Australia.

Purvis, M. (2010). *Seeking a good life: Human goods and sexual offending.* Saarbrücken, DE: Lambert Academic Press.

Purvis, M., Ward, T., & Willis, G. (2011). The good lives model in practice: Offence pathways and case management. *European Journal of Probation, 3*(2), 4–28.

Rogers, C. R. (1959). A theory of therapy, personality, and interpersonal relationships, as developed in the client-centered framework. In S. Koch (Ed.), *Psychology: A study of a science: Vol. 3.* New York, NY: McGraw-Hill.

Rogers, C. R. (1961). *On becoming a person: A therapist's view of psychotherapy.* Boston, MA: Houghton Mifflin.

Schunk, D. H., Meece, J. L., & Pintrich, P. R. (2014). *Motivation in education: Theory, research, and applications* (4th ed.). Boston, MA: Pearson.

Seligman, M. E. P. (2002). *Authentic happiness.* New York, NY: Free Press.

Seligman, M. E. P., & Csikszentmihalyi, M. (2000). Positive psychology: An introduction. *American Psychologist, 55,* 5–14.

Serran, G., & Marshall, W. (2010). Therapeutic process in the treatment of sexual offenders: A review article. *The British Journal of Forensic Practice, 12*(3), 4–16.

Thakker, J., & Ward, T. (2010). The good lives model and the treatment of substance abusers. *Behaviour Change, 27,* 154–175.

Thakker, J., Ward, T., & Chu, C. M. (2013). The good lives model of offender rehabilitation: A case study. In W. O'Donohue (Ed.), *Case studies in sexual deviance* (pp. 79–101). London: Routledge.

Ward, T. (2002a). Good lives and the rehabilitation of offenders: Promises and problems. *Aggression and Violent Behavior, 7,* 513–528.

Ward, T. (2002b). The management of risk and the design of good lives. *Australian Psychologist, 37,* 172–179.

Ward, T. (2011). Human rights and dignity in offender rehabilitation. *Journal of Forensic Psychology Practice, 11,* 103–123.

Ward, T. (2013a). Addressing the dual relationship problem in forensic and correctional practice. *Aggression and Violent Behavior, 18,* 92–100.

Ward, T. (2013b). The heart of offender rehabilitation: Values, knowledge, and capabilities. In L. A. Craig, L. Dixon, & T. A. Gannon (Eds.), *What works in offender rehabilitation: An evidence based approach to assessment and Treatment* (pp. xxi–xxii). West Sussex: John Wiley & Sons.

Ward, T., & Birgden, A. (2007). A Human rights and correctional clinical practice. *Aggression and Violent Behavior, 12,* 628–643.

Ward, T., & Brown, M. (2004). The good lives model and conceptual issues in offender rehabilitation. *Psychology, Crime, & Law, 10,* 243–257.

Ward, T., & Fortune, C. A. (2013). The good lives model: Aligning risk reduction with promoting offenders personal goals. *European Journal of Probation, 5,* 29–46.

Ward, T., & Gannon, T. A. (2006). Rehabilitation, etiology, and self-regulation: The comprehensive good lives model of treatment for sexual offenders. *Aggression and Violent Behavior, 11,* 77–94.

Ward, T., & Hudson, S. M. (1998). The construction and development of theory in the sexual offending area: A metatheoretical framework. *Sexual Abuse: A Journal of Research and Treatment, 10,* 47–63.

Ward, T., & Hudson, S. M. (2000). A self-regulation model of relapse prevention. In D. R. Laws, S. M. Hudson, & T. Ward (Eds.), *Remaking relapse prevention with sex offenders: A sourcebook* (pp. 79–101). Thousand Oaks, CA: Sage.

Ward, T., Louden, K., Hudson, S. M., & Marshall, W. L. (1995). A descriptive model of the offence chain for child molesters. *Journal of Interpersonal Violence, 10,* 452–472.

Ward, T., Mann, R., & Gannon, T. (2007). The good lives model of offender rehabilitation: Clinical implications. *Aggression and Violent Behavior, 12,* 87–107.

Ward, T., & Marshall, W. L. (2007). Narrative identity and offender rehabilitation. *International Journal of Offender Therapy and Comparative Criminology, 51,* 279–297.

Ward, T., & Maruna, S. (2007). *Rehabilitation: Beyond the risk paradigm.* New York, NY: Routledge.

Ward, T., Melser, J., & Yates, P. M. (2007). Reconstructing the risk need responsivity model: A theoretical elaboration and evaluation. *Aggression and Violent Behavior, 12,* 208–228.

Ward, T., & Stewart, C. A. (2003). Criminogenic needs and human needs: A theoretical model. *Psychology, Crime, & Law, 9,* 125–143.

Ward, T., Yates, P. M., & Long, C. A. (2006). *The self-regulation model of the offence and relapse process, volume II: Treatment.* Victoria, BC: Pacific Psychological Assessment Corporation.

Ward, T., Yates, P. M., & Willis, G. M. (2012). The good lives model and the risk-need-responsivity model: A critical response to Andrews, Bonta, and Wormith (2011). *Criminal Justice and Behavior, 39,* 94–110.

Webster, S. D. (2005). Pathways to sexual recidivism following treatment: An evaluation of the Ward and Hudson self-regulation model of relapse. *Journal of Interpersonal Violence, 20,* 1175–1196.

Whitehead, P., Ward, T., & Collie, R. (2007). Time for a change: Applying the good lives model of rehabilitation to a high-risk violent offender. *International Journal of Offender Therapy and Comparative Criminology, 51,* 578–598.

Willis, G. M., & Grace, R. C. (2009). Assessment of community reintegration planning for sex offenders: Poor planning predicts recidivism. *Criminal Justice and Behavior, 36,* 494–512.

Willis, G. M., Prescott, D. S., & Yates, P. M. (2013). The good lives model in theory and practice. *Sexual Abuse in Australia and New Zealand, 5*(1), 3–9.

Willis, G. M., & Ward, T. (2013). The good lives model: Does it work? Preliminary evidence. In L. Craig, L. Dixon, & T. Gannon (Eds.), *What works in offender rehabilitation: An evidence-based approach to assessment and treatment* (pp. 305–317). London: Wiley-Blackwell.

Wilson, R. J., & Yates, P. M. (2009). Effective interventions and the good lives model. *Aggression and Violent Behavior, 14,* 157–161.

Yates, P. M., Prescott, D. S., & Ward, T. (2010). *Applying the good lives and self regulation models to sex offender treatment: A practical guide for clinicians.* Brandon, VT: Safer Society Press.

Yates, P. M., & Ward, T. (2008). Good lives, self-regulation, and risk management: An integrated model of sexual offender assessment and treatment. *Sexual Abuse in Australia and New Zealand: An Interdisciplinary Journal, 1,* 3–20.

Ziegler, D. J. (2002). Freud, Rogers, and Ellis: A comparative theoretical analysis. *Journal of Rational-Emotive and Cognitive-Behavior Therapy, 20*(2), 75–91.

6

BUILDING GOOD LIVES THROUGH CORRECTIONAL INTERVENTION

Since first proposed by Ward and Stewart in 2003, advocates of the Good Lives Model (GLM) have explored the implications of the model's general and etiological assumptions (e.g., Ward & Stewart, 2003a, 2003b, 2003c; Ward & Mann, 2004; Ward & Gannon, 2006; Ward & Maruna, 2007). Initially, scholars tended to provide only general guidance for applying the GLM in correctional assessment and treatment. In recent years, however, Ward and his colleagues have presented more systematic directions outlining how to integrate the GLM into treatment programs (Willis, Yates, Gannon, & Ward, 2012; Purvis, Ward, & Shaw, 2013; Purvis, Ward, & Willis, 2011; Yates, Kingston, & Ward, 2009; Yates, Prescott, & Ward, 2010). They note that the effectiveness of a treatment program "rests on the correct operationalization of the GLM in practice" (Willis, Ward, & Levenson, 2014, p. 61). By contrast, they warn that a "misguided operationalization of the GLM could result in ineffective treatment and ultimately higher rates of reoffending" (p. 61; see also Willis et al., 2012).

In brief, within the GLM, the role of correctional interventions is to assist offenders in achieving their primary goods in both personally meaningful and prosocial ways. Specifically, the therapist should help each offender to construct a highly individualized "Good Life Plan" (GLP). This plan consists of the distinctive conditions that are likely to lead the individual toward happiness, a good life, and well-being. According to the GLM, following such a GLP is also "likely automatically to eliminate or modify commonly targeted dynamic risk factors (i.e., criminogenic needs)" (Ward & Maruna, 2007, p. 108).

Ward and his colleagues have given explicit directions on how to deliver an effective GLM treatment. They have used the conceptual underpinnings of the GLM to provide guidance in five distinctive domains of treatment interventions: the program aims and orientation, assessment, intervention planning, treatment content, and delivery of service (Willis et al., 2012). In addition, Willis et al. (2014) took this effort a step forward in their investigation of the operationalization of the GLM in North America treatment programs. In this study, they present a protocol that contains 11 "items," which describe the "GLM consistent practice" in each of the five domains.

Essentially, this current chapter presents Willis et al. (2014)'s 11 items as 11 correctional principles for effective GLM interventions. These items can also be seen as principles because they represent the GLM's overarching correctional framework. In this regard, each of them is consistent with the GLM's general and etiological assumptions. Moreover, each of them is consistent with the literature that suggests general treatment implications of the GLM.

Overall, this chapter consists of six sections. The first five sections discuss the five distinctive domains of treatment interventions. The first domain is *programs aims and orientation* (the first section). This domain includes only one principle (principle 1) that emphasizes the "dual aims" of the GLM's interventions (i.e., the focus on both risk reduction and good promotion). The second domain (the second section), *offender assessment*, includes three principles (principles 2, 3, and 4). These principles direct the assessment of empirically informed static and dynamic risk factors (principle 2), offenders' heavily weighted primary goods (principle 3), and offenders' full aspects of primary and secondary goods (principle 4). The third domain (the third section), *intervention planning*, guides the development of intervention plans to achieve the primary goods prosocially (principle 5). The fourth domain (the fourth section) includes three principles that direct the *intervention content* (principles 6, 7, and 8). This domain contains directions for integrating the GLM's dual aims approach in treatment (principle 6), and guides the attention to the full range of primary goods (principle 7) and offender's social ecology (principle 8). The fifth domain (the fifth section), *program delivery*, presents three principles that direct the therapists' approach to treatment (principles 9 and 10), and the delivery of an individualized services in each domain (principle 11).

The sixth and last section in this chapter evaluates the empirical status of the GLM. This section focuses on the studies that have evaluated the impact of correctional interventions that followed the GLM. The analysis in this section encompasses studies that have explicitly integrated the GLM as an overarching framework.

Domain 1: Program Aims and Orientation

Principle 1: "The Aims of the Treatment Program Include Both Risk Reduction and Well-Being Enhancement" (Willis et al., 2014, p. 63)

As noted, the first correctional principle guides the programs' aims and orientation. In essence, this principle follows the GLM's literature that "a central aim of rehabilitation according to the GLM is to build client capacity to live a satisfying life that does not involve harming others" (Willis et al., 2012, p. 127). In other words, this principle applies the assumption that addressing both good promotion and risk reduction will result in more effective treatment programs. Specifically, principle 1 directs correctional interventions to manage the balance between the avoidance goal of reducing risk and the approach goal of promoting personal goods. According to Ward and Maruna (2007), such balance is crucial because "erring on the side of either goal can result in disastrous social and personal consequences for the therapist and the client" (p. 125; see also Ward, Mann, & Gannon, 2007).

In this regard, Ward and Maruna (2007) argue that a therapeutic effort that focuses only on increasing the well-being of offenders may "result in happy but dangerous individual" (p. 125). According to Willis et al. (2012), this undesired outcome contrasts "the very reason treatment programs exist" (p. 127). Yates et al. (2010) share this notion in their practical guide for clinicians. In the opening page, they state that "the ultimate goal of sexual offender treatment is to prevent a recurrence of re-offending" (p. 3).

By contrast, Ward and Maruna (2007) argue that correctional interventions should not solely focus on managing the individuals' risk because it can "lead to punitive practices and a defiant or disengagement client" (p. 125). According to this perspective, the focus only on reduction offenders' risk is unethical and ineffective. Thus, in practice, interventions with such focus have a limited ability to deal with issues of motivation, identity, and lifestyle. That is, they have difficulties to persuade offenders to reorient their core values and, subsequently, to change their criminal lifestyle.

In this context, principle 1 directs correctional interventions to communicate the dual aims of treatment to the offenders. According to Willis et al. (2012), such communication should result in offenders who enter treatment "with the knowledge that the program is designed to assist them develop skills to live a personally meaningful, offense-free life" (p. 128). For example, correctional interventions can communicate such knowledge through "the name of a program and any associated workbooks, treatment consent forms or contracts, and any other introductory material clients receive that describe the program" (Willis et al., 2014, p. 63).

Domain 2: Offender Assessment

Principle 2: Treatment Programs Should Assess the Offender's Level of Risk, Therapeutic Needs (i.e., Treatment Targets), and Responsivity Factors

Principle 2 is the first principle (out of three) that guides correctional programs in the domain of offender assessment. In general, assessment in the GLM refers to any activity that intends to discover more about the offender. Within this context, principles 2 to 4 guide interventions in collecting information that will eventually be integrated into offenders' intervention plan. Specifically, principle 2 directs correctional interventions to use empirically supported measures to identify offenders' (1) level of risk, (2) therapeutic needs, and (3) responsivity factors.

First, this principle advises correctional interventions to use empirically validated risk assessment instruments to identify offenders' static and dynamic risk factors. According to Willis et al. (2012), the use of such assessment tools assists interventions to determine "the intensity of intervention required" (p. 128). In this regard, Ward and his colleagues recommend that intervention use empirically validated risk assessment instruments (Ward & Maruna, 2007; Langlands, Ward, & Gilchrist, 2009; Yates et al., 2010). Specifically, Yates et al. (2010) suggest that "to be effective, treatment intensity (i.e., duration, number, and frequency of contact hours), should be higher for those clients who are at higher risk to re-offend, while minimal or no intervention should be applied to clients at lower risk to re-offend" (p. 105). According to these authors, information about offenders' level of risk allows correctional agencies to allocate their limited treatment resources in more accurate ways. In addition, such information assists to avoid the negative consequences of intervention that provides intensive service to low-risk offenders (e.g., increasing their tendency to recidivate).

Second, principle 2 also directs correctional interventions to use empirically supported assessment tools that were designed to identify offenders' criminogenic needs. These needs are considered dynamic risk factors that, when changed, are associated with changes in the tendency to recidivate. Within the GLM's approach to assessment, criminogenic needs are "range riders"—indicators of "problems in the way goods are being sought" (Ward & Maruna, 2007, p. 164). In other words, correctional interventions should assess the problems that undermine "the offenders' ability to live a good life" and "the severity of these problems" (Ward & Gannon, 2006, p. 89).

Third, principle 2 directs correctional interventions to use assessment tools that provide information about offenders' responsivity factors. These factors encompass any factor that influences offenders' engagement and participation in treatment, or factors that facilitate offenders' capacity to change (e.g., level of cognitive functioning, mental health, attachment problems, motivation, learning styles, personality disorder, culture). According to the GLM's correctional framework, interventions should consider the influence of responsivity factors on risk factors and criminogenic needs (Ward & Maruna, 2007). For example, Yates et al. (2010) assert that the assessment of static and dynamic risk factors serves only as "a baseline level of risk" for determining treatment intensity (p. 113). That is, the final decision about the adequate treatment intensity for offenders depends on their responsivity factors.

In practice, the GLM encourages correctional interventions to use any structured or unstructured assessment that provide reliable information about responsivity issues. For example, Yates et al. (2010) specify assessment tools and scales that provide measures of cognitive flexibility (e.g., Wisconsin Card Sort), learning disability (e.g., identifying Attention Deficit Hyperactivity Disorder), personality (e.g., Millon Clinical Multiaxial Inventory), and psychopathic traits (e.g., Psychopathy Checklist-Revised).

Principle 3: GLM-Informed Assessment Should Identify Offender's Heavily Weighted Primary Goods

Principle 3 is the second principle that directs correctional programs in offender assessment. This principle focuses on identifying what the offender values most in life (i.e., the "heavily weighted primary goods" or "overarching goods"). In essence, principle 3 is based on the assumption that offenders' heavily weighted primary goods reflect their values and priorities. Thus, in addition to *risk, needs,* and *responsivity,* the GLM's correctional framework directs interventions to assess offenders' *priorities* (Ward & Maruna, 2007). This fourth area of assessment includes offenders' "own goals, life priorities, and aims for the intervention" (Ward & Mann, 2004, p. 604). This assessment allows interventions "to understand how a client prioritizes and operationalizes the primary human goods" (Ward & Maruna, 2007, p. 132). Within the GLM, this assessment provides essential knowledge for interventions because offenders' heavily weighted primary goods are designated to build the basis of their future GLP.

According to principle 3, the offenders' heavily weighted primary goods are assessed through "exploring offenders' future goals and priorities as well as goods evident in offending" (Willis et al., 2014, p. 63). In this regard, Ward and Maruna (2007) suggest "two primary procedures" for identifying these goods (p. 132). The first primary procedure is to observe offenders' behavior and infer "what kind of goals are evident in their offense-related actions and general life functioning" (pp. 132–133). According to this procedure, knowledge about offenders' general life functioning reveals their "aspirations, future plans, and fundamental commitments" (Yates et al., 2010, p. 67). Accordingly, knowledge about offenders' offense-related behavior involves "the examination of the individual's offense patterns and associated developmental history" (pp. 66–67).

The second primary procedure for identifying heavily weighted primary goods is clinical interview. The need for clinical interview arises because offenders do not explicitly express themselves in terms of their life goals (Willis, Prescott, & Yates, 2013). Rather, they typically respond to questions about their priorities in life in terms of the activities and strategies they use. Therefore, advocates of the GLM recommend to conduct a semi-structured interview with "a series of increasingly detailed questions about the activities, situations, and experiences that are important to the [offender] in his life and the activities into which he puts his energies on a regular basis" (Yates et al., 2010, p. 66). Importantly, assessors are instructed to identify "the goods evident in client's responses through reflective listening, paraphrasing, and summarizing" (Willis et al., 2012, p. 129). According to Willis et al. (2012), assessors can complete this procedure by using questionnaires such as the Personal Concerns Inventory or the Quality of Life Inventory. In addition, these scholars call attention to and favor the use of the structured interview developed by Yates, Kingston, and Ward. This structured interview was designed to assess offenders' heavily weighted goods.[1]

Recently, Purvis et al. (2013) suggested an assessment guideline for practitioners (The Primary Human Goods—Acquisition Analysis) (PHG-AA). This structured guideline assists practitioners to evaluate how offenders secure each of their primary goods, and should be completed every six months. In this regard, the PHG-AA provides a table that summarizes this assessment. In this table, the assessor should identify the relative weight of each primary good (High/Moderate/Low) and highlight whether each good was previously implicated in offending. In addition, the assessor should evaluate the offenders' achievement of each primary goods according to the following levels: optimal, progressing, active, inactive, blockages, and disengaged.

Principle 4: Correctional Interventions Should Assess the Full Aspects of Primary Goods

Principle 4 directs correctional interventions toward a complete understanding of offenders' primary human goods. Within the GLM's correctional framework, this assessment should provide a reliable description of offenders' good lives conceptualization. In general, this assessment should identify "what the individual has done in the past, or does presently, to achieve the primary good" (Willis et al., 2012, p. 130). Specifically, an assessment of each offender's good lives conceptualization seeks three types of understanding: (1) what the offender "values in life," (2) how the offender's "valued goods were associated with offending," and (3) what problems the offender "is currently encountering while implementing his good life plan" (Yates et al., 2010, p. 84).

In practice, the assessment of the full aspects of primary goods should be built on the information about offenders' most heavily weighted primary goods. In other words, the weight and value that the offender ascribes to each of the 10 primary goods is the basis of this individual's good lives conceptualization. Therefore, within the GLM's correctional framework, interventions should assess offenders' full aspects of the primary goods (principle 4) during the assessment of their heavily weighted primary goods (principle 3). In this regard, according to Ward and his colleagues, the assessment process in principle 4 should gain information about three elements: (1) the offender's specific secondary goods, (2) the relationship between the offender's primary goods and offending, and (3) the problems in the offender's GLP.

First, the assessment of offenders' good lives conceptualization involves an identification of the concrete activities and strategies that offenders use to obtain their primary goods (i.e., to identify secondary goods). This element of the assessment is expected to provide information about strategies that "have worked well" to achieve offender's primary good and strategies that "have not worked to achieve the good" (Willis et al., 2012, p. 130). Such assessment should also classify the offender's strategies to those that inflicted harm to society (i.e., inappropriate secondary goods), and those that have not resulted in harm to others (i.e., appropriate secondary goods). Importantly, the assessment of appropriate secondary goods is crucial because these goods represent the offender's strengths. Thus, at the end of the assessment process, the GLM will integrate these strengths as "skills upon which treatment can build" (see principle 6) (p. 130).

Second, the assessment of offenders' good lives conceptualization should examine the offense progression. Within the GLM, this means to provide information about "the role that each primary good plays in offending" (Yates et al., 2010, p. 76). That is, principle 4 directs therapists to investigate how offenders' "actions at the time of the offense related to their pursuit of primary goods" (Willis et al., 2010, p. 130). This element is important for correctional interventions because some of these instrumental means "also represent the client's dynamic risk factors for offending" (Yates et al., 2010, p. 85). In practice, this examination of offense progress also requires the therapist to identify whether offenders seek the primary goods by using a direct or indirect route to offending. As mentioned in the previous chapter, a direct route to offending occurs when the person intentionally uses inappropriate strategies to attain the primary good, whereas an indirect route to offending is evident when the person's problems to attain the goods lead to the offense.

Another aspect of the relationship between primary goods and offending relates only to correctional interventions that integrate the GLM and the Self-Regulation Model (i.e., GLM/SRM-R). Within the GLM/SRM-R, the goal of assessing the offense progression is to determine the offense pathway. In this regard, the GLM's literature often refers to a structured assessment protocol that was developed by Yates et al. (2009) (Willis et al., 2012, Willis et al., 2014; Yates et al., 2010; Kingston, Yates, & Olver, 2014). This assessment protocol includes seven items that evaluate the offense-related goals (avoidant/approach goals) and offense strategies (active/passive). Specifically, the assessment of the offense-related goals includes four items: (1) "the individual's desire to prevent or avoid offending," (2) "the individual's overall attitude toward offending," (3) "cognitive distortion in the offense progression," and (4) "post offense evaluation of self, the offending, and the behavior enacted during the offense" (Yates et al., 2010, pp. 96–97). In addition, the assessment of offense strategies includes three items: (5) "the individual's self-regulation skills," (6) "the degree of planning the offense," and (7) "the individual's control, or perceived control, over his offending behavior" (p. 100). Overall, this assessment protocol should integrate the assessments of offense-related goals and offense strategies into four combinations: avoidant-passive, avoidant-active, approach-automatic, and approach-explicit (see the previous chapter for more details on these combinations).

The third element in the assessment of offenders' good lives conceptualization involves an identification of any activities and strategies that can lead to problems in attaining each primary good (Willis et al., 2012). Within the GLM, this assessment examines the specific flaw in the offenders' GLP (i.e., problems in the way individuals live their life or plan to live their life). Thus, principle 4 directs interventions to assess the four following considerations (see the previous chapter for more details). First, whether the person lacks the internal capacity or external opportunities to secure the primary goods. Second, whether the person's GLP is restricted in scope (i.e., neglects important primary goods). Third, whether the person's GLP involves inappropriate and/or counterproductive means. Fourth, whether lack of coherence in the person's GLP creates conflict among goods (i.e., "situations in which the client indicates priorities or goals that cannot co-exist easily") (Yates et al., 2010, p. 83).

Domain 3: Intervention Planning

Principle 5: Correctional Interventions Should Construct Individualized Intervention Plans

Once all assessment has been completed, the GLM's correctional framework directs interventions to construct individualized intervention plans. In essence, principle 5 is about translating the information from the assessments to intervention goals with the offender. Such translation is assumed to provide "greater understanding of the offender's commitments, priorities, desires, motivations, challenges and strengths" (Purvis et al., 2011, p. 15). Thus, at this point in the intervention, the therapist should evaluate the accumulated information and develop a comprehensive intervention plan that "explicitly and actively helps the client to attain what he values most in life" (Yates et al., 2010, p. 115). According to Willis et al. (2012), such "GLM-based intervention plans provide a roadmap for working toward the dual aims of treatment—enhanced well-being and reduced risk—and form the basis of a future-oriented GLP, the life toward which clients will work during treatment" (p. 131).

Within the GLM's literature, the concept of intervention plans has four basic characteristics. First, intervention plans describe the factors that made each offender susceptible to committing an offense (Yates et al., 2010). Second, intervention plans are "oriented toward understanding what is important to clients in their lives and what their strengths and areas of need are" (p. 146). Third, the elements of intervention plans are constructed in a collaborative manner with the offender (Ward & Maruna, 2007; Ward & Mann, 2004). Fourth, the construction of intervention plans is a dynamic process. That is, therapists should refine the offenders' intervention plan "as treatment progresses and as clients build strengths and competencies to satisfy primary goods in prosocial ways" (p. 131). Overall, as mentioned above, intervention plans serve "as a basis of a Good Life Plan produced at the end of the program" (Willis et al., 2014, p. 64).

More specifically, within the GLM's correctional framework, intervention plans aim to elaborate the following elements: "dynamic factors, responsivity factors, treatment components, primary and secondary goods, and potential flaws in the client's attempts to achieve [the primary and secondary goods]" (Yates et al., 2010, p. 146). In this regard, Ward and his colleagues suggest that the construction of an intervention plan involves several distinctive phases (e.g., Ward & Gannon, 2006; Ward & Maruna, 2007; Yates et al., 2010). For the purpose of clarity, this section describes the six phases suggested by Yates et al. (2010).[2]

In phase 1, the construction of intervention plans begins with "the inclusion of primary human goods that are important to the client and that he actively seek out or what he would like to have in his life" (Yates et al., 2010, p. 128). In other words, within the intervention plans, the heavily weighted primary goods represent the person's fundamental commitments and "how [this] person sees his or her world" (i.e., his or her personal identity) (Ward & Maruna, 2007, p. 135).

Phase 2 involves evaluations of "the secondary (instrumental) goods associated with obtaining primary goods—that is, the means by which the individual goes about obtaining those things that are important in his life" (Yates et al., 2010, p. 130). In essence, this phase focuses on acknowledging, reinforcing, and incorporating the offender's strengths into the therapeutic process (Willis et al., 2012, p. 132). Thus, therapists and offenders should identify and evaluate the socially excepted activities and strategies that offenders used to acquire primary goods (i.e., the appropriate secondary goods). In practice, these strengths are used as the building blocks of the intervention plan (Ward & Gannon, 2006, p. 90).

In phase 3, the therapist and offender should evaluate the problems "that are evident in the client's good life plan" (Yates et al., 2010, p. 131). In the intervention plan, such analysis consists of both problems that are not related to offending and problems that are more directly related to offending (e.g., criminogenic needs). Within this evaluation, "flaws in the individual's good life plan are also identified, helping all parties to better understand the specific problems—i.e., scope, means, conflict, or capacity—that the client experiences in implementing the plan, since these flaws may lead to offending" (p. 131).

Phase 4 involves "understanding all clinical phenomena implicated" in offending (Yates et al., 2010, p. 132). Based on the information gained from the assessments, the intervention plan should explain "the causal connections between the Good Lives plan, criminogenic needs (i.e., problems in the internal and external conditions), offending route [(i.e., direct or indirect link to offending)], and the person's psychosocial development" (Ward & Gannon, 2006, p. 90).

Phase 5 in the development of intervention plans "involves identifying the context and environment in which the client is living or will be living upon completion of treatment" (Yates et al., 2010, p. 133). According to Ward and Gannon (2006), "the key factors to consider are the interests and preferences of the offender, the competencies they need, the opportunities for work and leisure etc., resources that are available (e.g., training schemes, interest groups), the attitudes and supportiveness of the local community, and possible living arrangements" (p. 90).

In phase 6, the therapist and offender discuss all the evaluations conducted in the previous phases and construct an agreed-upon individualized treatment plan. In this regard, Yates et al. (2010, p. 116) recommend to set up the formal treatment plan according to the following five parts: (1) "a description of a specific concern or treatment area"; (2) "a carefully stated [specific, measurable, attainable, realistic, and time-limited] goal"; (3) "a handful of strategies for achieving the goal"; (4) "a description of who is responsible for each of the strategies"; (5) "operational definitions of progress in these areas that includes specific, measurable indicators."

More specifically, according to Yates et al. (2010, pp. 134–135), the collaborative approach should lead to the construction of a treatment plan with the following elements: (1) "intensity (duration and frequency of contact) of treatment based on risk assessment"; (2) "dynamic risk factors"; (3) "responsivity factors and comprehensive plans to address [the dynamic risk factors]"; (4) "specific treatment components required, based on assessed criminogenic needs"; (5) "treatment targets based on dynamic risk factors"; (6) "treatment targets based on the offense pathway(s) and self-regulation styles and issues,"[3] or on the particular route to offending (direct/indirect); (7) "treatment targets based on primary and secondary goods and flaws in good lives plans"; (8) "existing strengths on which treatment will build"; (9) "specific skills and strategies to be developed in collaboration with the client, timeframes to re-visit, and/or revised treatment goals"; (10) "objective, operationalized indicators of treatment progress."

In recent years, advocates of the GLM have presented two management tools that aim to assist programs in analyzing offenders' current life and past offending for constructing intervention plans. First, Purvis et al. (2011) developed the offender's individual GLM Mapping Table. This documentation tool aims to translate the data from the assessments into "workable intervention targets" (p. 15). The GLM Mapping Table includes four main columns that summarize the data for each primary good. These columns present the evaluations of (1) whether the offender consider this good as a heavily weighted good, (2) the offender's internal and external strengths (capabilities) and weaknesses (obstacles) (four sub-columns in the table), (3) the type of means the offender uses (appropriate/inappropriate), and (4) the relationship between offender's behavior and offending (direct, indirect, protective, or unrelated). See Thakker, Ward, and Chu, 2013 for a detailed example of how correctional interventions should use this table in a specific case. In addition, see Purvis et al. (2013) for a more recent version of this table.

The second management tool is the GLM Analysis Table. This table was designed to assist in summarizing the analyses of the following aspects (Purvis et al., 2011, p. 16): (1) "issues related to the offender's previous and current life plan, including pathways to offending"; (2) "the offender's most pressing individual criminogenic needs, that is, those internal obstacles (and his stage of change in reference to each) and external obstacles that impede his pro-social securing of goods"; (3) "the level of scope present in the offender's life (and distinction between those goods that are secured pro-socially and those that are sought via inappropriate means, or not sought at all)"; (4) "the nature and degree of horizontal conflict" ("discrepancy between his behaviour and the actual desired outcome"; and (5) "the level of vertical coherence of the offender's current life plan (making sure to cross-check with the offender's previous life plan at the time of his offending)."

Domain 4: Intervention Content

Principle 6: All Program Components/Modules/Assignments Should "Attend to Goods Promotion Alongside Risk Reduction." The End Product of the Therapeutic Process Should Be a Future-Oriented Good Lives Plan (Willis et al., 2014, p. 64)

Principle 6 is one of the three correctional principles that guide the content of treatment programs. According to this principle, the content of the therapeutic process should promote offenders' psychological well-being alongside the goal of reducing their likelihood to reoffend (i.e., consistent with the intervention's dual aims). Specifically, the therapeutic process is expected to address both goals that aim to realize desired situations (i.e., approach goals) and avoid undesired outcomes (i.e., avoidant goals). Importantly, principle 6 directs treatment programs to take a strength-based approach to correctional rehabilitation. In practice, it means that the content of treatment programs should be built around the offender's approach goals. That is, according to principle 6, the "goal of each component/module/assignment are framed using approach goals . . . and linked to the fulfillment of primary goods" (Willis et al., 2014, p. 64). In this regard, the end product of such treatment process should be a "component/module/assignment of a program [that] involves clients consolidating their Good Life Plan" (p. 64).

Overall, treatment ends when offenders are ready to live a fulfilling life. According to Ward and Mann (2004), such end point depends on two broad therapeutic outcomes. First, "offenders must construe themselves as people who can secure all the important human goods in socially acceptable and personally rewarding ways" (p. 609). In other words, offenders are expected to experience an increase in their self-efficacy "with respect to managing risk and implementing [their] good life plan" (Yates et al., 2010, p. 271). In essence, this also includes the establishment of a new personal identity as non offenders.

The second necessary treatment outcome for living a fulfilling life is to fix the flaws in offenders' GLP. That is, at the end of treatment, offenders should obtain "the scope, capacities, coherence, and strategies necessary for a healthy personal good lives plan" (Ward & Mann, 2004, p. 609). In practice, this means a therapeutic process that equips offenders with a comprehensive understanding of the relationship between their life goals and offending. In addition, it means that the treatment process equips offenders with the ability to translate their understanding into activities and strategies that secure their life goals. Specifically, Ward and Stewart (2003a) argue that the typical content of such treatment programs should involve "the acquisition of cognitive skills, values that support prosocial behaviour, social and intimacy skills, empathy for others, vocational and educational competencies, and the motivation to live a different kind of life" (p. 141).

Overall, principle 6 also directs the therapeutic efforts to reach a specific final stage: the development and implementation of offender's GLP. Indeed, the GLP is a central theme in the GLM correctional framework. In this regard, Ward and Maruna (2007) argue that "for normative and practical reasons, individual clients need *only* undertake those treatment activities that provide the ingredients of their own particular [Good Lives] plan" (p. 129; emphasis added). For example, when treatments addresses the offenders' dynamic risk factors (i.e., criminogenic needs), "the goal is always to reinforce and strengthen a client's existing skills and to develop new skills and capacities, in the context of" their GLP (Yates et al., 2010, p. 160). Moreover, when treatment programs use Cognitive-Behavioral Therapy, this therapeutic method should be "wrapped around" the goal of individuals' good fulfilling (Ward et al., 2007; Willis et al., 2012). That is, because the goal within the GLM's framework "is always to create new skills and capacities within the context of individuals' good lives plans and to encourage fulfillment through the achievement of human goods" (Ward & Mann, 2004, p. 613).

Thus, at this final stage of a treatment program, therapist and offender should be ready for writing down the individualized future-oriented GLP. According to Yates et al. (2010), the construction of the GLP has two "unique goals": (a) "the development and implementation of a comprehensive 'map for living' that includes all the ingredients of a good life; and (b) the identification of strategies needed to respond to problematic situations that may disrupt or threaten the client's functioning in other areas of his life" (p. 246).

In this regard, Yates et al. (2010, p. 247) also summarize the eight elements that should be included in the offenders' post-treatment GLP: (1) "primary goods identified in assessment and treatment as important to the client and specific plans to attain them"; (2) "secondary goods that represent the ways primary goods will be attained"; (3) "specific indicators (to the client and to others) that goods are being acquired and his good life plan is being implemented effectively"; (4) "specific indicators (to the client and to others) when the good life plan may be threatened or in jeopardy, and plans assembled to address this issue"; (5) "similarly, specific indicators (to the client and to others) of flaws in the good life plan, and plans to address these, as well"; (6) "specific ways that self-regulation will be attained and maintained, including skills developed and rehearsed during treatment"; (7) "specific risk factors and plans to manage risk"; and (8) "specific indicators (to the client and others) that risk may be re-emerging or becoming acute (i.e., warning signs)."

In addition, Yates et al. (2010) provide the Good Lives/Self-Regulation Plan Template as a tool for practitioners. This template guides the intervention in how to translate the therapeutic process into a GLP. Within this template, the analysis of each primary goods inserts to six columns with the following headlines: (1) "ways to obtain goods," (2) "how I will know I am getting these,"

(3) "problems I will need to manage," (4) "risk factors," (5) "warning signs for risk," and (6) "self-regulation style" (p. 272).

Principle 7: Program Content Should "Attend to the Full Range of Primary Goods" (Willis et al., 2014, p. 64)

Principle 7 is the second principle that guides the content of treatment. Within the GLM's correctional framework, this principle advises treatment programs to address the full range of primary goods. According to Ward et al. (2007), such an approach is needed because "a flourishing, satisfying life requires the presence of all the goods in some form" (p. 98). In addition, such attention to the full range of primary goods is important because a specific program component (e.g., module assignment) focuses only on "one or more primary goods" (Willis et al., 2014, p. 64; see also Ward et al., 2007). In this regard, principle 7 directs interventions to attend also the primary goods that are not targeted directly by the program components. For example, Willis et al. (2014) suggest that such attention to the less desired primary goods can be achieved "through the format of group session" (p. 64).

Principle 8: Programs Should Promote Offenders' "Social Capital Through Attending to [Their] Social Ecology" (Willis et al., 2014, p. 64)

Principle 8 guides correctional programs in how to prepare post–treatment maintenance and supervision. In general, this principle outlines the practices needed to assist offenders to "re-enter and reintegrate into the community in ways that promote their well-being and in ways that reduce their risk to re-offend" (Yates et al., 2010, p. 281). Specifically, it emphasizes the importance of conducting a post-treatment assistance to ensure that the offenders' GLP is translated into their lives in the community. In brief, *release planning* and *community supervision* involve "both carrying out court orders and supporting efforts at rehabilitation simultaneously and in equal measure" (p, 279). Accordingly, *post-treatment maintenance* is considered "an essential part of treatment that assists clients to integrate and entrench progress made during more formal treatment" (p. 178).

Similar to other parts in the GLM's therapeutic framework, post-treatment maintenance and supervision should build "upon clients' values, interests, and primary goods in addition to addressing and monitoring risk" (Yates et al., 2010, p. 277). In other words, "it is essential that maintenance and supervision focus on assisting clients to implement their goods and develop positive approach goals in addition to manage risk" (p. 284). In practice, it means that the post-treatment services should "actively assist clients to reinforce and entrench self-regulation skills and strategies not only to manage risk, but in the service of implementing their good lives plans" (p. 291).

According to principle 8, treatment programs should "anticipate the social and personal environment into which clients will most probably be released so as to best prepare for their transition into the community" (Yates et al., 2010, p. 285). Such preparations include a GLP that contains "emergency instructions and well-rehearsed strategies that are designed to help clients react quickly and adaptively to threats" to their GLP (i.e., potential solutions when things go wrong) (p. 285). In addition, the preparations for post-treatment supervision include "monitoring and reinforcing clients' progress and the implementation of effective self-regulation skills and good lives plans, along with providing assistance to clients to actively achieve their goals to manage risk" (i.e., monitoring and reinforcing when things go right) (p. 290).

In practice, treatment programs have to ensure that offenders' release plans are available to the community supervision agent, the case management team, and other support persons. In addition, Ward and his colleagues argue that a major challenge in the post-treatment mainte- nance and supervision is to ensure the availability of environmental resources and support that offenders need for implementing their GLP. That is, the human services in the post-treatment maintenance and supervision are expected to "explicitly create opportunities for clients to attain important primary goods in their lives and to apply their self-regulation skills to attaining these" (p. 291).

In this regard, Willis et al. (2012) suggest that the involvement of "multidisciplinary team mem- bers (i.e., correctional workers, nurses, health care workers, therapeutic activity workers) is crucial in ensuring the necessary environmental conditions are in place, as is establishing the external conditions and opportunities to ensure that clients can attain primary goods" (p. 137). Moreover, according to Yates et al. (2010), some aspects of offenders' functioning "are best addressed by ser- vices and workers outside the immediate therapy team" (p. 285). Such external assistance can be provided by offenders' peers, significant others, teachers, chaplains, employers, social workers, and recreation instructors.

Domain 5: Program Delivery

Principle 9: Therapists Should "Approach Clients in a Manner That Acknowledges Their Status as Fellow Human Beings, of Equal Intrinsic Value" (Willis et al., 2014, p. 64)

Principle 9 is one of the three principles (principles 9, 10, and 11) that direct therapists and other correctional personnel (e.g., parole and probation officers) in the domain of program delivery (Willis et al., 2012; Willis et al., 2014). In general, within the GLM's correctional framework, principle 9 guides therapists to adopt a positive approach to rehabilitation. According to this principle, therapists should approach offenders with attitude and language that convey respect. In addition, therapists should display characteristics that facilitate ethical and effective therapy (Willis et al., 2014; Willis & Ward, 2010). Overall, Ward and Maruna (2007) argue that such positive therapeutic approach results in strong therapeutic alliance and therefore effective treatment programs.

Principle 9 thus advises therapists to find ways to overcome their tendency to condemn offend- ers for their harmful acts (Ward et al., 2007) and to approach offenders as "people like us" (Willis et al., 2012, p. 136). As Serran and Marshall (2010) note, practice that conveys dignity and respect "tells the clients that they are valued and accepted" (p. 6). Within the GLM's correctional frame- work, Ward and Maruna (2007) argue that offenders should "warrant our respect for their capacity to change and the fact that their offending is directly or indirectly associated with the pursuit of the ingredients of a good life" (p. 125; see also Ward & Stewart, 2003a). In this regard, Willis et al. (2012) suggest that therapists should address responsively issues with a respect to offenders and their circumstances. For example, therapists ought to express a "respect for individuals' history and past selves, which is in keeping with cultural and social perspectives that place great value on the past and its meaning" (Ward et al, 2007, p. 95).

Within this general attitude toward offenders, principle 9 also instructs therapists to use certain therapeutic language. As Ward and Maruna (2007) argue, "the kind of language associated with GLM interventions should be future-oriented, optimistic and approach-goal focused" (p. 127). Thus, in correctional programs, "language associated with avoidance goals should be changed to language associated with approach goals" (Ward & Mann, 2004, p. 613). For example, GLM's treatment programs should rename the following concepts: "intimacy building" instead of "intimacy deficits," "treatment need" instead of "dynamic risk factor," and "self-management" instead of "relapse prevention" (Ward & Maruna, 2007; Ward & Mann, 2004).

Another aspect of principle 9 deals with the characteristics that therapists need to possess in order to facilitate therapeutic changes. According to Willis et al. (2014), these characteristics include "warmth, empathy, praise, some directedness and no confrontation" (p. 64; see also Ward & Birgden, 2009; Ward et al., 2007; Ward & Maruna, 2007). Specifically, within the positive psychological approach, therapeutic *warmth* "is displayed as acceptance, caring and support, and encourages clients to examine their problem behavior" (Serran & Marshall, 2010, p. 5). Accordingly, treating offenders with *empathy* "refers to the ability of the therapist to understand and respond emotionally to the client" (p. 5). Next, the provision of *praise* (or rewards) to offenders involves "the therapists offering verbal encouragement to clients for small steps toward whatever goal was being sought" (Marshall, 2005, p. 114). In addition to warmth, empathy, and praise, some degree of *directiveness* is important because it equips offenders with alternatives ways to handle situations. According to Serran and Marshall (2010), such a directive approach "includes encouraging clients to practice skills outside the treatment session . . . and helps clients develop problem solving skills" (p. 6).

The last characteristic that is mentioned in principle 9 is a non confrontational therapeutic style. By contrast, a confrontation style in treatment is defined by "aggressive, critical, hostile, and sarcastic behavior" (Marshall et al., 2011, p. 68; see also Serran & Marshall, 2010). According to McMurran and Ward (2004), therapists' use of confrontation "removes autonomy from the client" because it "presents the client with the problem and prescribes the therapy that the client should undertake" (p. 8). That is, such practice does not involve a collaborative therapeutic effort. In addition, under such therapeutic style, offenders may experience their treatment as a punishment rather than an opportunity for constructing a better life.

Principle 10: Therapists Should Deliver Programs With a "Collaborative and Transparent Approach to Assessment, Intervention Planning, and Intervention Content" (Willis et al., 2012, p. 136)

Principle 10 directs therapists to seek collaboration with offenders in every aspect of program delivery. In essence, this collaborative approach "involves a commitment from the therapist to working transparently and respectfully" (Ward & Maruna, 2007, p. 131). Within the GLM's theoretical framework, this approach conveys an ethical commitment to offenders' agency and autonomy (Willis et al., 2012).

In practice, offenders who have experienced a collaborative approach in programs are expected to recognize how the therapeutic process respects their values and aims to promote their life goals. According to Ward and his colleagues, such recognition leads to a strong therapeutic alliance between therapists and offenders. In addition, Ward and Maruna (2007) argue that when offenders experience a therapeutic process that is relevant to their life, they tend "to engage enthusiastically in treatment" (p. 134). Moreover, according to Ward and Mann (2004), this perception of relevancy is also "associated with reduced risk of future offending" (p. 606).

Specifically, principle 10 directs therapists to use a collaborative approach in assessment, intervention plan, and intervention content. First, a collaborative approach in the assessment process requires an open discussion about the assessments' outcomes and its therapeutic consequences. In practice, it means that the therapist should work with the offender "to define together the nature of the client's problems and to agree on a process for working toward solutions" (Ward & Mann, 2004, p. 607). Ward and Mann (2004) argue that a collaborative approach to assessment can "lead a client to start thinking about change or to gain insight into problems not previously recognized" (p. 604). Ward et al. (2007) content that such an approach during the assessment process also leads to a stronger therapeutic alliance and a "subsequent positive effect on motivation and retention in treatment" (p. 96).

Second, as mentioned in principle 5, the collaborative and transparent approach has an important role in the development of an intervention planning. According to this perspective, offenders and therapists should collaborate in the development of treatment targets and therapeutic content. As noted by Ward and his colleagues, such collaborative approach to treatment planning serves as a motivational factor that assists offenders to "undertake treatment" (Willis et al., 2012, p. 131). In addition, they argue that a collaborative work on offenders' final good life plan results in a stronger therapeutic alliance (Ward et al., 2007; Ward & Maruna, 2007; Yates et al., 2010).

Principle 11: The "Intensity, Content, and Process of Intervention [Should Be] Individually Tailored" (Willis et al., 2014, p. 65)

Principle 11 is the last principle that directs the GLM's program delivery. This principle emphasizes "the importance of tailoring interventions to each client's unique intervention plan" (Willis et al., 2012, p. 137). In essence, principle 11 follows the GLM's perspective that treatment process is an "exploratory process in which clients are active participants, and the therapist is generally a guide" (p. 137). Specifically, this principle of program delivery elaborates the individualistic aspects of (1) the intensity of interventions, (2) the content of the intervention plan, and (3) the therapeutic process.

First, Willis et al. (2014) suggest that "the intensity and content of interventions [should be] individually tailored according to each client's intervention plan" (p. 65). According to this perspective, the intensity of treatment depends on the value offenders ascribe to the particular primary good. For example, "a client valuing relatedness who has poor interpersonal skills receives a higher intensity of interventions designed to satisfy this good compared with a client who doesn't place as much emphasis on interpersonal relationships and/or has well-developed interpersonal skills" (p. 65).

Second, as Ward and Maruna (2007) observe, the "therapeutic tasks within standard program should be shaped to suit the person in question based on their own life plan" (e.g., variation in homework tasks) (p. 126). Thus, Willis et al. (2014) argue that "clients [should] only receive those interventions directly related to their intervention plan" (p. 65). Essentially, during the intervention, therapists should update the offenders' intervention plan in a way that reflects their individual progress toward the GLP.

Third, principle 11 also guides interventions to tailor the therapeutic process individually. Within the GLM, this individualization refers "to the systematic delivery of modules/interventions, such that clients are continually reminded how each module/intervention coheres with their unique intervention plan" (Willis et al., 2014, p. 65). According to Ward and Maruna (2007), such an approach allows programs to "address responsivity issues and helps to focus interventions around genuine concern of correctional clients" (p. 168).

In sum, this section followed the effort of Ward and his colleagues to operationalize the GLM. As detailed above, these scholars equipped the correctional field with general guidelines for practitioners (Yates et al., 2010; Yates et al., 2009), treatment modules (Ward et al., 2007), and management tools (Purvis et al., 2011; Purvis et al., 2013; Yates et al., 2010). In addition, Willis et al. (2014) distilled the GLM's general and etiological assumptions to 11 distinctive items. These items were designed to cover the optimal integration of the GLM in correctional interventions. Thus, in this section, the 11 items were rephrased as principles of effective correctional intervention. Overall, these principles aim to direct practitioners how to establish an effective GLM-consistent treatment program.

It is important to note, however, that the typical reference groups in these studies consist of individuals convicted of sexual offenses. That is, although consistent with the GLM's theoretical and practical framework, Ward and his colleagues have not explicitly generalized the 11 principles to the general offenders' population. Therefore, it is too soon to conclude whether these principles represent an agreed-upon set of directions that transcends all correctional interventions. In other words, the overall effort to translate the GLM's theoretical assumptions into practice is still in its early stage.

The next section examines a related issue—the empirical evaluations of treatment programs that followed the GLM's correctional framework. This analysis aims to identify the unique GLM's elements in evaluations of programs that adopted this model of offender rehabilitation. In addition, the next section aims to present the current empirical status of the GLM.

The Empirical Status of the GLM

Since first presenting the GLM, the model's advocates have endorsed the "massive, sophisticated and seemingly incontrovertible evidence" that was presented by the "What Works Movement" (Ward & Maruna, 2007, p. 9). In this regard, they appreciated the fact that the evidence-based approach to treatment reaffirmed rehabilitation in the correctional system (Ward & Maruna, 2007; Yates et al., 2010). In addition, they contended that ethical reasons support the use of evidence-based practice because "we should not subject individuals to empirically unsupported interventions" (Day & Ward, 2010, p. 291; Ward et al., 2007, p. 212).

Thus, Ward and his colleagues argue that the GLM should guide interventions in developing empirically supported therapies (Ward & Maruna, 2007; Ward & Mann, 2004). Specifically, they assert that correctional interventions that follow the GLM's theoretical framework should result in two outcomes. First, they should "reduce the likelihood of individuals committing additional crimes" (Ward & Maruna, 2007, p. 143). Second, they should engage "participants in the rehabilitation process and [promote] desistence from crime" (Willis & Ward, 2013, p. 305). In practice, this effectiveness criterion expects that correctional programs will demonstrate both the reduction in offenders' recidivism (i.e., reduce the risk to the society) and the enhancement of offenders' psychological well-being (increase the chance of achieving better lives).

This section reviews the extant studies that have evaluated the implementation of GLM-consistent interventions (i.e., treatment programs consistent with the GLM's theoretical assumptions).

These studies are presented in two parts. The first part includes three studies that evaluated the application of the GLM without any comparison (or control) group. The second part includes three studies that used a control group in their evaluation.

Evaluations Without Any Comparison Group

Three studies evaluated the implementation of GLM-consistent interventions in the correctional system without any control comparison. Two of these studies were clinical case studies, and the third study was a qualitative analysis of a group-based application. These studies aimed to demonstrate how the GLM principles integrated into treatment programs for sex offenders (Lindsay, Ward, Morgan, & Wilson, 2007; Gannon, King, Miles, Lockerbie, & Willis, 2011) and violent offenders (Whitehead, Ward, & Collie, 2007). In general, advocates of the GLM refer to these studies as preliminary evidence of "positive results" (Casey et al., 2013; Ward & Maruna, 2007; Ward & Fortune, 2013). Specifically, these studies are suggestive of the positive effect that can be achieved through the "GLM's attention to the social ecology of offenders [and] its focus on offenders' values and life priorities" (Scoones, Willis, & Grace, 2012, p. 233).

The first evaluation study is by Lindsay et al. (2007), a clinical case study that was conducted in the correctional system of Scotland. This study presents a preliminary attempt to operationalize the theoretical principles of the GLM and the Self-Regulation Model (SRM). In general, Lindsay et al. (2007) sought to examine the effectiveness of a therapeutic method that used GLM and SRM principles in the treatment of sex offenders. Specifically, they integrated *a life map* that was designed to trace "personal development from birth" and to incorporate offenders' "long-term future projections" (p. 37). Their study evaluated the impact of this therapeutic method on two sex offenders. These offenders entered this intervention after completing another treatment that focused on their deficits and risk management (e.g., anger management, control of alcohol abuse, reduction of risk factors).

Lindsay et al. (2007) concluded that the GLM's approach affected the two offenders in three main ways. First, due to the GLM's dual aims (the focus on building capacities alongside with managing risk), "both men felt that the therapists were genuinely interested in them and their lives and were not intent simply on ensuring that they did not offend again" (p. 49). Second, the focus "on developing a more adaptive lifestyle plan makes a great deal of intuitive sense to both the men and the therapists" (p. 49). Third, "the constructive nature of the GLM helped to allay [offenders'] suspicions [about the treatment] and to appreciate that one of their therapist's aims was to ensure they lived better lives as well as less harmful ones" (p. 49). In addition, Lindsay et al. (2007) mention that both offenders had not recidivated during a five-year follow-up period. Overall, according to Whitehead et al. (2007), this study "provides some very preliminary evidence concerning the empirical adequacy and heuristic value of the GLM" (p. 582).

The second clinical case study that applied the GLM was conducted in the correctional system of New Zealand. In this single case study, Whitehead et al. (2007) describe how the GLM guided an "ongoing treatment with a high risk, violent offender" (p. 582). They also note that during the offender's past two periods of incarcerations, he "completed two intensive cognitive-behavioural, group-based treatment programmes targeting his criminogenic needs (dynamic risk factors)" (p. 585). Essentially, this therapeutic background led therapists to conclude that "the standard Risk-Management, cognitive-behavioural treatment options available for Mr. C [(i.e., the offender)] were exhausted" (p. 587).

Thus, Whitehead et al. (2007) designed a treatment program that applied the principles of the GLM for this particular offender. Specifically, this treatment program aimed to "establish relevant treatment goals," "identify dominant human goods," "increase treatment readiness," enhance understanding how the most valued goals interacted with primary goods and criminogenic needs, "develop a Good Lives case formulation," "develop a detailed Good Lives plan based on the case formulation," "work on goal attainment," and "monitor progress via regular supervision" (pp. 587–592).

According to Whitehead et al. (2007), "the true value of the GLM was in facilitating treatment readiness . . . and promoting [the offender's] long-term reintegration goals, while creating a more adaptive personal identity" (p. 595). They argued that the key therapeutic change occurred when the offender visualized his "new me." That is, they concluded that the GLM enabled the offender "to visualize and begin working toward a life for himself that he would never have previously considered" (p. 588). In addition, they reported that this offender did not recidivate during the 14-month follow-up period (according to Willis & Ward, 2013, this offender had not been convicted for six years).

Overall, Whitehead et al. (2007) assert that these findings "illustrated the promise that the GLM hold" (p. 595). However, they are also aware that this is only a single clinical case study. In this regard, they suggest that for an "empirical 'acid test' of the value of the GLM," a control trial should compare between the effect size of "the Risk-Management approach and the combined Risk-Management plus Good Lives approach" (p. 596).

The third evaluation study was conducted by Gannon et al. (2011), who presented a qualitative analysis of a new GLM-consistent intervention in the correctional system of England and Wales. This study evaluates the impact of treatment on five mentally disordered sex offenders in a mental health hospital. Essentially, this group of offenders "differed on age, intellectual ability, experience of previous sexual offender treatment, psychiatric diagnoses, offending history and treatment need" (p. 164). For example, this group consisted of one high-risk offender with borderline intelligence, one moderate-risk offender with low-average intelligence, one moderate-risk offender with average intelligence, and two low-risk offenders with average intelligence.

The treatment program for this heterogenic group was designed to reflect both the RNR model (the risk, need, and responsivity principles) and the GLM model (assessment of primary goods, support the attainment of these goods, and understanding the relationship between the attainment of the goods and offending). Before the offenders entered the program, the therapists collaborated with them to assess their previous sexual offense history, underlying motivations, and the relationship between these motivations and offending. The treatment content in this program delivered the following nine modules that adopted a GLM approach: general group formation, understanding good lives and risk factors, understanding offending, sexual arousal and fantasy, coping skills, offense-supportive thinking, victim awareness and empathy, intimacy and relationships, and recognizing risk and leading a good life.

Gannon et al. (2011) evaluated the impact of this program on each offender and presented several findings. First, all five offenders completed the program. Second, all of them understood "the meaning of each of the goods . . . and how they should attempt to gain each of these Goods—prosocially—within their daily lives in order to protect themselves from future offending" (p. 164). Third, offenders with "lower intelligence levels and/or indirect pathways to offending . . . struggled to understand the links between the GLM and their own risk factors for sexual offending" (p. 164).

Fourth, offenders with higher intelligence levels "focused so much on the Good Lives aspect of the group that they failed to fully appreciate the importance of their own risk and treatment factors and required some significant support on this aspect" (p. 164). Overall, Gannon et al. (2011) are aware of the limits of their qualitative analyses. Thus, they stated that "because a control group is not included and the effectiveness of this group is still being evaluated, the conclusions and recommendations that we make in this section are necessarily speculative" (p. 164).

Evaluations With a Comparison Group

Three studies evaluated the application of the GLM in the correctional system by using a control or comparison group. Essentially, all of these studies evaluated treatment programs for sex offenders that changed their therapeutic focus from avoidant goals to approach goals. Specifically, the programs in these studies rewrote their Relapse Prevention (RP) module and implemented a new module with a GLM approach to treatment. The evaluation studies, thus, compared offenders who participated in the RP-based programs to offenders who participated in the GLM-based programs. These studies are discussed in chronological order.

The first evaluation that compared a GLM-based program to a RP-based program was undertaken by Simons, McCullar, and Tyler (2006, 2008). The results of these studies were presented at two annual conferences but were never published in a journal.[4] Therefore, the description here about this study is drawn from other scholars' works that reported on this evaluation. Based on this information, this study was conducted in the corrections system of Colorado. In this regard, Willis and Ward (2013) reported that Simons et al. (2006, 2008) evaluated a new "GLM approach to treatment planning at a prison-based sex offender treatment programme" (p. 312). Essentially, this new GLM approach—a collaborative therapeutic process that focused on offenders' approach goals—replaced the RP-based treatment. Thus, Simons et al. (2006, 2008) compared 100 offenders who received the RP-base treatment to 96 offenders who received the GLM-based treatment.

The extant literature reports that this study provides evidence that the GLM "can enhance client engagement in treatment and reduce dropouts from programmes" (Willis et al., 2012, p. 124; see also Andrews, 2011; Willis & Ward, 2013; Wilson & Yates, 2009). In addition, according to Willis and Ward (2013), "Pre/post-treatment comparisons on a range of measures revealed that clients who received either RP-or GLM-based treatment planning improved similarly on social skills and victim empathy" (p. 312). Another finding was that the GLM-based treatment planning demonstrated significantly better problem-solving ability and coping skills. In addition, offenders in this program "were more likely to have a social support system post-treatment compared to clients who received RP" (p. 312). Overall, based on this literature, Simons et al. (2006, 2008) appear to provide evidence that support the use of the GLM approach to treatment. However, the findings from this study reflected preliminary findings, and Simons et al. have yet to present follow-up data.

The second evaluation study comparing GLM-based treatment and RP-based treatment was conducted by Harkins, Flak, & Beech (2012), who evaluated a new therapeutic approach in community-based treatments for sex offenders in England (see also Harkins, Flak, & Beech, 2008). Prior to this change, the programs for sex offenders consisted of a Core module (144 hours that covered therapeutic areas such as victim empathy, problem-solving, and cognitive distortions) and a RP module (36 hours). After this change was implemented, the RP module was replaced with a

Better Lives (BL) module (also 36 hours). This administrative change aimed to implement a module that "was derived from a GLM rehabilitation framework" (p. 535).

In essence, the program with the BL module had three sections. First, the program "aimed to build motivation and acquaint offenders with the treatment approach" (sessions 1–4) (p. 523). Second, the program "focused on skills practice in relation to meeting individual needs in prosocial ways and managing obstacles" (p. 523) (sessions 5–11). Third, the program assisted offenders to present their GLP (session 12). Importantly, Harkins et al. (2012) noted that the BL module was not "entirely consistent with the GLM approach" (p. 537). This inconsistency is because the module encourages offenders to find a "roughly equal balance of all the goods rather than determining which were the most heavily weighted for them" (p. 537). Within the GLM's correctional framework, ignoring the heavily weighted primary goods is considered problematic because these goods are supposed to establish the basis of offenders' future GLP.

Harkins et al. (2012) evaluated the implementation of the BL module in four parts. First, they compared the attrition rates before and after the implementation of this module. In this statistical analysis, they found that the attrition rates between the RP group (n = 182) and the BL group (n = 87) did not differ significantly. Second, Harkins et al. (2012) compared the changes that occurred in treatment areas targeted under each module. For this analysis, they examined the pre- and post-treatment psychometric data for 643 offenders (the data were collected from a national psychometric database). Then, they translated this information into a therapeutic change in three main treatment areas: (1) pro-offending attitudes, (2) socioaffective measures, and (3) relapse prevention skills. The statistical analysis revealed "no significant differences between the modules for the proportion of individuals who had achieved treatment change for any of the areas targeted in treatment" (p. 528).

The third and fourth parts of the evaluation examined the perceptions of therapists and offenders. In this analysis, Harkins et al. (2012) used semi-structured interviews conducted with 11 therapists ("a number of them also had experience running the RP module") and with 20 offenders (only five of them participated in the RP module) (p. 529). Notably, due to the small number of interviewees, the study did not conduct a statistical analysis to compare between the modules. Instead, this study presented and compared the within-groups proportion.

First, Harkins et al. (2012) found that 83% (10 of 12) of the participants in the BL module "thought [that] the module was positive or had positive aspects" (compared to 4 of 5 in the RP module) (p. 531). Second, 46% of them (6 of 13) reported that "they improved their understanding of themselves as related to their offending" (compared to 4 of 5 in the RP module) (p. 532). In this regard, 61% (8 of 13) also reported that they have "a better understanding of the positive aspects of themselves" (compared to 1 of 5 in the RP module) (p. 532). Third, 27% (4 of 15) of the participants in the BL module reported that "their thoughts and attitudes had changed in a way that they were better able to manage themselves or their reoffending" (compared to 4 of 5 in the RP module) (p. 532). Relatedly, 47% (7 of 15) reported that "their thoughts and attitudes about themselves or the future were more positive" (compared to 1 of 5 in the RP module).

Fourth, according to Harkins et al. (2012), 90% (10 of 11) of the therapists reported that they liked the BL's "positive and future-focused elements," and 72% (8 of 11) noted that the BL module had "a positive influence on the [offenders'] motivation" (p. 529, p. 530). Fifth, 64% (7 of 11) of the therapists "did not feel the module would be appropriate for high-risk or unmotivated men" (p. 529). Sixth, 73% (8 of 11) of them thought the BL module was "missing important element," and 64% (7 of 11) specified that "the BL module was missing a sexual offending/risk component" (p. 529).

The last evaluation study that compared between GLM-based treatment and RP-based treatment is Barnett, Manderville-Norden, and Rakestrow (2014). This study was designed to examine the implementation of the BL module in two community treatment programs for sex offenders in the correctional system of England and Wales. Impotently, the BL modules in these programs were revised to address the problematic aspects that revealed in Harkins et al. (2008, 2012). In other words, Barnett et al. (2014) evaluated BL modules that gave more attention to risk than the BL module that was evaluated in Harkins et al. (2008, 2012).

Similar to Harkins et al. (2008, 2012), Barnett et al. (2014) compared between the attrition rates of offenders who participated in the BL group (n = 610) and the RP group (n = 785). Their statistical analysis did not find an "association between attrition rate and program approach" (p. 27). In addition, similar to Harkins et al. (2008, 2012), Barnett et al. (2014) used the available pre- and post-treatment psychometric data to measure the relative impact of the BL and RP modules on offenders. Accordingly, the data from the psychometric scores were translated into a therapeutic change in (1) pro-offending attitude, (2) socioaffective measures, and (3) relapse prevention skills. The results from this analysis showed that the BL module did not differ significantly from the RP module. In addition, according to psychometric measures, both GL and RP versions of the program did not affect "the majority of people that required change" (i.e., the offenders who were assessed as dysfunctional in pretreatment psychometric measures) (p. 29).

In sum, the review of the six studies revealed that only two studies evaluated the long-term outcome of treatment (Lindsay et al., 2007; Whitehead et al., 2007). These two case studies reported the time that the offenders have remained offense-free. The other four studies evaluated only within-treatment goals (i.e., the effectiveness to change offenders on the targets addressed in treatment). Thus, overall, the literature that evaluated the GLM-consistent interventions did not provide much evidence about the actual ability of these programs to prevent reoffending. Due to this lack of evidence, it is important to introduce another evaluation study that examined the integration of the GLM in a correctional program. In this study, Marshall et al. (2011) evaluated the primary program of the Rockwood Psychological Service (RPS) programs, which "has been evolved over the past 40 years" (p. 125).

Marshall et al. (2011) presented the reoffending rates of a program that treated 535 sex offenders in prison within the England and Wales correctional system. Essentially, the RPS was not designed to reflect the GLM's assumptions (i.e., it is not a GLM-consistent intervention). Rather, this program is considered an intervention with a "GLM-related concepts" (Willis & Ward, 2013, p. 310). In general, this program was designed as a strength-based approach to treatment that incorporates elements from Miller and Rollnick's (2002) Motivational Interviewing, Andrews and Bonta's RNR model, and Ward and his colleagues' GLM.

Specifically, the RPS integrated the GLM in its last phase of treatment (Phase 3). Within the RPS, the first phase of the program "aimed exclusively at engaging each client and winning his trust and confidence in the therapist" (Marshall, Marshall, Serran, & O'Brien, 2013, p. 182). Although this phase outlined the GLM framework, the main focus remains targeting offenders' self-esteem, sense of shame, copping skills, and mood management. In the second phase, the RPS addresses known criminogenic needs such as offenders' attitudes and cognition, self-regulation, relationships, and sexual issues. This treatment involves "assisting the clients in developing the skills, attitudes and self-confidence necessary to meet their relationship needs in prosocial and effective ways" (p. 183).

In the third phase, the RPS integrates the GLM. In this modified version of the GLM, the program advises offenders to focus only on two or three of their most important primary goods. The program also encourages them to choose the goods of knowledge, creativity, and excellence in work and play as their therapeutic targets (Marshall et al., 2013). In addition, phase 3 assists offenders to construct a released plan with their approach goals and to identify community support groups that can encourage "their pursuit of the identified GLM goals" (p. 184).

Marshall et al. (2011) reported the reoffending rates of 535 offenders who were treated in the RPS during the period 1991–2001. This study found that after an average of 5.4 and 8.4 years of follow-up, the sexual reoffending rates were 3.2% and 5.6%, respectively. In addition, this study found that after an average of 5.4 years of follow-up, the nonsexual reoffending rate was 13.6%, and after an average of 8.4 years of follow-up, the violent reoffending rate was 8.4%. Notably, Marshall et al. (2011) evaluated the relative effectiveness of the RPS by comparing these reoffending rates with the offenders' "expected recidivism rate of reoffending, derived from sound risk assessment instruments" (p. 98). According to this comparison method, the expected reoffending rates for sexual offenses after 5.4 and 8.4 years are 16.8% and 28.2%, respectively. Accordingly, the reoffending rate for nonsexual offenses after 5.4 years is 40%, and the reoffending rate for violent offenses after 8.4 years is 34.8%. Thus, Marshall et al. (2011) concluded that the RPS "effectively reduced reoffending" (p. 160).

Overall, the evaluation studies that were presented in this section show that the implementation of the GLM in the correctional system is still in its exploratory stage. First, all of these evaluations provided only preliminary findings about the effectiveness of the GLM in the correctional system. That is, the GLM-consistent treatment programs produced very little empirical evidence that the GLM can achieve its rehabilitative goals. Second, most of these studies (5 of 6) evaluated treatment programs that were exclusively designed for sex offenders. Thus, to date, it is unknown if the implementation of the GLM principles impacts other offender populations. Third, only one of the above evaluations (Barnett et al., 2014) was designed to measure the impact of a GLM-consistent treatment programs over a matched group of offenders. Fourth, as mentioned above, all of the evaluations that compared the GLM-consistent treatment with the RP treatment did not follow the reoffending rates of their participants.

Conclusion

This chapter followed the efforts of Ward and his colleagues to operationalize their theoretical assumptions. As discussed in the first five sections, these scholars provide explicit directions on how correctional intervention should follow the GLM's theoretical premises. Their explicit guidance consists of 11 correctional principles in five domains of treatment interventions. In essence, these principles cover the correctional framework of the GLM and were designed to direct interventions toward a successful application of the GLM in the correctional system. Specifically, these five domains cover the programs' aims and orientation (the first section), offender assessment (the second section), intervention planning (the third section), intervention content (the fourth section), and program delivery (fifth section). Essentially, Ward and his colleagues also developed practical tools that assist practitioners in assessment and treatment.

Overall, advocates of the GLM present a systematic theoretical and correctional framework for undertaking the rehabilitation enterprise. This approach promises to help offenders in achieving better lives and, simultaneously, to reduce the tendency of offenders to inflict harm on society. To date, the GLM has been applied within the correctional systems of Ireland, England, Canada, Australia, New Zealand, and United States.

Despite its theoretical development and growing popularity among treatment programs for sex offenders (e.g., McGrath, Cumming, Burchard, Zeoli, & Ellerby, 2010), empirical evidence in support of the GLM is scarce and inconsistent. As reviewed in the final section of this chapter, very few studies have evaluated interventions that are, in the least, consistent with the GLM. Moreover, findings from the extant evaluations have not yet provided strong empirical evidence that GLM-based intervention "work." In other words, it is still unknown if a correctional program that applies the GLM can both enhance offenders' level of psychological well-being and reduce their risk of reoffending.

Thus, the next chapter aims to understand how advocates of the GLM and RNR model view each other's model—what they perceive as their relative deficits and strengths. Such discussion is essential for any attempt to integrate these models because the GLM was developed as a critique of the RNR model. Therefore, Chapter 7 conveys the nature of the dispute between the two models and shows the potential points of agreement. The goal of this chapter is to reveal the extent to which these models are compatible or incompatible approaches to offender treatment. Such conclusion will set the basis for Chapter 8—an attempt to build a new vision for offender rehabilitation.

Notes

1. Unfortunately, I could not find an access to this document or more details about its components. In the GLM's literature, this document is often cited as: Yates, P. M., Kingston, D. A., & Ward, T. (2009). *The self-regulation model of the offence and re-offence process: A guide to assessment and treatment planning using the integrated good lives/self-regulation model of sexual offending.* Victoria, British Columbia, Canada: Pacific Psychological Assessment Corporation.
2. As mentioned above, this publication provides a comprehensive practical guide for practitioners. Willis et al. (2012) refer to Yates et al. (2010) "for elaboration of what GLM-guided treatment could look like" (p. 133).
3. This element is relevant only for correctional interventions that endorse the GLM/SRM approach.
4. The literature referred to this study as either (1) Simons, D. A., McCullar, B., & Tyler, C. (2006). *Evaluation of the good lives model approach to treatment planning.* Paper presented at the 25th Annual Association for the Treatment of Sexual Abusers Research and Treatment Conference, September, Chicago; or (2) Simons, D., McCullar, B., & Tyler, C. (2008). *Evaluation of the good lives model approach to treatment planning.* Presented at the 27th Annual Research and Treatment Conference of the Association for the Treatment of Sexual Abusers, Atlanta, GA.

References

Andrews, D. A. (2011). The impact of nonprogrammatic factors on criminal-justice interventions. *Legal and Criminological Psychology, 16,* 1–23.

Barnett, G., Manderville-Norden, R., & Rakestrow, J. (2014). The good lives model or relapse prevention: What works better in facilitating and maintaining change? *Sexual Abuse: A Journal of Research and Treatment, 26,* 3–33.

Casey, S., Day, A., Vess, J., & Ward, T. (2013). *Foundations of offender rehabilitation*. New York, NY: Routledge.

Day, A., & Ward, T. (2010). Offender rehabilitation as a value laden process. *International Journal of Offender Therapy and Comparative Criminology, 54*, 289–306.

Gannon, T., King, T., Miles, H., Lockerbie, L., & Willis, G. M. (2011). Good lives sexual offender treatment for mentally disordered offenders. *British Journal of Forensic Practice, 13*, 153–168.

Harkins, L., Flak, V., & Beech, A. (2008). *Evaluation of the N-SOGP better lives program*. London, UK: Report prepared for the Ministry of Justice.

Harkins, L., Flak, V. E., & Beech, A. R. (2012). Evaluation of a community-based sex offender treatment program using a good lives model approach. *Sexual Abuse: A Journal of Research and Treatment, 24*, 519–543.

Kingston, D. A., Yates, P. M., & Olver, M. E. (2014). The self-regulation model of sexual offending: Intermediate outcomes and posttreatment recidivism. *Sexual Abuse: A Journal of Research and Treatment, 26*, 429–449.

Langlands, R., Ward, T., & Gilchrist, L. (2009). Applying the good lives model to male perpetrators of domestic violence. *Behaviour Change, 26*, 113–129.

Lindsay, W., Ward, T., Morgan, T., & Wilson, I. (2007). Self-regulation of sex offending, future pathways and the good lives model: Applications and problems. *Journal of Sexual Aggression, 13*, 37–50.

Marshall, W. L. (2005). Therapist style in sexual offender treatment: Influence on indices of change. *Sexual Abuse: A Journal of Research and Treatment, 17*, 109–116.

Marshall, W. L., Marshall, L. E., Serran, G. A., & O'Brien, M. D. (2011). *Rehabilitating sexual offenders: A strength-based approach*. Washington, DC: American Psychological Association.

Marshall, W. L., Marshall, L. E., Serran, G. A., & O'Brien, M. D. (2013). What works in reducing sexual offending. In L. Craig, L. Dixon, & T. Gannon (Eds.), *What works in offender rehabilitation: An evidence-based approach to assessment and treatment* (pp. 173–191). London: Wiley-Blackwell.

McGrath, R., Cumming, G., Burchard, B., Zeoli, S., & Ellerby, L. (2010). *Current practices and emerging trends in sexual abuser management: The safer society 2009 north American survey*. Brandon, VT: Safer Society Press.

McMurran, M., & Ward, T. (2004). Motivating offenders to change in therapy: An organizing framework. *Legal and Criminological Psychology, 9*, 295–311.

Miller, W. R., & Rollnick, S. (2002). *Motivational interviewing: Preparing people for change* (2nd ed.). New York, NY: Guilford.

Purvis, M., Ward, T., & Shaw, S. (2013). *Applying the good lives model to the case management of sexual offenders: A practical guide for probation officers, parole officers, and case workers*. Brandon, VT: Safer Society Press.

Purvis, M., Ward, T., & Willis, G. (2011). The good lives model in practice: Offence pathways and case management. *European Journal of Probation, 3*(2), 4–28.

Scoones, C., Willis, G. M., & Grace, R. C. (2012). Beyond static and dynamic risk factors: The incremental predictive validity of release planning in sex offender risk assessment. *Journal of Interpersonal Violence, 27*, 222–238.

Serran, G., & Marshall, W. (2010). Therapeutic process in the treatment of sexual offenders: A review article. *The British Journal of Forensic Practice, 12*(3), 4–16.

Simons, D. A., McCullar, B., & Tyler, C. (2006, September). *Evaluation of the good lives model approach to treatment planning*. Paper presented at the 25th Annual Association for the Treatment of Sexual Abusers Research and Treatment Conference, Chicago, IL.

Simons, D. A., McCullar, B., & Tyler, C. (2008). *Evaluation of the good lives model approach to treatment planning*. Presented at the 27th Annual Research and Treatment Conference of the Association for the Treatment of Sexual Abusers, Atlanta, GA.

Thakker, J., Ward, T., & Chu, C. M. (2013). The good lives model of offender rehabilitation: A case study. In W. O'Donohue (Ed.), *Case studies in sexual deviance* (pp. 79–101). London: Routledge.

Ward, T., & Birgden, A. (2009). Accountability and dignity: Ethical issues in forensic and correctional practice. *Journal of Aggression and Violent Behaviour, 14*, 227–231.

Ward, T., & Fortune, C. A. (2013). The good lives model: Aligning risk reduction with promoting offenders personal goals. *European Journal of Probation, 5*, 29–46.

Ward, T., & Gannon, T. A. (2006). Rehabilitation, etiology, and self-regulation: The comprehensive good lives model of treatment for sexual offenders. *Aggression and Violent Behavior, 11,* 77–94.

Ward, T., & Mann, R. (2004). Good lives and the rehabilitation of offenders: A positive approach to sex offender treatment. In P. A. Linley & S. Joseph (Eds.), *Positive psychology in practice* (pp. 598–616). Hoboken, NJ: John Wiley.

Ward, T., Mann, R., & Gannon, T. (2007). The good lives model of offender rehabilitation: Clinical implications. *Aggression and Violent Behavior, 12,* 87–107.

Ward, T., & Maruna, S. (2007). *Rehabilitation: Beyond the risk paradigm.* New York, NY: Routledge.

Ward, T., Melser, J., & Yates, P. M. (2007). Reconstructing the risk need responsivity model: A theoretical elaboration and evaluation. *Aggression and Violent Behavior, 12,* 208–228.

Ward, T., & Stewart, C. A. (2003a). Criminogenic needs and human needs: A theoretical model. *Psychology, Crime, & Law, 9,* 125–143.

Ward, T., & Stewart, C. A. (2003b). The relationship between human needs and criminogenic needs. *Psychology, Crime, & Law, 9,* 353–360.

Ward, T.; & Stewart, C. A. (2003c). The treatment of sex offenders: Risk management and good lives. *Professional Psychology: Research and Practice, 34,* 353–360.

Whitehead, P., Ward, T., & Collie, R. (2007). Time for a change: Applying the good lives model of rehabilitation to a high-risk violent offender. *International Journal of Offender Therapy and Comparative Criminology, 51,* 578–598.

Willis, G. M., Prescott, D. S., & Yates, P. M. (2013). The good lives model in theory and practice. *Sexual Abuse in Australia and New Zealand, 5*(1), 3–9.

Willis, G. M., & Ward, T. (2013). The good lives model: Does it work? Preliminary evidence. In L. Craig, L. Dixon, & T. Gannon (Eds.), *What works in offender rehabilitation: An evidence-based approach to assessment and treatment* (pp. 305–317). London: Wiley-Blackwell.

Willis, G. M., Ward, T., & Levenson, J. S. (2014). The good lives model (GLM): An evaluation of GLM operationalization in North American treatment programs. *Sexual Abuse: A Journal of Research and Treatment, 26,* 58–81.

Willis, G. M., Yates, P. M., Gannon, T. A., & Ward, T. (2012). How to integrate the good lives model into treatment programs for sexual offending: An introduction and overview. *Sexual Abuse: A Journal of Research and Treatment, 25,* 123–142.

Willis, G. W., & Ward, T. (2010). Striving for a good life: The good lives model applied to released child molesters. *Journal of Sexual Aggression, 17,* 290–303.

Wilson, R. J., & Yates, P. M. (2009). Effective interventions and the good lives model. *Aggression and Violent Behavior, 14,* 157–161.

Yates, P. M., Kingston, D. A., & Ward, T. (2009). *The self-regulation model of the offence and re-offence process: Volume III: A guide to assessment and treatment planning using the integrated good lives/self-regulation model of sexual offending.* Victoria, BC: Pacific Psychological Assessment Corporation.

Yates, P. M., Prescott, D. S., & Ward, T. (2010). *Applying the good lives and self regulation models to sex offender treatment: A practical guide for clinicians.* Brandon, VT: Safer Society Press.

PART IV

The Future of Rehabilitation

7

THE RNR-GLM DEBATE

The debate between the Risk-Need-Responsivity (RNR) model and Good Lives Model (GLM) reveals many controversial issues in the field of offender rehabilitation (hereinafter referred to as the RNR-GLM debate). This debate began when Tony Ward and Claire Stewart proposed their strength-based approach to offender rehabilitation. During the early 2000s, their approach challenged the dominance of the RNR model because it shifted the focus of correctional intervention from addressing criminogenic needs to promoting primary human goods. Since then, Ward and his colleagues have been developing this alternative approach within a systematic rehabilitation theory—the GLM of offender rehabilitation.

The goal of this chapter is to analyze this debate and find ways to bridge between the two models. This debate is analyzed in two main sections. The first of these sections aims to conclude if the two theoretical frameworks can be bridged. For this purpose, this section discusses the debate from the GLM's theoretical perspective. Specifically, it presents seven issues in offender rehabilitation that Ward and his colleagues consider as unique aspects of the GLM. These controversial issues are (1) the role of offender motivation in rehabilitation; (2) the role of values in offender rehabilitation; (3) the role of needs in offender rehabilitation (criminogenic needs versus human needs); (4) the role of risk in offender rehabilitation (individualistic versus multifaceted aspects of risk); (5) the role of contextual factors in offender rehabilitation; (6) the role of personality in offender rehabilitation; (7) the role of human agency in offender rehabilitation. Overall, this discussion is expected to mark the unique theoretical contributions of the GLM over the RNR model.

Accordingly, the second of these sections discusses the correctional implications of these issues. For this purpose, this section examines the RNR-GLM debate within the RNR's correctional framework—the principles of effective intervention. These principles serve as a benchmark because RNR-consistent interventions demonstrated clear success to achieve the ultimate goal of correctional rehabilitation: a reduction in offenders' tendency to reoffend. In addition, new interpretations of these principles may assist to bridge between the correctional frameworks of the RNR and GLM. According to Ward, Yates, and Willis (2012), this is a realistic goal because "the RNR principles all have their counterparts within the GLM" (p. 100). Accordingly, Andrews, Bonta, and Wormith

(2011) argued that "GLM-based interventions may not be that different from soundly implemented RNR interventions" (p. 750). Specifically, this section examines if the operationalization of the GLM is compatible with the RNR model's core correctional principles (part 1), key clinical issues (part 2), and organizational principles (part 3).

Before analyzing these theoretical and correctional issues, it is also important to introduce the more heated, if not acrimonious, aspects of the RNR-GLM debate. Indeed, the presence of the GLM dragged the advocates of both models "into an almost caustic exchange" (Ogloff & Davis, 2004, p. 236). Thus, a full understanding of the RNR-GLM debate requires a brief chronicle of the replies and rebuttals of those on both sides of the RNR-GLM debate. This discussion includes the background of the exchanges and the way each camp responded to the criticism.

The Chronicle of the RNR-GLM Debate

From the GLM's perspective, the roots of the RNR-GLM debate can be traced back to the mid-1990s. Back then, Ward and his colleagues challenged the preeminence of the Relapse Prevention (RP) model in the sex offending field (Ward, Hudson, & Siegert, 1995; Ward et al., 1995; Ward & Stewart, 2003c). In brief, the RP model directs clinicians and researchers to use their "understanding of the process of relapse" to design treatments for sex offenders (Ward & Mann, 2004, p. 598). In practice, it means that treatment programs should identify high-risk situations for particular cases and develop cognitive-behavioral strategies to cope with those situations. Ward and his colleagues opposed the rigid risk management approach of the RP model. They asserted that this rehabilitative model concentrates on relapse management rather than assisting offenders "to achieve important goods through the construction of a meaningful life plan" (Ward, 2002a, p. 522).

In the early 2000s, Ward and his colleagues argued that there was a connection between the RP model and the RNR model. Although it predates the RNR model, they saw the RP model as a variation of this approach (Ward, Mann, & Gannon, 2007). Accordingly, they argued that the RNR model is the rehabilitative approach of risk management in the criminal justice system because its major aim is to target dynamic risk factors that relate to future offending (i.e., criminogenic needs).

In 2003, Ward and Stewart published an article named "Criminogenic Needs and Human Needs: A Theoretical Model" (Ward & Stewart, 2003a). This article criticized the RNR model (i.e., the "risk-need model") and, in particular, its conceptualization of offenders' needs. In a nutshell, their criticism consisted of the following issues: "criminogenic needs are value laden; [criminogenic needs] are effectively only range riders (i.e., do not inform clinicians what to do in therapy); the use of the term 'need' is inappropriate and misleading; the relationship between the four principles comprising the model is not specified; the relationship between criminogenic needs is not clear (in our model it is); the relationship between the vocational and therapeutic aspects of treatment is unclear; there is no explanation as to why criminogenic needs arise; and the neglect of the essential role of noncriminogenic needs in practice" (Ward & Stewart, 2003b, p. 220). Then, Ward and his colleagues proposed the GLM as a better alternative to approach offender rehabilitation.

Essentially, when Ward and Stewart presented the GLM, the status of rehabilitation within the criminal justice system in the United States was fragile. Although the rehabilitative ideal continued to regain its legitimacy, the criminal justice system still relied on punitive reaction to

offending (Currie, 1998; Clear, 2009). In this regard, Garland (2001) observed that the "rehabilitative possibilities of criminal justice measures [were] routinely subordinated to other penal
goals, particularly retribution, incapacitation, and the management of risk" (p. 8). Thus, during
the early 2000s, advocates of the RNR model considered the criticism of the model's theoretical foundation as an act that weakened their fight against conservative perspectives that wish to
punish and incapacitate offenders.

Andrews and Bonta published their commentary on Ward and Stewart's model of human
needs in the same volume. Their reaction was sharp and clear: Ward and his colleagues are
"theoriticists"—scholars who accept or reject knowledge in accordance with their "personal views
and not in accordance with evidence" (Bonta & Andrews, 2003, p. 215). They also stated that the
GLM approach "is long on popular appeal but short in evidence" (p. 216). Specifically, Bonta and
Andrews contended that Ward and Stewart "ignore the evidence that reductions in criminogenic
needs are associated with reduced criminal behaviour, turn a blind eye to the fact that there is not a
shred of evidence that psychodynamic interventions reduce recidivism, and simply assert that [their]
approach makes the most sense" (p. 217).

During the 2000s, Ward and his colleagues continued to develop the GLM without demonstrating success. Even so, their criticism of the theoretical framework of the RNR model and advocacy
of a strength-based approach inspired other scholars to embrace their approach to correctional
treatment. In this regard, Cullen (2012) reviewed three important books trumpeting the GLM
and what was called "creative correctives." He concluded that the GLM was part of "a growing
movement . . . that seeks to replace the Canadians' paradigm in favor of interventions rooted on
desistence theory and research" (p. 95). In essence, this movement challenges the RNR model by
shifting the rehabilitative question from "what works" in correctional rehabilitation to "what do
offenders want" in their rehabilitative process.

Ten years later, at the beginning of the 2010s, this ongoing criticism led the advocates of the
GLM and RNR model to participate in another critical exchange (Andrews et al., 2011; Ward et al.,
2012; Wormith, Gendreau, & Bonta, 2012). Andrews et al. (2011) initiated this exchange with an
assertion that the "RNR already subsumes many of the features of the GLM" (p. 737). Therefore,
they argued, "there is nothing unique in GLM other than the encouragement of weak assessment
approaches . . . and the addition of confusion in service planning" (p. 751).

In response, Ward et al. (2012) tried to explain the incremental value of the GLM and correct
common misrepresentations of this model. In their critical commentary, they concluded that the
GLM's rehabilitation framework "can accommodate all that is valuable in the RNR, but the reverse
is not true" (p. 107). Therefore, they asserted, "the GLM has greater scope and applicability" than
the RNR model (p. 107). This exchange ended with a rejoinder that was published in the same
volume. In brief, Wormith et al. (2012) argued that the incremental value of the GLM in offender
rehabilitation remains puzzling. In addition, they compared the empirical status of the two models
and criticized the fact that Ward and his colleague promote the GLM in the correctional system
with very little scientific support.

Overall, the chronicle of the RNR-GLM debate leads this introduction to the discussion in the
next sections. Together with the previous chapters (the theoretical and correctional frameworks of
each model), the next sections are ready to examine the extent to which these models of offender
rehabilitation can be bridged. That is, the next sections will lead to a conclusion if the RNR-GLM
debate can be resolved on a common theoretical and correctional ground.

The Incremental Value of the GLM's Theoretical Framework

As mentioned above, scholars who developed the GLM continuously criticized the RNR model. In particular, they argue that the RNR's theoretical framework represents a limited approach to rehabilitation. According to this criticism, the RNR model concentrates on the evidence-based aspects of what works to change offenders and therefore neglects or ignores other relevant aspects that contribute to the treatment process. By contrast, the GLM is envisioned as a broader perspective on offender rehabilitation—a model that reflects the diverse dimensions of this field. Ward and his colleagues assert that the GLM's comprehensive theoretical framework encompasses the theory and the research that underlies the RNR model. But by then moving beyond the RNR to develop a richer perspective, advocates of the GLM propose to save correctional rehabilitation from hitting "a kind of effective practice 'glass ceiling' in the field" (Porporino, 2010, p. 63).

Specifically, this section discusses seven theoretical issues that Ward and his colleagues describe as controversial. This discussion consists of theoretical issues that concern broader perspectives on concepts such as motivation, values, needs, risk, ecology, personality, human nature, and methodology. For each controversial issue, this section addresses four aspects: (1) the limitation that advocates of the GLM recognize in the RNR model; (2) the GLM's perspective on this issues; (3) the response of advocates of the RNR model to the criticism; and (4) a summary that evaluates how the GLM's theoretical framework potentially expands our perspectives of offender rehabilitation.

Table 7.1 summarizes the essence of these seven theoretical issues within the RNR–GLM debate. That is, for each theoretical controversial issue, Table 7.1 presents the RNR model's theoretical perspective (the middle column) and the GLM's theoretical incremental value for improving offender rehabilitation.

Controversial Issue 1: The Role of Offender Motivation in Rehabilitation

Since first presented, advocates of the GLM have criticized the RNR model's approach to rehabilitation (Ward & Stewart, 2003a, 2003b). In general, they assert that this framework endorses the faulty presumption that "the major aim of rehabilitation is to reduce the chance of harm to the community and that this is best achieved by managing these risks" (Ward & Maruna, 2007, p. 83). By contrast, they developed the GLM as a paradigm of offender rehabilitation that addresses risk through the improvement of "offenders' quality of life" (Ward, 2002b, p. 172; see also: Ward & Maruna, 2007; Ward & Stewart, 2003a). Their assumption is that the GLM's approach will result in correctional rehabilitation with greater capacity to motivate offenders toward social reintegration.

In this regard, Ward and his colleagues criticized the RNR model for choosing risk management as its major strategy to deal with criminality. Their general argument is that risk management policies overemphasize the avoidance of harmful consequences, and that such an approach is unlikely to motivate offenders to change their criminal lifestyle. According to Ward and Maruna (2007, p. 83), "it is unclear how an approach focused on the prevention of harmful consequences to others can encourage offenders to change their own behavior in fundamental ways" (i.e., in ways that lead them to social reintegration).

Specifically, Ward and his colleagues assert that "motivating offenders by concentrating on eliminating or modifying their various dynamic risk factors is extremely difficult", because offenders

TABLE 7.1 The incremental value of the GLM's theoretical framework

Theoretical Controversial Issue	The RNR's Theoretical Perspective	The GLM's Incremental Value
Controversial Issue 1. The role of offender motivation in rehabilitation.	• External incentives (reward-cost contingencies) motivate offenders. • The role of offender motivation is to assist in achieving treatment goals.	• Internal incentives (primary human goods) are another powerful source of motivation. • The role of offender motivation is also to achieve offenders' personal goals.
Controversial Issue 2. The role of values in offender rehabilitation.	• Values have a moderating role: It reflects the standards of accumulating knowledge (epistemic values) and of adequate correctional service (ethical values).	• Values also have a mediation role: It reflects what is important in offenders' social reintegration (prudential values).
Controversial Issue 3. The role of needs in offender rehabilitation.	• Offender needs are personal deficits that relate to offenders' criminal lifestyle. • Offender needs is a practical concept—it assists to focus on the therapeutic efforts (treatment's needs).	• Offender needs are also internal drives to attain offenders' primary human goods. • Offender need is a personal concept—it reflects what offenders want in life (offender's needs).
Controversial Issue 4. The role of risk in offender rehabilitation.	• Risk is a psychometric and practical concept (an estimation of offenders' tendency to reoffend).	• Risk is also a holistic concept (a multifaceted observation about offenders' criminal lifestyle).
Controversial Issue 5. The role of contextual factors in offender rehabilitation.	• Contextual factors assist interventions within the correctional system to address offenders' criminogenic needs.	• Contextual factors also assist the criminal justice system to address offenders' social reintegration.
Controversial Issue 6. The role of personality in offender rehabilitation.	• Offenders' personality reflects the interactions between offenders' traits and how they interpret the immediate situation of action.	• Offenders' personality reflects the interactions between offenders' traits, personal striving, and self-narratives.
Controversial Issue 7. The role of human agency in offender rehabilitation.	• Humans follow their external contingencies to align with the standard of conduct.	• Humans also follow their innate desires to achieve a good life.

may feel alienation when they view the rehabilitative services as irrelevant to their life (Ward & Maruna, 2007, p. 22). In other words, the attempt "to have offenders internalize societal laws and norms simply because we want them to is likely to fail" (Ward et al., 2012, p. 99). Thus, they conclude that the capacity of the RNR model to generate behavioral change and prosocial reintegration is limited.

Ward and his colleagues contend that the GLM is a model that provides a broader perspective of offender motivation. They argue that their perspective considers the influence of both external incentives (i.e., behavioral contingencies) and internal incentives (i.e., intrinsic drive toward the primary human goods). Their assumption is that the GLM's primary goods are intrinsically beneficial for offenders and thus motivate offenders to seek them for their own sake.

Moreover, Ward and Maruna (2007) assume that the GLM's approach to motivation may result in stronger therapeutic alliances because it leads therapists to be more attuned to offenders' psychological needs. Accordingly, it may signal to offenders that the correctional system cares as much about their life as it does about their potential risk to society. Thus, advocates of the GLM expect that their broader perspective of motivation will increase the chance to engage offenders in treatment strategy and goals. Specifically, they assume that "it is easier to motivate individuals to change their offense-related characteristics by focusing on the perceived benefits (primary goods) they accrue from their offending and by exploring more appropriate means (secondary goods) to achieve what is of value to them" (p. 108).

Advocates of the RNR model reject the assertion that their model concentrates solely on managing offenders' risk. According to Polaschek (2012), such rigid approaches to rehabilitation "differ in important ways from both the letter and the spirit of the RNR model" (p. 10). That is, the RNR model encourages the correctional system to provide human service (i.e., rehabilitative efforts) "*for the offender*" (p. 10, emphasis in original). This model aims to benefit both society and offenders by using "some combination of avoidance and approach goals for offenders" (p. 10). In this regard, Polaschek concluded that some differences between the RNR perspective and the GLM that "seem substantive on paper, evaporate, or at most, become differences in emphasis when the models are applied" (p. 11; see also Andrews et al., 2011). Overall, advocates of the RNR model assert that they "remain very open to RNR being informed by psychological models of motivation" (Andrews et al., 2011, p. 739). Moreover, they "do not dismiss the possibility that a more generalized and perhaps innate needs is important" (i.e., primary human goods may generate intrinsic motivation) (p. 739). However, the fact that the current RNR version does not consider primary human goods limits its theoretical perspective on motivation and social reintegration.

In sum, from a theoretical perspective, the GLM do presents a broader perspective of motivation than the RNR model. Two considerations are relevant. First, while the RNR model understands motivation through the impact of reward-cost contingencies (external motivation), the GLM understands motivation also through humans' strive for their primary goods (intrinsic motivation). Second, while the RNR model uses motivation to achieve treatment goals (e.g., minimum attrition, change in dynamic risk factors) and social goals (e.g., reduction in recidivism), the GLM also uses motivation to achieve personal goals (e.g., optimal psychological functioning and prosocial reintegration).

Controversial Issue 2: The Role of Values in Offender Rehabilitation

The second controversial issue questions the attention that models of offender rehabilitation should pay to values. Advocates of the GLM criticize the RNR model for downplaying the role of values in offender rehabilitation. They argue that the RNR model considers values only within the context of empirical validity and service delivery. First, they assert that the RNR model's empirical orientation conveys the false impression that the therapeutic process in this model is value-free. According to Ward and Maruna (2007), values in the RNR model can be viewed as "equivalent to subjective preferences of individuals, along the lines of taste preferences for certain foods" (p. 77). That is, the RNR ignores the fact that rehabilitation is a value-laden process. For example, it ignores that "every rehabilitation program presupposes conceptions of possible good lives for offenders and, associated with this, an understanding of the necessary internal and external conditions for living such lives" (Ward, 2002a, p. 513). Second, values in the RNR model mainly serve to constrain undesired attempts to study or practice correctional rehabilitation. According to this criticism, values within the RNR model "seem to play a *moderating role*" in correctional rehabilitation (Ward et al., 2012, p. 105, emphasis added).

Thus, Ward and his colleagues proposed the GLM as a model that endorses a value-laden perspective of rehabilitation and considers the *mediating role* of values in the reintegration process (Ward et al., 2012). In brief, this is a comprehensive perspective that presupposes three types of values in offender rehabilitation: (1) prudential values (i.e., primary human goods), which represent the good for a person in the broadest sense; (2) ethical values, which represent the core standards of living and behaving in a particular community; and (3) epistemic (or cognitive) values, which represent the standards for conducting the best rehabilitative practice. In terms of this typology of values, advocates of the GLM criticize the RNR model for focusing on epistemic values and professional ethics while paying little attention to the prudential values that underlie delivery of service. Then, they argue that values in the GLM serve to identify therapeutic goals, and to direct the delivery of psychological needs and social resources that are essential for offender prosocial reintegration.

Within the GLM's literature, the debate on this issue is often demonstrated through the comparison between the GLM's primary human goods and the RNR model's criminogenic needs. According to Ward and Maruna (2007), the primary human goods represent "objective" values because they are "motives that incline individuals to seek types of experiences and objects, outcomes that objectively result in greater physical health and well-being" (p. 77). In essence, these values also "reflect individuals' judgments about what kind of activities and experiences are worth pursing in their lives and likely to meet their core and related interests" (Day & Ward, 2010, p. 290). According to this perspective, the values that underlie the RNR model's criminogenic needs are "subjective" values because they reflect "normative judgments that such risk factors or predictors are needs" (Ward, 2002a, p. 525). That is, they represent ethical or epistemological values, but not prudential values.

Advocates of the RNR model agree that the criminogenic needs were not constructed to reflect objective prudential values (i.e., are not considered intrinsic benefits for offenders). According to Andrews and Bonta (2010), the term "need" in the concept "criminogenic needs" is used for a "practical reason" (p. 28). Their practical expectation is that "if criminogenic need factors are reduced, the chances of criminal involvement will decrease" (p. 28). In fact, within the RNR model, criminogenic needs are not intrinsic benefits for offenders, but "simply predictors of future criminal conduct" that were identified on single-wave longitudinal studies (i.e., changes from intake to retest in these factors were linked with reoffending) (p. 28). In that sense, the goodness of criminogenic needs for offender rehabilitation resides in their empirical validity and human service orientation (i.e., their epistemic and ethical values).

More broadly than criminogenic needs, it seems that the RNR theoretical framework—the psychology of criminal conduct (PCC) and the general personality and cognitive social learning model (GPCSLP)—pays little attention to prudential values. First, according to Andrews and Bonta (2010), the values "at the base of PCC" include the respect for human diversity (i.e., individual differences) and human behavior complexity (i.e., the multiple influences on behavior) (p. 5). In essence, this respect for diversity and complexity reflects epistemic and ethical values rather than prudential values. That is, values in the PCC serve the "interests of all who are interested in the criminal behavior of individuals," but not the offenders' own core preferred primary goods or commitments (p. 6).

Second, the little attention to values can also be demonstrated by another core value of the PCC: the respect for personal autonomy. Notably, this value was added only in a recent version of the PCC (Andrews & Bonta, 2010). This inclusion reveals how advocates of the RNR model and the GLM differ in how they perceive the concept of personal autonomy. Whereas Ward and his colleagues perceive personal autonomy as a prudential value that guides personal choices, Andrews and Bonta perceive this concept as an ethical value that aims to protect offenders from the punitive nature of correctional systems.

In sum, the GLM expands the perspective on values in offender rehabilitation. The inclusion of the primary human goods along the rehabilitative process allows for a comprehensive evaluation of what offenders need and want in their way out of crime. That is, the GLM's unique contribution resides in its consistent effort to understand and address offenders' core values (human primary goods as prudential values). This approach fosters discussions about the priorities that each society chooses for this complex task. Accordingly, advocates of the GLM assume that such orientation persuades "individuals to reorient (and at times replace) their core values and the way these values are instantiated in their lifestyles" (Ward, 2013, p. xxii). That is, to motivate offenders toward choice behavior that will reduce their future offending and enhance their social reintegration.

However, the GLM's theoretical framework seems to have a major flaw. Its emphasis on prudential values seems to downplay the importance of epistemic values in the correctional systems. Such values are expected to restrain inappropriate applications of the GLM's theoretical ideas. Essentially, Ward and his colleagues are well aware of this risk. For example, Ward and Maruna (2007) stated that values in rehabilitation should prevent attempts to "subject individuals to empirically unsupported interventions" (p. 37). In addition, Day and Ward (2010) remind us that the punitive nature of the correctional systems tends to distort therapeutic practices that aim to promote offenders' well-being. That is, within a correctional system, even forensic psychologists with good intentions are not immune from such undesired outcomes in treatment delivery.

Despite these self-warnings, the GLM's theoretical framework does not require rigorous scientific examinations before applying its theoretical ideas (see Chapters 5 and 6). As opposed to the RNR model, the development of the GLM has not followed knowledge from successful attempts to reduce reoffending. Thus, overall, the GLM is a model of offender rehabilitation without strong epistemic values. Inevitably, this fact lessens its potential contribution to the field of rehabilitation.

Controversial Issue 3: The Role of Needs in Offender Rehabilitation

The third controversial issue between the GLM and the RNR model involves the conceptualization of offender needs. In general, both models agree that the concept of offender needs "indicates a lack or deficiency of some kind, a lack of valued good" (Ward & Stewart, 2003a, p. 128). However, the RNR model and GLM differ in their perspective of this "valued good." While advocates of the GLM conceptualize some personal needs as internal drive to attain human goals, advocates of the RNR model conceptualize needs as personal deficits that are associated with criminal behavior.

According to advocates of the GLM, offenders' needs motive them to attain what they perceive as their most important goals in life—their primary human goods. In essence, they take a "naturalistic and humanistic" perspective of needs that focuses on what offenders want for their optimal functioning (Ward & Maruna, 2007). Specifically, needs "are concerned with attainment of objective goods that sustain or enhance an individual's life, their absence will harm a person in some way or else increase the chances of harm occurring in the future" (Ward & Stewart, 2003a, p. 128). For these scholars, such understanding of offenders' needs "stipulates that effective rehabilitation ultimately requires articulating a view of human well being" (p. 126).

According to the RNR perspective, needs are a practical concept. Thus, needs should be identified and classified according to their potential to be changed (stable or acute dynamic factors) and according to the relative impact of such change on offenders' tendency to reoffend (criminogenic or noncriminogenic needs). Within the RNR model, such potential is determined by research that seeks an empirical understanding of criminal behavior. Thus, overall, advocates of the RNR model perceive the concept of needs as "treatment needs" for reducing offenders' tendency to reoffend, rather than as "offender needs" for attaining his or her most valued goals (Ogloff & Davis, 2004).

By contrast, Ward and his colleagues suggest the GLM as a model that describes a better conceptualization of offender needs. First, they criticize the RNR model for endorsing an "inappropriate and misleading" perspective of needs (Ward & Stewart, 2003b, p. 220). Ward and Maruna (2007, p. 78), admittedly with a touch of hyperbole, depicted the RNR's perspective as setting forth an "Orwellian redefinition of needs." As an alternative, they offered the concept of primary human goods as a more adequate way to envision the needs relevant in offenders' lives. Notably, within this reconceptualization of needs, Ward and his colleagues also redefine the RNR model's concept of criminogenic needs. Within the GLM, they redefine such needs as any dynamic risk factors that signal the lack of internal and external conditions necessary to attain given primary human goods. For example, criminogenic needs signal the required skills, capabilities, opportunities, and supports that offenders need for achieving primary goods in a socially appropriate manner. Thus, overall, they assert that their perspective advances the field of offender rehabilitation because it specifies the values that underlie the therapeutic process and because it provides a coherent explanation about the relationship between various needs.

Advocates of the RNR model do not reject the potential contribution of this reconceptualization. In this regard, they accept the possibility that the inclusion of the primary human goods may lead to a redefinition of criminogenic needs. According to Bonta and Andrews (2003), "perhaps, basic human needs can account for a link to criminogenic needs and explain the inter-relationships among criminogenic needs" (p. 218). However, they consistently require that such reconceptualization of needs has to be operationalized and tested (Andrews et al., 2011; Bonta & Andrews, 2003; Wormith et al., 2012).

Controversial Issue 4: The Role of Risk in Offender Rehabilitation

As mentioned in previous chapters, the GLM and RNR model agree that their ultimate goal is to reduce offenders' future reoffending. However, advocates of these models disagree on the adequate perception of risk in correctional rehabilitation. Proponents of the GLM assert that risk is a multifaceted and contextualized concept. They view risk as a broad concept that encompasses both the offenders' character and lifestyle and the social and cultural factors that generate the common perception of risk (e.g., degree of social exclusion, opportunities for prosocial lifestyle) (Ward & Maruna, 2007).

In this regard, Ward and his colleagues criticize the RNR model for adopting a narrow perspective of risk. According to their argument, the RNR model embraces an "individualistic or psychometric" perspective of risk that "is most concerned with the issues of offender management, and not with questions of value or character (unless the latter are viewed as measurable sources of antisocial behavior)" (p. 81). In other words, they argue that by viewing risk as a predictor of criminal behavior, the RNR model reduces this multifaceted concept to its empirical aspects.

Ward and Maruna (2007) assert that this narrow perspective of risk stems from the RNR model's narrow perception of human being. That is, it reflects the perspective's "core idea" that "individuals are basically a bundle or cluster of properties that are in principle observable and measurable" (p. 79). Thus, they argue that the RNR model's concept of risk "creates the impression that offenders are intrinsically bearers of risk and that specific risk factors inhere or are embedded in them" (p. 81). In this regard, Ward and his colleagues often use the analogy "pin cushion model" of offender rehabilitation to describe the RNR's approach to risk (e.g., Ward & Mann, 2004).

Advocates of the GLM suggest their model as a perspective of risk that also accounts for the psychological, social, situational, and cultural contexts of risk factors (Ward & Maruna, 2007). They argue that, for any potential risk factor, the GLM considers both actuarial measures (for indicating the potential magnitude of risk) and holistic clinical examinations (for revealing the development and maintenance of risk). Thus, they assert that the GLM provides a broader perspective of risk than the RNR model.

Once again, advocates of the RNR model respond to this criticism with their practical perspective of offender rehabilitation. First, Andrews et al. (2011) argue that establishing a psychometric perception of risk is a desired task for a model of offender rehabilitation. That is, "any model and clinical intervention should be based on structured assessments with reliable and valid instruments that have been designed with reference to the underlying theory and to the task at hand" (p. 746). They view this criticism as a "compliment" for their model.

Second, advocates of the RNR model assert that their model considers both personal and contextual aspects of risk. According to Andrews and Bonta (2010), their perception of risk is broad because it is based on a comprehensive examination of variables from multiple disciplines. This includes personal and contextual variables that were found "in biology, personality, attitude and belief, aptitudes and skills, learning history, family, peer relationships, broader social arrangements, and the immediate situation of action" (p. 13). However, within the RNR model, the relative attention to these variables is determined by their practical value—the demonstrated prediction of criminal behavior.

In sum, it seems that the GLM expands the theoretical definition of risk in offender rehabilitation. While proponents of the RNR model follow the evidence-based perception of risk, advocates of the GLM endorse a more holistic approach to this concept. Essentially, Ward and his colleagues reject the notion that empirical methods can encompass its multifaceted aspects of risk. That is, they claim that taken in isolation, the RNR's evidence-based risk factors cannot explain the risk that individual offenders impose on the society. For these scholars, a reliable understanding of such risk can only be achieved during a therapeutic process that considers these risk factors within the context of personal striving toward human primary goods.

Controversial Issue 5: The Role of Contextual Factors in Offender Rehabilitation

The fifth controversial issue between the GLM and the RNR model revolves around the adequate attention to contextual factors in offender rehabilitation. Advocates of the GLM criticize the RNR model for minimizing the role of personal situations and social network in its explanation of criminal behavior. They assert that a model of offender rehabilitation should actively build and strengthen environmental opportunities, resources, and support. Advocates of the RNR model reject the criticism that their theoretical framework underemphasizes contextual and ecological factors. However, they argue, correctional interventions should be aware of their limited capacity to change the social environment.

Specifically, Ward and his colleagues criticize the role of contextual factors in the RNR's theoretical framework (Ward & Gannon, 2006; Ward & Maruna, 2007; Ward & Stewart, 2003a, 2003b). According to Ward and Maruna (2007), "the RNR model explicitly underplays the contextual nature of human behavior and seeks to build general principles that are applied without much consideration of the local circumstances and macro-economic forces impacting individual lives" (p. 82) (see also Ward, Melser, & Yates, 2007). According to Casey, Day, Vess, and Ward (2013), attention to the impact of ecological factors on offenders' behavior is a crucial aspect because "environmental factors have the potential to facilitate or impede the maintenance of treatment-related changes to dynamic risk factors" (p. 41). In essence, this criticism views the RNR model's rehabilitative efforts as less realistic and relevant to offenders' life and, therefore, less effective in facilitating reintegration into social environment.

Ward and his colleagues contend that the GLM is a model that gives more attention to contextual factors because its general assumption posits that any person depends on other people and social institutions in pursuing commitments and interests. They assert that this interdependency perspective on human being explains criminality because offenders' social networks determine the opportunities that individuals can use to pursue their goals in life in a prosocial way.

Advocates of the RNR reject the criticism that their model does not consider contextual factors. According to Andrews et al. (2011), the RNR's theoretical framework "was explicitly designed to reflect both personal risk factors and contextual or ecological factors" (p. 746). Specifically, the General Personality and Cognitive Social Learning (GPCSL) perspective represents behavioral and criminological theories that explain criminal behavior through the social contexts in which offenders are embedded (e.g., differential association theory, social learning theory, social bond theory, general strain theory). Moreover, this perspective consists of an important assumption that human functioning is a result of continuous reciprocal interaction of personal and environmental factors (Andrews & Bonta, 2010).

For example, Andrews et al. (2011) assert that the RNR model's criminogenic needs "include such external factors as family relationships, the influence of peers, and the work or educational environment in which the offender might spend a good part of the day" (p. 746). Within the RNR model, the therapeutic process is expected to address these contextual issues by building "rewarding alternatives to procriminal ways of thinking, feeling, and acting," and by enhancing "rewards and satisfactions for prosocial pursuits in the context of peers, family, school/work, and leisure/recreation" (p. 743). In addition, Andrews and Bonta (2010) assert that the RNR model considers ecological factors in its attention to relapse-prevention plans and aftercare services. Such practices are used with offenders in their natural environment to assist them in maintaining and enhancing the changes that occurred during the therapeutic process.

In addition, advocates of the RNR model oppose the notion that a model of offender rehabilitation has to expend its services beyond the justice context. In brief, they assert that such practice entails an unwise and unrealistic goal for a model of offender rehabilitation. First, they argue that it is unwise to expand the power of justice by adding the task of attaining offenders' optimal functioning. They assert that, despite the good intentions, the nature of correctional systems is the restriction of liberty and managing criminal sanctions, not fulfilling offenders' good lives (Andrews et al., 2011). Thus, they prefer to leave this task to others in the health, mental health, education, welfare, recreation, and psycho-recreation systems, and to ask them "to recognize crime prevention as a legitimate pursuit" (p. 750).

Second, advocates of the RNR model assert that the achievement of both the basic task of treatment and social reintegration is an unrealistic goal for correctional interventions. In this regard, Andrews et al. (2011) argue that evaluation studies have shown that it is difficult enough to conduct therapeutic processes that result in a reduction of offender recidivism. Therefore, they contend that broadening the focus of the rehabilitative process "to include the pursuit of excellence across the whole domain of human needs may be asking too much" (p. 750). Relatedly, without demonstrating clear success in reducing recidivism, the allocation of social resources to solve offenders' problems may undermine the legitimacy of correction rehabilitation. Without proven effectiveness, it is difficult to justify correctional interventions that equip offenders with opportunities and resources that nonoffenders with similar environmental problem do not receive (Cullen & Jonson, 2012).

In sum, the GLM's theoretical perspective expands the role of contextual factors in offender rehabilitation. While the RNR model focuses on these factors within the correctional system, the GLM also aims to address their larger sources in society. As will be presented in the next section, the challenge to using these theoretical ideas resides in their implementation within the criminal system justice. As Willis et al. (2012) observe, "we acknowledge that external constraints such as resourcing and legislative demands might present barriers to fully integrating a GLM approach" (p. 138).

Controversial Issue 6: The Role of Personality in Offender Rehabilitation

The sixth controversial issue revolves around the way that each model understands and approaches offenders' personality. Advocates of the GLM argue that the RNR model presents a static perception of human personality because it involves "little more than one's dispositional traits" (Ward & Maruna, 2007, p. 84). They set forth the GLM as a broader theoretical framework to understand antisocial personality. They assert that the GLM explains both the static and more dynamic aspects of human personality.

Specifically, advocates of the GLM follow McAdams's (1994) three-level perspective on human personality. The first level is trait ("the 'having' aspects of the self") (Maruna, 2001, p. 87). According to Ward and Maruna (2007), individual's *traits* are "characteristic ways of behaving [that] are thought to have strong genetic component, tend to be shaped early in an individual's development, and are unlikely to change substantially over the life course" (p. 84). The second level of personality is personal striving ("the 'doing' aspects"). This level expresses the ongoing interaction between individuals' personal goals and the actual achievement of these goals (Maruna, 2001). According to Ward and Maruna (2007), this sense of the self is more dynamic than traits because personal strivings "change over the life course in response to changes in context and normative, social expectations" (p. 85).

McAdams's third level of human personality is self-narratives ("the 'making' aspects") (Maruna, 2001, p. 87). Within the GLM, this is the most significant domain of personality. Ward and Maruna (2007) assume that self-narratives are important because "modern adults create an internalized life-story—or personal myth—in order to provide their lives with unity, purpose and meaning" (p. 85). In that sense, personal identity is considered as "a lifelong project that individuals continuously restructure in light of new experiences and information" (Maruna, 2001, p. 42). According to the GLM, ongoing criminality and desistance from crime exist in this level of personality. Thus, changes in offenders' antisocial behavior require a new personal story about the self. As described in Chapters 5 and 6, advocates of the GLM assume that offenders develop their new prosocial personal identity through a process of self-reflection that examines the priority they ascribe to primary human goods.

Thus, based on these three levels of human personality, advocates of the GLM criticize the RNR model for focusing on offenders' traits and neglecting the role of personal striving and personal identity. They argue that this limited RNR model's approach to personal change process decreases its capacity to guide changes in offenders' antisocial lifestyle.

In response to this criticism, advocates of the RNR model assert that their explanation of human conduct is more sophisticated than the simplistic argument that traits control such behavior. They present their general definition of human personality as a "characteristic pattern of thinking, feeling and acting that may be evident among individuals within any particular social location that may be defined according to age, gender, race, ethnicity or geographical area" (Andrews & Bonta, 1994, pp. 59–60; see also Andrews & Bonta, 2010). That is, they argue that the RNR model explains human personality as the product of dynamic relationships between cognitive, affective, and behavioral factors.

Indeed, during its early development, the RNR model approached human personality with an emphasis on the scientific evidence that supported the trait perspective of personality (Andrews & Bonta, 1994, 1998; Andrews & Wormith, 1989). However, according to Bonta and Andrews (2017), the RNR's theoretical framework also endorses the situational/psychological-processing perspective of personality. In essence, this perspective explains human behavior by "specifying under what situational conditions a trait was expressed" (p. 91). Thus, they argue that, within the RNR model, the way in which individuals perceive and respond to situations vary from relatively stable to more dynamic interactions (e.g., McGuire, 2004).

Specifically, this approach aims to understand human personality through the elements of the situation of action, and how the individual (with particular traits) interprets this situation (i.e., the cognitive and social-emotional processes that he or she uses in the situation). For example, Andrews and Bonta (2010) cite Walter Mischel's integrative theory. This theory posits that cognitive-affective processing—such as encoding, affect, expectancies, and self-regulatory planning—act as potential "mediators between personality traits and the situation" (p. 197). In addition, they mention John Mayer's ideas about human personality. According to this perspective, personality consists of systems frameworks such as "motives, emotions . . . memory, intelligence, social attachments, and attitude and expectation" (p. 198).

In sum, both the GLM and the RNR model view personality as involving stable personality traits and cognitive processes. However, the GLM presents a broader theoretical perspective to explain changes in antisocial personality. First, while the RNR model explains the development of personality through interactions that reoccur in the immediate situation of action (i.e., traits–situation interactions), the GLM also explains this development as a continuing effort toward the attainment of primary human goods (i.e., personal striving). Second, while the RNR model explains changes in offenders' reactions through the balance in the perceived reward-cost contingencies, the GLM also explains such reactions through the experiences and information processing that structures the way offenders perceive their life (i.e., also through changes in individuals' self-identity).

Controversial Issue 7: The Role of Human Agency in Offender Rehabilitation

This controversial issue revolves around the adequate attention to human agency in offender rehabilitation. Ward and his colleagues criticized the RNR model for taking a "restricted and passive view of human nature" (Ward & Maruna, 2007, p. 22). They argue that the RNR model's overemphasis on radical behaviorism creates a view of persons as a "passive recipient of behavioral contingencies" (Ward et al., 2012, p. 101). That is, the RNR model explains human behavior only in terms of internal and external pressures that bring behavior in alignment with a socially accepted standard of conduct. According to Ward and Marshall (2007), this "narrow notion of human nature" "ignores the fact that as evolved, biologically embodied organisms, humans naturally seek and require certain goods to live fulfilling and personally satisfying lives" (p. 283).

Thus, advocates of the GLM contend that their model offers a broader theoretical perspective of human nature. They assert that, within the GLM, human behavior is a function not only of reinforcement but also the product of innate desire to fulfill basic human goals that are "intrinsically beneficial" for them (Ward et al., 2012, p. 95). Relatedly, Ward and Maruna (2007) assert that these basic humans goods—the GLM's primary human goods—also expand the potential rewards that are typically sought by individuals. That is, the GLM provides offenders with rewards that not only keep them within the standard of conduct (e.g., away from criminality) but also serve as independent personal incentives to live a prosocial fulfilling life (e.g., the reward of increasing their sense of autonomy and success) (Yates, Prescott, & Ward, 2010).

Advocates of the RNR model view this controversy issue from their practical point of view. Essentially, as Ward and Maruna (2007) mentioned, the RNR model "does not preclude primary human goods and human needs" (p. 88). According to Andrews et al. (2011), they "appreciate that human beings seek goods in pursuit of personal well-being", but also remind that there is no scientific evidence that the psychological functioning of human beings is determined by the fulfillment of inner needs (p. 745). They follow the evidence that supports the impact of behavioral contingencies on human psychological functioning and conclude that "in practice, in the clinical situation, the social learning principles are the stronger elements of effective services" (p. 745).

In sum, while the GLM embraces a broader theoretical perspective of human nature and behavior, the RNR model adheres to the evidence-based aspects of behavioral change. In essence, this reflects a general pattern of the RNR-GLM debate. As presented in previous theoretical controversial issues, Ward and his colleagues have consistently criticized the RNR model for endorsing a limited perspective of offender rehabilitation. In turn, they offered the GLM as a comprehensive model of offender rehabilitation—a model that uses both evidence-based and holistic perspectives when undertaking the complex task of reducing offender reoffending. In response, advocates of the RNR model did not dismiss these theoretical perspectives as a potential enhancement to their model. This openness to the GLM's ideas is due to the current lack of scientific studies that have evaluated whether, in fact, they have incremental value for improving offender rehabilitation. These scholars consistently insist that the GLM's theoretical ideas must be operationalized, tested, and shown to impact recidivism before they can be integrated within the RNR model.

Thus, overall, it seems that the GLM fulfills its promise to provide a broad theoretical framework that encompasses the RNR model's evidence-based perspectives and intends "to augment and enhance intervention delivered within the framework of the Risk/Need/Responsivity Model" (Yates et al., 2010, p. ix). The next section will examine how this promise is operated within the RNR's correctional framework. That is, the section will discuss the pattern of the RNR-GLM debates within a common correctional framework.

The Correctional Framework of the RNR-GLM Debate

Advocates of both the GLM and the RNR model agree that the models are compatible approaches to correction rehabilitation. Ward and Maruna (2007, p. 142) argue, for example, that the GLM is "a complementary theory" to the RNR model because it is "able to incorporate the principles of the Risk-Need Model while expending on them" (see also Whitehead, Ward, & Collie, 2007, p. 596). Thus, according to the GLM, "applying treatment on the basis of the GLM can be effectively implemented in conjunction with" the RNR model approach (Marshall, Marshall, Serran, & O'Brien, 2011, p. 20). However, within the GLM's literature, it is unclear if advocates of the GLM consider the integration of only the major RNR model's principles (i.e., the three risk-need-responsivity principles) or the entire principles that comprise the RNR model (e.g., Ward & Maruna, 2007; Willis, Ward, & Levenson, 2014). Similarly, advocates of the RNR model support the notion of compatible models and assert that some of the "alleged differences between RNR and GLM are illusory" and "mostly semantic" (Wormith et al., 2012, p. 112). They assert that the "RNR already subsumes many of the features of GLM" (Andrews et al., 2011, p. 737).

This section examines the above statements within the RNR perspective's correctional framework. Specifically, this section uses the RNR model's correctional domains to examine whether the GLM and RNR model are compatible or incompatible approaches to offender treatment. These domains include the RNR model's core principles, key clinical issues, and organizational principles. Within each domain, this section discusses the agreed and controversial correctional issues for each of the RNR paradigm's principles in these domains. The goal of this section is to provide a better view on the correctional boundaries of each model, as well as to examine their potential integration. In this regard, Table 7.2 summarizes the correctional framework of the RNR-GLM debate. This table shows the potential agreements (the middle column) and disagreements (the left column) within the RNR-GLM debate for each RNR model's principle.

Note that this section does not include the RNR approach's overarching principles domain (the principles of respect for the person and the normative context, psychological theory, and general enhancement of crime prevention services). That is because most of the relevant issues in this domain were already discussed in the previous section. Nevertheless, to complete the overarching correctional perspective of the RNR-GLM debate, this section begins with a discussion about the role of psychological theories within the debate.

The Psychological Theories Within the RNR-GLM Debate

Both the GLM and RNR model adopt a psychological perspective of criminal behavior. In general, theories that explain human behavior suggest individual variables and behavioral strategies that have a potential to modify criminality. In that sense, the two models differ from mainstream criminology

TABLE 7.2 The correctional framework of the RNR-GLM debate

Adherence to the RNR's Correctional Principles	Potential Agreements Within the RNR-GLM Debate	Potential Disagreements Within the RNR-GLM Debate
Adherence to the psychological perspective of criminal conduct.	Correctional intervention should follow a social psychology perspective of crime.	Correctional interventions should also follow the perspectives of the humanistic and positive psychology. GLM: Within the social psychology perspective, it is better to follow the social cognitive approach to treatment than the cognitive social learning approach.
Adherence to the provision of human services.	Correctional intervention should provide human services.	None.
Adherence to the risk principle.	The intensity of correctional services should be matched to offenders' level of risk.	RNR model: The GLM's holistic approach to risk may lead to different characteristics of low-, medium, and high-risk offenders. RNR model: The GLM's dynamic perception of risk may lead to intensity of services that varies too often. RNR model: The GLM may provide too much service to low-risk offenders.
Adherence to the need principle.	"Criminogenic needs" (empirically validated dynamic risk factors) are important intermediate targets.	GLM: the "Criminogenic needs" should not be targeted predominantly. GLM: Correctional interventions should examine the relative importance of each dynamic factor within the particular therapeutic context.
Adherence to the general responsivity principle.	Behavioral and cognitive-behavioral treatment modalities demonstrated success in correctional settings. Cognitive-behavioral and social learning strategies demonstrated success in correctional settings.	GLM: The content of correctional intervention should consist of more cognitive strategies than behavioral strategies. GLM: Correctional intervention should focus more on offenders' strengths than on offenders' deficits. GLM: Correctional intervention should use self-reflection as their major therapeutic strategy (promotes the attainment of human primary goods).
Adherence to the specific responsivity principle.	Correctional interventions should conduct a collaborative and transparent therapeutic process. The content of the therapeutic intervention should not be unstructured or overly structured.	GLM: Correctional interventions should collaborate with offenders in a way that express their human agency and autonomy. GLM: Correctional interventions should use treatment guides over treatment manuals.
Adherence to the breadth (or multimodal) principle.	High-risk offenders need multimodal interventions.	GLM: It is a mistake to determine a strict ratio between criminogenic and noncriminogenic needs.
Adherence to the strength principle.	Offenders' strengths are important factors of the therapeutic process.	GLM: Offenders' strengths are independent factors for behavioral change, not only factors that facilitate change.

Adherence to the RNR's Correctional Principles	Potential Agreements Within the RNR-GLM Debate	Potential Disagreements Within the RNR-GLM Debate
Adherence to the structured assessment principle.	Correctional intervention should use structured assessment instruments. Correctional intervention should conduct a structured assessment process.	GLM: The assessments of primary and secondary goods should not be limited to structured empirically validated assessment instruments. GLM: Correctional interventions should use clinical discretion to integrate assessment and treatment rather than estimations of actuarial-based assessment instruments.
Adherence to the professional discretion principle.	Deviation from the RNR's principles is an inevitable practice.	GLM: Correctional intervention should not limit the therapists' "very specific reasons" to deviate from the RNR's principles.
Adherence to the community-based principle.	Correctional interventions are more effective in community settings than in institutional settings. Offenders' natural environment is an important aspect of any rehabilitative process.	None.
Adherence to the core correctional staff practice.	Therapists in correctional interventions should have the skills for developing and establishing good therapeutic relationship with offenders.	RNR model: Correctional interventions should structure the therapists' collaborative process with offenders.
Adherence to the management principle.	Correctional interventions should employ organizational aspects, including a quality assurance mechanism.	RNR model: Quality assurance mechanism requires a structured supervision on therapists' clinical discretion.

that embraces a more sociological perspective on crime. However, within their psychological perspective, the GLM and RNR model hold different approach to offender rehabilitation.

First, while advocates of the RNR model concentrate on social psychology, advocates of the GLM also consider the humanistic psychology (focus on capabilities and potentialities for positive experience) and positive psychology (focus on optimal human functioning). Second, within their social psychology perspective on human behavior, each model focuses on a different theory of human behavior.

In general, the social psychology perspective on human behavior is "the scientific study of how we feel about, think about, and behave toward the people around us and how our feelings, thoughts, and behaviors are influenced by those people" (Stangor, 2011, p. 10). Within this context, whereas advocates of the RNR model adopt a *cognitive social learning perspective*, advocates of the GLM endorse a *social cognitive perspective*.

The RNR's theoretical framework assumes that the ongoing person–environment interactions determine the person's psychological functioning. According to this assumption, the main source of behavioral learning involves the observation of others. Thus, the RNR's *cognitive social learning* perspective of human behavior integrates operant conditioning (reward–cost contingencies) and the impact of cognitive events on the person ("a crucial mediator of action") (McGuire, 2004, p. 53).

By contrast, the GLM's theoretical framework focuses on cognitive explanations of human behavior—the mental activity that relates to social activities (i.e., social cognitive explanations). In essence, advocates of this model assume that psychological functioning is determined through cognitive, vicarious, self-regulatory, and self-reflective processes. That is, they assume that the main source of behavioral change consists of internal personal factors. Thus, they use the humanistic and positive psychology to provide alternative theoretical explanations to behavior (alternatives to explanations that focus on the impact of behavioral contingencies). Overall, the GLM explains behavior also through the peoples' intrinsic motivation that pushes their behavior toward what is perceived as the most important goals in life.

According to Andrews et al. (2011), practical reasons lead the RNR model to focus on the social learning perspective over the social cognitive perspective. Simply, empirical studies suggest that this psychological approach to offender rehabilitation is an appropriate way to provide effective correctional services. In this regard, they argue that neither the elements of the social cognitive approach nor the operationalization of the humanistic and positive psychology gain the necessary empirical support for guiding therapeutic strategies with offenders.

Despite the clear empirical evidence, advocates of the GLM continue to follow the humanistic theories' approach. In general, they argue that the importance of the problem is more important than the quality of methodology. That is, "the justifications for rehabilitation are essentially moral arguments about what society ought to do in relation to offenders, and arguments about what we ought to do cannot simply be derived from evidence about what we can do" (Raynor & Robinson, 2009, p. 17). In other words, they assert that changes in criminality can be explained through various cognitive processes, and the development of these processes within the field of correctional rehabilitation should not be blocked by a rigid evidence-based approach.

Domain 1: The RNR-GLM Debate and the RNR's Core Principles

The Provision of Human Service Within the RNR-GLM Debate

As models of rehabilitation, both the GLM and RNR model highly support the provision of human service to offenders. In essence, these models direct correctional interventions to respond to criminality by offering rewarding prosocial alternatives rather than by inflicting punitive sanctions. Essentially, this approach in corrections has theoretical reasons as well as very strong empirical support (Bonta & Andrews, 2017; Lipsey & Cullen, 2007).

The Adherence to the Risk Principle Within the RNR-GLM Debate

Within the RNR's correctional framework, the risk principle links offenders' level of risk to effective correctional treatment. According to this principle, correctional interventions should match the intensity of human service with offenders' level of risk (i.e., with the categorical chance that a person will reoffend). In practice, medium-risk and high-risk offenders should receive more rehabilitative services than low-risk offenders (see Chapter 4). This approach reflects a correctional policy to allocate resource to those who need it most (i.e., more risk means more problems to address). In addition, the risk principle reflects the need to protect low-risk offenders from the negative influence of dangerous offenders who tend to participate in intensive interventions. Essentially, both theoretical and empirical research lend support to the risk principle (Andrews, 2011; Lipsey, 2014).

Advocates of the GLM endorse this general notion of the risk principle (Ward & Maruna, 2007; Willis et al., 2012). However, within the RNR-GLM debate, each model may apply the risk principle in a different way. First, interventions that follow the two models may not agree upon the factors that constitute the labels low-risk, moderate-risk, or high-risk offender. While the RNR model explains risk through offenders' criminogenic needs (i.e., higher risk means more problems in the criminogenic domains), the GLM argues that the symmetric relationship between criminogenic needs and offenders' risk does not reflect the complexity of this concept (Ward & Maruna, 2007). As mentioned in the previous section, GLM-consistent interventions are expected to examine risk also in accordance with the person's attainment of primary human goods.

Second, interventions that follow the two models may not agree about the stability of offenders' risk to reoffend. The RNR model views risk as a relatively stable concept and therefore suggests that interventions should conduct only periodic reassessments on offenders (e.g., before and after the treatment program). The GLM views risk as a more dynamic concept and therefore requires that treatment staff conduct an ongoing reassessment of risk. In practice, this differential use of assessment means that while the intensity of services in RNR-based interventions will tend to be stable, the intensity of services in GLM-consistent interventions may be more dynamic. For example, therapists who follow the GLM may change the intensity of treatment based on new information about offender's overall risk. Thus, within the RNR-GLM debate, the risk principle may be applied in a more flexible manner than in the RNR model.

Third, interventions that follow the two models may not agree about the intensity of services that low-risk offenders should receive. As discussed above, the RNR model argues that correctional interventions should allocate "minimal or even no" therapeutic resources to offenders with low potential to reoffend (Bonta & Andrews, 2017, p. 179). Advocates of this model support correctional assistance that will improve the reintegration process of low-risk offenders without increasing their tendency to reoffend. By contrast, the GLM endorses different perspective on correctional intervention for low-risk offenders. This model advises staff to provide therapeutic resources according to the potential "benefit" that these will bring to offenders (Ward & Maruna, 2007, p. 99). In other words, advocates of the GLM support the provision of services to low-risk offenders as long as they promote the attainment of offenders' primary goods in a socially accepted way. Thus, overall, GLM-consistent interventions may determine the intensity of services by integrating offenders' level of risk (high, moderate, or low) and psychological needs (e.g., activities that enhance their psychological functioning). Within the RNR-GLM debate, such practice means a potential distortion of the RNR model's risk principle.

The Adherence to the Need Principle Within the RNR-GLM Debate

The need principle asserts that during treatment, correctional interventions should target for change dynamic factors. In essence, this principle distinguishes between two categories of dynamic risk factors. One category consists of dynamic factors that, when changed, reduced offenders' tendency to reoffend. These are called "criminogenic needs." The second category consists of dynamic factors that, when changed, are unlikely to reduce offenders' future criminality. These are called "noncriminogenic needs." Within the RNR model, the risk principle directs correctional interventions to target criminogenic needs "predominantly" (Bonta & Andrews, 2017, p. 176).

According to the RNR model, criminogenic needs are necessary intermediate targets that correctional interventions seek to change, with the ultimate goal of offender rehabilitation—the reduction of offenders' tendency to reoffend. As described in Chapter 4, this model identifies seven general criminogenic needs. Essentially, advocates of the RNR model use both criminological theories and empirical research to establish the causal importance of these criminogenic needs. Notably, the predictive validity of the seven criminogenic needs in the field of corrections is now supported by meta-analyses (Bonta & Andrews, 2017).

Advocates of the GLM appreciate the role of the RNR model's criminogenic needs in the rehabilitative process (Ward & Stewart, 2003a). They also accept the empirical distinction between criminogenic and noncriminogenic needs (Ward & Maruna, 2007). However, as discussed in the previous section, the GLM and RNR model differ in how they view the role of needs in offender rehabilitation. Accordingly, they differ in how they apply the need principle in correctional rehabilitation.

Specifically, Ward and Maruna (2007) argue that the distinction between criminogenic and non-criminogenic "makes less sense" during the therapeutic process and "might even be impossible in some cases" (p. 102). They explain that "targeting non-criminogenic needs may be a necessary precondition for being able to effectively target and reduce criminogenic needs" (p. 41). In other words, noncriminogenic needs should not be considered discretionary targets in offender rehabilitation. Rather, they should play an essential role in any therapeutic process that aims to rehabilitate offenders.

Relatedly, within the GLM, the clinical significance of each dynamic factor determines its label as a relevant risk factor. According to Ward and his colleagues, the distinction between criminogenic and noncriminogenic needs should not be a priory. They argue that correctional interventions should determine the relevance criminogenic needs only within the clinical context of each individual. In practice, such clinical significance is concluded by therapists who aim to build a strong therapeutic alliance with offenders and increase offenders' motivation to change their lifestyle.

Thus, within the RNR-GLM debate, the GLM does not guide correctional interventions to target the RNR model's criminogenic needs predominantly. GLM-consistent interventions may address the RNR model's criminogenic needs only as a (important) part of their overall strategy to assist offenders to achieve their primary human goods in a prosocial way (i.e., the GLM's dual aims). However, advocates of the RNR model insist that criminogenic needs should play the primary role in correctional interventions. They explain this position by citing practical reasons (Andrews et al., 2011). First, there is no clear evidence that the GLM's approach to criminogenic/noncriminogenic needs results in reduction of future reoffending. Second, they argue that "targeting criminogenic needs is the more direct and less risky approach to reducing criminal behavior rather than by enhancing human goods" (p. 740). Third, they assert that success in targeting of the areas covered by the RNR's criminogenic needs "leads to personal fulfillment" and thus improve offenders' life (p. 743).

The Adherence to the General Responsivity Principle Within the RNR-GLM Debate

The responsivity principle aims to guide correctional interventions toward the most effective treatment strategies to achieve prosocial change. In this regard, the RNR model distinguishes between the general responsivity of offenders to different styles and modes of service and their specific responsivity to the delivery of particular services.

The RNR model's general responsivity principle advises those providing correctional interventions about the best way to modify offenders' criminogenic needs (i.e., to achieve the interventions' intermediate goals). As mentioned above, advocates of the RNR model rely on their cognitive social learning perspective on human behavior to explain behavioral change among offenders. They argue that the empirical literature on offender rehabilitation consistently shows that behavioral and cognitive-behavioral programs are more successful than other treatment approaches (Ogloff & Davis, 2004). Thus, the RNR model guides correctional interventions to focus on cognitive-behavioral and cognitive social learning strategies (e.g., modeling, role-playing, graduate practice, external and internal reinforcement, skill building, and cognitive restructuring).

Essentially, the underlying assumptions of the GLM provide a different guidance to achieve prosocial behavioral change. As opposed to the RNR-based interventions, GLM-consistent interventions do not build around changing offenders' criminogenic needs. Rather, Ward and his colleagues adopt a theoretical approach that explains criminality through the attainment of primary human goods. As discussed in Chapter 5, they assume that correctional interventions have the potential to reduce future criminality when they enable offenders to secure primary human goods in prosocial ways. In practice, GLM-consistent interventions focus on person-centered strategies such as empathic understanding, skill building, strengths building, self-reflection, self-regulation, and unconditional positive regard (i.e., to "value a person no matter what they do, say, think, and feel") (Van Voorhis & Salisbury, 2014, p. 95). Theoretically, these modalities are drawn from humanistic and positive psychology approaches in conjunction with the social-cognitive perspective of human behavior.

In essence, due to their focus on person-centered strategies, advocates of the GLM tend to present the RNR model's responsivity principle in terms of specific responsivity. For example, Ward and Maruna (2007) explain that "the intent of the responsivity principle is to ensure that therapeutic and other style of correctional intervention are implemented in a way that is likely to make sense to offenders and thus enable them to absorb the program content and make the changes necessary in their life to desist from further offending" (p. 22; see also Willis et al., 2014; Yates et al., 2010). They emphasize the need to tailor the therapeutic process for each offender but pay only little attention to the empirical evidence that supports their general treatment modality. By doing so, they ignore the evidence that client-centered therapy "and other unstructured approaches are contra-indicated with criminal populations" (Ogloff & Davis, 2004, p. 234; see also Van Voorhis & Salisbury, 2014).

The GLM's approach to the general responsivity principle can also be demonstrated by its application of the cognitive-behavioral therapy (CBT). Advocates of the GLM encourage correctional interventions to apply "empirically supported interventions such as CBT" (Willis et al., 2012, p. 126; see also Ward & Stewart, 2003a; Willis et al., 2014). However, the GLM's therapeutic approach may lead correctional intervention to deliver a therapy that is predominantly cognitive. In essence, such practice may lead the GLM-consistent interventions to deliver less structured CBT than that delivered by RNR-based interventions. For example, Marshall et al. (2011) observe that "most sexual offender programs" that were described as CBT did not employ behavioral techniques "and when they are present, they do not seem to be systematically or extensively used" (pp. 77–78).

Thus, it seems that the GLM's overreliance on cognitive strategies (over behavioral strategies) creates its own version of CBT. Within the RNR-GLM debate, it means that GLM-consistent interventions may not apply the same CBT that research has demonstrated empirically as successful in reducing recidivism in the correctional system. Moreover, the GLM's version to CBT may explain the past difficulties of such interventions to reduce recidivism.

As the following principles show, the issue of structured versus semi-structured delivery of treatment remains a permanent controversy within the RNR–GLM debate. Advocates of the RNR model constantly try to bolster the structure of service delivery in correctional rehabilitation (therapeutic content, offender assessments, and organizational aspects). Advocates of the GLM take a different approach to service delivery. From the GLM's perspective, highly structured practice means less attention to what offenders want and need in their rehabilitation process. Thus, overall, the application of the general responsivity principle remains a controversial issue. It seems that a common ground might be found when, during an intervention, advocates of the GLM choose to integrate a systematic use of behavioral techniques that aim to change offenders' antisocial behavior.

The Specific Responsivity Principle Within the RNR-GLM Debate

In general, specific responsivity is a multifaceted construct that considers the impact of offenders, therapists, program characteristics, and the interactions among them on the effectiveness of correctional interventions (Bonta & Andrews, 2017; Gendreau, 1996; Ward & Maruna, 2007; Wormith et al., 2012). Within the RNR model, this is the principle that guides correctional interventions in how to take into account service delivery factors such as offenders' amenability or level of motivation to engage in treatment, biodemographic profiles (e.g., age, gender, race, and culture), personality and cognitive styles, and the potential relevance of noncriminogenic needs (Bonta & Andrews, 2017).

Within the evidence-based literature, "the effects of specific responsivity on treatment outcomes remain relatively unexplored" (Ward & Maruna, 2007, p. 94; see also Bonta & Andrews, 2017). In practice, this means that the extant literature can provide only limited guidance to correctional interventions in how best to apply this principle. For that reason, Andrews (2011) concludes that the specific responsivity principle is considered "a weakness in the RNR approach" (p. 13). Essentially, within the RNR–GLM debate, the underdeveloped empirical status of this principle opens up the door for the GLM to suggest creative ways to apply the style and mode of service to each offender. Indeed, as described in the previous section, advocates of the GLM suggest theoretical explanations that have a potential to expand the RNR model's perspective on issues such as offender motivation, values, offender needs, contextual factors, and offender personality.

In general, both the GLM and RNR model propose that interventions should implement treatment strategies that are "carefully matched to the preferred learning styles of the treatment recipient" (Ward & Maruna, 2007, p. 72). Moreover, both models accept that correctional therapy should be "tailored to each offender . . . while still being administered in a systematic and structured way" (Ward & Mann, 2004, p. 612). Despite these agreements, the models differ in the way they apply the specific responsivity principle. Within the RNR–GLM debate, the controversy includes two interrelated issues: the adequate level of collaboration in therapeutic process (an issue of therapeutic relationship between offender and service deliverer), and the appropriate degree of programs' manualization (an issue of structured services). These issues are discussed in more detail below.

The first controversial issue is how much therapists' collaboration with offenders is required to result in maximum specific responsiveness. In this regard, advocates of the GLM emphasize the importance of staff collaborating or consulting with offenders during the entire rehabilitative process (see the GLM' general assumption 7 in Chapter 5 and correctional principle 10 in Chapter 6).

Thus, therapists delivering GLM-consistent interventions are expected to seek to work closely with and seek input from each offender during the assessment process, making an intervention plan, deciding on intervention content, and developing the final good life plan. Such interventions should pay close attention to what offenders want during this process. In practice, it also means that therapists should conduct a completely transparent therapeutic process. That is, offenders should always understand how every aspect of program delivery can "directly benefit them in terms of goods that they value" (Ward & Mann, 2004, p. 606; see also Ward et al., 2007).

Similarly, the RNR model considers the issue of collaboration with offenders as an important aspect of correctional interventions. In this regard, Bonta and Andrews (2017) include this practice as one of the skills that therapists must acquire (see the RNR's 14 principle—Core Correctional Staff Practice). That is, they accept the possibility that collaborative treatment planning may enhance the motivation of offenders or assist the intervention in establishing effective treatment goals (Andrews et al., 2011).

Thus, within the RNR-GLM debate, the two models agree upon collaborative and transparent practice. However, potential disagreement may occur in the application of these norms. In this regard, advocates of the GLM perceive the goal of collaboration as something more powerful than a strategy for engaging offenders in the therapeutic process. They view collaboration also as a way to ensure that correctional interventions are committed to ensuring offenders' agency and autonomy. Within the RNR-GLM debate, such commitment may have practical implications. For example, GLM-consistent interventions may deviate or ignore a particular aspect of evidence-based practice because the offender is resistant to this experience. In contrast, RNR-based interventions oppose making such an adjustment based on what offenders want in their rehabilitative process. That is, within the RNR model, offenders' treatment preferences have a limited ability to veto the use of the empirically supported elements of treatment.

The second controversial issue around the specific responsivity principle is the appropriate degree of programs' manualization—or the extent to which a manual directs therapists on the specific dosage, strategy, techniques, and outcomes of administering the particular treatment. Essentially, the degree of programs' manualization determines the interventions' level of structure. Advocates of the GLM argue that the RNR's embrace of manualization "often results in a mechanistic, one-size-fits-all approach to treatment" (Ward & Mann, 2004, p. 601; see also Ward, 2002a; Ward & Maruna, 2007). According to this criticism, the RNR's approach to treatment is a mistake because it "fails to take critical individual needs and values into account" (Ward & Maruna, 2007, p. 103). That is, it "tends to downplay the role of context and relationship variables (e.g., therapeutic alliance or therapists' attitudes to offenders) in favor of a one-size-fits all approach (e.g., use of manuals)" (Ward & Gannon, 2006, p. 79). In this regard, Ward (2002a) argues that such practice results in therapeutic content that suffers from "irrelevance and meaninglessness" when applied to the life of offenders (p. 525). Thus, Ward et al. (2012) conclude that the RNR model is problematic because it has "led to overly structured interventions that allow for little clinical service in practice" (p. 103).

Advocates of the RNR model partly agree with the above criticism. They are aware that following its development, the RNR model has at times been implemented in a mechanistic way. According to Andrews et al. (2011), correctional agencies that implemented the RNR model on a large scale tended to "overmanualizing their training of service providers and the delivery of their intervention" (p. 747). They explain this problematic practice through agencies' "zeal to maintain program integrity" and, in particular, their effort "to adhere to the need principle" (p. 747).

Moreover, Polaschek (2012) concludes that correctional agencies in countries such as the United Kingdom, Canada, and New Zealand translated the RNR model into one version of RNR-based intervention: "structured, cognitive-behavioural closed-group based treatment programmes" (p. 11; see also Porporino, 2010).

Within the RNR-GLM debate, this reality raised the question of the appropriate balance between structured and highly structured delivery of therapeutic content. In practice, this controversy reflects different perspectives of the degrees of manualization in correctional rehabilitation. Importantly, advocates of the RNR model and the GLM agree that any extreme degree of manualization is not a desired practice in their interventions. First, both models reject the notion of not providing therapists with any guidance (i.e., no directions of how the intervention should change offenders' criminality). In this regard, Ward and Mann (2004) conclude that such "unstructured treatment programs have been found to have no impact on recidivism rates and, therefore, presumably, are not sufficiently targeting offense-relevant areas of pathology" (p. 609). Second, both models reject the notion of generic programs that provide services without considering the individual differences. According to Andrews et al. (2011), such consideration is relevant "even among those who may exist at the same level of risk and share the same need" (pp. 746–747).

Thus, in practice, the RNR-GLM debate revolves around the midpoints of programs manualization—that is, whether correctional interventions should adhere rigidly to treatment manuals (highly structured delivery of service) or avoid manuals in favor of less detailed or prescriptive "treatment guides" (structured delivery of service). Advocates of the RNR model prefer the use of treatment manuals because they address the types of problems that many offenders experience and verify the delivery of empirically supported services. In addition, they argue that this highly structured method to deliver services enhances the integrity of program delivery (Andrews, 2011; Bonta & Andrews, 2017; Gendreau, French, & Gionet, 2004). That is, "the goal of such manuals is to ensure that each group will address the same issues, in the same order, and follow the same approach" (e.g., the program uses "a set of fixed specific treatment targets" with "a specified procedure for each of these targets" along "a fixed number of treatment sessions for the program") (Marshall et al., 2011, pp. 50–51). Essentially, they assert that such stability in service delivery is an important feature in the correctional interventions because the pressing daily problems tend to push their focus of treatment "away from long-term behavior change" (e.g., away from the task of changing offenders' criminogenic needs) (Mann, 2009, p. 122).

In general, advocates of the GLM perceive the notion of manual-based programs as a problematic aspect of interventions that aim to rehabilitate offenders. Ward and Maruna (2007) lament that such programs "tend to have built into them generic conceptions concerning what kinds of goods or goals should be achieved rather than taking into account individual offenders' capabilities, preferences and likely living circumstances" (p. 103). Ward (2002a) argues that manual-based programs "fail to consider the appropriate form of life for a given individual" (i.e., they provide "prepackaged lives") (pp. 525–526). Thus, according to Ward and Mann (2004), highly structured programs "may not be consistent with the GLM's emphasis on person-centered values" (p. 609).

Ward and his colleagues criticize the RNR model's tendency to rely on treatment manuals. They argue that this practice of treatment manuals represents the major problematic aspect of the RNR model: the focus on the success of treatment programs rather on the success of individual offenders. Accordingly, they propose that interventions should approach correctional rehabilitation "from the perspective of the individual offender (stressing autonomy and empathic concern) rather than of maximizing outcome for the benefit of the community" (Ward & Salmon, 2011, p. 402).

According to Ward and his colleagues, the solution to this problem is for correctional interventions to use treatment guides. They assert that treatment guides are less structured than program manuals and therefore more suitable to providing the flexibility that therapists need to tailor therapeutic content to offenders' needs (Willis et al., 2012; Marshall et al., 2011; Polaschek, 2012). In practice, GLM would advise staff to assess the relevant therapeutic aspects for each offender and then, in deciding what intervention to use, to consult and select information from a pool of treatment guides relevant to a given offender's specific needs.

Another aspect of this solution to overly structured, non-individualized, treatment is to run open-ended (rolling) groups. That is, advocates of the GLM recommend treatment programs in which participates can be added over time and receive services according to their progress. According to Marshall et al. (2011), this flexible frame of service delivery "allows the therapists to pay attention to the responsivity principle" (p. 56). Specifically, in open-ended groups, therapists can tailor the therapeutic assignments to the unique characteristics or learning style of each offender (Ward & Mann, 2004).

Finally, Mann (2009) has attempted to detail the key elements of an effective treatment manual and has derived six features. First, a manual should focus on goals; it "sets out, and justifies, the targets of a particular intervention and by omission (or explicitly) clarifies what targets are inappropriate" (p. 126). In this regard, it should "explain aims as well as procedures" and be arranged in a way that "the modules that each offender needs to attend could be selected easily rather than applying inefficiently the entire set of options to every offender" (p. 126). Second, a good manual should "specify the desired interpersonal and group processes for the intervention, and to suggest the techniques for achieving these aspects of treatment" (p. 127). In addition, it should specify the promising "targets and methods that are best employed to achieve those goals" (p. 127).

Third, a good treatment manual should be "preceded by comprehensive assessment" and should present "treatment strategies in terms of the need or risk they address" (p. 127). In that sense, a manual should be considered as "a menu" for treatment providers that "can choose to employ some treatment strategies from the menu and follow the manualized instructions for those strategies, but need not apply the full range of possible treatment techniques" (p. 127). Fourth, "treatment manuals can describe the ideal interpersonal style of the treatment delivery" (p. 127). Essentially, a manual should be based on the assumption that the therapists have the interpersonal skills, the experience, and adequate training to approach the particular intervention (p. 127). Fifth, a good manual maintains the balance between structure and flexibility by keeping "an intermediate level of specificity so that guidelines are adequate but not too overwhelming to implement" (p. 128). In this regard, it also requires the flexibility to address the offenders' pressing issue or daily crisis on time. Sixth, good treatment manuals should not be "too scripted" (p. 129).

In sum, the above two controversial issues demonstrate the difficulty of implementing the specific responsivity principle. Doing so requires reliable individual assessments, high-quality therapists, and individualized therapeutic attention. Moreover, very little is known about the best way to tailor the rehabilitative efforts to the particular offender. That is, correctional interventions that aim to reduce offenders' tendency to reoffend need more knowledge about the right balance between structured and high delivery of therapeutic services.

Thus, within the RNR–GLM debate, it is still unknown how much flexible services should be allowed to enhance the effectiveness of specific responsivity to offenders. Andrews (2011) argues that the existing evidence shows the limits of "exquisite matching of services to the unique characteristics of the individual case" (p. 14). Moreover, the evidence suggests that "effective services that are sensitive to a few key characteristics of individuals for the most part are widely applicable regardless of the uniqueness of individuals" (e.g., Lipsey, 2009) (p. 14). As discussed in Chapter 6, GLM-consistent interventions have not yet demonstrated what an effective balance between structured and flexible practice is. That is, such interventions are yet to show better outcomes than the highly structured approach of the RNR model.

Within the correctional system, it seems that the lack of high-quality therapists in correctional settings explains the struggles of GLM-consistent interventions to implement their flexible approach to treatment. In this regard, Mann (2009) observes that "much correctional treatment (at least in the United Kingdom and Canada) is delivered by paraprofessionals (albeit supervised by professionals)" (p. 129). Based on this reality, Marshall et al. (2011) wonder if the use of treatment guides (over manuals) "is perhaps better suited to small operations where on-site supervision is continuous" (p. 52). Relatedly, Andrews et al. (2011) suggest that such small operations with high-quality treatment providers may explain the consistent success of controlled demonstration projects to reduce recidivism. That is, these projects may have found a more flexible way to tailor the RNR's therapeutic process to each individual than the routine correctional interventions.

Domain 2: The RNR-GLM Debate and the RNR's Key Clinical Issue

The Breadth Principle Within the RNR-GLM Debate

In general, breadth (or multimodal) principles emphasize the importance of multimodal interventions for high-risk offenders. According to Glick (2006), such interventions use a combination of reliable methods that can address several relevant targets simultaneously. Within the RNR model, this principle presents a narrower therapeutic pathway: "target a number of criminogenic needs relative to noncriminogenic needs" (Bonta & Andrews, 2017, p. 177). In other words, correctional interventions should concentrate on criminogenic needs rather than on noncriminogenic needs. Andrews et al. (2011) explain this strict direction as the result of their "frustration with ineffective treatment and with clinical attempts to block effect treatment" (p. 746).

Within the RNR–GLM debate, advocates of the GLM cannot accept a principle that directs interventions to focus predominately on criminogenic needs. In essence, the GLM rejects the RNR model's strict distinction between criminogenic and noncriminogenic needs. For example, Ward et al. (2012) argue that "we do not refer to noncriminogenic needs in the construction of the GLM except in reference to the weaknesses and criticisms of the RNR. Our point is that it is sometimes essential to pay attention to addressing noncriminogenic needs to effectively target criminogenic needs" (p. 102).

Thus, overall, it seems that the GLM and RNR model cannot find a common ground for the breadth principle. From the GLM's perspective, scholars reject any rigid therapeutic structure that chooses to see the RNR model's criminogenic needs as the a priori target and hence treatment solution in every correctional case. By contrast, RNR scholars view the criminogenic needs as fundamental to the practice of effective correction interventions. In addition, they argue that the results of meta-analyses that support this focus should not be ignored (Dowden, Antonowicz, & Andrews, 2003; Dowden & Andrews, 1999a, 1999b, 2000, 2003).

The Strength Principle Within the RNR-GLM Debate

The GLM and RNR model both endorse the use of offenders' strengths in the therapeutic process. However, advocates of these competing perspectives differ on how to integrate offenders' strengths in treatment. According to the RNR model, offenders' strengths are independent variables that are the person characteristics and circumstances that potentially predict low probability of offending (Andrews & Bonta, 2010). Thus, advocates of the RNR model propose that correctional interventions should include strengths when developing assessment tools and consider strengths as factors that affect an offender's specific responsivity to treatment. However, as Farrington, Loeber, and Ttofi (2012) conclude, there is very little knowledge about these factors and their protective mechanism. The research does not provide much evidence about the potential interactions of strength factors in practice (Andrews, 2011). Thus, when advocates of the RNR model argue that the "RNR is about building on strengths," they mean that interventions should seek and reward prosocial factors manifested by offenders. Within the RNR-based interventions, such prosocial aspects are often found during the assessment of the criminogenic needs' domains (e.g., positive aspects in offenders' attitudes, belief, values, personality, associates, social achievement in school/work, familial affection, and conventional leisure-time activities) (Andrews et al., 2011).

As a strength-based approach to offender rehabilitation, the GLM gives a more salient role to offenders' strength factors than does the RNR model. According to the GLM, offenders' strengths are the activities and strategies that are used to achieve the primary human goods in a socially acceptable way (i.e., the individual capabilities to attain prosocial knowledge, healthy life, inner peace, friendship, communal belonging, happiness, creativity, and excellence in work, play, and agency). Thus, within the GLM, strength factors are the building blocks of the therapeutic process—the main way to achieve offenders' optimal functioning in society (Ward & Gannon, 2006; Ward & Maruna, 2007). In practice, GLM-consistent interventions are expected to assess offenders' strengths and use them to offset offenders' dynamic risk factors.

Overall, the consideration given to strength factors in each model seems to be more than a semantic issue. That is because the RNR-based interventions are expected to use offenders' strength factors as a specific responsivity to offenders, whereas the GLM-consistent interventions are expected to use offenders' strength factors as a general responsivity to offenders. That is, RNR-based interventions use strength factors in a therapeutic process that focuses on the best way to change the RNR model's criminogenic needs. Within this process, offenders' strengths are important to the extent that they assist to facilitate such change (i.e., a specific responsivity element). By contrast, GLM-consistent interventions use offenders' strengths as an integral part of the main therapeutic change process. The design of such interventions is based on offenders' strengths and the commitment to use these strengths while promoting offenders' primary goods (i.e., the GLM dual aims).

The Structured Assessment Principle Within the RNR-GLM Debate

Both the GLM and RNR model follow the general direction of this principle and seek to establish a structured offender assessment process that uses structured assessment instruments. In addition, both models view the assessment process as the baseline of their overall therapeutic process. They agree that correctional interventions should include information from the assessments in the offenders' structured intervention plan. Despite these similarities, the GLM and RNR model adopt different approaches to offender assessment. The major differences reside in the domains that each model assesses, the role that they ascribe to empirically validated assessment tools, and the way they translate the information into practice.

First, although advocates of the GLM endorses the RNR model's assessment domains, they also argue that additional domains should be assessed. That is, while the RNR model uses assessments to identify offenders' (1) level of risk, (2) relevant criminogenic needs, and (3) specific responsivity issues, the GLM also seeks knowledge about (4) offenders' priorities of primary and secondary goods (Ward & Maruna, 2007; Ward & Mann, 2004). Specifically, within the GLM, uncovering the priority that offenders ascribe to each primary human good is the basic task of any GLM-consistent intervention. As described in the previous chapter, such assessment seeks information about offenders' general life functioning and offense-related behavior. Accordingly, the GLM's assessment process involves a comprehensive assessment of offenders' secondary goods. This type of assessment reveals the essential information about the specific activities and strategies used to achieve the primary goods, the relationship between the primary goods and offending (i.e., offenders' good lives conceptualization), and the problems in the offenders' good lives plan. Within the RNR–GLM debate, these additional assessments in GLM-consistent interventions have a practical implication. While the RNR-based interventions use assessment tools that provide specific information about offenders' level of risk and relevant criminogenic/noncriminogenic needs, the GLM-consistent interventions also use any other structured instrument that provides information about offenders and their circumstances.

Second, the GLM and RNR model have a different perspective on what constitutes an adequate structured assessment. While the RNR model favors the use of validated actuarial-based assessment instrument (i.e., highly structured assessment tools), the GLM supports the use of any structured assessment tool. Within the RNR-GLM debate, the RNR model's actuarial-based assessment instrument has demonstrated its predictive validity. However, scholars have yet to conduct a study that examines the relative impact of a highly structured assessment system compared to only a structured assessment system.

In this regard, advocates of the RNR model insist that correctional interventions should focus on an evidence-based approach to offender assessment. That is, in RNR programs, staff are expected to adhere to the outcomes of empirically validated actuarial-based assessment tools when determining the intensity of intervention or developing treatment plans. As mentioned above, advocates of the GLM have also embraced these empirically validated assessment instruments in their interventions. However, the GLM does not insist on a similar scientific standard in the GLM's unique assessment instruments. That is, the assessment of offenders' primary and secondary goods is based on structured clinical interviews and observations. Essentially, the development of the GLM's unique assessment instruments is still in its early stage. Thus, the empirical validity and reliability of these instruments is still unclear.

Third, within the RNR-GLM debate, advocates of the RNR model also argue that the GLM allows therapists to exercise too much discretion when integrating assessment information into treatment practice. That is, while RNR-based interventions use quantitative analyses to ensure the predictive validity of assessments instruments, the GLM relies on the assessors' personal discretion to synthesize the overall information about offenders into effective practice. Andrews et al. (2011) assert that such practice "may dilute the validity of the RNR-based assessments and the RNR-based ability to influence criminal conduct" (p. 737). They also argue that such an unstructured assessment process adds "confusion in service planning" (p. 751). In this regard, they are concerned about "the risk of slipping back to the pre-RNR days," when the field of correctional rehabilitation was characterized by invalided assessment tools and ineffective programs (p. 741). This broader controversial issue of therapists' discretion will be discussed next.

The Professional Discretion Principle Within the RNR-GLM Debate

Advocates of both the GLM and RNR model agree that service delivery can deviate from the structured directions of their model. They also agree that the scientific evidence does not cover the entire individual factors that correctional interventions may need to address when conducting an effective rehabilitative process (e.g., aspects of treatment alliance and motivation) (Ward & Maruna, 2007). They believe that treatment based on professional observation and discretion will always be a step ahead of evidence-based practice or any other structured guidance (Andrews et al., 2011).

Specifically, advocates of the RNR model understand that the deviation from the model's principles is sometimes inevitable because the evidence-based literature cannot solely govern the complex task of changing human behavior. They are also aware of the methodological limitations of empirical studies and of the fact that many research studies omit offenders' contextual factors from their analysis (Andrews & Bonta, 2010). Similarly, advocates of the GLM perceive the RNR model's principle of professional discretion as important in that it "allows for treatment flexibility and innovation under certain circumstances" (Ward & Stewart, 2003a, p. 128).

Despite the above agreement, the GLM and RNR model endorse different versions of the professional discretion principle. Advocates of the RNR model emphasize that the decision to deviate from any RNR principle should be an exceptional practice. According to this perspective, the strength of the RNR model derives from the adherence to its Risk-Need-Responsivity principles as well as to its key clinical principles.

Andrews (2011) concludes that "the evidence is reasonably strong in regard to the principles of human service, risk, criminogenic need, general responsivity, and the principle of breadth" (all of the above principles were supported by meta-analyses) (p. 9). Thus, deviation from these principles may result in ineffective correctional intervention and are recommended for very specific reasons. Regarding the other RNR principles (specific responsivity, strengths, and structured assessment), the research that has examined their impact on correctional intervention is limited (in the RNR's terms, this means a lack of support from meta-analytic studies). In practice, such relatively weak empirical status makes these principles more susceptible to professional overrides. Thus, in order to improve their scientific knowledge, advocates of the RNR model mandate that service providers conduct a systematic monitoring of their overrides and its consequences.

In essence, advocates of the GLM are reluctant to accept any principle that constrains their professional discretion in managing the rehabilitative process. They perceive the leverage in discretion as an inevitable practice for correctional interventions that focus on the attainment of individuals' primary and secondary goods. Thus, in GLM-consistent interventions, staff have much leeway to find the "very specific reasons" that are required to justify deviating from the RNR model's principles. However, as discussed above, the GLM's flexible interpretation of the RNR's principles may result in GLM-consistent interventions that distort the very essence of these principles.

Domain 3: The RNR-GLM Debate and the RNR's Organizational Principles

The Community-Based Principle Within the RNR-GLM Debate

The GLM and RNR model agree upon this principle. Both models prefer rehabilitative processes that take place in community settings. For RNR-based interventions, behavioral change is more likely to occur when offenders practice the learned prosocial skills in their natural environment. For the GLM-consistent interventions, meaningful attainment of primary human goods can be achieved only when offenders reintegrate into their society. Nevertheless, advocates of both models believe in the power of their model to guide the delivery of effective interventions in institutional settings.

The Core Correctional Staff Practice Within the RNR-GLM Debate

Advocates of the GLM and RNR model agree that therapists' practical skills have a major impact on offender rehabilitation. Essentially, both models endorse the work of Carl Rogers (1961), "who first brought our attention to those important therapist qualities of empathy, warmth, being open, and being genuine" (Andrews et al., 2011, p. 745). Ward and Maruna (2007) also assert that strong therapeutic alliances between therapists and offenders result in effective correctional programs. Accordingly, Andrews et al. (2011) argue that therapists are "the greatest asset of any intervention" and "the therapeutic relationship between offender and therapist is a key ingredient of offender service" (p. 750).

In general, advocates of the RNR model argue that therapists in effective correctional rehabilitation exercise a dual set of core practical skills: high-quality relationship skills and high-quality structuring skills (Bonta & Andrews, 2017). First, humanistic psychology influenced Andrews and Bonta to establish the RNR model's *relationship principle* that states the importance of therapists' developing a strong therapeutic relationship with offenders (see Chapter 4). Second, behavioral theories influenced Andrews and Bonta to require therapists to collaborate with offenders through structured modeling, reinforcement, and disapproval—the *structuring principle*. Essentially, within the RNR model, these two core correctional principles are interrelated. According to Andrews et al. (2011), "building a therapeutic alliance is a step in establishing the power of therapist's use of core structuring practices" (p. 746). In practice, such combination is expected to influence offenders' criminogenic needs and, consequently, their tendency to reoffend.

Notably, within the RNR-GLM debate, advocates of the RNR criticize the GLM for overemphasizing the power of the therapeutic relationship to reduce offenders' tendency to reoffend. They argue that the GLM tends to downplay the importance of structuring skills when therapists collaborate with offenders. For example, Andrews et al. (2011) assert that the GLM views "therapy as more an art than an applied science, and not wanting to restrict their freedom to experiment with individual cases" (p. 741). They conclude that "appeals to relationship and alliance as the major or sole source of therapeutic change do not fit at all with the findings of meta-analyses of the effect of correctional treatment with moderate and higher risk cases" (p. 745).

Indeed, within the GLM, therapists must have high-quality interrelationship skills but they are not required to practice structuring skills. According to Ward et al. (2012), the GLM-consistent intervention "is an art in the sense that there is no prescriptive set of procedures available to guide every aspect of intervention" (p. 105). Instead, they "must be skilled at motivating offenders, building an effective working alliance, and being change agents" in a treatment that is "not overly structured and manualized" (p. 105).

Thus, advocates of the GLM respond to their critics by arguing that the RNR model's structured approach provides insufficient therapeutic attention to what the individual offender wants in life. They insist that attention to what offenders want results in a stronger therapeutic alliance, which leads to a higher level of motivation to engage in treatment and, in turn, achieves a higher chance to reduce offenders' tendency to reoffend (Ward & Maruna, 2007). Ward and Mann (2004) argue that one of the major problems in the RNR-based interventions is that they give little therapeutic attention to "the crucial importance of human needs and their influence in determining offending behavior" (p. 601). Thus, overall, Ward and his colleagues concluded that their emphasis on therapists' positive approach to offender rehabilitation (i.e., their humanistic strength-based approach) generates more effective influence on offenders than the RNR model's structured approach to therapeutic relationship.

However, within the strength-based approach literature, not all scholars have reached the same conclusion. Several scholars who support the positive approach to offender rehabilitation also recognize the importance of therapists' structuring skills. For example, Marshall et al. (2013) suggest that the therapists' training "should involve not only targeting the specific criminogenic features and implementing appropriate procedures to change them but also emphasizing the important aspects of the delivery of treatments" (p. 177). More specifically, Polaschek (2011) argues that the role of therapists as "vehicles for achieving the general responsivity principle" has two effective components: "the ability to develop a good working alliance, and skill in effecting change in participant through the use of cognitive-behavioral methods" (p. 24). In this regard, Marshall et al. (2011) observed that a common problem in correctional interventions that employ CBT is their inappropriate use of reinforcement (as well as lack of other useful behavioral techniques).

From the RNR's model perspective, scholars argue that it is still unknown if the GLM's therapeutic approach results in more effective correctional interventions than the RNR's approach. There is no evidence that GLM-consistent interventions that focus on establishing strong a therapeutic alliance with offenders (with or without structured responses to offenders' behavior) result in offenders' lower tendency to reoffend (see Chapter 6).

In sum, within the RNR-GLM debate, it seems that the role of therapists in GLM-consistent intervention is fundamentally different than the role of therapists in RNR-based interventions. Although both models emphasize on developing therapists' high-quality relationship skills, only the RNR model insists on having structuring skills. In practice it means that the RNR model imposes more restrictions on therapists' therapeutic discretion than the GLM. Essentially, the experience from the past unrestricted therapeutic programs in correctional rehabilitation (see Chapter 1) and the demonstrated success of the RNR model's therapists to reduce reoffending (see Chapter 4) support the development of structuring skills. Thus, the models can find a common ground only if advocates of the GLM will encourage therapists to develop their therapeutic alliance in a more structured way. As described above, advocates of the positive approach to correctional rehabilitation argue that such practice assists therapists to achieve therapeutic goals without losing their humanistic strength-based approach to collaboration with offenders.

The Management Principle Within the RNR-GLM Debate

According to the management principle, program managers have a salient role in correctional interventions. Managers in such programs are responsible for the correct implementation of the therapeutic elements during the rehabilitative process. Within the RNR model, this task includes the establishment of a therapeutic environment that constantly follows the principles of effective intervention. In addition, managers in RNR-based interventions should select skilled staff members, ensure relevant training and support, and supervise the quality of treatment delivery (Bonta & Andrews, 2017).

The GLM endorses many similar directions for managers in GLM-consistent interventions. Specifically, advocates of the GLM often refer to practice in terms of ensuring appropriate therapists' characteristics and therapeutic environment, providing adequate environmental resources and support, and verifying the attention to the specific responsivity process. Nevertheless, the GLM literature often omits the element of quality assurance mechanisms in correctional interventions (e.g., Willis et al., 2012; Willis et al., 2014; Yates et al., 2010). Within the correctional system, such mechanisms are required to ensure that interventions follow their theoretical and correctional assumptions (i.e., interventions' integrity).

Within the GLM literature, research by Willis et al. (2014) has demonstrated the importance of such mechanisms in the field of sex offender rehabilitation. These scholars showed that even among treatment programs that "reported using the GLM as a main theory informing their treatment approach," most of the programs were not consistent with the GLM. Specifically, this study evaluated 13 programs and found that only 4 programs integrated the GLM "into programs content" (in other 7 programs, only the "GLM spirit was evident") (p. 75).

In recent years, advocates of the GLM have paid more attention to quality assurance in correctional interventions (Purvis, Ward, & Willis, 2011; Purvis et al., 2013). For example, Purvis et al. (2011) described how the correctional system in Victoria, Australia (VC) was the first justice organization to operationalize the GLM in case-management practices. According to this initiative, "serious sex offenders who are subject to post-sentence supervision orders will receive intensive case management based on the Good Lives Model (GLM)" (Post-sentence Supervision and Detention Scheme for Serious Sex Offenders, 2012, p. 11). According to Purvis et al. (2011), the organizational aspects of such intensive case management include "high level organizational support and stable resourcing," "quality training," "monitoring program," "case management forum," and "quality assurance" (p. 18). In this regard, the quality assurance mechanism includes "monitoring drift in practice, competency standards, knowledge gaps and training needs and the quality of case management reports" (p. 18). Overall, this initiative reflects the ongoing developments in the GLM's attention to the various aspects of operating interventions in a correctional system. Moreover, this initiation seems to establish a solid platform to examine systematically the GLM's correctional framework in the real world of correctional rehabilitation. However, even though this project has been in operation since 2008, it is yet to be evaluated.

In sum, recent developments in the GLM's organizational aspects show that the RNR's management principle can be integrated into the GLM. Within the RNR-GLM debate, it seems that the major challenge is to find an agreed-upon approach to clinical supervision. For example, due to the vast therapeutic discretion in GLM-consistent interventions, it is unclear how managers can determine that the therapeutic process incorporated all the relevant primary goods or how they ensure that the needed internal and external support for the offender were provided.

Conclusion

This chapter sought to convey and assess the theoretical and correctional debates that have occurred between advocates of the Risk–Need-Responsivity model (the RNR model) and advocates of the Good Lives Model (the GLM). The first section chronicled the nature of the RNR-GLM debate and how this controversy led scholars from both camps to offer strident criticisms on opposing visions of how best to undertake correctional rehabilitation. In turn, the chapter's second and the third sections tried to examine these issues by clarifying each position and the potential to establish a common ground between the RNR model and the GLM.

The second section elaborated the extant theoretical controversial issues and examined whether the GLM has provided incremental value to the offender rehabilitation enterprise. As described above, such discussion was needed because advocates of the RNR model have concluded that the GLM's incremental value is unclear (Wormith et al., 2012). Thus, this section discussed seven theoretical controversial issues that were suggested by Ward and his colleagues. The RNR model's perspective on each of these issues was presented. Based on these theoretical discussions, it was suggested that the GLM provides a broader theoretical perspective on offender rehabilitation. Essentially, this perspective offers insights into offender rehabilitation that remain beyond the confines of the RNR model's evidence-based approach. As summarized in Table 7.1, the GLM's theoretical framework expands the RNR model's perspective in rehabilitative issues such as motivation, values, needs, risk, social context, personality, and human agency.

Accordingly, the third section assessed the correctional controversial issues of the RNR-GLM debate. As noted, despite the mutual criticism inherent in the paradigms' debate, the advocates of both the GLM and RNR model admit that the two correctional frameworks are, in many ways, compatible. Thus, the third section examined this assumption through the models' potential agreements and disagreements on each of the RNR model's correctional principles. As summarized in Table 7.2, this analysis found that the GLM's theoretical framework may lead to substantially different correctional interventions than the RNR-based interventions. That is, correctional interventions that follow the GLM's dual aims—that is, of risk reduction and the promotion of goods—may distort the essence of the RNR model's principles or even resist their practical implications. As a result, this chapter shows that the integration between the GLM and RNR model may be more challenging than many scholars have assumed.

The next chapter will recap the overall conclusions of the seven chapters and discuss the future of offender rehabilitation. In general, Chapter 8 suggests two possible futures for offender rehabilitation in corrections. Within one realistic future, advocates of the GLM and RNR model continue to develop their models independently. That is, each model remains a distinctive perspective of correctional rehabilitation. The second realistic future of offender rehabilitation suggests the development of a new, alternative perspective. This perspective uses the strengths of each model to propose an integrated paradigm of offender rehabilitation. In essence, within such a paradigm, the two models would work together to achieve their ultimate goal—the reduction of offenders' future reoffending. These two futures of offender rehabilitation will be discussed next.

References

Andrews, D. A. (2011). The impact of nonprogrammatic factors on criminal-justice interventions. *Legal and Criminological Psychology, 16,* 1–23.
Andrews, D. A., & Bonta, J. (1994). *The psychology of criminal conduct.* Cincinnati, OH: Anderson.
Andrews, D. A., & Bonta, J. (1998). *The psychology of criminal conduct* (2nd ed.). Cincinnati, OH: Anderson.
Andrews, D. A., & Bonta, J. (2010). *The psychology of criminal conduct* (5th ed.). New Providence, NJ: Anderson/ LexisNexis.
Andrews, D. A., Bonta, J., & Wormith, J. S. (2011). The risk–need–responsivity (RNR) model: Does adding the good lives model contribute to effective crime prevention? *Criminal Justice and Behavior, 38,* 735–755.
Andrews, D. A., & Wormith, J. S. (1989). Personality and crime: Knowledge, destruction and construction in criminology. *Justice Quarterly, 6,* 289–309.
Bonta, J., & Andrews, D. A. (2003). A commentary on Ward and Stewart's model of human needs. *Psychology, Crime & Law, 9,* 215–218.
Bonta, J., & Andrews, D. A. (2017). *The psychology of criminal conduct* (6th ed.). New York, NY: Routledge.
Casey, S., Day, A., Vess, J., & Ward, T. (2013). *Foundations of offender rehabilitation.* New York, NY: Routledge.
Clear, T. (2009). *Imprisoning communities: How mass incarceration makes disadvantage neighborhoods worst.* New York, NY: Oxford University Press.
Cullen, F. T. (2012). Taking rehabilitation seriously: Creativity, science, and the challenge of offender change. *Punishment & Society, 14,* 94–114.
Cullen, F. T., & Jonson, C. L. (2012). *Correctional theory: Context and consequences.* Thousand Oaks, CA: Sage.
Currie, E. (1998). *Crime and punishment in America: Why the solution to America's most stubborn social crisis have not worked—and what will.* New York, NY: Metropolitan Books.
Day, A., & Ward, T. (2010). Offender rehabilitation as a value laden process. *International Journal of Offender Therapy and Comparative Criminology, 54,* 289–306.
Dowden, C., & Andrews, D. A. (1999a). What works in young offender treatment: A meta-analysis. *Forum on Corrections Research, 11,* 21–24.
Dowden, C., & Andrews, D. A. (1999b). What works for female offenders: A meta-analytic review. *Crime and Delinquency, 45,* 438–452.
Dowden, C., & Andrews, D. A. (2000). Effective correctional treatment and violent reoffending: A meta-analysis. *Canadian Journal of Criminology, 42,* 449–467.
Dowden, C., & Andrews, D. A. (2003). Does family intervention work for delinquents? Results of a meta-analysis. *Canadian Journal of Criminology and Criminal Justice, 45,* 327–342.
Dowden, C., Antonowicz, D., & Andrews, D. A. (2003). The effectiveness of relapse prevention with offenders: A meta-analysis. *International Journal of Offender Therapy and Comparative Criminology, 47,* 516–528.
Farrington, D. P., Loeber, R., & Ttofi, M. M. (2012). Risk and protective factors for offending. In D. P. Farrington & B. C. Welsh (Eds.), *The Oxford handbook of crime prevention* (pp. 46–69). Oxford: Oxford University.
Garland, D. (2001). *The culture of control: Crime and social order in contemporary society.* Chicago, IL: University of Chicago Press.
Gendreau, P. (1996). The principles of effective intervention with offenders. In A. T. Harland (Ed.), *Choosing correctional interventions that work: Defining the demand and evaluating the supply* (pp. 117–130). Thousand Oaks, CA: Sage.
Gendreau, P., French, S. A., & Gionet, A. (2004). What works (what doesn't work): The principles of effective correctional treatment. *Journal of Community Corrections, 13,* 4–30.

Glick, B. (2006). Multimodal interventions. In B. Glick (Ed.), *Cognitive behavioral interventions for at-risk youth* (pp. 4-1–4-8). Kingston, NJ: Civic Research Institute.

Lipsey, M. W. (2009). The primary factors that characterize effective interventions with juvenile offenders: A meta-analytic overview. *Victims and Offenders, 4*, 124–147.

Lipsey, M. W. (2014). Interventions for juvenile offenders: A serendipitous journey. *Criminology and Public Policy, 13*, 1–14.

Lipsey, M. W., & Cullen, F. T. (2007). The effectiveness of correctional rehabilitation: A review of systematic reviews. *Annual Review of Law and Social Science, 3*, 297–320.

Mann, R. E. (2009). Sex offender treatment: The case for manualization. *Journal of Sexual Aggression, 15*, 121–131.

Marshall, W. L., Marshall, L. E., Serran, G. A., & O'Brien, M. D. (2011). *Rehabilitating sexual offenders: A strength-based approach.* Washington, DC: American Psychological Association.

Marshall, W. L., Marshall, L. E., Serran, G. A., & O'Brien, M. D. (2013). What works in reducing sexual offending. In L. Craig, L. Dixon, & T. Gannon (Eds.), *What works in offender rehabilitation: An evidence-based approach to assessment and treatment* (pp. 173–191). London: Wiley-Blackwell.

Maruna, S. (2001). *Making good: How ex-convicts reform and rebuild their lives.* Washington, DC: American Psychological Association.

McAdams, D. P. (1994). Can personality change? Levels of stability and growth in personality across the life span. In T. F. Heatherton & J. L. Weinberger (Eds.), *Can personality change?* (pp. 299–313). Washington, DC: American Psychological Association.

McGuire, J. (2004). *Understanding psychology and crime: Perspectives on theory and action.* New York, NY: Open University Press.

Ogloff, J. R. P., & Davis, M. R. (2004). Advances in offender assessment and rehabilitation: Contributions of the risk-needs-responsivity approach. *Psychology, Crime and Law, 10*, 229–242.

Polaschek, D. L. L. (2011). Many sizes fit all: A preliminary framework for conceptualizing the development and provision of cognitive-behavioral rehabilitation programs for offenders. *Aggression and Violent Behavior, 16*, 20–35.

Polaschek, D. L. L. (2012). An appraisal of the risk-need-responsivity (RNR) model of offender rehabilitation and its application in correctional treatment. *Legal and Criminological Psychology, 17*, 1–17.

Porporino, F. J. (2010). Bringing sense and sensitivity to corrections: From programmes to 'fix' offenders to services to support desistence. In J. Brayford, F. Cowe, & J. Deering (Eds.), *What else works? Creative work with offenders* (pp. 61–85). Cullompton, Devon: Willan.

Purvis, M., Ward, T., & Shaw, S. (2013). *Applying the good lives model to the case management of sexual offenders: A practical guide for probation officers, parole officers, and case workers.* Brandon, VT: Safer Society Press.

Purvis, M., Ward, T., & Willis, G. (2011). The good lives model in practice: Offence pathways and case management. *European Journal of Probation, 3*(2), 4–28.

Raynor, P., & Robinson, G. (2009). *Rehabilitation, crime and justice.* Hampshire: Palgrave Macmillan.

Rogers, C. R. (1961). *On becoming a person: A therapist's view of psychotherapy.* Boston, MA: Houghton Mifflin.

Stangor, C. (2011). *Social psychology principles.* Nyack, NY: Flat World Knowledge.

Van Voorhis, P., & Salisbury, E. (2014). *Correctional counseling and rehabilitation* (8th ed.). Cincinnati, OH: Elsevier/Anderson.

Ward, T. (2002a). Good lives and the rehabilitation of offenders: Promises and problems. *Aggression and Violent Behavior, 7*, 513–528.

Ward, T. (2002b). The management of risk and the design of good lives. *Australian Psychologist, 37*, 172–179.

Ward, T. (2013). The heart of offender rehabilitation: Values, knowledge, and capabilities. In L. A. Craig, L. Dixon, & T. A. Gannon (Eds.), *What works in offender rehabilitation: An evidence based approach to assessment and Treatment* (pp. xxi–xxii). West Sussex: John Wiley & Sons.

Ward, T., & Gannon, T. A. (2006). Rehabilitation, etiology, and self-regulation: The comprehensive good lives model of treatment for sexual offenders. *Aggression and Violent Behavior, 11*, 77–94.

Ward, T., Hudson, S. M., & Siegert, R. J. (1995). A critical comment on Pithers' relapse prevention model. *Sexual Abuse: A Journal of Research and Treatment, 7,* 167–175.

Ward, T., Louden, K., Hudson, S. M., & Marshall, W. L. (1995). A descriptive model of the offense chain for child molesters. *Journal of Interpersonal Violence, 10,* 452–472.

Ward, T., & Mann, R. (2004). Good lives and the rehabilitation of offenders: A positive approach to sex offender treatment. In P. A. Linley & S. Joseph (Eds.), *Positive psychology in practice* (pp. 598–616). Hoboken, NJ: John Wiley.

Ward, T., Mann, R., & Gannon, T. (2007). The good lives model of offender rehabilitation: Clinical implications. *Aggression and Violent Behavior, 12,* 87–107.

Ward, T., & Marshall, W. L. (2007). Narrative identity and offender rehabilitation. *International Journal of Offender Therapy and Comparative Criminology, 51,* 279–297.

Ward, T., & Maruna, S. (2007). *Rehabilitation: Beyond the risk paradigm.* New York, NY: Routledge.

Ward, T., Melser, J., & Yates, P. M. (2007). Reconstructing the risk need responsivity model: A theoretical elaboration and evaluation. *Aggression and Violent Behavior, 12,* 208–228.

Ward, T., & Salmon, K. (2011). The ethics of care and treatment of sex offenders. *Sexual Abuse: A Journal of Research and Treatment, 23,* 397–413.

Ward, T., & Stewart, C. A. (2003a). Criminogenic needs and human needs: A theoretical model. *Psychology, Crime, & Law, 9,* 125–143.

Ward, T., & Stewart, C. A. (2003b). The relationship between human needs and criminogenic needs. *Psychology, Crime, & Law, 9,* 219–224.

Ward, T., & Stewart, C. A. (2003c). The treatment of sex offenders: Risk management and good lives. *Professional Psychology: Research and Practice, 34,* 353–360.

Ward, T., Yates, P. M., & Willis, G. M. (2012). The good lives model and the risk-need-responsivity model: A critical response to Andrews, Bonta, and Wormith (2011). *Criminal Justice and Behavior, 39,* 94–110.

Whitehead, P., Ward, T., & Collie, R. (2007). Time for a change: Applying the good lives model of rehabilitation to a high-risk violent offender. *International Journal of Offender Therapy and Comparative Criminology, 51,* 578–598.

Willis, G., Ward, T., & Levenson, J. S. (2014). The good lives model (GLM): An evaluation of GLM operationalization in North American treatment programs. *Sexual Abuse: A Journal of Research and Treatment, 26,* 58–81.

Willis, G. M., Yates, P. M., Gannon, T. A., & Ward, T. (2012). How to integrate the good lives model into treatment programs for sexual offending: An introduction and overview. *Sexual Abuse: A Journal of Research and Treatment, 25,* 123–142.

Wormith, J. S., Gendreau, P., & Bonta, J. (2012). Deferring to clarity, parsimony, and evidence in reply to Ward, Yates, and Willis. *Criminal Justice and Behavior, 39,* 111–120.

Yates, P. M., Prescott, D. S., & Ward, T. (2010). *Applying the good lives and self regulation models to sex offender treatment: A practical guide for clinicians.* Brandon, VT: Safer Society Press.

8

BEYOND THE RNR-GLM DEBATE

Two Futures for Offender Rehabilitation

At the core of the Risk-Need-Responsivity–Good Lives Model (RNR-GLM) debate is the challenge of how best to grow knowledge about treatment effectiveness and to improve offenders' lives. Toward this goal, two possible futures for offender rehabilitation seem possible. One concludes that the RNR model and the GLM are fundamentally incompatible and thus should remain independent treatment paradigms that are left to compete with one another. The other future sees special value in each model and encourages the two perspectives to seek judicious integration. Such integration might involve a complete merger into a single overarching perspective, whereas another integration might involve mutual influence where the RNR model and the GLM continue to exist but in a different way.

In choosing these two futures—which are not mutually exclusive—it is important to realize that a similar controversy has existed in criminological theory for more than four decades. Beginning with his publication of *Causes of Delinquency* in 1969, Travis Hirschi has trumpeted the value of clearly demarcating rival, independent theories that are tested systematically against one another (Hirschi, 1969). Hirschi argues that, at least within criminology, theoretical paradigms start with inconsistent assumptions about human nature that cannot be reconciled—a fact that dooms any true merger. Further, he contends that competition leads to a more concerned effort by advocates to improve individual paradigms and to amass supportive empirical evidence. "A successful integration," he observes, "would destroy the healthy competition among ideas that had made the field of delinquency one of the most interesting and exciting fields in sociology for some time" (Hirschi, 1979, p. 37; see also Hirschi, 1989). Accordingly, he advises that when it comes to the growth of knowledge, "separate and unequal is better" (p. 34).

The counterargument, however, is that Hirschi's rigid independence strategy ignores empirical reality. Most theoretical paradigms capture a slice, not the whole, of reality. By focusing on a delimited set of causal factors, they turn a blind eye to all others. The failure to integrate thus forfeits the possibility of taking into account causal processes that matter. At a certain point, a theory being wrong—even partially wrong—restricts its ability to be a truly general, unifying perspective (for a general discussion, see Messner, Krohn, & Liska, 1989).

Similar issues thus face the growth of the RNR model and the GLM. Are they best left alone to develop internally without much thought of the other? Will this lead them to develop conceptually and empirically more fully? Or will this approach eventually reach a glass ceiling and limit what the models might become? If integration is to occur, however, is this possible? And if possible, how would such integration be undertaken? Should the goal be a full merger and true integration, or should advocates of the RNR model and GLM look to the other approach as a means of elaborating their favored treatment paradigm (see Thornberry, 1989)? In a way, these questions will be answered only in the time ahead. Even so, this chapter discusses what these futures might entail.

Specifically, the first section of this chapter discusses a future with the RNR model and GLM as independent models of offender rehabilitation. This section presents the models' unique theoretical and correctional aspects that seem incompatible. Then, the second section discusses a future with the RNR model and GLM as integrated models of offender rehabilitation. Given its theoretical specificity and empirical support, the RNR model is chosen as the foundational treatment paradigm for this integration effort. However, GLM offers crucial reminders of the therapeutic importance of both encouraging offender motivation for change and helping offenders to pursue good lives. Accordingly, the potential for the GLM to enrich the RNR model is incorporated into the new integrated perspective—to be called the *Risk-Need-Responsivity-Motivation model* or the *RNRM model*.

The First Future: Independent Models

This section discusses the future of offender rehabilitation with two independent models of offender rehabilitation. Advocates of this vision may argue that the integration of the RNR model and GLM is impossible without substantially altering at least one of these models. In this regard, the assumption is that such alteration would impede the potential of each model to reduce reoffending. Essentially, the practical implication of such future is that each of the opposed models would be developed independently, including their theoretical ideas and their applied correctional strategies.

When the Theoretical Frameworks of the RNR Model and GLM Hold Opposed Views of Offender Rehabilitation

Since the GLM was first developed, the model's advocates have presented their humanistic strength-based approach to offender rehabilitation as an alternative model to the RNR's evidence-based approach. Indeed, these scholars designated the GLM as a distinctive model of offender rehabilitation. Thus, the theoretical differences between the RNR model and GLM may not reflect merely differences in the models' focus or emphasis. Rather, these differences reflect two models that are not the same for all intents and purposes. Thus, a realistic future of offender rehabilitation consists of the RNR model and GLM as independent models that each keep their theoretical framework clear and consistent.

From the GLM's theoretical perspective, the concept of primary human goods demonstrates the vitality of two independent models in correctional rehabilitation. In essence, the consistent role of this concept gives the GLM its distinctive theoretical framework. First, the GLM's naturalistic view of human beings assumes that the concept of primary human goods is the major source of offenders' motivation and change (i.e., goals held and sought by all offenders). Second, within the GLM, the concept of primary human goods determines the role of all other GLM's theoretical concepts. For example, the concepts of offenders' needs and risk are evaluated according to their potential to attain or block the person's most important primary human goods. In addition, the concepts of values and contextual factors are expected to mediate the notion of primary human goods throughout the rehabilitative processes.

Thus, any integrated theoretical framework will inevitably diminish the explanatory power of the concept of primary human goods. In this regard, such an integrated model cannot ignore the lack of existing empirical evidence showing that the idea of primary human goods explains variation in the criminal behavior of individuals. Accordingly, within an integrated model, the limited role given to primary human goods will substantially curtail the GLM's unique theoretical explanation and therapeutic spirit. Thus, overall, it does seem that any attempt to integrate the RNR model and GLM would not preserve the GLM's core theoretical explanatory approach. That is, from the GLM's perspective, the field of offender rehabilitation should continue in an independent development of the GLM's theoretical framework rooted in the concept of primary goods.

From the RNR model's perspective, a future with two independent models also seems more promising than a future with an integrated model. First, as an independent model, the RNR model can continue to maintain and develop its strict evidence-based approach to correctional rehabilitation. Second, the RNR model can continue to secure the theoretical elements that reaffirmed the legitimacy of rehabilitation in the correctional system. That is, the RNR model remains a consistent theoretical framework that demonstrates predictive power, reflects interdisciplinary criminology, and enables the incorporation of new promising rehabilitative elements.

In fact, as opposed to the GLM, the theoretical development of the RNR model was based on empirical evidence and followed by empirical tests that guided its theoretical construction. That is, while the RNR model was designed as an evidence-based theoretical framework, the GLM was designed as a holistic rehabilitation framework that provides practitioners with a broader perspective of therapeutic aims and values. Thus, an integration of the models' theoretical frameworks will inevitably impede the already long enterprise to develop the most effective evidence-based correctional intervention. In addition, such integration may impede the legitimacy that the field of correctional rehabilitation gained since the RNR model's theoretical framework used the empirical evidence to demonstrate success. Thus, from the RNR model's theoretical perspective, an independent development of the model has a greater potential of success than an integrated model.

When the Correctional Frameworks of the RNR Model and GLM Hold Opposed Views of Offender Rehabilitation

In accordance with their unique theoretical perspectives of offender rehabilitation, the RNR model and GLM also hold a distinct perspective of correctional rehabilitation. As discussed in Chapters 4 and 6, each model has its own consistent approach to offender assessment and therapeutic strategies. Moreover, since first presented, advocates of each model continue to develop their correctional approach and argue for its therapeutic power. Within this context, a future of offender rehabilitation with the RNR model and GLM as independent models is supported by the fact that each model has (1) a unique therapeutic orientation and (2) therapeutic elements with distinctive levels of structure.

First, although both models agree that the ultimate goal of offender rehabilitation is to reduce future reoffending, advocates of the RNR model and GLM differ in their therapeutic orientation to achieve this goal. For example, while the RNR model is concerned with the appropriate management of correctional interventions, the GLM is concerned with the appropriate management of individual cases. That is, the RNR's correctional framework was designed to maximize the potential of correctional interventions, whereas the GLM's correctional framework was designed to maximize the potential of individual offenders. In addition, the RNR model and GLM have a different orientation toward the rehabilitative outcome. That is, while the RNR-based interventions aim to achieve reduction in participants' recidivism, the GLM-consistent interventions aim to achieve offenders' prosocial reintegration.

Accordingly, the RNR model and GLM differ in their therapeutic process. Specifically, RNR-based interventions are designed to change offenders' dynamic risk factors that relate to recidivism (i.e., to identify and address criminogenic needs), whereas the GLM-consistent interventions are designed to address offenders' psychological needs and social resources that promote prosocial reintegration (i.e., to identify and address primary and secondary human goods). Essentially, each correctional framework also has its own orientation to offender assessment (focus on offenders' risk and needs versus on offenders' strengths), treatment strategies (focus on offenders' perceived reward-cost contingencies versus on their self-reflection), and delivery of services (limited versus wide therapeutic discretion).

Second, advocates of the RNR model and GLM implement their unique therapeutic orientation with a distinctive level of structure. In general, on a hypothetic scale of structured practice, the RNR's correctional framework consists of structured and highly structured therapeutic elements. By contrast, on the same scale, the GLM's correctional framework consists of structured and unstructured therapeutic elements. In other words, while RNR-based interventions tend to vary between structured and highly structured practice, the GLM-consistent interventions tend to vary between structured and unstructured practice.

For example, while RNR-based interventions use actuarial-based instruments to integrate offender assessment and treatment (i.e., highly structured assessment tools), GLM-consistent interventions use structured clinical interview for such integration. In addition, while RNR-based interventions endorse a therapeutic practice that systematically uses structured behavioral procedures (e.g., behavioral rehearsal, classical or operant conditioning, role playing), GLM-consistent interventions endorse a therapeutic practice that employs mainly structured and unstructured cognitive strategies. Moreover, while the RNR model encourages therapists to practice structuring skills (e.g., effective reinforcement, effective disproval, effective authority), the GLM views this practice as an unnecessary constraint on the therapists' professional discretion. Relatedly, advocates of the RNR model recommend correctional interventions to use treatment manuals when delivering therapeutic content, whereas advocates of the GLM recommend interventions to use treatment guides for this task (less structured manualization).

Overall, the RNR model and GLM seem to hold opposing views of correctional rehabilitation. Thus, an integrated model is likely to curtail or distort their independent potential to reduce reoffending. In other words, an integrated model is expected to be less effective than the original models. A better solution for offender rehabilitation might be to keep the RNR model and GLM as rival models that challenge each other within the correctional system. Essentially, advocates of these models will continue to develop and implement their unique correctional frameworks. Within such future, each model will be evaluated by its ability to achieve the definitive goal of offender rehabilitation—reduction in reoffending.

The Second Future: The RNRM Integrated Model

If successful, the first future outlined above will produce either a single, dominant effective treatment model or potentially two independent models that are equally effective. The second outcome might be preferable because it would give the field two distinct strategies from which to select. This option might then allow agencies in different contexts to select either the RNR model or the GLM according to how each perspective matches their orientation to the correctional enterprise.

As also noted, the incompatibility of the RNR model and the GLM means that these approaches cannot be easily merged. There is a tendency to assume that integration is the best option because the best from both approaches can be combined. However, this view can be mistaken if the models are not equally developed or if they have incompatible components. In this context, it does not appear that it is possible to integrate the RNR model and the GLM as co-equal treatment partners. At this point in time, the RNR model has far more clearly specified its statement of principles and has achieved far more empirical support. In offering an integrated theory of rehabilitation, therefore, it seems that the foundation for this approach should be the RNR model.

The difficulty for the RNR model is that it may have reached, or at least be approaching, a glass ceiling in how much effectiveness it can achieve. It is not clear within this paradigm where the next conceptual development will occur that will significantly advance its efficacy. Of course, it is possible to improve its impact through more advanced training of correctional staff and by improving program implementation. But avenues for theoretical advance remain unclear. With the passing of Donald Andrews and the retirement (though not inactivity) of James Bonta and Paul Gendreau, the leadership for paradigmatic advance is declining.

Although still in a developmental stage and in need of true evidence-based verification, the GLM seeks to add something that the RNR model lacks. Although not the intention of its advocates, there is a tendency in the RNR model to reduce offenders to a set of risk factors that should be targeting to reduce recidivism—the gold standard of any RNR-based correctional intervention. By its nature, the LSI-R seeks to separate the criminogenic wheat from the chaff—to focus on what really matters to reduce reoffending. But the GLM starts from a different vantage point. Its strength is seeing offenders as whole people and envisioning corrections as not only reducing their future criminality but also improving their future lives. Its advocates remind us that therapists should take the time to talk with offenders and understand their life goals—and then use this knowledge to motivate their treatment and help them achieve good lives that involve less offending.

Thus, it seems possible to envision an integrated model that starts with the RNR model as the foundation that is then elaborated by integrating the strengths of the GLM. It is unclear that this approach would be more effective than independent models; such a claim would await empirical test. Still, the GLM identifies areas that plausibly would enrich the RNR model. In particular, the GLM has made a strong case for the use of the good lives goals as a means to motivate offenders to enter and sustain treatment. For this reason, the integrated approach being proposed is called the "Risk-Need-Responsivity-Motivation" model, or the RNRM model.

To identify the contents of the RNRM model, the following strategy is used. First, given that the RNR model is conceived as the foundational perspective, its 15 principles are listed. For each principle, it is noted whether the principle stays unchanged or is revised by integrating insights from the GLM. If there is a revision offered, then a rationale for the elaboration is explained under the principle. Further, new principles are also integrated into the RNR model's list of principles. When this is done, a rationale is provided. Finally, when new text is added to an existing RNR principle or a new principle is added, then this text is noted in italics.

Overarching Principles

Principle 1: Respect for the Person and the Normative Context. Services are delivered with respect for the person, including respect for personal autonomy, being humane, ethical, just, legal, decent, and being otherwise normative. Some norms may vary with the agencies or the particular settings within which services are delivered. For example, agencies working with young offenders may be expected to show exceptional attention to education issues and to child protection. Mental health agencies may attend to issues of personal well-being. Some agencies working with female offenders may place a premium on attending to trauma and/ or to parenting concerns.

The words of this principle remain unchanged. However, the RNRM expands the interpretation that the RNR model gives to personal autonomy in correctional rehabilitation. As discussed in Chapter 7, the RNR model provides a limited explanation of why correctional interventions should respect the personal autonomy. According to the RNR model, such respect aims to ensure that correctional interventions will secure the physical and psychological health of offenders (i.e., an ethical norm). In this regard, the RNRM model draws from the GLM and approaches offenders' autonomy also as a personal choice. That is, the RNRM model directs correctional interventions to respect the need of offenders to engage in rehabilitative process because they want to improve their lives. In other words, correctional interventions should respect offenders' personal autonomy to choose a rehabilitative process that reflects their values, goals, or interests.

Principle 2: The Major Goal of Correctional Rehabilitation Is to Improve Offenders First by Reducing Their Recidivism and, Second, by Enhancing Their Well-Being. The overall goal of corrections is improving offenders through rehabilitation. Within this general aim, the primary goal of correctional rehabilitation is to reduce offenders' tendency to recidivate. The secondary goal of correctional rehabilitation is to enhance offenders' well-being.

This RNRM's new principle reflects the consensus among both the RNR model and the GLM that the goal of offender rehabilitation is to improve offenders through rehabilitation. However, within this general goal, the RNRM prioritizes two major goals of correctional rehabilitation.

First, according to the RNRM model, the primary goal of correctional rehabilitation is to improve the offender through reduction of his or her tendency to recidivate. This goal reflects the view that the public mandate to intervene in offenders' lives while they are under state supervision is based on evidence that correctional interventions reduce offenders' recidivism (Andrews, 1982; Ward & Maruna, 2007). In addition, this goal reflects the fact that the legitimacy of the RNR model in the corrections was founded on ample empirical research that appropriate treatment reduced recidivism—which the model's advocates embraced as the goal standard outcome of correctional intervention. Thus, within the RNRM, the primary task of correctional interventions is to improve the offender in a way that protects the members of the community from being victimized. Essentially, this primary goal directs practitioners to build their correctional interventions on therapeutic elements that were found as associated with recidivism (e.g., associated with offender's rearrest, reconviction, and re-incarceration).

Second, according to the RNRM model, the secondary goal of correctional rehabilitation is to improve the offender through enhancement of his or her well-being. In essence, this goal reflects the view that, implicitly or explicitly, all interventions in correction rehabilitation assume that offenders can achieve good lives and aim to address internal and external conditions that impede or facilitate such lives (Cullen, 2013; Ward, 2002). In addition, this principle reflects the salient role of the discipline of psychology in the field of correctional rehabilitation. As discussed in Chapters 3 and 5, the GLM and RNR model are rooted in the psychological perspective of criminal conduct, and their advocates seek better understanding of the cognitive processes in offenders' personality and behavior.

Thus, within the RNRM model, the legitimacy of applying psychological explanations in correctional rehabilitation also depends on practice with a focus on the goal of improving the person (being well) alongside the goal of protecting society (interventions that reduce victimization). Accordingly, the RNRM model directs practitioners to search for ways to engage offenders with the challenges and opportunities that the therapeutic process offers to their lives. Relatedly, this model encourages researchers to explore the direct and indirect impact of enhancing offenders' well-being on recidivism.

> ***Principle 3: Psychological Perspective and Theories.*** *Base interventions on the social psychology perspective of criminal behavior and, within this perspective, apply the positive psychology framework. Specifically, a perspective that combines the general personality, social learning theory, and social cognition theory is the most promising, empirically supported way to reduce recidivism. Within such a perspective, the application of theoretical concepts and strategies from positive psychology is expected to enhance the interventions' capacity to reduce recidivism and the offenders' well-being.*

Within the RNRM model, the original RNR model's "Psychological Theory" principle is revised. According to the RNRM model, correctional interventions should follow the social psychology perspective on human behavior and apply theoretical concepts and strategies from the positive psychology framework. In general, this principle takes a broader perspective on the psychological framework of offender rehabilitation than the RNR model. According to this framework, the RNRM model consists of two integrated psychological perspectives.

First, similar to the RNR model, the RNRM model advises that correctional interventions be based on the social psychology perspective of human behavior. As discussed in Chapter 3, this perspective establishes a solid theoretical foundation because it bridges the discipline of psychology and criminological theories and because of its demonstrated success in predicting and providing a basis for changing criminality. Specifically, the RNRM model endorses the RNR model's perspective that explains human behavior through an interaction between the general personality, social learning theory, and social cognition theory. That is, human behavior is explained through dynamic psychological processes that mediate between the genetic predisposition and personal, interpersonal and community-based factors.

Essentially, this is a powerful perspective because it combines empirically defensible theories. Relatedly, the following features reflect the practical merit of this perspective for correctional rehabilitation: (1) it has a proven applicability across the human being; (2) it seeks to identify the immediate causal factors that influence criminality; (3) it seeks to identify the major factors that predict criminal or noncriminal lifestyle; (4) it aims to identify ways to influence criminality by guiding the learning of alternative noncriminal behavior and thinking process; (5) it supports efforts to explore the integration of theoretical elements from alternative perspectives of human behavior (e.g., humanistic and positive psychology perspectives of human behavior); and (6) it is flexible enough to incorporate new therapeutic strategies from other perspectives.

Second, similar to the GLM, the RNRM model uses the conceptual framework of positive psychology to illuminate factors or strategies that increase offenders' motivation to improve their lives. As discussed in Chapter 5, applied positive psychology aims to identify offender's strengths, capacities, and resources for assisting offenders to meet their needs and interests. Specifically, advocates of this perspective seek therapeutic ways to enhance offenders' subjective well-being (developing positive emotions toward life experiences), psychological well-being (developing full engagement in life), and collective well-being (developing a meaningful life as community members). In essence, a major value of the GLM is that, more than the RNR model and other approaches, it explains the importance of achieving these outcomes in treatment interventions (Marshall, Marshall, Serran, & O'Brien, 2011).

Essentially, according to the RNRM model, positive psychology serves as a psychological framework that is integrated within the social psychological perspective of criminality. Within this integration, positive psychology helps to identify sources of internal incentives that can assist to achieve the goals of correctional rehabilitation. Specifically, the RNRM assumes that offenders, as is true for all human beings, have inner motivation to attain the GLM's primary human goods. However, within the RNRM model, primary human goods do not have the central role in the treatment process. That is, this model assumes that correctional intervention that focuses on the attainment of primary human goods is not the most effective way to attain reduction in recidivism. Instead, the role of primary human goods is to increase offenders' motivation to learn skills, attitudes, and behavior that reduce their tendency to recidivate. In addition, these goods have a salient role in improving offenders through enhancement of their well-being.

> *Principle 4: General Enhancement of Crime Prevention Services.* The reduction of criminal victimization may be viewed as a legitimate objective of service agencies, including agencies within and outside of justice and corrections.

Within the RNRM model, this principle remains unchanged. In general, agencies that provide services within and outside corrections and criminal justice can use the RNRM model to guide their efforts to prevent crime. Thus, because there is strong empirical evidence supporting the principle of using a human service approach to intervention, the risk principle, and the general responsivity principle, it is likely that these principles have broad applicability across agency settings. Further, a rehabilitative model that integrates strategies that aim to reduce victimization and enhance well-being offers an attractive practice for agencies that see their clients not only at risk of offending but as having other personal needs (e.g., mental health).

Core RNRM Principles and Key Clinical Issues

> *Principle 5: Introduce Human Service.* Introduce human service into the justice context. Do not rely on the sanction to bring about reduced offending. Do not rely on deterrence, restoration, or other principles of justice.

Within the RNRM model, this principle remains unchanged. Similar to the GLM and RNR model, the RNRM model views human services as the general strategy to attain the goals of correctional rehabilitation. First, the RNRM model prefers the provision of human services over strategies based on punitive sanctions (deterrence or incapacitation) or justice (retribution, restorative justice). Second, within the RNRM model, the provision of human services aims to address offenders' recidivism and improve their quality of life.

> ***Principle 6: Risk.*** Match intensity of service with risk level of cases. Work with moderate and higher risk cases. Generally, avoid creating interactions of low-risk cases with higher risk cases.

Within the RNRM, this principle remains unchanged. In this regard, the RNRM follows the RNR model's conception of risk. First, the level of risk is determined according to the offenders' likelihood to recidivate. Second, although risk is a dynamic factor, changes in the level of offenders' risk can occur only periodically (while aging or after completion of the treatment program).

> ***Principle 7: Need.*** Target criminogenic needs predominately *for achieving reduction in recidivism. Promote the attainment of primary human goods for enhancing offenders' well-being.*

Within the RNRM model, this principle is expanded. First, the RNRM model endorses the major role that the RNR model gives to criminogenic needs in correctional interventions. As discussed in Chapter 4, criminogenic needs are empirically supported dynamic risk factors. In essence, these are "characteristics of people and/or their circumstances that signal reward–cost contingencies favorable to criminal activity relative to noncriminal activity" (Andrews, Bonta, & Wormith, 2011, p. 738). Within the RNR model's correctional framework, these factors determine offenders' category of risk and the therapeutic areas that the rehabilitative process should target. Thus, similar to the RNR model, the RNRM model guides correctional interventions to target criminogenic needs predominately, and it predicts that a change in these factors affects criminality and reduces offenders' recidivism.

Second, the RNRM model adds to the RNR model by inserting the concept of primary human goods as a concept that directly highlights the importance of targeting the secondary goal of correctional rehabilitation—the enhancement of offenders' well-being. In essence, these primary human goods serve as the RNRM model's explicit efforts to improve the quality of offenders' lives. In this regard, the RNRM model relies on the GLM's primary human goods as personal targets that reflect what offenders want most during their rehabilitative process. In essence, the RNRM model's underlying assumption is that addressing primary human goods has an indirect incremental impact on offenders' recidivism and a direct impact on offenders' well-being.

Specifically, the RNRM model assumes that the primary goods have only an indirect impact on offenders' recidivism because there is no empirical evidence that satisfying any of these primary human goods has ever achieved such an impact (see Chapter 6). In fact, the research that aims to specify, operationalize, and test these goods is still in its developmental stage (see Table 5.1 and Purvis, Ward, & Shaw, 2013, pp. 41–45 for the current developmental stage of primary human goods). Nevertheless, the RNRM model expects that the direct impact of primary human goods on offenders' well-being will result in an indirect incremental reduction in offenders' recidivism. That is, the enhancement of offenders' well-being through the promotion of their primary human goods is expected to increase offenders' level of engagement in the process of change. Accordingly, high levels of such engagement are expected to significantly decrease the chance that offenders will recidivate.

> *Principle 8: General Responsivity. Target criminogenic needs by employing* behavioral, social learning, and cognitive-behavioral influence and skill building strategies. *Promote the attainment of primary human goods by employing motivational strategies that enhance offenders' core commitments in the process of behavioral change.*

Within the RNRM model, this principle is expanded. Essentially, the RNRM model's general responsivity consists of two types of styles and modes of service that aim to achieve the major goals of correctional rehabilitation (reduction in recidivism and enhancing well-being). One type of services aims to generate changes in offenders' criminogenic need, whereas the other type aims to promote the attainment of offenders' primary human goods.

First, the RNRM model follows the RNR model and the consistent empirical findings that specify how to achieve direct changes in offenders' criminality. Thus, to achieve the primary goal of reduction in offenders' recidivism, the RNRM model endorses using behavioral, social learning, and cognitive-behavioral therapies. Similar to the RNR model, the RNRM model favors rehabilitation practice that focuses on changing the criminogenic needs through strategies such as role-modeling, role-playing, graduate practice, external and internal reinforcement, cognitive restructuring, and building behavioral and cognitive skills (see Chapter 4). In this regard, within the RNRM, the therapeutic process should build the offenders' prosocial capabilities through a systematic use of behavioral techniques (reward–cost contingencies).

In addition, similar to the RNR model, the RNRM model assumes that teaching offenders low-risk alternative behaviors, thoughts, and emotions that aim to change their dynamic risk factors will also enhance their well-being. However, in contrast to the RNR model, the RNRM model pays explicit attention to the distinctive styles and modes of service that achieve this secondary goal of correctional rehabilitation. In this regard, the RNRM model uses offenders' inner motivation to attain primary human goods as a general therapeutic strategy that motivates offenders' commitment to the process of behavioral change. That is, the RNRM model uses primary human goods to directly enhance offenders' well-being and to indirectly reduce their recidivism.

Essentially, the RNRM model focuses on the primary human goods that the offender values most. Thus, this model guides correctional interventions to assess the weight that offenders ascribe to each primary human good (i.e., offenders' priority). For this task, practitioners may use the GLM's Primary Human Good Acquisition Analysis (the PHG-AA) that was designed to determine the priority of offenders' primary human goods acquisition (see Chapter 6).

Overall, thus, the responsivity principle reflects a substantial difference between the correctional frameworks of the RNR model and the RNRM model. While the RNR model views offender motivation as a specific responsivity issue, the RNRM model views offender motivation as a general responsivity issue. In other words, while the RNR model uses motivational techniques to facilitate changes in offenders' criminogenic needs, the RNRM model also uses motivation as a major strategy to achieve the goals of correctional rehabilitation.

Specifically, within the RNRM model, two main sets of motivational strategies aim to promote the attainment of primary human goods. The first set consists of strategies that increase offenders' awareness of the challenges and opportunities that the therapeutic process holds for their lives. In essence, these strategies are designed to increase offenders' understanding of how the therapeutic process relates to their personal goals. Thus, in practice, correctional interventions should use motivational strategies that assist offenders in realizing the internal and external conditions for attaining their primary human goods.

For example, correctional intervention may provide pretreatment sessions to increase offenders' treatment readiness. Within such sessions, offenders may discuss which primary human goods are most important to them and what expectations they have for participating in a program that aims to change their criminal lifestyle. A second possible example involves case managers and offenders meeting to discuss what set of interventions they believe is likely to promote desirable prosocial change. As a third example, offenders might be taught to verbalize their personal goals during treatment sessions that teach them specific behavioral and cognitive skills. That is, the substance of offenders' role playing (e.g., a vignette that shows the steps of the skill-related caveats) and homework explicitly reflect the challenges that offenders face while attaining their primary human goods.

The second major set of strategies that enhance offenders' well-being consists of teaching offenders basic cognitive capabilities that facilitate the attainment of their primary human goods. Specifically, drawing from social cognitive theory, correctional interventions should apply three related concepts that construct a powerful way to attain the desired primary goods: (1) goal setting, (2) self-efficacy, and (3) self-regulation.

Within the RNRM model, goal setting is a motivational process that is directed toward the attainment of offenders' primary human goods. Thus, within this perspective, correctional interventions should teach offenders the skill of setting a series of goals where each goal is (1) desired by the offender, (2) proximal, (3) concrete, and (4) perceived by the offender as challenging but attainable. Essentially, such progress toward each goal is expected to increase offenders' self-efficacy—a concept defined by Bandura (1986, p. 391) as "people judgment of their capabilities to organize and execute courses of action required to attain designated types of performances." In turn, increasing offenders' self-efficacy is expected to sustain their motivation to achieve the next intermediate goal. As mentioned above, the overall aim of this process is to instigate and sustain offenders' inner motivation to attain their personal goals through goal-directed activities.

Essentially, such an overall aim requires that offenders will learn how to self-regulate themselves during this process—that is, how to "activate and sustain cognitions, behaviors and affects that are systematically oriented toward attainment of their goals" (Schunk, Meece, & Pintrich, 2014, p. 158). In this regard, goal setting and self-efficacy influence offenders' self-regulation. In practice, intervention should teach offenders the three activities that comprise the self-regulation process: self-observation, self-judgment, and self-reaction (Bandura, 1986). Specifically, correctional interventions should encourage offenders to record "the frequency, intensity, or quality of behavior" (self-observation), to compare the "current performance level with one's goal" (self-judgment), and to conduct "behavioral, cognitive, and affective responses to self-judgment" (self-reaction) (Schunk et al., 2014, pp. 159–160).

Principle 9: Specific Responsivity. Adapt the style and mode of service according to the setting of service and to relevant characteristics of individual offenders, such as their strengths, motivations, preferences, personality, age, gender, ethnicity, cultural identifications, and other factors. *Test the impact of these adaptations on offenders' recidivism and well-being. Communicate these adaptations in terms of assistance to attain offenders' primary human goods.*

The evidence in regard to specific responsivity is generally favorable but very scattered, and it has yet to be subjected to a comprehensive meta-analysis. Some examples of specific responsivity considerations follow:

a. When working with the weakly motivated: Build on strengths; reduce personal and situational barriers to full participation in treatment; establish high-quality relationships; deliver early and often on matters of personal interest; and start where the person "is at."
b. Attend to the evidence in regard to age-, gender-, and culturally responsive services.
c. Attend to the evidence in regard to differential treatment according to interpersonal maturity, interpersonal anxiety, cognitive skill levels, and the responsivity aspects of psychopathy.
d. Consider the targeting of noncriminogenic needs for purposes of enhancing motivation, the reduction of distracting factors, and for reasons having to do with humanitarian and entitlement issues.

Within the RNRM model, the specific responsivity principle is revised. Similar to the GLM and RNR model, the RNRM model guides correctional interventions to adapt therapeutics to the setting in which the service is provided and the characteristics of the individuals being treated. In this regard, all three models share the assumption that specific offender responsivity helps offenders to overcome internal and external barriers to their engaging in the rehabilitative process. Notably, these models also are limited by the lack of empirical research that can be used to guide how correctional interventions should follow this principle.

In this regard, the RNRM model endorses the RNR model's orientation to specific responsivity. First, within this model, correctional interventions should follow the empirical evidence in regard to offenders' biodemographics and amenability to treatment. Second, as a model that expands the role of motivation in the RNR model, the RNRM model endorses practice that provides specific attention to offenders' level of motivation. Third, the RNRM model accepts the priority of criminogenic needs over noncriminogenic needs. That is, targeting criminogenic needs are an integral part of any rehabilitative process, whereas noncriminogenic needs are employed based on professional discretion.

The RNRM model also has its own orientation to offenders' specific responsivity. In accordance with the model's evidence-based approach, the RNRM model advises correctional interventions to test the impact of service adaptations on both offenders' recidivism and well-being. In addition, the RNRM instructs correctional interventions to communicate these adaptations with offenders in terms of potential obstacles or facilitators to the attainment of their primary human goods.

Essentially, regarding the GLM–RNR debate over the issues of offenders' specific responsivity, the RNRM model stands beside the RNR model. As discussed in Chapter 7, the major controversial issues between the GLM and RNR model revolve around the adequate level of responsivity to what the offender wants (i.e., offenders' preferences), and around the appropriate degree of structure that interventions should use while delivering services. Two considerations are relevant.

First, the RNRM model views collaborative (and transparent) rehabilitative process as a desirable practice. Nevertheless, the RNRM model also views its correctional principles as a guidance that limits offenders' personal preferences. For example, correctional interventions should not dismiss the Risk–Need–Responsivity principles because offenders prefer an alternative course of action. Second, the RNRM model views the effort to tailor rehabilitative content to each offender as a desired practice. Nevertheless, this model also sets limitations to the flexibility of such service delivery. In this regard, the RNRM model follows the evidence that supports using a highly structured rehabilitative process over an unstructured process. This model also assumes that correctional interventions can deliver highly structured processes that offenders perceive as relevant and meaningful to their lives.

Thus, in practice, the RNRM model guides correctional interventions to use detailed program manuals that enhance service integrity and elaborate how to target common types of offender-related needs. Accordingly, the RNRM model also favors interventions that conduct close group–based treatments with multiple entry points over open-ended groups. Such practice is believed to generate interventions with sufficient flexibility to tailor rehabilitative services (e.g., needs and dosage) to offenders' individual characteristics.

> ***Principle 10: Breadth (or Multimodal).*** *Employ multimodal interventions for high-risk offenders. Within such interventions, rehabilitative services that aim to reduce offenders' recidivism should* target a number of criminogenic needs relative to noncriminogenic needs.

Within the RNRM model, the breadth principle is clarified. First, this principle guides only correctional interventions that provide services to medium to high-risk offenders. Second, this principle emphasizes that correctional interventions that aim to change high-risk offenders' behavior are required to target several criminogenic needs. Thus, this principle directs correctional interventions to focus on modifying criminogenic needs and minimizes their attention to noncriminogenic needs.

> ***Principle 11: Offenders' Personal Strengths.*** Assess *offenders' personal* strengths to enhance prediction *of recidivism and to promote attainment of primary human goods.*

Within the RNRM model, the strength principle is revised. Similar to the GLM and the RNR model, the RNRM model aims to integrate offenders' personal strengths into therapeutic processes. However, the scientific knowledge regarding the effects of these strengths is very limited (see Chapter 4). For example, it is still unknown whether the opposite manifestation of empirically based risk factors protects the person from a criminal lifestyle (Farrington, Loeber, & Ttofi, 2012). Accordingly, it is still unknown whether assessment tools that are based on personal strengths, or integrate them into a broader instrument, improve the prediction of offenders' recidivism. Similarly, how the inclusion of personal strengths in the therapeutic process impacts the effectiveness of correctional interventions remains unknown.

Nevertheless, the RNRM model follows the empirical enterprise that aims to increase the current knowledge. This research seeks to identify personal factors that can be shown empirically to protect offenders from engaging in criminality or, if involved in such conduct, to pull them out of crime. Hopefully, empirical studies will not only identify these strength factors but also illuminate the mechanisms that allow such factors to protect against criminal involvement. In the future, such findings may assist the RNRM model to predict and address offenders' recidivism and well-being.

Due to this lack of empirical guidance, the RNRM model draws from the GLM's perspective on strengths. That is, according to the RNRM model, personal strengths are also the activities and strategies that offenders use to attain their primary human goods in socially accepted ways. Correctional interventions should reward these activities and strategies and may use them to promote the attainment of other primary human goods. Thus, in practice, correctional interventions should assess which of the primary human goods are attained in a prosocial way and what strategies offenders use during this process. For gathering such information, practitioners may use the following procedures: (1) observe offenders' offense-related actions and general life functioning; (2) conduct semi-structured clinical interviews that focus on offenders' important activities, situations, and experiences; (3) use the RNR-based risk-need-responsivity assessment instruments to gain information about offenders' prosocial aspects.

Principle 12: Structured Assessment.

a. Assessments of Risk-Need-Specific Responsivity Factors: Employ structured and validated assessment instruments.
b. Integrated Assessment and Intervention: Every intervention and contact should be informed by the assessments.

Within the RNRM model, the structured assessment principle remains unchanged. First, the RNRM model views the assessment of level of risk, relevant criminogenic needs, and relevant responsivity factors as the backbone of effective correctional interventions. Thus, similar to the RNR model, the RNRM model advises that therapists providing interventions should base their decisions on structured and validated assessment instruments (see Chapter 4). Second, similar to the RNR model, the RNRM model argues that the primary goal of correctional rehabilitation is to influence criminality—to reduce offenders' recidivism. Thus, this model emphasizes the importance of integrating assessment and intervention.

Principle 13: Release Process and Continuity of Care. *Develop a release process that assists offenders to avoid criminality, maintain therapeutic changes, and implement personal goals.*

a. *Teach offenders skills that help them to avoid high-risk situations, develop social support, and plan the attainment of their personal goals.*
b. *Collaborate with offenders to develop a future-oriented plan for implementing their primary human goods.*
c. *Collaborate with other agencies to establish continuity of care.*

This RNRM model's new principle reflects the attention that this model pays to successful termination of services in correctional interventions. In general, correctional interventions that provide services to offenders should extend to the point when offenders are discharged from treatment. Thus, the RNRM model advises correctional interventions to develop a release process that has clear objectives of how to terminate services successfully. In essence, this release process should include the development of a release plan that assists offenders to avoid criminality, maintain therapeutic changes, and implement personal goals. Overall, such practice is expected to serve the two major goals of correctional rehabilitation—reduction offenders' recidivism and enhancement of their well-being.

Specifically, the RNRM model requires correctional interventions to complete the following tasks before the formal termination of services. First, correctional interventions should equip offenders with skills that assist them to maintain the behavioral and cognitive changes that were gained in treatment. Such practice consists of skills that help offenders to achieve the following objectives: (1) Identifying high-risk situations that may lead them to offending behavior and respond to these situations with a low-risk alternative course of action (e.g., through relapse-prevention strategies); (2) sustaining progress toward the attainment of their primary human goods (e.g., teaching planning skills); and (3) identifying and developing social support that can maintain their prosocial lifestyle.

Second, during the therapeutic process, staff conducting correctional interventions should collaborate with offenders to develop a concrete individualized future-oriented plan. In essence, this plan is designed to assist offenders in achieving their primary human goods. Within the RNRM model, correctional interventions are expected to include the development of this plan while the therapeutic process concentrates on offenders' criminogenic needs. That is, intervention therapists should help offenders understand how the therapeutic process relates to their most important primary human goods (see the RNRM model's general responsivity principle).

In general, such practice aims to enhance offenders' intrinsic motivation to face the challenges and opportunities that awaits them outside the intervention. Such individualized future-oriented plans may consist of (1) offenders' most important primary goods, (2) the strategies to achieve these goods in a prosocial way, (3) indicators that signal the attainment of these goods, and (4) indicators that signal threat to the attainment of these goods (for the GLM's version, see Chapter 6 and the Good Lives Plan Template in Yates, Prescott, & Ward 2010).

Third, the successful termination of human services also requires correctional interventions that provide offenders with continuity of care. In general, the practice of continuity of care aims to prevent the interruption of service when offenders leave the intervention and move to another correctional agency or to an agency outside the correctional system (Van Voorhis & Salisbury, 2016). In essence, such practice allows different correctional and criminal justice agencies to deal with offenders while speaking "the same language" (p. 329). Thus, the RNRM model instructs correctional interventions to make sure that offenders who complete the formal intervention continue to receive the support that they need to maintain their rehabilitative process. Overall, the RNRM model assumes that such interagency communication and aftercare services reduce offenders' recidivism and enhance their well-being.

> ***Principle 14: Professional Discretion.*** Deviate from recommendations only for very specific reasons. For example, functional analysis may suggest that emotional distress is a risk/need factor for this person.

Within the RNRM model, this principle remains unchanged. First, similar to the RNR model, the RNRM model states a clear default that correctional interventions should adhere to its principles. In essence, this guidance reflects a consensus in the field of correctional rehabilitation that adherence to the principles of the RNR model results in the reduction in offenders' recidivism (i.e., the primary goal of correctional rehabilitation) (Bonta & Andrews, 2017; Ward & Maruna, 2007). Relatedly, this position also reflects advocacy of correctional principles as a strategy to transfer the scientific knowledge to practitioners in a way that can be tested (Cullen, 2005).

Second, similar to the RNR model, the RNRM model elaborates the general conditions under which it is permissible for practice to deviate from its principles. That is, correctional intervention can deviate from the model's core principles (human service, risk, need, and general responsivity principles) only when a reliable empirical research suggests taking an alternative course of action. In addition, according to the RNRM model, any deviation should be explicitly explained and systematically monitored. In this regard, the RNRM model assumes that such practice allows correctional interventions to have a sufficient therapeutic flexibility to produce further developments of this model while continuing to achieve the major goals of correctional rehabilitation.

Organizational Principles: Settings, Staffing, and Management

> *Principle 15: Community-Based.* Community-based services are preferred but the principles of RNR also apply within residential and institutional settings.

Within the RNRM model, this principle remains unchanged. Similar to the GLM and the RNR model, the RNRM model prefers to conduct therapeutic processes in offenders' natural environment.

> *Principle 16: Core Correctional Staff Practices.* Effectiveness of interventions is enhanced when delivered by therapists and staff with high-quality relationship skills in combination with high-quality structuring skills. Quality relationships are characterized as respectful, caring, enthusiastic, collaborative, and valuing personal autonomy. Structuring practices include prosocial modeling, effective reinforcement and disapproval, skill building, problem-solving, effective use of authority, advocacy/brokerage, cognitive restructuring, and motivational interviewing. Motivational interviewing skills include both relationship and structuring aspects of effective practice.

Within the RNRM model, this principle remains unchanged. Similar to the RNR model, the RNRM model endorses the importance of therapists who approach offenders with both high-quality relationship skills and high-quality structuring skills (see Chapter 4).

> *Principle 17: Management.* Promote the selection, training, and clinical supervision of staff according to the *RNRM model* and introduce monitoring, feedback, and adjustment systems. Build systems and cultures supportive of effective practice and continuity of care. Some additional specific indicators of integrity include having program manuals available, monitoring of service process and intermediate changes, adequate dosage, and involving researchers in the design and delivery of service.

This principle remains unchanged. Similar to the RNR model, managers of correctional interventions have a pivotal role in the capacity of the RNRM model to achieve the major goals of correctional rehabilitation.

Conclusion

This chapter has presented two possible futures for offender rehabilitation. One future views the GLM and RNR model as incompatible and thus as offering two independent, rival treatment paradigms. Within such a future, advocates of these models would continue to develop the distinctive theoretical and correctional perspectives of their model. The second future for offender rehabilitation envisions the possible integration of the GLM and the RNR model. Toward this end, it was proposed that the most defensible integrated approach would use the RNR model's framework as its theoretical and correctional foundation and the GLM's primary human goods as a source of intrinsic motivation to attain offenders' personal goals.

Specifically, the first section discussed a future with scholars who believe that any integration between the GLM and RNR model will severely curtail the models' unique perspective (see also Chapter 7). In this regard, an integrated model seems to force the RNR model to compromise the role of the evidence-based practice in correctional rehabilitation. Indeed, for many of its advocates, such concession may be perceived as a malpractice because it can undermine the legitimacy of rehabilitation in the criminal justice system. Accordingly, any integrated model inevitably seems to force the GLM to compromise the role of offenders' primary human goods as the main rehabilitative concept. Thus, advocates of the GLM may view the consequences of such an integration with the RNR as unacceptable in practice because the GLM prioritizes tailoring the rehabilitative process around what the offender values most in life. Overall, scholars who share the notion of a future with an independent GLM and the RNR model believe that treatment effectiveness is best advanced by encouraging both models to develop their "internal consistency and conceptual clarity" (Hirschi, 1989, p. 42). The resulting competition would yield either a single model that empirically is shown to reduce recidivism more substantially or two models that might be equally effective. This latter possibility would mean that the field of corrections would have two options when undertaking offender treatment.

The second section discussed a future in which scholars would seek to advance correctional rehabilitation by creating an integrated RNR-GLM model. Such a model would embrace both a strong scientific orientation and ethics of care. Toward this end, a specific integrated model of offender rehabilitation was presented—the *Risk-Need-Responsivity-Motivation model* (RNRM model).

In essence, this integration aims to guide correctional interventions to achieve the two major goals of correctional rehabilitation: reduction in offenders' recidivism (as the primary goal) and the enhancement of offenders' well-being (as the secondary goal). Recognizing the existing theoretical sophistication and empirical support achieved by the RNR model's development over the past quarter century (Bonta & Andrews, 2017), the RNRM model accepted the RNR model as its correctional foundation. However, it also was proposed to integrate the GLM as an integral part of this model. Specifically, within the RNRM model's correctional framework, the RNR model's principles serve as a baseline. Then, the GLM's concept of primary human goods is integrated into the RNR model to create the RNRM model. Taken together, the RNRM model presents 17 principles that guide evidence-based interventions on how best to reduce future criminal involvement and to promote offenders' personal goals in prosocial ways. Importantly, the effectiveness of this new model in correctional setting should be tested.

Overall, within the above two futures for offender rehabilitation, correctional interventions have three legitimate models of offender rehabilitation: the RNR model, the GLM, and the RNRM model. As the history of correctional rehabilitation shows, the main challenge of these models is to secure and promote the legitimacy of offender rehabilitation. Thus, as the 21st century moves forward, a successful development of these models depends on scientific evidence that demonstrates their capacity to reach their goals—of reducing recidivism and improving offenders' lives.

References

Andrews, D. A. (1982). *The supervision of offenders: Identifying and gaining control over the factors that make a difference*. Program Branch User Report. Ottawa, ON: Solicitor General of Canada.

Andrews, D. A., Bonta, J., & Wormith, J. S. (2011). The risk-need-responsivity (RNR) model: Does adding the good lives model contribute to effective crime prevention? *Criminal Justice and Behavior, 38*, 735–755.

Bandura, A. (1986). *Social foundations of thought and action: A social cognitive theory*. Englewood Cliffs, NJ: Prentice Hall.

Bonta, J., & Andrews, D. A. (2017). *The psychology of criminal conduct* (6th ed.). New York, NY: Routledge.

Cullen, F. T. (2005). The twelve people who saved rehabilitation: How the science of criminology made a difference. *Criminology, 43*, 1–42.

Cullen, F. T. (2013). Rehabilitation: Beyond nothing works. In M. Tonry (Ed.), *Crime and justice in America, 1975 to 2025—crime and justice: A review of research* (Vol. 42, pp. 299–376). Chicago, IL: University of Chicago Press.

Farrington, D. P., Loeber, R., & Ttofi, M. M. (2012). Risk and protective factors for offending. In D. P. Farrington & B. C. Welsh (Eds.), *The Oxford handbook of crime prevention* (pp. 46–69). Oxford: Oxford University.

Hirschi, T. (1969). *Causes of delinquency*. Berkeley: University of California Press.

Hirschi, T. (1979). Separate but unequal is better. *Journal of Research in Crime and Delinquency, 16*, 34–38.

Hirschi, T. (1989). Exploring alternatives to integrated theory. In S. F. Messner, M. D. Krohn, & A. E. Liska (Eds.), *Theoretical integration in the study of crime and deviance: Problems and prospects* (pp. 37–49). Albany, NY: State University of New York Press.

Marshall, W. L., Marshall, L. E., Serran, G. A., & O'Brien, M. D. (2011). *Rehabilitating sexual offenders: A strength-based approach*. Washington, DC: American Psychological Association.

Messner, S. F., Krohn, M. D., & Liska, A. E. (Eds.). (1989). *Theoretical integration in the study of crime and deviance: Problems and prospects*. Albany, NY: State University of New York Press.

Purvis, M., Ward, T., & Shaw, S. (2013). *Applying the good lives model to the case management of sexual offenders: A practical guide for probation officers, parole officers, and case workers*. Brandon, VT: Safer Society Press.

Schunk, D. H., Meece, J. L., & Pintrich, P. R. (2014). *Motivation in education: Theory, research, and applications* (4th ed.). Boston, MA: Pearson.

Thornberry, T. P. (1989). Reflections on the advantages and disadvantages of theoretical integration. In S. F. Messner, M. D. Krohn, & A. E. Liska (Eds.), *Theoretical integration in the study of crime and deviance: Problems and prospects* (pp. 51–60). Albany, NY: State University of New York Press.

Van Voorhis, P., & Salisbury, E. (2016). *Correctional counseling and rehabilitation* (9th ed.). New York, NY: Routledge.

Ward, T. (2002). Good lives and the rehabilitation of offenders: Promises and problems. *Aggression and Violent Behavior, 7*, 513–528.

Ward, T., & Maruna, S. (2007). *Rehabilitation: Beyond the risk paradigm*. New York, NY: Routledge.

Yates, P. M., Prescott, D. S., & Ward, T. (2010). *Applying the good lives and self regulation models to sex offender treatment: A practical guide for clinicians*. Brandon, VT: Safer Society Press.

INDEX

Note: Page numbers in italics denote tables.